Parcella'86

Mathematical Research · Mathematische Forschung

Wissenschaftliche Beiträge
herausgegeben von der
Akademie der Wissenschaften der DDR
Karl-Weierstraß-Institut für Mathematik

Band 29

Parcella'86

Herausgeber:

Dr. Tamás Legendi
Hungarian Academy of Sciences
Research Group on Automata Theory, Szeged

Prof. Dennis Parkinson
DAP Support Unit, Queen Mary College, London

Prof. Dr. Roland Vollmar
Institut für Informatik,
Technische Universität Braunschweig

Dr. Gottfried Wolf
Akademie der Wissenschaften der DDR
Zentralinstitut für Kybernetik und Informationsprozesse, Berlin

---

Die Titel dieser Reihe werden vom Originalmanuskript der Autoren reproduziert

ISBN 3-05-500175-3
ISSN 0138 - 3019

Erschienen im Akademie-Verlag Berlin,
DDR-1086 Berlin, Leipziger Straße 3-4

Lizenznummer: 202 • 100/411/86
Printed in the German Democratic Republic
Gesamtherstellung: VEB Kongreß- und Werbedruck, 9273 Oberlungwitz
Lektor: Dipl.-Phys. Gisela Lagowitz
LSV 1095
Bestellnummer: 763 476 4 (2182/29)
03600

Parcella '86

Proceedings of the III. International Workshop on Parallel Processing by Cellular Automata and Arrays held in Berlin (GDR), September 9–11, 1986

edited by

Tamás Legendi
Dennis Parkinson
Roland Vollmar
Gottfried Wolf

Akademie-Verlag Berlin 1986

P R E F A C E

The volume contains the papers of Parcella '86 - the III. International Workshop "Parallel Processing by Cellular Automata and Arrays" held in Berlin from September 9 to 11, 1986.
International activities show the continuously increasing role of cellular and array structures for parallel and distributed computing. Deeper understanding of these structures permits a high speed and structural flexibility, i. e. well-algorithm-adapted computer architectures, and helps to overcome the challenge to future computer generations. Focusing the interest on regular computing structures, Parcella '86 kept the profile of its predecessors and gathered those scientists who were interested in presenting and discussing new results and ideas in this field. The aim was find common aspects for parallel processing on these two closely related types of structures and to stimulate the process of research. Important information on the state-of-the-art in the different research institutions was exchanged concerning problems and future projects.

T. Legendi (Szeged) and G. Wolf (Berlin) cooperated as organizers and chairman. Their efforts were supported by work done by International Program Committee, where M. Harao (Yonezawa), F. Hoßfeld (Jülich), A. Jugel (Dresden), N. Kasabov (Sofia), E. Katona (Szeged), D. Maritsas (Patras), J. Miklosko (Bratislava), H. Nishio (Kyoto), D. Parkinson (London), J. Prangishvili (Moscow), A. Salomaa (Turku), U. Schendel (Berlin-West), J. Toth (Szeged), R. Vollmar (Braunschweig), W. Wilhelmi (Berlin), G. Wunsch (Dresden) were working.

Fortunately, the size of the volume has increased compared with the previous ones but, unfortunately, not enough to include all papers submitted to the editors. Nevertheless the editors would like to express their thanks to the members of International Program Committee, the chairmen of sessions and to all contributors and speakers who helped to achieve a full success.

Finally the editors are very much obliged to Prof. Dr. sc. V. Kempe, Director of the Central Institute Cybernetics and Information Processes, and to Prof. Dr. H. Fuchs, Deputy Director of this institute, for their untiring efforts made in organizing the workshop, as well as to Mrs. Dipl.-Phys. G. Lagowitz and Dr. R. Höppner from Akademie-Verlag Berlin as the publishing house, providing excellent conditions for the edition of this volume.

Furthermore, our thanks are due to Mrs. Böttcher and Dr. Köles for their organizational assistance.

Looking forward to Parcella '88.

T. Legendi
D. Parkinson
R. Vollmar
G. Wolf

TABLE OF CONTENTS

DATA ORGANISATION FOR THE EFFECTIVE USE OF PROCESSOR ARRAYS

Dr. Peter M. Flanders[1]
&
Prof. Dr. Dennis Parkinson[2]

ABSTRACT

Experience of developing applications for parallel processors reveals that the major problem is one of data communication. Even in the case of synchronous SIMD systems the problem is not well understood and ad-hoc techniques are usually employed to handle data mapping and routing. This paper provides an introduction to a theory of data organisation which permits the mapping of algorithms on to processor arrays to be analysed systematically and rigorously. The benefits of this have been demonstrated on the ICL DAP and include: simplification of the description of data mapping and movement leading to more effective solutions; ease of production of software for parallel processing; and, a better understanding of the effects of different processor interconnection networks.

1. INTRODUCTION AND OVERVIEW

The nature of processing on a parallel SIMD (Single Instruction stream Multiple Data stream) processor array such as the ICL DAP [5] is fundamentally different from that on a conventional sequential processor. The latter involves repeatedly operating on individual data which are accessed via address computation. In contrast to this, the basic profile of a parallel computation is shown in figure 1. It involves an interleaving of two phases: one is a computation phase which performs identical operations simultaneously in every processor on data local to the processor, and the other phase routes data between the processors. The purpose of the data routing phase is to bring together data which needs to interact during the next computation phase.

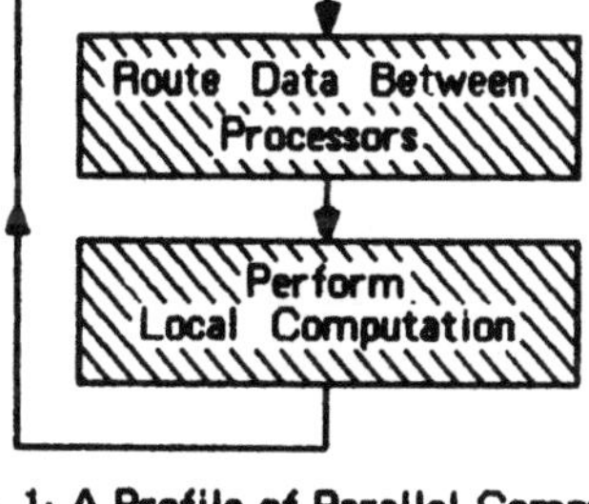

Fig. 1: A Profile of Parallel Computation

1) Systems Strategy Centre, ICL, Lovelace Rd., Bracknell, Berkshire RG12 4SN, England.
2) DAP Support Unit, Queen Mary College, University of London, Mile End Rd., London E1 4NS, England.

Much attention has been given elsewhere to "optimal" ways of mapping and routing data on parallel processor arrays for specific algorithms. Usually a single specific case is studied for which the the amount of data directly matches the number of processors in the array. Even in the simplest cases the pattern of interaction of data is complex and it is not therefore surprising that the claim to having the optimal solution is often short-lived. There is therefore a requirement for a general theory of data organisation to handle complex data mapping and routing. The theory described here for this purpose is known as "musical-bits"[1] and is particularly relevant in the context of SIMD processor arrays. The use of such a theory in place of ad-hoc methods results in the following benefits:

(a) simplification of the description of data mapping and movement, especially in cases where both the data and the memory are multi-dimensional;
(b) better insight into how to solve problems on parallel hardware leading to more sophisticated, high performance, solutions;
(c) better engineered and more easily produced software for parallel processing;
(d) systematic evaluation of the effects of different processor interconnection networks;
(e) provision of a theoretical basis for the design of a class of parallel hardware.

The role of musical-bits in generating efficient algorithms for data routing can be compared with the role of the FFT in providing efficient numeric computation. Improvements in routing performance are a consequence of elegant solutions made possible by the reduction in complexity brought about by the theory. This report provides an introduction to the basic concepts of musical-bits. Only the basic notation and simplified examples are given here in order to demonstrate the nature of the approach rather than prove its validity. Some indication of the wider applicability is given at the end. A more complete introduction is given in ref[1]. Ref[2] provides a formal description of these concepts and describes various advanced applications; ref[3] looks in more detail at the use of musical-bits in the context of processor interconnection networks.

The essence of musical-bits is that, rather than considering the physical mapping of data directly, we consider an alternative representation for which each mapping is described by a "mapping vector". Mapping vectors are defined for only a subset of all possible data mappings but it turns out that the subset covered is relevant to the solution of a number of important problems. By restricting the set of mappings handled we are able to significantly simplify the description of data mappings, the mapping vectors being concise one-dimensional objects. Furthermore the analysis and implementation of data routing can then be simplified by treating it as transformations between these simplified mapping descriptions. These transformations are decomposed into more elementary transformations termed "generators" which are efficiently

1) The art of music is concerned with structuring sounds to produce a harmonious result rather than noise. By analogy musical-bits is concerned with building structure into data routing operations to extract elegant and efficient solutions from the plethora of possibilities.

implemented on processor arrays. Thus we are employing the device (fig. 2) which is found in other contexts, such as the Fourier Transform, of working (at least conceptually) in a different space in order to gain advantages in terms of efficiency and reduction of complexity; the space in which we are working we refer to as "mapping vector space". The decomposition of transformations into generators is also an important and familiar technique; as shown in figure 3 there is a corresponding decomposition in the original physical space with each elementary change in the physical mapping corresponding to the application of a single generator. This decomposition process enables the implementation of transformations to be constructed from a small set of primitive functions supplied by the system and highly tuned for optimal performance. "Programming" the data routing covered by musical-bits for an application is thereby reduced to the invocation of the appropriate generator functions at the appropriate time.

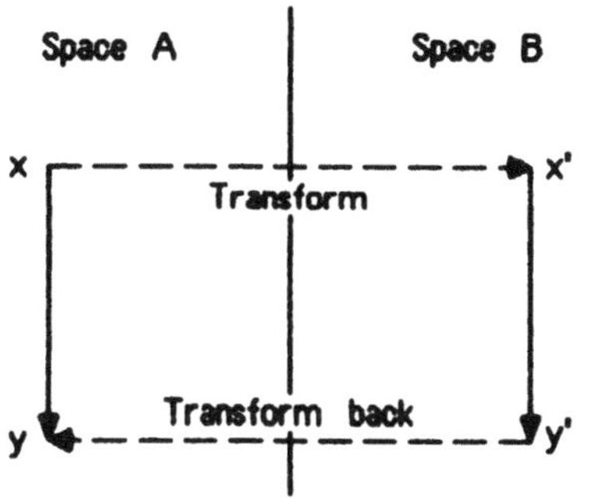

Fig 2: Working in a Different Space

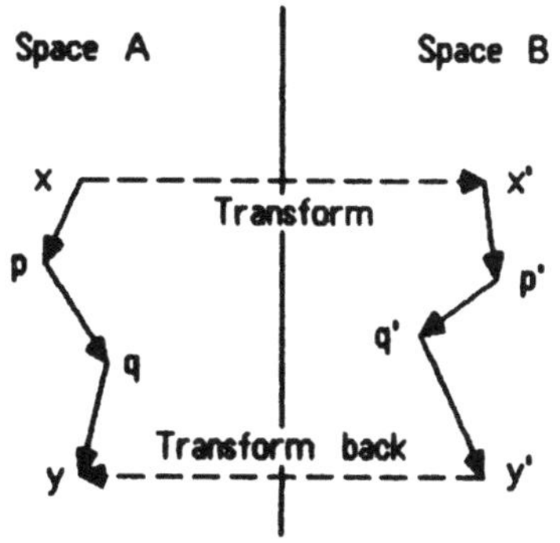

Fig 3: Decomposing Transformations

2. A BASIC HARDWARE MODEL AND ASSOCIATED MAPPING VECTORS

We describe first a basic form of computational model to which the theory of musical-bits may be applied. The theory is applicable to many parallel systems and has been used as the theoretical basis for the data reorganisation hardware described in reference [4]. Here we are primarily concerned with its application to SIMD processor arrays where a large number of processing elements (PEs) execute the same instruction stream simultaneously under the direction of a single control unit. Each PE is assumed to have its own local memory which it can randomly access. The PEs, including their local memory, are connected in the form of an array so that data can be transferred between them. The simplest arrangement is a linear chain with each PE connected to its two nearest neighbours. The resulting parallel system is then as shown in figure 4. In general musical-bits enables us to consider the effects of connecting the PEs in different ways, but to exemplify the basic principles it is convenient to introduce a further restriction as follows. We assume that for a system of N PEs, the memory of each PE contains one data item and any temporary working data; thus we are initially concerned with how N data items are mapped on to the local memories of N PEs, subject to the restriction of one item per PE.

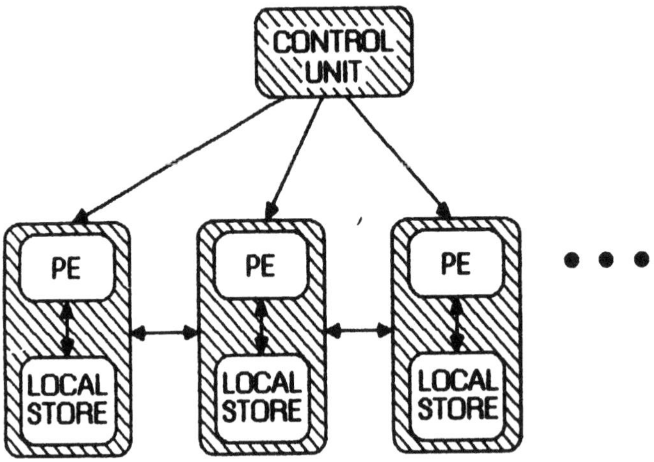

Fig. 4: Schematic of Simple Processor Array

This is analogous to the classical problem of placing N distinct items into N boxes; the "items" being fixed size data items and the "boxes" being single memory locations in each of the PEs. It is well known that there are N! ways in which the allocation, or data mapping, can be done. Representing a given mapping is equivalent to representing a given permutation of the numbers 0 to N-1. The simplest way to do this is to lay out the numbers in the desired order, for example:

[0 4 1 5 2 6 3 7]

represents a mapping for which data item 0 is in PE 0, data item 4 is in PE 1, data item 1 is in PE 2, etc.. This representation of the mapping directly describes the physical arrangement of data and is referred to as the "physical mapping". It can describe any of the N! mappings of N data items on to N PEs but is very cumbersome for large N, requiring N symbols for its denotation. In many practical applications the mapping has some regularity and by restricting ourselves to a subset of the N! mappings we can reduce the information required to specify each mapping. In the notation used here each mapping is denoted by a mapping vector having $\log_2 N$ symbols.

Consider the problem of mapping 8 data items on to our linear array of 8 PEs. Each data item d is stored at PE p where both d and p are integers in the range 0 to 7. Let the binary representation of d be $d_2d_1d_0$. For a given mapping of the subset of mappings in which we are interested, the binary value of p is obtained for each data item by taking a specific ordering of the values of the bits d_2,d_1, and d_0; the particular ordering taken defines that particular mapping.

An example should clarify this. Suppose we take the bits d_2,d_1,d_0 in the order $d_1d_0d_2$;

this defines a mapping of data known as "shuffled" mapping with the property that data item $d_2d_1d_0$ is stored in PE $d_1d_0d_2$. We illustrate this pictorially as follows:

For example data item 3 has the binary form 011 and hence d_2=0, d_1=1, and d_0=1; taking d_2,d_1, and d_0 in the order $d_1d_0d_2$ gives the binary number 110 indicating that data item 3 is stored in PE 6. Pictorially we have:

The complete physical mapping is derived by repeating this process for all values of d in the range 0 to 7 as shown in figure 5; this shows that the mapping derived in this way corresponds to the physical mapping [0 4 1 5 2 6 3 7] shown above. (Note that indices of data items in the physical mapping are numbered from left to right starting with zero.)

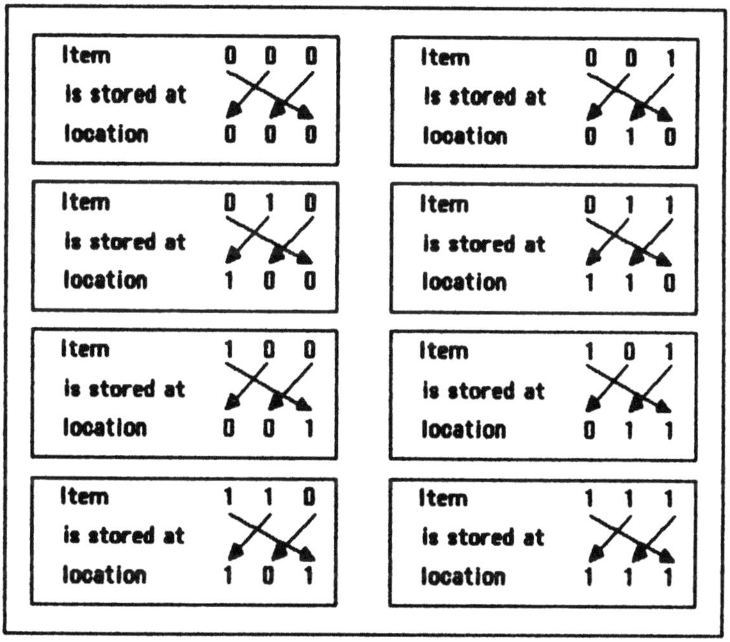

Fig. 5: Derivation of Shuffled Mapping

The mapping vector describing this mapping simply needs to specify the order in which the data index bits d_2, d_1, d_0 are taken; it does this in a manner similar to that used to specify the physical mapping, thus in this example we represent the ordering $d_1 d_0 d_2$ by the mapping vector (1 0 2). Like the physical mapping, the mapping vector is a permutation of numbers but in this case it specifies a permutation of data index bits rather than a permutation of data items; to differentiate between physical mappings and mapping vectors we use square brackets for the former and parentheses for the latter.

The following table shows mapping vectors and corresponding physical mappings for some mappings of 8 items on to an 8 PE array.

TABLE I: SAMPLE MAPPINGS OF 8 DATA ITEMS ON A LINEAR ARRAY OF 8 PEs

DESCRIPTION OF MAPPING	MAPPING VECTOR	PHYSICAL MAPPING
Identity mapping	(2 1 0)	[0 1 2 3 4 5 6 7]
Bit-reversed mapping	(0 1 2)	[0 4 2 6 1 5 3 7]
Shuffled mapping	(1 0 2)	[0 4 1 5 2 6 3 7]
Inverse shuffled mapping	(0 2 1)	[0 2 4 6 1 3 5 7]

3. EXTENSION OF MAPPING VECTORS TO INCLUDE BIT INVERSION

A useful extension to the class of mappings covered by mapping vectors is obtained by allowing the location of an item to be formed from the inverses of index bits as well as the index bits themselves. For example a mapping of 8 items could be defined by taking the index bits in order and inverting just b_2; pictorially the location of each item is obtained from the index bits as follows:

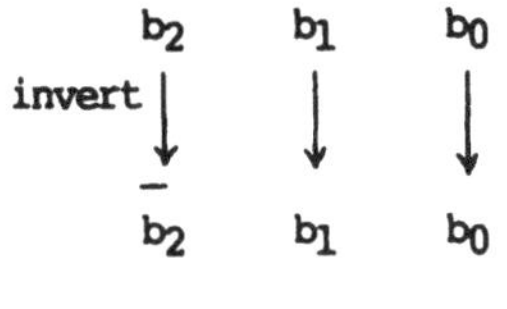

The corresponding physical mapping, [4 5 6 7 0 1 2 3], has both halves interchanged.

The notational form of the mapping vector indicates inverted bits by placing a bar over them so that the mapping vector for the above example is $(\bar{2}\ 1\ 0)$.

Inversion can be applied independently to any elements of the mapping vector and combined with any particular ordering, so for example the mapping vector $(\bar{2}\ 0\ \bar{1})$ is equivalent to the physical ordering [6 4 7 5 2 0 3 1].

Taking the inverse of all index bits in natural order, as described for 8 items by the mapping vector $(\bar{2}\ \bar{1}\ \bar{0})$ gives rise to the physical mapping [7 6 5 4 3 2 1 0] which is a complete reversal of the identity mapping (2 1 0).

The extension to include inversion increases the number of mappings which can be represented by mapping vectors to $N(\log_2 N)!$ where N is the number of data items.

4. DATA ROUTING IN THE BASIC HARDWARE MODEL

We have introduced the basic concept of a mapping vector and a notation adequate for representing simple mapping vectors. In this section we examine the process of data routing in this somewhat limited context. Data routing corresponds to changing the mapping of data on to PEs and we demonstrate that viewing such changes in terms of mapping vectors, that is in mapping vector space, is simpler than trying to follow the corresponding changes in physical space.

Thus the question we are addressing here is "given that we have two different mappings of data, how do we transform from one to the other?" For example after performing a Fast Fourier Transform which leaves its results in bit-reversed order (see table I) we may wish to put the results into sequential order; this entails transforming between the bit-reversed mapping and the identity mapping. The transformation required for the basic hardware model with a linear array of 16 PEs (N = 16) is shown below both for the physical mapping and the corresponding mapping vector:

(a) Changes to physical mapping:

```
Initial Mapping: [0  8  4 12  2 10  6 14  1  9  5 13  3 11  7 15]
Final Mapping:   [0  1  2  3  4  5  6  7  8  9 10 11 12 13 14 15]
```

(b) Changes to mapping vector:

```
Initial Mapping:     (0  1  2  3)
Final Mapping:       (3  2  1  0)
```

The data movement implied by (a) could be done by breaking it down into a sequence of pair-wise exchanges of data. Each exchange gives rise to an intermediate mapping; an example sequence is shown pictorially as follows:

```
[  0  8  4 12  2 10  6 14  1  9  5 13  3 11  7 15]
      └────────────────────┘
[  0  1  4 12  2 10  6 14  8  9  5 13  3 11  7 15]
                                    └─────┘
[  0  1  4 12  2 10  6 14  8  9  5 11  3 13  7 15]
         └─────┘
[  0  1  2 12  4 10  6 14  8  9  5 11  3 13  7 15]
               └─────────────────┘
[  0  1  2 12  4  5  6 14  8  9 10 11  3 13  7 15]
            └──────────────────────────┘
[  0  1  2  3  4  5  6 14  8  9 10 11 12 13  7 15]
                        └────────────────────┘
[  0  1  2  3  4  5  6  7  8  9 10 11 12 13 14 15]
```

In our basic hardware model with 16 PEs linearly connected each PE can simultaneously send an item of data to one of its neighbours and receive an item of data from its opposite neighbour. All PEs are simultaneously passing data in the same direction so the overall effect is to shift the complete vector of data across the linear array of PEs. Typically the time to execute the shift of the vector of data is proportional to the number of PEs through which the data is shifted. Each pairwise exchange of data may be trivially implemented on this processor array by shifting the whole vector of data both to the left and the right and selectively overwriting the original data. There are more efficient (and more complex) ways to perform the remapping but for our purposes here that is of little consequence.

Alternatively, we can solve the problem in terms of mapping vectors. We can decompose the changes to the mapping vector into a sequence of elementary changes (or "generators") in a similar fashion to that above. Taking pair-wise exchanges of mapping vector elements as the generators gives rise to the following pattern of generators and intermediate mappings:

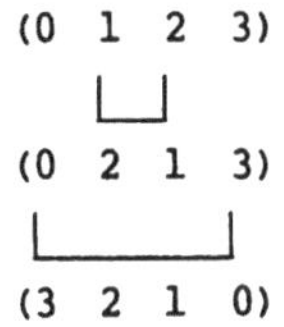

The solution is greatly simplified by working in mapping vector space because of the reduction in the amount of information needed to specify each mapping. This of course raises the question "how do we implement the generators?" We shall comment briefly on that after looking at the physical mappings and data movements corresponding to the mapping vectors and generators shown above. These are shown below with the mapping vectors and generators on the left and the corresponding physical mappings and data movements on the right; thus the left hand side is a diagram of the transformation in mapping vector space and the right hand side is a diagram of the corresponding transformation in physical space.

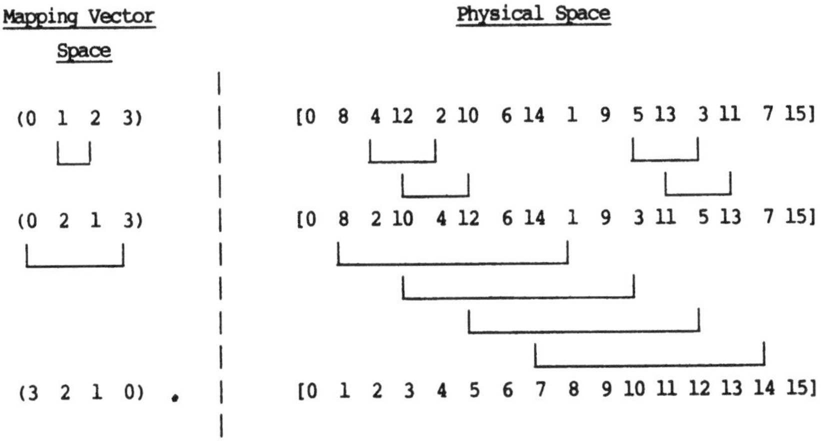

The physical data movements corresponding to the two generators used above are seen to be very regular; in particular each pair of data exchanged during the implementation of one generator requires the same amount of shift. Thus the exchange of two elements of a mapping vector is a good candidate for a generator in that the corresponding data movement is simple and efficient to implement on a processor array with nearest neighbour connectivity. Furthermore if the data movements corresponding to these pair-wise exchanges of mapping vector elements are supplied as macros or subroutines, the user need not be concerned about the details of the physical data movement at all.

Pair-wise exchanges of mapping vector elements are good candidates for generators for another reason, namely that any permutation of mapping vector elements can be obtained by a suitable sequence of pair-wise exchanges. Thus we have a technique for transforming between any two mapping vectors (ignoring for a moment the question of inversion). In general there is no unique sequence of pair-wise exchanges for a given transformation; even in the simple example given above one alternative would be to reverse the order of the generators.

As a second example of a transformation consider the perfect shuffle of 16 data items. In physical space the transformation between the identity mapping and the shuffled mapping may be shown diagrammatically as:

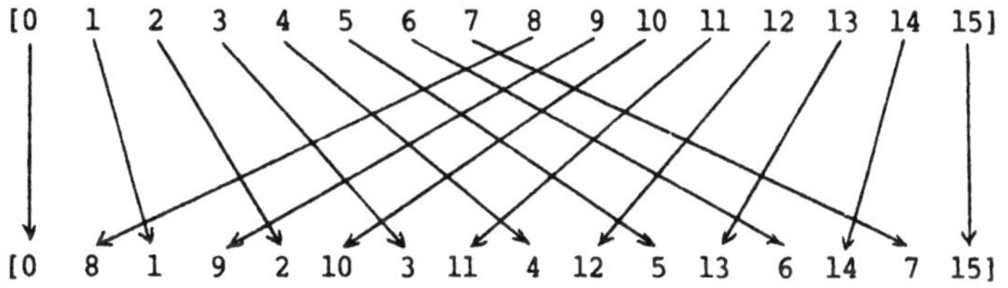

and the corresponding transformation in mapping vector space as:

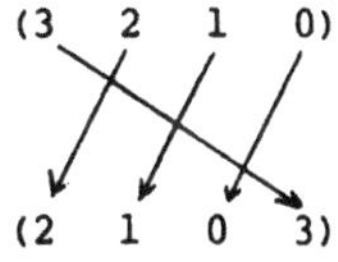

In mapping vector space it is simply a cyclic shift to the left of the mapping vector which may be implemented by the following sequence of generators:

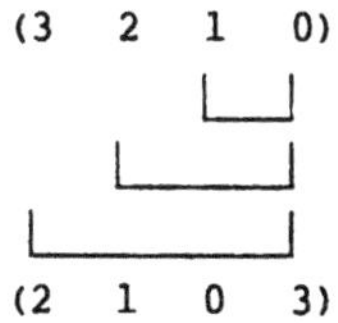

Note that the inverse transformation, in this case an inverse shuffle, can be performed by the same sequence of generators in reverse order.

So far in our discussion of transformations we have ignored inversion of mapping vector elements. However just as any permutation of mapping vector elements may be decomposed into a sequence of pair-wise exchanges, any inversions of mapping vector elements can be done one at a time. The order in which they are done is immaterial. For example consider the problem of reversing the order of the 8 items in a vector. We show below how this can be done by inverting the mapping vector elements in turn; alongside the transformations in mapping vector space are the corresponding transformations in physical space.

	Mapping Vector Space	Physical Space
Identity mapping:	(2 1 0)	[0 1 2 3 4 5 6 7]
Invert bit 0:		
	(2 1 $\bar{0}$)	[1 0 3 2 5 4 7 6]
Invert bit 1:		
	(2 $\bar{1}$ $\bar{0}$)	[3 2 1 0 7 6 5 4]
Invert bit 2:		
Final mapping:	($\bar{2}$ $\bar{1}$ $\bar{0}$)	[7 6 5 4 3 2 1 0]

Again it can be seen that the individual inversions, which are the generators, have corresponding data movements which are simple and efficient on processor arrays with nearest neighbour connectivity.

Rather than drawing the sequence of generators required to produce a transformation between two mapping vectors, it is convenient to have a notation; this enables a more mathematical approach to the specification of data routing. For a single pair-wise exchange we need to identify the two mapping vector elements exchanged and for a single inversion we need to identify the mapping vector element inverted. We therefore use E(x;y) to denote an exchange of elements at positions x and y in the mapping vector and I(x) to denote inversion of the mapping vector element at position x. Note that the parameters x and y refer to the <u>positions</u> of elements of the mapping vector and <u>NOT</u> the values of the elements; note also that the positions of mapping vector elements are numbered from the right starting at zero. For example the exchange E(0;2) applied to the mapping vector (2 0 1 3) has the effect:

Initial mapping:	(2 0 1 3)
Exchange E(0;2):	
Final mapping:	(2 3 1 0)

To describe a sequence of pair-wise exchanges of mapping vector elements it is convenient to use the product notation of mathematics. For example the sequence:

E(1;0) E(2;0) E(3;0) (read from left to right) described previously to implement a perfect shuffle of 8 items is written more concisely as:

$$\prod_{i=1}^{3} E(i;0)$$

As noted previously this is a cyclic shift of the mapping vector by one place to the left. The order of the E(i;j) is important. The inverse of a transformation can always be obtained by reversing the order of the E(i;j). Thus for example the inverse shuffle of 8 data items can be performed by the sequence: E(3;0) E(2;0) E(1;0)

i.e.

$$\prod_{i=0}^{2} E(3-i;0)$$

The product notation is also used to denote other sequences; for example the sequence of inversions: I(0) I(1) I(2) discussed previously transforms the mapping vector (2 1 0) into $(\bar{2}\ \bar{1}\ \bar{0})$. It reverses the order of data in the physical mapping. To represent this sequence of inversions using the product notation we write:

$$\prod_{i=0}^{2} I(i)$$

To summarize this section, we have shown that any transformation (or data reordering) can be viewed in terms of changes to the mapping vector or as changes to the physical mapping. In either case a complex transformation can be decomposed into a sequence of elementary transformations. We have also shown that working with mapping vectors (i.e. working in mapping vector space) is very much simpler than working with physical mappings (i.e. working in physical space). The elementary transformations in mapping vector space are (a) pair-wise exchanges of mapping vector elements and (b) inversions of individual mapping vector elements. They are termed "generators" and for any two mapping vectors there is always at least one sequence of generators which will transform one into the other; the reverse sequence of generators will perform the inverse transformation. In a similar way to that in which we derived an algebraic form of the mapping vector from its pictorial form, we also derived an algebraic notation to denote sequences of generators.

5. DATA REORDERING AS AN INTEGRAL PART OF COMPUTATION

In section 4 we gave some simple examples of data reordering operations using musical-bits. There are a number of important data transformations which are best handled using musical-bits and appreciation of this increases as the notation is extended to cover multi-dimensional data and multi-dimensional processor arrays with different interconnection networks [1,2]. In this section we illustrate that as well as being useful for generating one-off data reorderings, musical-bits is an invaluable tool during the implementation of certain algorithms on processor arrays.

As stated previously and illustrated in figure 1, parallel computation on a processor array is organized as a sequence of cycles and each cycle involves, firstly, data routing and, secondly, computation on data held locally within each PE. Musical-bits enables us to describe and perform the data routing simply and efficiently and also to keep track of where the data is during computation.

The purpose of routing the data prior to each stage of local computation is to pair up data items which need to interact during the local computation. Because the binary form of divide-and-conquer strategy underlies many important algorithms it is a common requirement to have interaction between pairs of data whose indices differ in just one bit when represented in binary form. To develop this further it is necessary to introduce the following definition.

Definition of the term "k-apart":

Let i and $i^{(b)}$ be two natural numbers whose binary representations differ only in position b; in other words if the binary representation of i is:

$$(\ldots\ i_{b+1}\ i_b\ i_{b-1}\ \ldots\ i_1\ i_0)$$

then:

$$(\ldots\ i_{b+1}\ i'_b\ i_{b-1}\ \ldots\ i_1\ i_0)$$

is the binary representation of $i^{(b)}$, where i'_b is the binary complement of the bit i_b. The pair of numbers $(i, i^{(b)})$ are said to be "2^b-apart" (or B-apart where $B=2^b$).

For example the numbers 9 and 13 have binary representations 1001 and 1101 respectively. They differ only in bit 2 and are therefore "2^2-apart" (i.e. 4-apart). The set of pairs of integers in the range 0 to 15 which are 2^3-apart (i.e. 8-apart) is:

$$\{(0,8)\ (1,9)\ (2,10)\ (3,11)\ (4,12)\ (5,13)\ (6,14)\ (7,15)\}$$

Note that the difference between two B-apart numbers is always equal to B, but not all pairs of numbers whose difference is B are B-apart. For example the numbers 1 and 2 are not 1-apart. We now use the concept of "apartness" to define an important property of mapping vectors which we shall subsequently refer to as the "adjacency property".

Definition of the "adjacency property":

For any mapping which can be represented by a mapping vector, data items whose indices are 2^i-apart are mapped in to locations (PEs) which are 2^j-apart where j is the position of the mapping vector element "i" within the mapping vector. (Note that positions of mapping vector elements are numbered from the right starting at zero)

This can be clearly seen if we revert to the diagrammatic view of the mapping vector. For example consider the mapping vector (2 0 1) of 8 data items. In diagrammatic form this is shown as follows:

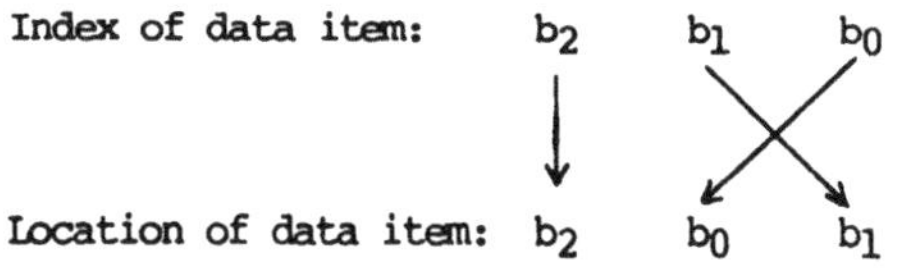

which brings out more clearly the way the location (PE number) of each data item is derived from its binary index. Since the location is obtained by simply permuting (and possibly inverting) the bits of the index, a pair of data whose indices differ in only one of the bits b_0, b_1, b_2 will be mapped into locations which differ in just one bit. Suppose the indices of a pair of data differ only in bit 0 (i.e. they are 2^0-apart); by reference to the diagram it should be clear that their locations will differ only in bit 1 (i.e. their locations are 2^1-apart). Comparison with the mapping vector confirms that mapping vector element "0" is at position 1 in accordance with the adjacency principle. For the above mapping the adjacency principle also tells us that:

(a) data items with indices 2^1-apart are mapped in to PEs which are 2^0-apart (since mapping vector element "1" is at position 0 in the mapping vector);

(b) data items with indices 2^2-apart are mapped in to PEs which are 2^2-apart (since mapping vector element "2" is at position 2 in the mapping vector).

Using this property of mapping vectors we can now illustrate how the musical-bits notation is used during the solution of a problem. The purpose of the following illustration is to demonstrate "how" and not "how well" this is done. An appreciation of the latter requires an analysis of the performance of specific hardware and will in general involve consideration of the effects of multi-dimensional data, multi-dimensional memories and mappings with more than one data item in each PE.

The illustration we use is that of sorting a bitonic sequence of numbers using the Batcher bitonic merge [6]; a bitonic sequence is defined as a sequence of numbers which when considered cyclicly has only one ascending and one descending part. We consider the special case of a sequence of 8 numbers on our basic hardware model with a linear array of 8 PEs, each connected to its nearest neighbour. No familiarity with the algorithm is assumed and, as far as possible, irrelevant details are omitted.

The flowgraph for the computation is shown in fig. 6. The data shown there is labelled with indices D0 to D7 and sample values are given to illustrate the working of the algorithm. The arrowed lines indicate the flow of data and each circular node denotes a comparison operation in which data on the two incoming lines are compared and the

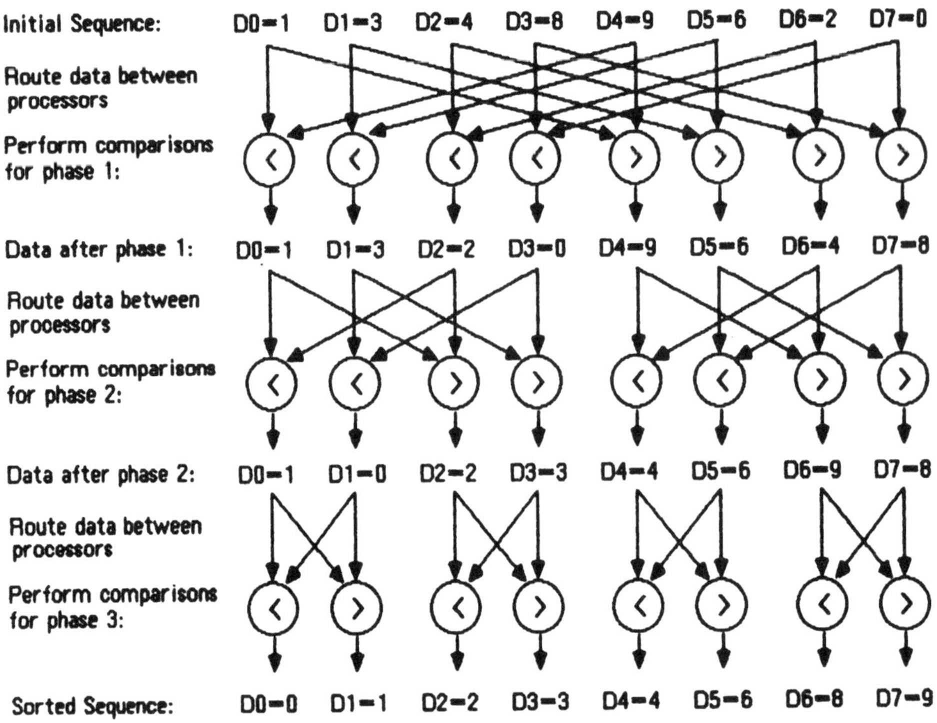

Fig. 6: Flowgraph of 8-point Bitonic Merge

larger (if the node is labelled ">") or the smaller (if the node is labelled "<") is passed to the output line below the node.

Examination of the flowgraph shows that there are three computation phases, each corresponding to one row of nodes in the flowgraph. Prior to each of these phases data is routed so that:

in the first phase data items with indices 2^2-apart are brought together;

in the second phase data items with indices 2^1-apart are brought together;

in the third phase data items with indices 2^0-apart are brought together.

With the algorithm expressed in this way we now make use of the adjacency property of mapping vectors to introduce an alternative solution to that implied by direct execution of the flowgraph of figure 6. We assume that each data item is located in a single PE and then we modify the mapping of data prior to each phase of computation in order to bring interacting data into adjacent locations. The algorithm is described in mapping vector space as follows:

(i) The initial mapping vector is that of the identity mapping, (2 1 0), and prior to the computation of the first phase we perform the exchange E(0;2) to give the mapping (0 1 2). Appealing to the adjacency property of mapping vectors, data items whose indices are 2^2-apart are now in PEs 2^0-apart.

Hence all comparisons for phase 1 can be done between data in adjacent PEs.

(ii) Prior to phase 2 we perform the exchange E(0;1) to transform from the mapping (0 1 2) to the mapping (0 2 1). For the latter, data items whose indices are 2^1-apart are in PEs 2^0-apart. Hence all the comparisons for this phase can be done between data in adjacent PEs

(iii) Prior to phase 3 we perform the exchange E(0;2) to transform from the mapping (0 2 1) to the mapping (1 2 0). For the latter, data items whose indices are 2^0-apart are in PEs 2^0-apart. Hence all the comparison-exchanges for this phase can be done between data in adjacent PEs.

The above algorithm can be summarized by saying that prior to each phase, interacting data is brought into adjacent PEs by transformations to the mapping vector which bring the mapping vector elements 2, 1, and 0 to position 0 in the mapping vector for each of the three phases respectively. The final mapping vector in the above algorithm is (1 2 0). If required natural ordering can be produced by applying the generator E(2;1). Thus the alternative algorithm including reordering is described in mapping vector space as shown in fig. 7. When working in mapping vector space there is no need to follow through the corresponding data movement in physical space. However, for the purposes of consolidating understanding, the corresponding physical movements are shown in fig. 8; the same sample data as before is given. Note that the positions of the indices D0 to D7 in figure 9 vary with changes to the mapping unlike figure 6 where the mapping is static. This method generalises quite simply for larger merges on correspondingly larger processor arrays. Thus for a 1024 point merge on a linear array of 1024 PEs the essence of the method is to bring mapping vector elements 9,8,7,6,5,4,3,2,1, and 0 to position 0 in the mapping vector for each of the ten stages respectively.

Steps of the Algorithm	Changes to the Mapping
Initial Mapping:	(2 1 0)
Remap using E(0;2):	(0 1 2)
Perform comparison-exchanges for phase 1:	(0 1 2)
Remap using E(0;1):	(0 2 1)
Perform comparison-exchanges for phase 2:	(0 2 1)
Remap using E(0;2):	(1 2 0)
Perform comparison-exchanges for phase 3:	(1 2 0)
Remap using E(1;2) to give identity mapping:	(2 1 0)

Fig. 7: A Merge of 8 Data Points in Mapping Vector Space

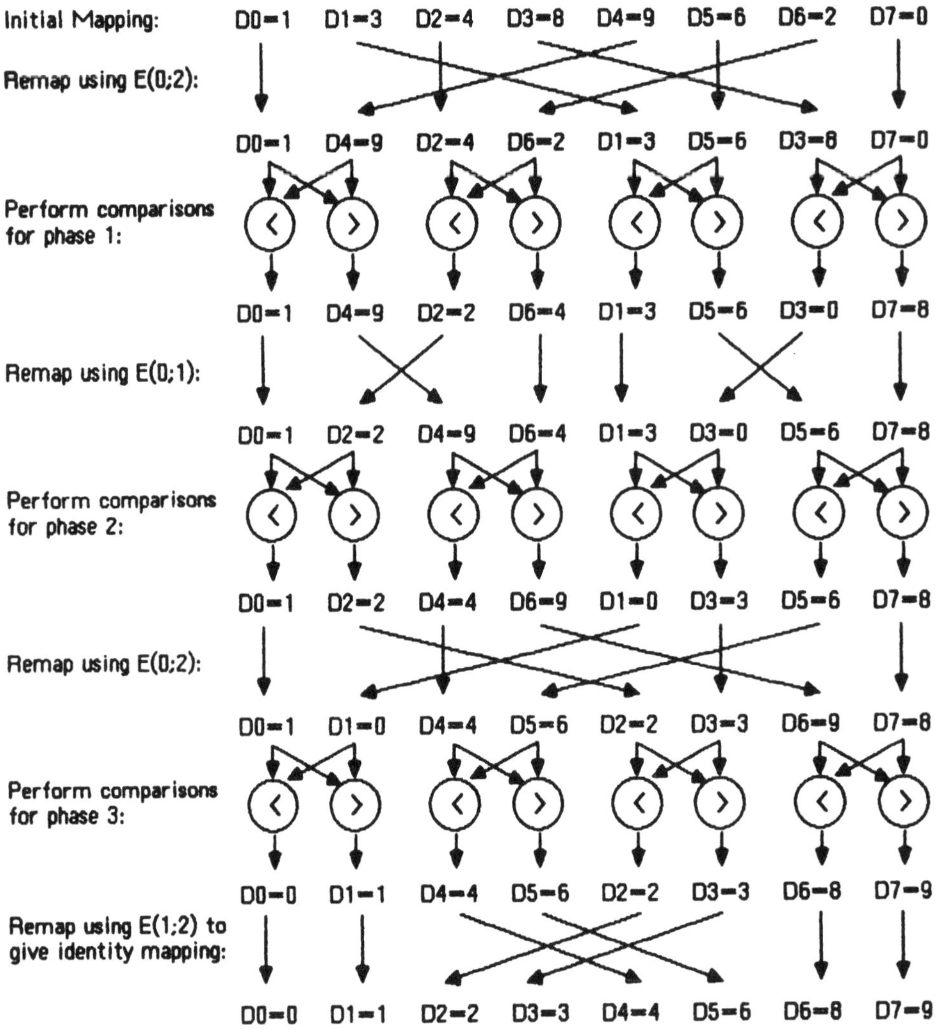

Fig. 8: Merge of Figure 7 in Physical Space

The Batcher bitonic merge is used repeatedlty to sort arbitrarily ordered data in the bitonic sort algorithm. For example 16 data items are sorted as follows:

Stage 1: Simultaneously perform 8 bitonic merges on sequences containing just 2 numbers. (note that a sequence of two numbers is trivially bitonic). This results in 8 sorted sequences and we arrange it so that alternate sequences are sorted in opposite directions so that each pair of sequences forms a single bitonic sequence. Thus as a result of this step we have 4 bitonic sequences each containing 4 numbers.

Steps of the Algorithm	Mapping Vector
Initial Mapping:	(3 2 1 0)
Stage 1:	
Do comparison-exchanges on data with indices 1-apart:	(3 2 1 0)
Stage 2:	
Remap using E(0;1):	(3 2 0 1)
Do comparison-exchanges on data with indices 2-apart:	(3 2 0 1)
Remap using E(0;1):	(3 2 1 0)
Do comparison-exchanges on data with indices 1-apart:	(3 2 1 0)
Stage 3:	
Remap using E(0;2):	(3 0 1 2)
Do comparison-exchanges on data with indices 4-apart:	(3 0 1 2)
Remap using E(0;1):	(3 0 2 1)
Do comparison-exchanges on data with indices 2-apart:	(3 0 2 1)
Remap using E(0;2):	(3 1 2 0)
Do comparison-exchanges on data with indices 1-apart:	(3 1 2 0)
Stage 4:	
Remap using E(0;3):	(0 1 2 3)
Do comparison-exchanges on data with indices 8-apart:	(0 1 2 3)
Remap using E(0;1):	(0 1 3 2)
Do comparison-exchanges on data with indices 4-apart:	(0 1 3 2)
Remap using E(0;2):	(0 2 3 1)
Do comparison-exchanges on data with indices 2-apart:	(0 2 3 1)
Remap using E(0;3):	(1 2 3 0)
Do comparison-exchanges on data with indices 1-apart:	(1 2 3 0)
Restore Identity Mapping:	
Remap using E(1;3):	(3 2 1 0)

Fig. 9: A Sort of 16 Data Points in Mapping Vector Space

Stage 2: Simultaneously perform 4 bitonic merges on the sequences resulting from the pair of sequences forms a single bitonic sequence. Thus as a result of this step we have 2 bitonic sequences each containing 8 numbers.

Stage 3: Simultaneously perform 2 bitonic merges on the sequences resulting from the execution of stage 1. This results in 2 sorted sequences and we arrange it so that they are sorted in opposite directions so that the result is a single bitonic sequence.

Stage 4: Perform a single bitonic merge on the sequence produced by stage 3 to complete the sort.

The sort performs comparison-exchanges on data as shown overleaf:

In stage 1: on data 2^0-apart;

In stage 2: on data 2^1-apart, 2^0-apart;

In stage 3: on data 2^2-apart, 2^1-apart, 2^0-apart;

In stage 4: on data 2^3-apart, 2^2-apart, 2^1-apart, 2^0-apart;

We can therefore use an algorithm for each stage similar to that described above for the bitonic merge. However it is not necessary to remap the data to produce the identity mapping after each stage, we can simply take whatever mapping is produced by one stage as the input mapping for the next stage and use mapping vectors to keep track of the data. The algorithm for sorting 16 numbers on the basic hardware model with 16 PEs is shown in mapping vector space in figure 9. Larger sorts follow a similar pattern. We do not try to show the corresponding data movement in physical space!

The algorithm described above is similar to that described in more detail in ref[2] for the more general situation where the number of items to be sorted is greater than the number of PEs and the PE array is two-dimensional. Its improved efficiency over other implementations of the Batcher bitonic sort given in the literature is only evident in this more general context and is a consequence of allowing the mapping to vary dynamically throughout the sort.

6. NOTES RELATING TO MORE REALISTIC APPLICATIONS

In the previous two sections we have illustrated in a simple way the reduction in complexity resulting from working in mapping vector space rather than in physical space. This is particularly so in more realistic situations involving multi-dimensional data, multiple data stored in each PE, and large numbers of PEs arranged as multi-dimensional arrays; in such situations the mapping vector retains its one-dimensional form and the solution of mapping and routing problems is not significantly more complex than for one-dimensional working. The adjacency principle extends naturally to these more realistic situations; it is particularly important when multiple data are stored in each PE since it then identifies mappings for which interacting data are in the memory of the same PE.

The physical data movements corresponding to individual generators are simple and efficient on processor arrays even in the multi-dimensional cases. Sophisticated implementations of these simple movements can achieve performance better than would be expected from a simple analysis; some details of this are given in [2]. The physical data movement corresponding to certain regular sequences of generators can be implemented more efficiently than if done by data movements corresponding to individual generators. Such "composite" transformations can be included in any implementation of a musical-bits system. The generators and some composite transformations are implemented as macros on the ICL DAP [5].

The nearest neighbour connections between the PEs of a processor array are sometimes supplemented by other PE interconnection networks. For example a perfect shuffle network is commonly proposed [7]. Musical-bits enables the wider exploitation of such a facility and enables its benefits to be assessed more systematically. It may be desirable to introduce new generators to reflect the capability of the network; for example if we have a bi-directional perfect shuffle network then unit shifts of appropriate groups of mapping vector elements are obvious candidates.

Musical-bits will handle multiple arrays, for example in executing a number of FFTs simultaneously. It will also handle "sub-atomic" operations where it is convenient to split individual data; this is often a requirement when, as is usually the case, the width of the PE data paths is less than the width of the data. In fact the width of PE data paths is frequently just one bit.

7. SUMMARY

We have described an index-based notation for denoting members of an important class of mappings of multi-dimensional data on to a multi-dimensional memory. Each mapping is represented by a mapping vector having important computational characteristics. Techniques are described for transforming between mappings to effect data routing, both as an end in itself and as an integral part of a computation. Working in the space of mapping vectors rather than in physical space results in considerable reduction in complexity leading to elegant solutions of complex routing problems. The reduction in complexity is largely due to two factors: a reduction by a factor of $N/\log_2 N$ in the amount of data needed to describe a mapping, and the reduction from multiple dimension to single dimension working. The relevance to parallel processing, in particular for SIMD processor arrays has been demonstrated by some simple examples. More advanced applications are described in references [1,2].

8. REFERENCES

[1] P.M. Flanders, D. Parkinson, "Musical-Bits, A calculus of data organisation for effective parallel processing", ICL SSC report CM99, Jan 86.

[2] P.M. Flanders, "A unified approach to a class of data movements on an array processor", IEEE Trans. Comp., Vol. C-31, No. 9, Sept. 82.

[3] P.M. Flanders, "A methodology for emulating sorting and routing networks on processor arrays", ICL SSC document CM 97, Oct. 85.

[4] D.J. Hunt, "Hardware for fast input-output and data reorganisation", ICL SSC document CM 81, Mar. 84.

[5] P.M. Flanders, D.J. Hunt, S.F. Reddaway, D. Parkinson, "Efficient high speed computing with the Distributed Array Processor", Symposium on High Speed Computer and Algorithm Organisation, University of Illinois, Academic Press, 1977.

[6] K.E. Batcher, "Sorting Networks and their Applications", Proc. AFIPS 1968 SJCC, Vol. 32, Montvale NJ, AFIPS Press, pp 307-314.

[7] H.S. Stone, "Parallel Processing with the Perfect Shuffle", IEEE Trans. Comp., Vol C-20, pp 153-161, Feb. 1971.

RECENT RESULTS IN THE THEORY OF HOMOGENEOUS STRUCTURES

VICTOR ALADYEV [1)]

1. INTRODUCTION

The homogeneous structure(HS) is an information parallel processing system consisting of intercommunicating identical finite automata. Although "homogeneous structures" will be the usual term throughout this work, it should be borne in mind that "cellular automata", "iterative networks", and so on are essentially synonymous. We can interpret HS not only as abstraction of biological cellular systems, but also as theotetical framework of artificial parallel information processing systems. From the logical point of view the HS is a infinite automaton with characteristic internal structure. The theory of HS can be considered to be the structural and dynamic theory of the infinite automata. At present, this theory forms original part of the modern cybernetics.

The modern point of view to the theory of HS has been formed under the influence of works of E.F. Moore, H. Yamada, A.R. Smith, A. Burks, H. Nishio, R. Vollmar, G. Wolf, T. Legendi, S. Toffoli and others.

During the recent years there has been considerable interest in the theory of HS about which many interesting results have been obtained. Much of this work has been motivated by the growing interest in computer science and biological modelling.

In our previous works [1-8] we investigated different aspects of the HS theory and their applications in computer science and biological modelling. Results in this directions contributed much that is new to the HS theory and its applications. Systematic survey of our publications in this direction over the years 1970-1985 can be found in work [16]. However, many questions still remaind open in the present topic. In this work we present our recent solutions of a number of open questions in the HS theory. This work is organized so as to discuss the more general problems and results obtained therein. It is rather unfortunate that we have no space here to discuss in detail the basic techniques for solving of problems. Exhaustive information about these can be found in our previous works [10-13]. The all general terms, notions and designations can be found in [5,7,8,10], in item 2 or are wellknown. All the others are introduced as the necessity arises.

---

1) Tallinn-35 Paldiski mnt 171-26 SKB MPSM ESSR

2. GENERAL DEFINITIONS AND NOTIONS

The classical d-dimensional HS(d-HS) is an ordered quadruple HS=$\langle Z^d, A, \tau^{(n)}, X \rangle$, where:

(1) Z^d is a d-dimensional regular array

(2) $A = \{0,1,2,\ldots,a-1\}$ is the alphabet of the HS

(3) $\tau^{(n)}$ is the global transition function of d-HS

(4) X is the neighbourhood index of HS

(5) n is the number of neighbouring machines in HS

Such models have been applied in the different areas and they present enough interesting independent objects of investigation as well.

The state of the entire array Z^d is called a configuration(CF) of the array and is simply the complete set of current states of each of the individual machines. A CF is any mapping CF: $Z^d \to A$; null-CF($\overline{0}$) is a mapping $\overline{0}$: $Z^d \to 0$. C_A denotes the set of all CF with respect to Z^d and A, i.e., $C_A = \{CF \mid CF: Z^d \to A\}$. Let c(z) be the current state of the machine located at cell $z \in Z^d$. The support of a CF c (denoted by [c]) is the set of all cells z such that $c(z) \neq 0$, i.e., the support is the nonquiescent part of CF c. CF with finite support are of considerable interest; the set of all such CF is denoted by $\overline{C}_A$. The set of all infinite CF of the d-HS is denoted by $\overset{\infty}{C}_A$; obviously, that $\overline{C}_A \cup \overset{\infty}{C}_A = C_A$ and $\overline{C}_A \cap \overset{\infty}{C}_A = \emptyset$.

The operation of the d-HS is specified by a local function $\sigma^{(n)}$ which produces the next state of an individual machine z in terms of the states of the machines which are directly connected to z. For the rest, a local function is any mapping $\sigma^{(n)}: A^n \to A$. The simultaneous application of a local function to the neighbourhood of every cell of the array Z^d defines a global function $\tau^{(n)}$ of the current CF c into the next CF c $\tau^{(n)}$. The operation of a d-HS is particularly simple. If $c=c_0$ is an initial CF of the array Z^d at time t=0, then the CF at time t=m is $c_0 \tau^{(n)m}$, the result of applying $\tau^{(n)}$ to the array m times. Let now $\langle c_0 \rangle_{\tau(n)}$ denote the CF-sequence generated by function $\tau^{(n)}$ from the CF $c_0 \in C_A$. CF c' is called the predecessor of CF $c \in C_A$ in d-HS if $c' \tau^{(n)} = c$; CF c is called periodical in d-HS with period k iff $c \tau^{(n)k} = c$.

A CF $c \in C_A$ will be said to be a self-reproducing in Moore's sense CF(SRCF) if for each positive integer m there exists a t such that CF $c^x = c \tau^{(n)t}$ contains m copies of a CF c; incidentally, we will say that a CF c^x contains m copies of a CF c, if there exist m disjoit subsets of the array of c^x and each of these subsets is a copy of c. We will say that d-HS possess universal reproductability in Moore's sense if any CF $c \in C_A$ is a SRCF. Definitions of nonconstructible CF(NCF and NCF-1), mutually erasable CF(MEC) and previous results in this direction can be found in our works[5,7,8,10].

Each d-HS($d \geq 1$) can be assumed as a parallel formal τ_n-grammar with an axiom $c_0 \in \overline{C}_A$(initial CF in d-HS) and productions $\tau^{(n)}$(global function of d-HS)[5-8]. It is most natural to define its language, denoted $L(\tau_n)$, as the set of all words(configurations, axiom included) that can be derived from axiom c_0 by means of applications of global function $\tau^{(n)}$; hence $L(\tau_n)= \{c \in \overline{C}_A | c_0 \xrightarrow{\tau^{(n)}} c\}$.

The general decomposition problem(GDP) of global functions in d-HS ($d \geq 1$) can be presented as follows: Can any global function $\tau^{(n)}$ of d-HS be presented in the form of composition of the finite number of more simple global functions $\tau^{(n_i)}$ ($n_i < n$; $i=\overline{1,k}$)?

Now we shall discuss the most significant, in my opinion, recent results in the HS theory and their applications. This work we have done over the years 1984-85 and the first quarter of 1986.

3. GENERAL RESULTS

Above all, we turn one's eyes again upon the general decomposition problem(GDP) of global functions in d-HS. The GDP was solved by Aladyev with the help of nonconstructibility approach in d-HS [4-7]. In our book [8] the GDP received further decisions on the basis of other interesting approaches, in the first place, with the help of Shannon's function and on the basis of results in K-valued logics($K \geq 2$). Using results on universal reproductability in Moore's sense in 1-HS, the following theorem can be proved [11].

<u>Theorem 1.</u> There exists the infinite set of binary global functions of 1-HS, which has negative solution of the GDP.

The GDP is the question whether or not any global function $\tau^{(n)}$ of d-HS will possess the following representation:

$$\tau^{(n)} = \tau_1^{(n_1)} \; \tau_2^{(n_2)} \; \ldots\ldots\ldots \; \tau_k^{(n_k)} \qquad (1)$$
$$(\forall j)(n_j < n)(j=\overline{1,k})$$

Representation (1) is called <u>minimal</u> for function $\tau^{(n)}$ if it has minimal length among all possible representations of type (1) for this function. Using this concept, we present the following result.

Let some function $\tau^{(n)}$ has the only possible representation (1). Clearly, this representation is minimal and maximal for function $\tau^{(n)}$ at the same time. Hence, for each function $\tau_i^{(n_i)}(i=\overline{1,k})$ from (1) the GDP has negative solution. On the other hand, there exist global functions having the only possible representation of type (1)[15]. Thus we receive just one more method of the GDP's solution.

Decidability results play extremely important role in modern mathematics. We extended this discussion to concern the problems studied in the HS theory[1-5,14,15]. The common problem of algorithmical solvability of the GDP for arbitrary function $\tau^{(n)}$ of d-HS($d \geq 1$) is open so far. The other picture can be seen in the case of some individual algorithmical problems. For example, is it decidable whether arbitrary function $\tau^{(n)}$ have representation of type (1), where $\tau_i^{(n_i)} \in G(i=\overline{1,k})$ and G is arbitrary subset of the set of all global functions $\tau^{(n)}$ of d-HS($d \geqslant 1$)? In this direction we have the following result [11].

Theorem 2. The GDP of global functions with respect to arbitrary subset G of the set of all global functions of d-HS($d \geqslant 1$) is undecidable.

On a level with well-known GDP it is interesting to investigate the so called global decomposition problem(GLDP) of global functions of d-HS ($d \geqslant 1$) [11]. This problem is the question whether or not arbitrary function $\tau^{(n)}$ will possess representation of type (1) on condition that functions $\tau_i^{(n_i)}$ are no linked the correlation $n_i < n(i=\overline{1,k})$, ignoring the trivial cases. This means that we may use arbitrary global functions as functions $\tau_i^{(n_i)}(i=\overline{1,k})$ in representation (1). Clearly, the positive solution of the GDP for function $\tau^{(n)}$ entail the positive solution of the GLDP for this global function. The inverse assertion is not true, broadly speaking [11]. Therefore, the GDP and the GLDP are not equivalent, generally. In connection with the GLDP we have interesting results [11].

Theorem 3. The GLDP for global functions $\tau^{(n)}$ has negative solutions, in general.

Theorem 4. If for some global function $\tau^{(n)}$ the GDP and the GLDP are equivalent, then for this functions these problems are decidable.

The utilization of possibility of representation of local functions $\sigma^{(n)}$ in the form of polynomial in modulo a(a - prime) [15] allow to receive the following interesting result [11].

Theorem 5. For any global function $\tau^{(n)}$ in alphabet $A_p=\{0,1,..,a-1\}$ (a - prime) the GDP and the GLDP are equivalent, and decidable.

Theorem 5 gives answers on a number of problems from our book [15]. Furthermore, theorems 4 and 5 show that structure of alphabet A of d-HS has of vital importance for the equivalence of the GDP and the GLDP. For alphabet A_p take place the equivalence and decidability of the GDP and the GLDP, whereas in the general case of alphabet A of d-HS these problems are not equivalent, generally; and the question of their decidability is open, so far. Using now theorem 5 and proof of theorem 3 the following theorem can be proved [11,12].

Theorem 6. The GDP and the GLDP for function $\tau^{(n)}$ in alphabet A_p have positive solutions iff the function $\tau^{(n)}$ can be presented in the form of composition $\tau^{(n)}= \tau^{(m)} \tau^{(q)}(m,q<n;\ m+q-1=n)$ of two functions in the same alphabet.

From theorem 6 the following interesting result may be drawn [11,12].

Theorem 7. For any integer $n \geqslant 3$ there exist functions $\tau^{(n)}$ in alphabet A_p, for which the GDP and the GLDP are equivalent and have negative solutions.

This theorem present just one more proof of negative solutions of the GDP and the GLDP. Using the proof of theorem 7, we can to estimate the quota of functions $\tau^{(n)}$ in alphabet A_p, for which the GDP and the GLDP have positive solutions [11,12].

Theorem 8. The GDP and the GLDP for "almost all" functions $\tau^{(n)}$

in alphabet A_p have negative solutions.

Thus, we receive slightly unexpected result, namely: quota of all functions $\tau^{(n)}(n \geqslant 3)$ in alphabet A_p, which have positive solutions of the GDP and the GLDP, is equal to zero. From results on the GDP and the GLDP [11,12] , it can be easily verified that among all functions $\tau^{(n)}$ $(n \geqslant 2)$ in alphabet A_p the infinite hierarchy of complexity with respect to the GDP/GLDP can be established. We shall say that function $\tau^{(n)}$ in alphabet A_p belongs to p-level of complexity(denotion: $\tau^{(n)} \in L(p)$)iff for it there exists representation

$$\tau^{(n)} = \tau_1^{(n_1)} \ldots\ldots \tau_k^{(n_k)} \quad (n_i \leqslant p < n;\ (\exists i)(n_i = p);(i=\overline{1,k}))$$

and there does not exist representation of the similar type with $n_i > p$ $(i=\overline{1,k})$. If the GDP(GLDP) for function $\tau^{(n)}$ has negative solution, then $\tau^{(n)} \in L(n)$. Using the above-mentioned results on the GDP and the GLDP, and the proof of theorem 8[11] we can receive the correlations:

$$(\forall p \geqslant 2)(\# L(p) \neq 0) \ ; \qquad \lim_{p \to \infty} \# L(p)/a^{a^p} \geqslant 1 \ (a \text{ - prime})$$

From theorem 5 and the definition of complexity with respect to the GDP/GLDP of global functions $\tau^{(n)}$ the following result can be drawn.

Theorem 9. The problem of determination of p-level of complexity with respect to the GDP/GLDP for arbitrary global function $\tau^{(n)}$ in alphabet A_p is algorithmically decidable.

In view of definition of complexity with respect to the GDP/GLDP of global functions, we can to receive a number of characteristics of global functions depending on their complexity. Thus, if function in alphabet A_p $\tau^{(n)} \in L(p)$ and $p < n$, then in conformity with theorem 5 it has representation $\tau^{(n)} = \tau^{(m)} \tau^{(q)}(m,q < n;\ m+q-1 = n)$ and, consequently, it has, for example, the same minimal size of MEC and NCF with functions $\tau^{(m)}$ and $\tau^{(q)}$, accordingly. Results on the GDP and the GLDP can be useful for solution of the problem of the existence of NCF and NCF-1 in d-HS(d>1) [11,12]. Moreover, in a series of cases we have the possibility to reduce solution of the existence problems for NCF and NCF-1 for d-dimensional functions $\tau^{(n)}$ in alphabet A_p to solution of the same problems for more simple global functions of the same dimensionality. Sometimes, such approach simplify the problem to a great extent, although in the common case the problem is open. It allow to present the following result [11,12].

Definition 1. The algorithm G for determination of the existence of MEC in d-HS(d>1) is called essentially constructive, if it for any global function $\tau^{(n)}$ of the structure give answer "yes-no" on the question of the existence of MEC for this function, and in the case of the positive answer are defined all typies of the existing pairs of MEC for global function $\tau^{(n)}$.

Using this definition and our previous results in d-HS [1], we can prove the following theorem [11,12].

Theorem 10. There exists no essentially constructive algorithm G, which solve the problem of the existence of MEC for d-dimensional functions $\tau^{(n)}(d \geqslant 2)$, in general.

From the theorem 10 we have the following conjecture: for solution of the problem of the existence of NCF in d-HS($d \geqslant 2$) algorithms(if such there exist) on the more high level than essentially constructive ones are required.

From above-mentioned results(theorems 5-9) it is clear that we essentially used the alphabet A_p, since the local function in this alphabet can be presented in the form of polynomial in modulo a of maximal degree n(a-1) over field A_p, and vice versa. In the case of composite integer a far from each function $\sigma^{(n)}$ in alphabet $A=\{0,1,2,\ldots,a-1\}$ cannot be presented in the polynomial form, generally speaking. The next theorem confirm this fact.

<u>Theorem 11.</u> For each alphabet $A=\{0,1,2,\ldots,a-1\}$(a - composite integer) the quota(g) of local functions $\sigma^{(n)}$ in the alphabet A, which are presented in the form of polynomial in modulo a, satisfy the following correlation

$$1/a^{a^n-4^n} \leq g \leq 1/a^{a^n-(a-2)^n}$$

Theorem 11 shows that for composite integers a "almost all" local functions in alphabet A cannot be presented in the form of polynomial in modulo a for enough large integers n or/and a. Thus, the well-known analitical method of investigation of d-HS($d \geqslant 1$) on the basis of the polynomial representation of local functions in the case of composite integer a is useless, in most cases. In the book [15] we formulated the following interesting problem: Is it possible to define the algebraical system, which permit the polynomial representation of local functions for case of composite integer a, like of the case of prime a. Various algebraical systems have been proposed to answer this question [15]. We present now an algebraical system, in which "almost all" local functions in alphabet A(a - composite integer) has representation in the form of polynomial in modulo a.

We define the algebraical system in the following way. Let $A=\{0,1,2,\ldots,a-1\}$(a - composite integer) be an arbitrary set of integers. On the set A the usual operation (+) of addition in modulo a is defined. At the same time, on the set A the binary operation of $\otimes$-multiplication is introduced in conformity with the following table

$\otimes$:	0	1	2	3	4	5	....	(a-1)
0 :	0	0	0	0	0	0	....	0
1 :	0	1	2	3	4	5	....	(a-1)
2 :	0	2	3	4	5	6	....	1
3 :	0	3	4	5	6	7	....	12
4 :	0	4	5	6	7	8	....	123
5 :	0	5	6	7	8	9	....	1234
....:	...	...	...	...	...	...	....	...
(a-1):	0	(a-1)	...			4	....	(a-3)(a-2)

(2)

It can be easily seen that operation $\otimes$-multiplication on the set $A\setminus\{0\}$ form the finite cyclic group $A^{\otimes}$ of degree (a-1). In view of our above-mentioned suppositions the following general result can be established [11,12].

<u>Theorem 12.</u> There exist an algebraical system $\langle A; +; \otimes \rangle$ in which "almost each " local function $\sigma^{(n)}$ in the alphabet A can be unequivocally presented in the form of polynomical $P_{\otimes}(n) \pmod a$, where:

1. (+) is operation of addition in modulo a, which form on the set A the finite additive cyclic group of degree a;
2. ($\otimes$) is operation of $\otimes$-multiplication, which is determined by table (2) and which form on the set $A \setminus \{0\}$ the finite cyclic group of degree (a-1);
3. polynomial $P_{\otimes}(n) = \sum_{i=1}^{a^n-1} c_i \otimes X_1^{k_{i_1}} \otimes X_2^{k_{i_2}} \otimes \ldots \otimes X_n^{k_{i_n}} \pmod a$ (3)
   contains no binomials of the form $P_k X_j^k + B_k X_j^{a-k-1}$
   $$(0 \leqslant k_{i_j} \leqslant a-1;\ \sum_{j=1}^{n} k_{i_j} \geqslant 1;\ X_j, c_i \in A;\ j=\overline{1,n};\ i=\overline{1,a^n-1};$$
   $$P_k + B_k = a;\ P_k, B_k \geqslant 1;\ k=\overline{1,[(a-2)/2]}).$$

Theorem 12 plays a very important role in investigations of dynamic properties of d-HS($d \geqslant 1$) in the case of alphabet $A=\{0,1,2,\ldots,a-1\}$ (a - composite integer). Furthermore, the theorem gives comfortable analytical representation of functions of a-valued logics in the case of composite integer a. To our knowledge this result is the best of its kind. Using now proofs of theorems 4 and 5, and the result of theorem 12 it is easily to receive the following theorem.

<u>Theorem 13.</u> The GDP and the GLDP with respect to the set of "almost all" global functions $\tau^{(n)}$ in alphabet $A=\{0,1,2,\ldots,a-1\}$ (a - composite integer), whose local functions $\sigma^{(n)}$ has polynomial representation in the form (3), are equivalent and decidable.

Thus, having a number of results on the problem of decidability of the GDP and the GLDP, we cannot spread this achievement on the general case of d-HS, so far. The further investigation on the GDP would be extremely desirable(unles necessary).

It is known, that the classical concept of d-HS($d \geqslant 1$) is based on the infinite homogeneous array Z^d. In cases where a finite arrays Z^d are considered, we deal with the finite d-HS($d \geqslant 1$). The finite d-HS are the theoretical foundation of a very wide class of electronic devices. They are, in principle, ordinary finite automata, but with specifical internal structure. Such d-HS are intensively investigated by Japanesse mathematicians, in general [1,3].

The problem of nonconstructibility in the classical d-HS is studied in detail enough [1-12]. In my opinion, this theme is the most developed in the mathematical theory of the infinite d-HS. However, in the case of the finite d-HS we have a series of unsolved problems and perspective directions of investigations, evidently, just owing to one's development. Now we shall present a result in this direction [11].

<u>Theorem 14.</u> If global function $\tau^{(n)}$ possesses NCF or/and NCF-1, then there exist enough wide class of the closed finite d-HS

(with such global function) which have NCF_f, and vice versa. Among NCF_f analogies of NCF and NCF-1 are distinguished.

In the common case of the finite d-HS the result of theorem 14 is false. For example, for the finite 1-HS with fixed boundary conditions each configuration can be constructible even if global function of such structure has NCF-1 without NCF. Consequently, it would be quite interesting to extend investigations in nonconstructibility to the finite d-HS($d \geqslant 1$).

The question of the investigation of algorithmical properties of global maps $\tau^{(n)}: \overset{\infty}{C}_A \to \overset{\infty}{C}_A$ for d-HS($d \geqslant 1$) presents considerable theoretical interest. In connection with this theme the following question arises: Is it decidable whether an arbitrary global map $\tau^{(n)}: \overset{\infty}{C}_A \to \overset{\infty}{C}_A$ is closed(Closed problem)? For 1-dimensional case we received the positive answer on this question [15]. This result can be spread on the case of dimensionality $d \geqslant 2$ [11].

<u>Theorem 15.</u> The closed problem for d-dimensional($d \geqslant 1$) global maps $\tau^{(n)}: \overset{\infty}{C}_A \to \overset{\infty}{C}_A$ is decidable.

Aladyev and others [1,15] investigated the problem of interconnection of the minimal size of NCF and MEC in d-HS. However, no one has been able, as yet, to receive a satisfactory solution of this problem. The following result elucidate the reason of this phenomenon [11].

<u>Theorem 16.</u> It is impossibly, in general, to receive a satisfactory numerical estimation of the minimal size of NCF in d-HS($d \geqslant 1$) depending on the minimal size of MEC, and vice versa.

This result explain the failure of all previous endeavours on this direction. At the same time we receive the answer on the problem 5 [15] about the dependence between the minimal size of NCF and MEC in d-HS.

The class of d-HS which has universal reproducing capability in the Moore's sense is enough exceptional in many respect. The next theorem to a certain extent define such class of d-HS($d \geqslant 1$) [11,12].

<u>Theorem 17.</u> If d-HS($d \geqslant 1$) possesses the universal reproduction in the Moore's sense then for it there exist NCF-1 without NCF. The inverse assertion is false, in general.

On the basis of theorem 17 can be solved the following extremely interesting question: Can a d-HS($d \geqslant 1$) double any finite CF $c \in \overline{C}_A$? [5]. At the same place we formulated the Hypothesis 4.2: There exists no formal system in alphabet A, which can double the arbitrary finite word in the same alphabet. The next theorem gives answer for case of d-HS($d \geqslant 1$).

<u>Theorem 18.</u> There exists no d-HS with alphabet A, which can double the arbitrary d-dimensional CF $c \in \overline{C}_A$ ($d \geqslant 1$).

In our monograph [5] the following interesting problem was formulated: Is it decidable whether an arbitrary infinite set $GS \subset \overline{C}_A$ is an $L(\tau_n)$-language? Now we define the constructive algorithm for solution of this problem as follows. The decisive algorithm is called <u>constructive</u> if it in case of positive answer give τ_n-grammars themselves which generate $L(\tau_n)$-language GS. In the light of this definition we present now the solution of the more common problem, actually.

Theorem 19. There exists no the constructive algorithm for solution of the problem: Is it decidable whether an arbitrary infinite set $GS \subset \overline{C}_A$ is an $L(\tau_n)$-language?

In the process of investigation of the GDP by the group methods, we proved [15] that a semigroup L(a,d) of all d-dimensional maps $\tau^{(n)}: C_A \to C_A$ can be presented in the form of union of subsemigroups L_i, L_j $\{(\forall i)(\forall j)(i \neq j \to L_i \cap L_j = \emptyset)\}$; $(i,j=\overline{1,4})$, which has no finite systems of generators and a maximum group G(d). At the same place we formulated The Hypothesis 2: G(d) is a single group, i.e. it consists of global functions which carry out identical maps $\tau^{(n)}: C_A \to C_A$, only. The further investigations [11,12] show that question with group G(d) is open to a certain extent up to this point. We attempted the detailed investigation of binary 1-HS with the purpose of discovering of an one-one map $\tau^{(n)}: C_A \to C_A$, which differ from identical ones. The attempted investigation proved to be a success. The next theorem present the best received result in this direction [11,12].

Theorem 20. For any integer $n \geqslant 3$ there exist at any rate $2^{n-1}-n$ binary 1-dimensional functions $\tau^{(n)}$, which possess the following properties, simultaneously:

1. $\tau^{(n)}$ has no NCF and NCF-1;
2. each CF $c \in \overline{C}_A$ is periodical for function $\tau^{(n)}$. There exist CF $c \in \overline{C}_A$ with the period p at any rate $(|c|+n-2)/(n-1) < p = 2^k$, where k is minimal integer which answer this inequality's demands;
3. map $\tau^{(n)}: \overset{\infty}{C}_A \to \overset{\infty}{C}_A$ is not one-one mapping;
4. for global function $\tau^{(n)}$ the GDP has negative solution.

This theorem is essential generalization of lemmas 7 and 9 from book [15] but it give not exhaustive solution of the problem for the case of binary 1-dimensional maps $\tau^{(n)}$, even. Whereas, for the case of nonbinary maps Hypothesis 2 [15] to be wrong, i.e. group G(d) contains nontrivial identical one-one maps. This affirmation is based on the following result [11,12].

Theorem 21. A semigroup $L(a,1)(a \geqslant 3)$ of all 1-dimensional maps $\tau^{(n)}: C_A \to C_A$ can be presented in the form of union of subsemigroups $L_i, L_j (i,j=\overline{1,4})$ $\{(\forall i)(\forall j)(i \neq j \to L_i \cap L_j = \emptyset)\}$, which has no finite systems of generators, and a maximum group G(1), which is union of subgroup T of all identical maps $\tau_0^{(n)} (n > 2)$, and symmetrical subgroup P(a) of periodical maps(functions) $\tau^{(n)} (n \geqslant 2)$ with finite system P(a,2) of generators and correlation $\tau^{(n)(a-1)!} = \tau_0^{(2)}$, and, possibly, subgroup of one-one maps, which differ from above-mentioned ones.

Theorem 21 shows that further work on this problem is badly needed. The complexity is one of the most intriguing and vague concepts in most cases. At present we know three approaches to the definition of complexity of the finite objects: combimatorical, probabilistic and algotithmical, which use the theory of recursive functions. For the last case N. Kolmogorov defined the relative complexity of some object G(comparatively of object S) by the minimum length of Turing Machine's programme of deriving of G from S. Our approach can be also called algorithmical but it differs from Kolmogorov's one [4–6,14,15]. The essence of our concept of complexity consists in the estimation of complexity of growing of arbitrary finite CF from some primitive CF c_p by means of the finite number of global functions from some set T_f. On the basis of introduced concept of complexity A(X) of the finite CF we presented solutions of a number of problems in the HS theory. The relation between the concept of complexity A(X) and the GDP in d-HS was stated. Furthermore, the relation between A(X) and other famous measures of complexity was presented [4–6,14,15]. However, it is known that our concept of complexity is based on the Hypothesis 3 [5]. In book [11] the proof of this Hypothesis was presented. The result is expressed by the following general theorem.

<u>Theorem 22.</u> For any finite alphabet A there exist no the finite sets of CF $c_i \in \overline{C}_A$ and global functions $\tau^{(n_i)}$ in alphabet A such that

$$\bigcup_i \langle c_i \rangle_{\tau^{(n_i)}} = \overline{C}_A \qquad (i=\overline{1,k})$$

Theorem 22 allows to give the clean mathematical reasons to a number of results, which were presented in our previous works [1–7,10]. On the basis of theorem 22 and the concept of complexity of the finite CF in d-HS(d $\geqslant$1) a number of interesting results can be proved [11,12].

<u>Theorem 23.</u> Supplement of the finite set of L(τ_n)-languages cannot be the language of the same type.

This theorem proves the truth of Hypothesis 4 [5], also. It was proved [5] that for d-HS without NCF, but with the global function $\tau^{(n)}$ and the set W of NCF-1 there exists no the finite set of CF $c_i \in \overline{C}_A$ such that $\bigcup_i \langle c_i \rangle_{\tau^{(n)}} = \overline{C}_A \setminus W$. Now we shall present essentially more general and very strong result [11,12], which give answer on a number of questions formulated in our previous works [1–8].

<u>Theorem 24.</u> Let $\tau^{(n)}$ be an arbitrary global function in alhabet A(a – prime), which has the set W of NCF and, possibly, NCF-1. Then there exists no the finite set of CF $c_i \in \overline{C}_A$ and functions $\tau^{(n_i)}$ in alphabet A such that:

$$\bigcup_i \langle c_i \rangle_{\tau^{(n_i)}} = \overline{C}_A \setminus W$$

or $\qquad (i=\overline{1,k})$

$$\bigcup_i \langle c_i \rangle_{\tau^{(n_i)}} = W$$

For the case of composite integer a take place the second correlation.

From this theorem we have a very interesting consequence: sets $\overline{C}_A \setminus W$ and W(W is a set of NCF and, possibly, NCF-1) in the case of prime a cannot be generated by means of the finite sets of CF $c_i \in \overline{C}_A$ and global functions in alphabet A regardless of function $\tau^{(n)}$ respect to which the nonconstructibility is considered. Thus, each set of nonconstructible CF(NCF or NCF-1) with respect to the completeness problem[5] possesse the same immunity with set $\overline{C}_A$.

In our monograph[5] in connection with the investigation of complexity problem of the finite CF in d-HS the following question was formulated: Can the set of CF of each level of complexity be finite? The next theorem to a certain extent clarifies the gist of the matter.

<u>Theorem 25.</u> There exist the infinite number of basic sets T_f of global functions $\tau^{(n_i)}(i=\overline{1,k})$ with respect to which there exist the infinite sets of the finite CF of the same complexity.

This theorem gives answers on a number of questions presented in our works[5,15]. However, for the complete solution it is necessary in detail to investigate global functions, which form the minimal basic set T_f. In this work we have defined the <u>minimal</u> basic set as a set contained a very insignificant number of global functions. In this direction we have a number of the interesting results[11].

<u>Theorem 26.</u> There exists a minimal basic set T_f, which contain only four 1-dimensional binary global functions. At any rate a function $\tau^{(n)}$ from the set T_f possesses NCF-1, to say the least.

<u>Theorem 27.</u> With respect to the minimal basic set T_f of 1-dimensional binary global functions, there exist infinite sets of the finite configurations of the same complexity.

Theorem 27 to a certain extent increases the result of theorem 25.

<u>Theorem 28.</u> There exist the minimal basic sets T_f of the binary global functions with respect to which take place the infinite sets of binary functions $\tau^{(n_i)}$ and binary CF $c_i \in \overline{C}_A$ such, that sequences of CF $\langle c_i \rangle_{\tau^{(n_i)}}$ contain the binary CF of any given complexity. There exist no the finite basic set T_f of binary global functions with respect to which each sequence $\langle c_o \rangle_{\tau^{(n)}}$ $(c_o \in \overline{C}_A)$ contains binary CF of the limited complexity, only.

Theorem 28 gives answer both on a question[15] and forms the basis of the following extremely interesting result[11,12]. Above we have noted the difference between concepts of complexity A(X) and K(X)(according to Kolmogorov) of the finite objects. Some of them are noted in our work[15]. Here is a typical example. One of Kolmogorov's results reads: any Turing machine(MT) with constant programme can print on one's own output tape binary words(configurations) of the limited complexity,only. Whereas in case of our concept of complexity we have the opposite picture, according to the theorem 28. The next theorem established the a difference between the concepts K(X) and A(X).

<u>Theorem 29.</u> There exists the difference of principle with respect to the concepts of complexity K(X) and A(X) between the generative possibilities of the infinite automata MT and 1-HS, which form a base for the above-mentioned concepts of complexity of the finite objects.

This theorem allows to elucidate the differences between of a number of Kolmogorov's and our results on the complexity of the finite objects. It is known [11,12] that for the proofs of theorems 24–28 the concept of the minimal basic set T_f and some properties of global functions of T_f were essentially used. Now we present more detailed properties of such minimal basic sets T_f. We consider the global functions $\tau_i^{(n_i)}$ such that its local functions $\sigma_i^{(n)}(i=\overline{0,3})$ are defined by the table

$\sigma(X)$	$\sigma_0^{(3)}(X)$	$\sigma_1^{(3)}(X)$	$\sigma_2^{(3)}(X)$	$\sigma_3^{(2)}(X)$
000	0	0	0	0
001	1	1	1	1
010	0	1	0	1
011	1	0	0	1
100	0	1	1	
101	1	0	1	
110	1	1	0	
111	0	0	0	

In connection with such definition of the global functions and new concept of nonconstructibility(NCF-2) in d-HS, which will be discussed further on, the following result can be presented [11,12].

Theorem 30. The minimal basic set $T_f = \{\tau_0^{(3)}, \tau_1^{(3)}, \tau_2^{(3)}, \tau_3^{(2)}\}$ consist of four 1-dimensional binary global functions having typies of nonconstructibility according to the following table

$\tau_i^{(n)}$	NCF	NCF-1	NCF-2
n=3, i=0	–	+	–
n=3, i=1	–	+	–
n=3, i=2	+	+	–
n=2, i=3	+	–	+

The minimal basic set T_f for non-binary 1-dimensional case consist of the global functions having NCF or/and NCF-1.

The given theorem allows to solve a number of problems from our book [5] and it can be used for investigation of the complexity problem in 1-HS with arbitrary alphabet A. For example, on the basis of theorem 30 can be received more simple substantiation of the introduced concept of complexity of the finite CF in 1-HS. The result of such substantiation take the form of the following theorem.

Theorem 31. Any binary 1-dimensional CF $c \in \overline{C}_A$ is monotonously generated from the primitive CF $c_p = \overline{0}1\overline{0}$ by the functions of set T_f. At the same time, there exists no the finite system of pairs $(c_j, \tau_{i_j}^{(n_j)})$ such that take place the following correlation

$$\bigcup_j \langle c_j \rangle_{\tau_{i_j}^{(n_j)}} = \overline{C}_A \qquad c_j \in \overline{C}_A$$

$$(n_j \in \{2,3\};\ i_j \in \{0,1,2,3\};\ j = \overline{1,k})$$

The set T_f can be chosen as a basic set, with respect to which the complexity of the finite binary 1-dimensional CF is defined.

It will be noted, that this theorem can be generalized on the case of an arbitrary alphabet A. On the basis of theorem 31 can be given more simple and, in a number of cases, constructive proofs of theorems 25–28, and some others results on the complexity of the finite CF in binary 1-HS. The result of theorem 31 in the first part can be essentially improved, namely, takes place the following theorem.

Theorem 32. As the finite system of pairs $(c_j, \tau_{i_j}^{(n_j)})$ of theorem 31 can be chosen system of pairs in which each global function is an arbitrary composition of the finite number of functions from the set T_f. There exist subsets of the set $\overline{C}_A$(A is binary alphabet), the cardinality of which averages 3/4 of cardinality of the set $\overline{C}_A$. Such subsets cannot be generated by the finite number of pairs $(c_i, \tau_i^{(n_i)}; c_i \in \overline{C}_A)$.

The complexity problem in d-HS is studied in detail enough. However, it has a series of unsolved problems and perspective directions of investigations, evidently, just owing to one's development.

Up to now, we considered two concepts of nonconstructibility in d-HS(NCF and NCF-1), only. Both concepts are based on the different possibilities of mapping $\tau^{(n)}: C_A \rightarrow C_A$ with respect to sets of the finite and the infinite CF. With the purpose of to embrace all possibilities in the problem, we introduce new type of nonconstructibility(NCF-2)[11].

Definition 2. CF $c \in \overline{C}_A$ is called NCF-2 for function $\tau^{(n)}$ iff there does not exist CF $\overset{\infty}{c} \in \overset{\infty}{C}_A$ such that $\overset{\infty}{c}\,\tau^{(n)} = c$ and there exists CF $c' \in \overline{C}_A$ such that $c'\,\tau^{(n)} = c$.

It is easy to verify that such nonconstructible CF there exist for d-HS(d$\geqslant$1). The next diagram illustrates the essence of all three typies of nonconstructibility in d-HS(d$\geqslant$1).

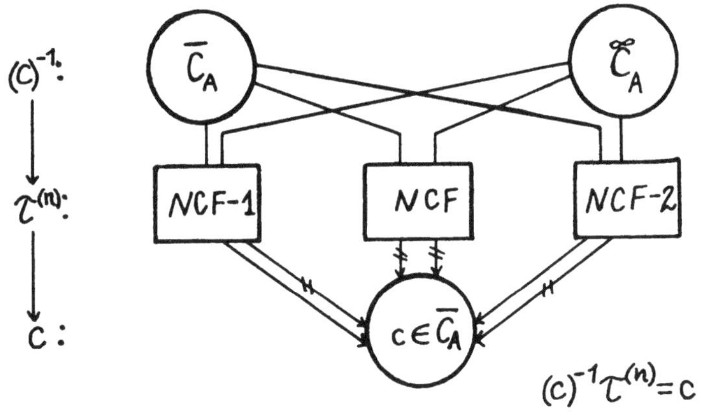

The diagram of nonconstructibility in d-HS

The interconnection of all typies of nonconstructibility in d-HS expresses the following general result[11,12].

Theorem 33. Each d-dimensional(d$\geqslant$1) global function $\tau^{(n)}$ possesses at least a type of nonconstructibility: NCF, NCF-1 or NCF-2 (the absence of absolute constructibility in d-HS). The non-empty sets of NCF, NCF-1 and NCF-2 in d-HS(d$\geqslant$1) is infinite, always. Each d-dimensional global function simultaneously has typies of nonconstructibility according to the following table

n/n	NCF	NCF-1	NCF-2	Possibility
1	+	+	+	there exists
2	+	+	–	-//-
3	+	–	+	-//-
4	–	+	+	is absent
5	+	–	–	there exists
6	–	+	–	-//-
7	–	–	+	-//-
8	–	–	–	is absent

The following theorem gives a criterion of the existence of NCF-2 in 1-HS without NCF [11,12].

Theorem 34. 1-dimensional global function $\tau^{(n)}$ without NCF has a NCF-2 iff the corresponding map $\tau^{(n)}: \overset{\infty}{C}_A \rightarrow \overset{\infty}{C}_A$ is closed.

This criterion is opposite, in a way, to the criterion of the existence of NCF-1 in 1-HS without NCF [5]. From criteria of the existence of NCF-1 and NCF-2 in 1-HS without NCF the following result can be essily received [11].

Theorem 35. If 1-dimensional mapping $\tau^{(n)}: \overset{\infty}{C}_A \rightarrow \overset{\infty}{C}_A$ is closed (is not closed), then the corresponding global function without NCF possesses NCF-2(NCF-1).

From theorem 33 and algorithmical decidability [5] of the problems of the existence of NCF and NCF-1 in 1-HS the following theorem can be proved [11,12].

Theorem 36. The problem of the existence of an arbitrary set of NCF, NCF-1 and NCF-2 in 1-HS is algorithmically decidable.

It is desirable to receive similar criteria in the geberal case d-HS($d > 1$). It is hardly too much to say, that detailed investigation of the concept of the MEC in d-HS present undoubted interest. This investigation will allow to clarify many dynamic properties of d-HS. Similar work we began in our previous work [1,5,15], and even on the basis of the received results we obtained a number of interesting dynamic properties of d-HS($d \geqslant 1$). Now we introduce the new concept of erasability in d-HS.

Definition 3. Two CF $c_1, c_2 \in C_A (c_1 \neq c_2)$ form for function $\tau^{(n)}$ a pair of the MEC-1 iff take place the correlation $c_1 \tau^{(n)} = c_2 \tau^{(n)} = c \in \overline{C}_A$.

The given generalization of the concept of erasability is directly linked with the nonconstructibility problem in d-HS($d \geqslant 1$). In view of definition 3 the following result can be established [11].

Theorem 37. 1-dimensional global function $\tau^{(n)}$ possesses NCF or/and NCF-1 iff for it there exists at least a pair of MEC-1.

This result is the essential generalization of the well-known Moore-Myhill's criterion of the existence of NCF in 1-HS. The next theorem present a kind of upper boundary for the existence of typies of nonconstructibility in d-HS($d \geqslant 1$) [11,12].

Theorem 38. Let NCF0, NCF1, NCF2 be sets of all NCF, NCF-1 and NCF-2 with respect to some global function $\tau^{(n)}$, accordingly. Then for each d-dimensional($d \geqslant 1$) global function $\tau^{(n)}$ take place the following correlation: NCF0 $\subset \overline{C}_A$, NCF1 $\subset \overline{C}_A$ and NCF0 U NCF1 $\subset \overline{C}_A$. There exist global functions $\tau^{(n)}$ for which take place the following correlation: NCF2= $\overline{C}_A$.

This result give one of argument in favour of the essential difference between typies of nonconstructibility NCF and NCF-1, on the one hand, and NCF-2, on the other hand. Using now the concept of NCF-2 and proofs of theorems 24,33, we can to generalize the theorem 24 on the case of NCF-2 [11,12].

<u>Theorem 39.</u> Let $\tau^{(n)}$ be an arbitrary global function in alphabet A(a - prime) having set G of NCF-2. Then there does not exist sets of CF $c_i \in \overline{C}_A$ and global functions $\tau^{(n_i)}_i$ in the same alphabet such that

$$\bigcup_i \langle c_i \rangle_{\tau^{(n_i)}_i} = G \qquad (i=\overline{1,k})$$

On the basis of new results on nonconstructibility in our works [10,11,12] the following theorem may be drawn.

<u>Theorem 40.</u> d-dimensional(d $\geqslant$1) global function $\tau^{(n)}$ without NCF possesses NCF-1 iff the corresponding mapping $\tau^{(n)}: \overset{\infty}{C}_A \rightarrow \overset{\infty}{C}_A$ is not closed,i.e. there exists CF $\overset{\infty}{c} \in \overset{\infty}{C}_A$ such that $\overset{\infty}{c}\ \tau^{(n)} = \overline{0}$.

This theorem gives answer both on a number of questions from our book [5] and the Problem 1 [15]. Furthermore, it can be used for generalisation of a number of the above-mentioned results on nonconstructibility.

<u>Theorem 41.</u> d-dimensional(d $\geqslant$1) global function $\tau^{(n)}$ without NCF possesses NCF-2 iff the corresponding mapping $\tau^{(n)}: \overset{\infty}{C}_A \rightarrow \overset{\infty}{C}_A$ is closed; if mapping $\tau^{(n)}: \overset{\infty}{C}_A \rightarrow \overset{\infty}{C}_A$ is closed(is not closed), then global function $\tau^{(n)}$ without NCF possesses NCF-2(NCF-1). D-dimensional(D $\geqslant$1) function $\tau^{(n)}$ possesses NCF or/and NCF-1 iff for it there exist MEC-1. The problems of the existence of NCF-1 and NCF-2 in d-HS(d $\geqslant$1) without NCF are algorithmically decidable. If for d-dimensional(d $\geqslant$1) global function $\tau^{(n)}$ there does not exist MEC-1, then for it there exist NCF-2; the inverse affirmation to be wrong, in general.

Theorem 41 essentially generalizes the well-known Moore-Myhill's criterion of the existence of NCF in d-HS(d $\geqslant$1).

At the end of the paper we shall present results on well-known Steinhays's problem "plus-minus"(S-problem) and on an Ulam's problem. S-problem can be formulated as follows(in our terms). Let p(1,1)p(1,2)....p(1,k) be the binary string of length k; $p(1,i) \in \{0,1\}$ $(i=\overline{1,k})$; values for k are chosen from set $M=\{3+4t, 4+4t / t=0,1,2,...\}$, only. Members of the j-th string of length k-j+1 are formed as

$$p(j,i)=p(j-1,i)+p(j-1,i+1)+1 \pmod 2 \qquad (i=\overline{1,k-j+1};\ j=\overline{2,k})$$

As a result we receive the triangular figure G_k which contains N=k(k+1)/2 symbols 1 and 0. Since N are even numbers for $k \in M$, then the following question can be formulated: Is it possible for each such permitted value k to determine figure G_k, which contains the same number k(k+1)/4 of symbols 1 and 0? In the positive case we shall say that string p(1,1).....p(1,k) is solution S(k) of the S-problem for the value k.

<u>Definition 4.</u> Solution S(k) of the S-problem for the value k is

called <u>derivative</u>(notation: D(k)), if it can be presented in the form of concatenation $S(k)=S(k_1)S(k_2).....S(k_n)$ of solutions for values $k_i < k$ with $\sum_i k_i = k (i=\overline{1,n})$. Let S(k) be the set of all kinds of S-problem's solutions for the value k. It is easily verified that $S(3)=\{000,011,110, 101\}$ and $S(4)=\{1101,1011,0011,1100,1010,0101\}$; these two sets are called <u>basis</u> sets. A derivative solution S(k) is called <u>basic</u>(notation: B(k)), if in its D(k)-representation $S(k_i) \in S(3) \cup S(4)$ $(i=\overline{1,n})$.

The sets of derivative and basic solutions(on a level with its elements) of the S-problem for the value k we shall denote D(k) and B(k), accordingly. For the purpose of modelling of the process of generation of the above-mentioned figures of type G_k, we define [11] 2-HS with alphabet $A=\{0,1,2\}$ and neighbourhood index $X=\{(o,o),(o,1),(1,1),(1,o)\}$. The detailed analysis of the behaviour of finite CF in such 2-HS, which use the profound properties of global function $\tau^{(4)}$, show that for each permitted value $k \geqslant 3$ the S-problem has positive solutions. At the same time, a series of the interesting properties of S-problem's solutions can be drawn. On the basis of such analysis we can formulate the following general result [11].

<u>Theorem 42.</u> Let S(k), D(k) and B(k) be the sets of all solutions, derivative and basic solutions of the S-problem for the value k, accordingly. Then for each permitted value $k \geqslant 11$ take place the following correlation: $\# S(k) > \# D(k) > \# B(k) > k$; for each permitted value $k \geqslant 3$ the set S(k) is not empty, where $\#$ P denotes the cardinality of the set P.

Thus, this theorem gives solution of the S-problem formulated for mathematicians(professionals and amateurs) more 25 years ago. For investigation of quantitative characteristics of S-problem's solutions the computer modelling was used. With that end in view the simulation program "PBM(+/-)" in Basic-language for personal computer ISKRA 226 was created. The utilization of the combined methods(computer simulation and theoretical researches) allow to receive a number of interesting results on the S-problem [13].

<u>Theorem 43.</u> The common number N(k) of S-problem's solutions for the value k satisfies the following condition: $N(k) \gg 2^{k-w(k)}$, where $w(k) \leqslant [k/2]$. Let the value k for the S-problem belongs to set $M=\{m+4t, n+4t/t=1,2,3,...\}$. Then number N'(k) of basic S-problem's solutions for the value k satisfy the inequalities $N'(k) \geqslant 2^{3t-2}$(for m=3) and (for n=4) $N'(k) \geqslant 2^{3t}$. Similar picture take place and for case of derivative S-problem's solutions.

It will be noted, that the S-problem can be essentially generalized as follows. Instead of two symbols 1 and 0 the alphabet $A=\{0,1,2,... ..,a-1\}$ and a string of k symbols from A are chosen. Members of the j-th string of length k-j+1 are formed as follows

$$p(j,i)=p(j-1,i)+p(j-1,i+1) \pmod a \quad (i=\overline{1,k-j+1};\ j=\overline{2,k})$$

With the result that the triangular figure T_k of $k(k+1)/2$ symbols from

A is formed. Since the values k(k+1)/2a are whole numbers for the infinite set of values k, then the following question can be formulated: Is it possible for each such permitted value k to determine figure T_k, which contains the same number k(k+1)/2a of each symbol from A? In such putting the S-problem is called <u>generalized</u> one. It is reasonable to suppose that the generalized S-problem can to receive the more wide interpretation, namely: neighbourhood index $X=\{0,1,2,\ldots,n-1\}$ for it must be an arbitrary. In such putting values k of the problem are chosen from the set $M=\{n+t(n-1)/t=0,1,2,\ldots\}$; we must substitute the triangular figures G_k and T_k for the stepped figure R_k, which contains $L=[(n-1)t^2+(3n-1)t+2(n+1)]/2$ symbols from A. The following question can be formulated: Are there for each permitted value k the stepped figures R_k, containing the same number L/a of each symbol from A? In such putting the S-problem with good reason is called <u>general</u> S-problem. Generalization of method of proof of the theorem 43 allows to formulate the following interesting result [11,12].

<u>Theorem 44.</u> For each alphabet $A=\{0,1,2,\ldots,a-1\}(a\geqslant 2)$ and the permitted value $k\geqslant 2a$ the generalized S-problem has at least 2a positive solutions. For each permitted value $k\in M=\{n+t(n-1)/t=0,1,2,\ldots\}$, alphabet A and neighbourhood index $X=\{0,1,2,\ldots,n-1\}$ the general S-problem has at least 2k positive solutions.

It is important to observe, too, that results of theorems 42–44 can be generalized on the case of the higher dimensionalities.

Heuristic studies of growth, already in two and three dimensions, show that the variety of growing figures is too great to allow simple characterizations. Therefore S. Ulam has attempted to make corresponding definitions in one dimension with the hope that some general properties of so-called "unique sum sequences"(USS) would be gleaned from them. V. Aladyev [1,5] using results on the HS theory proved a number of properties of the USS and formulated many interesting problems. Using computer modelling [15] a number of empirical results on the USS were presented. At the end of the paper we shall present a solution of the generalized Ulam's problem. The problem was investigated on the basis of computer simulation and our previous results on the HS theory.

<u>Definition 5.</u> Let $N'=N\setminus\{0\}$. Define binary operation w: x+y=z (for $x,y,z\in N'$) on the set N'. Elements z form a set $N_0\subset N'$. Two typies of binary operations w are considered:

(1) w_1: starting with the integers a and b we construct new ones in sequence by considering sums of two previously defined integers but not including in our collection those integers which can be obtained as a sum of previous ones in more than one way;

(2) w_2: by analogy with w_1, but on condition that the extreme right element of previously defined integers of sequence take part in addition. Such sequences of integers

obtained according to binary operations w_1 and w_2 are denoted POOS1(a,b) and POOS2(a,b). Twins of seduences POOS1(a,b) and POOS2(a,b) are integers in succession differing by value p=p(a,b).

The self-organizing program "POOS" in Basic-language for personal computer ISKRA 226 was created, which allows to investigate a number of properties of the USS experimentally. Combining the possibilities of this program and some methods of the HS theory the following interesting result can be proved [13].

Theorem 45. Let TW(p(a,b)) be the set of all twins of type p=p(a,b). Each POOS1(a,b) has infinite set of twins at least a type TW(a), TW(b) or TW(a+b). In POOS2(a,2a) there exist infinite set TW(2a); the density of POOS2(a,2a) relative to set N is equal to zero; for such USS there formulas $a_k=f(k,a)$, which present its elements a_k as functions of k and a. For each integer $b \geqslant 3$ POOS2(1,b) contains the infinite sets TW(b) and TW(b+1); for such USS take place the following formulas $a_k=f_3(k,b)$ (for b=3), $a_k=f_4(k,b)$ (for b=4) and $a_k=f_5(k,b)$ (for $b \geqslant 5$). For $a>1$ and $b/a - [b/a] > 0$ in POOS2(a,b) all elements of the sequence are defined by formula $a_k=b+(k-2)a$ (k=3,4,5,...); the set TW(a) in such POOS is infinite.

To our knowledge this result is the best of its kind for the USS.

It seems appropriate to note that the proofs of the theorems 42-45 once again corroborate the effectiveness of methods of the HS theory for the investigation of a number of the applied combinatorical problems. I hope that the presented results will help to clear up some new aspects to the mathematical theory of d-HS($d \geqslant 1$) as well as giving some information about our latest investigations in this direction.

4. CONCLUDING REMARKS

In conclusion of the present discussion of new results on the HS theory I should like once more to note about necessity of the very wide popularisation of the theory and their possibilities in modelling for the purpose of attracting the largest number of researches in the different areas to investigations on the theory of HS and their application in modelling. It is important direction for the further development of the HS theory, also! Indeed, many aspects of HS theory demand active participation of scientists of the different areas: pure and applied mathematics, physics, theoretical and mathematical biology, programming, engineering and many others. On the other hand, the HS theory can exercise considerable influence on a number of areas. The appearance of great many new problems in the theory of HS is waited for employment of HS for modelling in a new areas. It is hardly too much to say that the theory of HS is in the making, and further work on this theme is badly needed.

LITERATURE

1 Aladyev, V.: To Theory of Homogeneous Structures. Estonian Academic Press, Tallinn 1972.

2 Aladyev, V.: Survey of research in the theory of homogeneous structures and their applications. Math. Biosci. 22 (1974),121-154.

3 Aladyev, V.: The behavioural properties of homogeneous structures. Math. Biosci. 24 (1976),147-163.

4 Aladyev, V.: Some new results in the theory of homogeneous structures. Proc. Intern. Symp. on Math. Topics in Biology, Kyoto, (September 1978),193-206.

5 Aladyev, V.: Mathematical Theory of Homogeneous Structures and Their Applications. Valgus Press, Tallinn 1980.

6 Aladyev, V. et al: Mathematical Developmental Biology. Nauka, Moscow 1982.

7 Aladyev, V.: New results in the theory of homogeneous structures. Beiträge zur Theorie der Polyautomaten. Informatik-Skripten, 8, Braunschweig 1984,3-15.

8 Aladyev, V.: New results in the theory of homogeneous structures. MTA Szamitastechnikai es Autom. Tanulmanyok 158 (1984),3-14.

9 Aladyev, V.: A criterion of nonconstructibility in homogeneous structures. II Intern. Workshop "PARCELLA-84".Abstracts, Berlin (1984),3.

10 Aladyev, V.: A few results in the theory of homogeneous structures. PARCELLA-84. Mathematical Research.Band 25.Academie-Verlag, Berlin 1985,168-175.

11 Aladyev, V.: Solutions of a Number of Problems in the Theory of Homogeneous Structures. TR-040684. P/A "Silikaat", Tallinn 1985.

12 Aladyev, V.: Recent Results on the Theory of Homogeneous Structures. TR-041285. P/A "Silikaat", Tallinn 1985.

13 Aladyev, V.: Architecture and Software of Personal Computer ISKRA 226. SKB MPSM ESSR, Tallinn 1986.

14 Parallel Processing and Parallel Algorithms(Ed. by V. Aladyev). Valgus Press, Tallinn 1981.

15 Parallel Processing Systems(Ed. by V. Aladyev). Valgus Press, Tallinn 1983.

16 Zinkevich, T.G.: Homogeneous Structures. TR-1285. P/A "Silikaat", Tallinn 1985.

DATA STRUCTURES AND PARALLEL MEMORIES

M. Gössel and B. Rebel[1)]

In this paper an overview on existing and projected parallel memories is given.
In the first chapter the basic notions and notations as data structure, parallel memory, module assignment function, address function, isotropic address function with respect to a data structure, window and conflictfree window, the needed set of permutations and others are explained.
Chapter 2 deals with parallel memories for data in a scanning field as two- or more-dimensional pictures or matrices. The relation of different classes of module assignment functions, the connection of conflict-free parallel access to the scanning points of a window and the possibility to tessellate the plane by use of this window are discussed. Moreover a short review of memories with N memory modules, where N is a prime or $N = p \cdot q + 1$ is given.
In Chapter 3 relatively new results concerning parallel memories for trees are presented.

1. Definitions and Notations

A data structure $D = (K,R)$ is defined as a set of nodes K and a set of relations R /1/.
For $r \in R$, $k,k' \in K$ the nodes k and k' are connected by an edge, which is directed from k to k', if $(k,k') \in r$. This edge can be labelled by r. To every node $k \in K$ an n_k-tupel of values $v_1(k), v_2(k), \ldots, v_{n_k}(k)$ is assigned.
Here we suppose that the set of relations of the considered data structures is described by a set $F = \{f_1, f_2, \ldots, f_s\}$ of unary functions $f_i: K \to K$, $i = 1, \ldots, s$.
Then for $k,k' \in K$ the nodes k and k' are connected by an edge, which can be labelled with f_i, if $k' = f_i(k)$.
Examples of data structures are linear fields, 2-dimensional pictures, binary trees and others (s. e. g. /2/).

1) Zentralinstitut für Kybernetik und Informationsprozesse der Akademie der Wissenschaften der DDR, DDR-1086 Berlin, Kurstraße 33

Fig. 1 shows a parallel memory. A parallel memory consists of N memory modules $S_o,\dots,S_{N-1}$, an address generator A and a permutation network π_N.

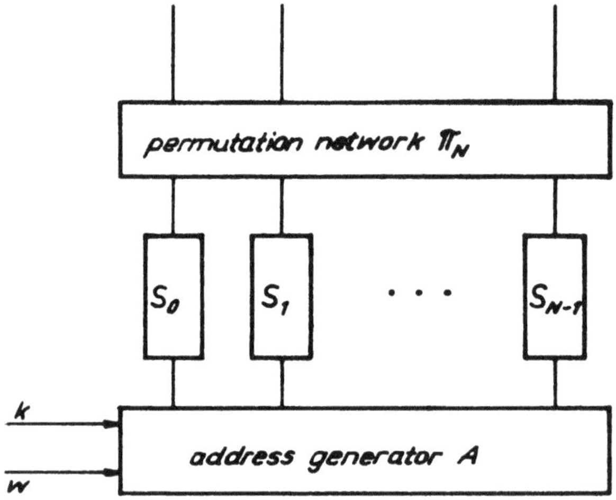

Fig. 1 Parallel Memory

If a data structure D = (K,F) is stored in a parallel memory, for every node k ∈ K the memory module and the address within the memory module where the values $(v_1(k),\dots,v_{n_k}(k))$ of the node k are stored, is to be determined.
Formally two functions, the module assignment function S and the address function a are to be determined.
The module assignment function $S: K \to \{0,\dots,N-1\}$ determines the index S(k) of the memory module where the values $(v_1(k),\dots,v_{n_k}(k))$ of the node k are stored.
The address function $a: K \to \{0,1,\dots,a_{max}\}$ determines the address a(k) under which $(v_1(k),\dots,v_{n_k}(k))$ is stored in S(k).
Generally a (parallel) processor needs a set of data in parallel in a special form, preferably in a special order, which is determined by the accessed window.
A window W of a data structure D = (K,F) can be described as an ordered set of unary functions $w_o,w_1,\dots,w_m$, $w_i: K \to K$, $i = 1,\dots,m$, where each of these functions w_i can be generated by superposition of some function $f_1^i,\dots,f_{n_i}^i \in F \cup \{f_o\}$ with $f_o(k) = k$ for all $k \in K$.

<u>Definition.</u> A window W is an ordered set of unary functions $W = (w_0, w_1, \ldots, w_m)$, $m \leq N - 1$, $w_i: K \to K$, with $w_0 = f_0, w_i = f_1^i f_2^i \ldots f_{n_i}^i$, $f_1^i, \ldots, f_{n_i}^i \in F$ for $i = 1, \ldots, m$
and with $w_i(k) \neq w_j(k)$ for $k \in K$ and $i \neq j$.

A window W(k) at the node $k \in K$ is the ordered subset of nodes

$$W(k) = (w_0(k) = k,\ w_1(k), \ldots, w_m(k)).$$

The node k is called the emphasized node of the window W(k).

A module assignment function S is called conflictfree with respect to a window F, if we have for $k \in K$, $k', k'' \in F(k)$

$$k' \neq k'' \text{ implies } S(k') \neq S(k'').$$

A window W(k) may be considered as a rigid template W placed in the emphasized node $k \in K$ of the data structure D.
To access data of a window W in parallel without conflict all the data of the accessed window had to be stored in different memory modules of the parallel memory.
A module assignment function S is called conflictfree with respect to a set of window $\mathcal{W} = \{W_1, \ldots, W_M\}$, if S is W_i conflictfree with respect to every window $W_i \in \mathcal{W}$.

For a given window W with $m = N - 1$ the permutation network of the parallel memory has to execute the following set P of permutations

$$P = \left\{ \begin{pmatrix} S(k) & S(w_1(k)) & \cdots & S(w_{N-1}(k)) \\ 1 & 2 & \cdots & N-1 \end{pmatrix},\quad k \in K \right\}.$$

This set is determined up to isomorphy. For $m < N - 1$ the corresponding permutations are partially determined.
The architecture of a parallel memory is strongly influenced by the choice of the memory function and the address function resp.
In the most of the known designs of parallel memories the module assignment functions are special cases of so called isotropic functions and even linear functions.

<u>Definition.</u> A module assignment function $S: K \to \{0, 1, \ldots, N-1\}$ is called isotropic with respect to a data structure $D = (K, F)$, if for all $k, k' \in K$ and for all $f \in F$

$$S(k) = S(k') \text{ implies } S(f(k)) = S(f(k')). \qquad (1)$$

A module assignment function $S: K \to \{0, 1, \ldots, N-1\}$ is called weakly isotropic with respect to a data structure $D = (K, F)$ if there exists a function $p: K \to \{0,1,2,\dots\}$ such that for all $k,k' \in K$ with $p(k) = p(k')$ and for all $f \in F$

$$S(k) = S(k') \text{ implies } S(f(k)) = S(f(k')). \qquad (1')$$

A proper subclass of the class of isotropic module assignment functions is the class of recursively linear functions.

<u>Definition.</u> A module assignment function $S: K \to \{0,1,\dots,N-1\}$ is called recursively linear with respect to a given data structure $D = \{K,F\}$ if for all $k \in K$ and for all $f \in F$

$$S(f(k)) = a_f \cdot S(k) + b_f \bmod N. \qquad (2)$$

The addition and multiplication in equation (2) are supposed to be modulo N.
Since we have for a recursively linear module assignment function for $k,k' \in K$, $f \in F$

$$S(f(k)) = a_f \cdot S(k) + b_f$$
$$S(f(k')) = a_f \cdot S(k') + b_f,$$

we conclude $S(f(k)) = S(f(k'))$ if $S(k) = S(k')$ and a recursively linear module assignment function is isotropic.
Of course isotropic address functions and recursively linear address functions are quite similarily defined.
It is easy to prove if an isotropic module assignment function is conflictfree with respect to a given window W or not. It is sufficient to choose N nodes $k_1,\dots,k_N \in K$ with

$$S(k_i) = i - 1, \quad i = 1,\dots,N,$$

and to investigate whether all components $w_1(k_i),\dots,w_m(k_i)$ of the window W are stored in different memory modules.
If S is a recursively linear module assignment function with a_f and N relatively prime it is even sufficient to choose an arbitrary node $k \in K$. If the components $w_1(k),\dots,w_m(k)$ of the window $W(k)$ are stored in different memory modules then S is conflictfree with respect to W.

If the module assignment function is isotropic the set of permutations P contains N elements only,

$$P = \left\{ \begin{pmatrix} S(k) & S(w_1(k)) & \dots & S(w_{N-1}(k)) \\ 1 & 2 & \dots & N \end{pmatrix}, \; k \in F(k') \right\},$$

where k' is an arbitrary node from K.
The trivial module assignment function $S(k) = k$ for $k \in K$ is isotropic with respect to an arbitrary data structure $D = (K,F)$. All the nodes of the data structure D are stored in different memory modules, which

has no sense from a technical point of view.
A theoretical problem of interest is:
Determine for a given data structure an isotropic (or recursively linear) module assignment function with a minimal ore fixed number N of memory modules which is conflictfree with respect to a given set $\mathcal{W}$ of windows.
Thereby the address computing corcuitry has to be "simple".
The set P of permutation has to be realized by a corresponding permutation network which is "simple structured" and "simple to control".

2. Parallel memories for scanning fields

A lot of papers is concerned with parallel memories for scanning fields or for data in matrix form. The first papers on this topic were /3, 4/.

A two-dimensional scanning field may be described as a data structure $D_s = (K,F)$ with

$$K = \{(i,j)/0 \leq i < R_x,\ 0 \leq j < R_y\},$$
$$F = \{O,\ W,\ S,\ N\}$$

with

$$O(i,j) = (i + 1,j),$$
$$W(i,j) = (i - 1,j),$$
$$S(i,j) = (i,j + 1),$$
$$N(i,j) = (i,j - 1),$$

where R_x and R_y are the lenghts of the scanning field. For more-dimensional scanning fields the data structure is quite similar. The considered classes of module assignment functions for scanning fields are periodic functions, isotropic functions and linear functions.

A module assignment function S is called (n_1,n_2)-periodic, if there exist integers n_1 and n_2 such that we have for all $(i,j) \in K$ and for all integers m_1 and m_2

$$S(i,j) = S((i,j) + (m_1 \cdot n_1, m_2 \cdot n_2)).$$

For $n_1 = n_2 = n$ S is called n-periodic.
In /5/ a somewhat artificial definition of a periodic module assignment function is given, and it is pretended in that paper, that a function is isotropic (in the terminology of /5/ regular) if and only if it is periodic.
A module assignment function which is 2^n-periodic but not isotropic is the module assignment function of the well known STARAN-computer, defined by

$$S(i,j) = (i \bmod 2^n) \bullet (j \bmod 2^n),$$

where $\bullet$ denotes the componentwise addition modulo 2 (s. e. g. /6, 7/).

Now we show that every isotropic module assignment function with finite N is periodic /6, 7/.
Since the module assignment function $S: K \to \{0,\ldots,N-1\}$ is supposed to be isotropic there exist uniquely invertible functions

$$\phi_x: \{0,1,\ldots,N-1\} \to \{0,1,\ldots,N-1\}, \quad \phi_y: \{0,1,\ldots,N-1\} \to \{0,1,\ldots,N-1\}$$

such that we have

$$S(i+1,j) = \phi_x(S(i,j)), \quad S(i,j+1) = \phi_y(S(i,j)).$$

Since the number of memory modules N is finite, there have to exist integers u_1 and u_2, $u_2 > u_1$, such that

$$\phi_x^{u_1}(S(i,j)) = \phi_x^{u_2}(S(i,j)).$$

Therefore the sequence $s = S(1,j),S(2,j),S(3,j),\ldots$ has to be of the form

$$s = S(1,j),\ldots,S(u_1-1,j),\underbrace{S(u_1,j),\ldots,S(u_2-1,j)}_{\text{periodic}}$$

and since ϕ_x is invertible, s is completely u_3-periodic with $u_3 = u_2 - u_1$ and u_3 minimal.
The same considerations are true for the j-coordinate.
Thus the class of isotropic functions is a proper subclass of periodic functions.
A module assignment function S for a scanning field is linear, if we have

$$S(i,j) = a \cdot i + b \cdot j + c \qquad (3)$$

where the addition and multiplication in (3) are modulo N.
Since we have

$$\begin{aligned} S(O(i,j)) &= S(i+1,j) = S(i,j) + a, \\ S(W(i,j)) &= S(i-1,j) = S(i,j) - a, \\ S(S(i,j)) &= S(i,j+1) = S(i,j) + b, \\ S(N(i,j)) &= S(i,j-1) = S(i,j) - b, \end{aligned}$$

a linear module assignment function is recursively linear.

The class of linear functions is a proper subclass of isotropic functions.
For N prime the class of linear functions is up to isomorphy equal to

the class of isotropic functions. For details s. /7/.
A new and interesting formulation of this facts in the terminology of so called "integral lattices" for arbitrary dimensions is given in /5/. Other theoretical considerations are concerned with the tesselation without rotation of a plane or a space by windows and the existence of different types of conflictfree module assignment functions.
Many of the practical relevant results as the possibility of parallel access to straight lines and generalized straight lines with equal distances between successing scanning points are contained in /8/ yet. The tesselation of a plane by polyominos is investigated in detail in /9/. In vector processing, image processing and raster graphics parallel access to special combinations of windows of straight lines, generalized straight lines and different rectangulars are of interest and are investigated in detail in many papers.
We mention some typical examples here.
In /10, 11/ the number of memory modules is a prime. Parallel access to almost all generalized straight lines is possible. Although the number of memory modules $N = 17 = 2^4 + 1$ is chosen to be a Fermat number the hardware costs for address circuitry and routing network are relatively high.
For the prime memory the set of needed permutations is

$$P(S,d) = \left\{ \begin{pmatrix} S & S+d & \cdots & S+(N-1)\cdot d \\ 0 & 1 & \cdots & N-1 \end{pmatrix}, \quad S,d \in \{0,1,\ldots,N-1\} \right\}.$$

S is the memory module where the emphasized scanning point of the window is stored and d is a parameter of the accessed generalized straight line. The decomposition of the corresponding permutation network is well understood (s. /12/).
An interleaved memory system with a prime number of memory modules is described in /13/.
If the number N of memory modules is 2^n, $n > 0$, the hardware costs are relatively low, but only a very few windows can be accesses in parallel. For $N = p \cdot q + 1$ (s. /14/) horizontal and vertical straight lines and $p \cdot q$-rectangulars can be accessed in parallel.
And interesting linear module assignment function which allows simultaneously parallel access to a lot of rectangulars, useful in raster graphics, is presented in /15/.
A parallel memory where both the module assignment function and the address function are isotropic is outlined in /7, 16/. The address computation is decentralized and even recursive.
Three-dimensional access to spheres and diamants is considered in /17/.
An interesting generalization of the memory of the STARAN-computer is contained in /18/.

3. Parallel memories for binary trees

Parallel access to complete subtrees of a given depth T of a given binary tree was investigated in /19/. In that paper a special recusively linear module assignment function was used. A detailed discussion of the results of /19/ is contained in /20/.
A complete binary tree can be described as a data structure

$$D_t^1 = \{K^1, F\} \quad \text{with} \quad K = \{0,1,\ldots\} \quad F = \{L,R\}$$

and

$$L(k) = 2 \cdot k + 1, \quad R(k) = 2 \cdot k + 2 \quad \text{for} \quad k \in K^1.$$

For binary trees we have investigated (together with J. Vilser) the existence of istropic module assignment functions which are conflict-free with respect to complete binary subtrees of the depth T for a fixed T and with respect to other subtrees by a computer.
To illustrate the method and the result we show: Let $S: K^1 \to \{0,1,\ldots,N-1\}$ be an isotropic module assignment function with respect to the data structure complete binary tree D_t^1 which is conflictfree with respect to a complete binary subtree of depth 3. Than N has to be at least 9.
At first we show that for N = 7 there does not exist an isotropic module assignment function which is conflictfree with respect to a complete binary subtree of depth 3.
In Fig. 2 a complete binary tree of depth 3 is represented. The root is stored in memory module 0. The nodes of the tree are labelled with the memory module where they are stored.

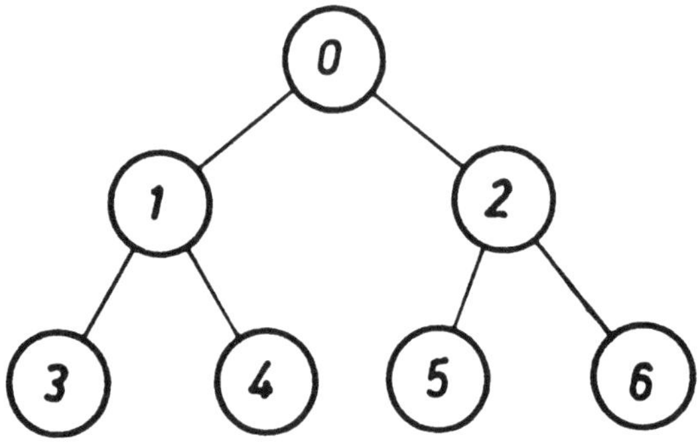

Fig. 2

We suppose without loss of generality

$$L(0) = 1, L(1) = 3, \quad L(2) = 5, \quad R(0) = 2, \quad R(1) = 4, \quad R(2) = 6.$$

To guarantee conflictfree access to the tree of depth 3 with the root stored in memory module 1, the sons of the nodes stored in memory modules 3 and 4 have to be stored in memory modules 0, 2, 5 and 6. Let $L(3) = 2$. Fig. 3 shows a tree with its root stored in memory module 1 under the assumption $L(3) = 2$.

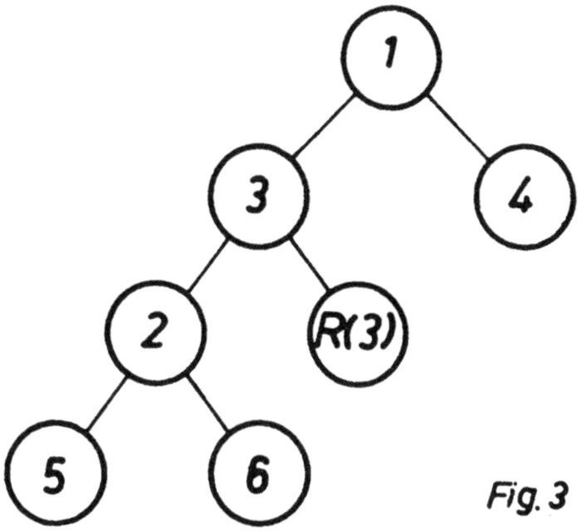

Fig. 3

$R(3) \in \{0,2,5,6\}$ gives raise to a conflict for a complete subtree with its root stored in memory module 3. Therefore $L(3) = 2$ is impossible. Analogeously it can be shown that $R(3) = 2$, $L(4) = 2$ and $R(4) = 2$ leads to a conflict. Therefore for $N = 7$ no isotropic module assignment function exists which is conflictfree with respects to a complete binary subtree of depth 3.
For $N = 8$ the proof is quite similar and left to a computer.

Two isotropic module assignment functions for $N = 9$ which are conflictfree with respect to a complete binary subtree of depth 3 are given in Table 1.

Table 1

S	0	1	2	3	4	5	6	7	8
L(S)	1	3	5	0	2	0	4	3	1
R(S)	2	4	6	6	7	7	8	8	5

S	0	1	2	3	4	5	6	7	8
L(S)	1	3	5	0	2	1	3	5	0
R(S)	2	4	6	7	8	8	4	6	7

Every isotropic module assignment function with $N = 9$ which is conflict-free with respect to a complete binary tree of depth 3 is isomorphic to one of these two functions. (This was shown by R. Creutzburg.)
The same method was applied to conflictfree access with respect to complete binary subtrees of depth greater than 3 and other subtrees.

Now we describe a complete binary tree as a data structure

$$D_t^2 = \{K^2, F^2\} \text{ with } K^2 = \{(l(x),x),\ x = 0,1,2,\ldots\}\ F^2 = \{\widetilde{L},\widetilde{R}\}$$

where $l(x)$ is the level of x and

$$\widetilde{L}(l(x),x) = (l(x) + 1,\ x + 2^{l(x)}) \quad (4)$$

$$\widetilde{R}(l(x),x) = (l(x) + 1,\ x + 2 \cdot 2^{l(x)}). \quad (5)$$

Then it is very simple to define a module assignment function $\widetilde{S}$ which is conflictfree to a binary subtree of depth T consisting of $2^T - 1$ nodes, by

$$S(l(x),x) = x \bmod N \quad (6)$$

with

$N \geq 2^T - 1$ and 2 and N relatively prime (i. e. N odd).

The nodes of a complete binary tree B_T of depth T with the root x are

$$B_T = \{x + i \cdot 2^{l(x)} / i = 0,1,\ldots,2^T-1\}.$$

Since 2 and N are relatively prime, the number $(2^{l(x)}) \bmod N$ is modulo N a generating element of the set $\{0,1,\ldots,N-1\}$, and therefore the nodes of B_T are stored in different memory modules.

Since 2 and 2^T-1 are relatively prime, conflictfree access to complete subtrees of depth T with 2^T-1 nodes with $N = 2^T-1$ memory modules is possible.

For $T = 3$ the successor nodes of the root x are shown in Fig. 4.
$2^0 = 1 \bmod 7$, $2^1 = 2 \bmod 7$, $2^2 = 4 \bmod 7$, $2^3 = 1 \bmod 7, \ldots$ are modulo 7 generating elements of $\{0,1,\ldots,6\}$.
From the equations (4), (5) and (6) we have

$$\widetilde{S}(\widetilde{L}(l(x),x)) = S(l(x) + 1,\ x + 2^{l(x)}) = S(x) + S(2^{l(x)})$$
$$= S(l(x),x) + (2^{l(x)}) \bmod N$$
$$\widetilde{S}(\widetilde{R}(l(x),x)) = S(l(x) + 1,\ x + 2 \cdot 2^{l(x)}) = S(x) + S(2 \cdot 2^{l(x)})$$
$$= S(l(x),x) + (2 \cdot 2^{l(x)}) \bmod N$$

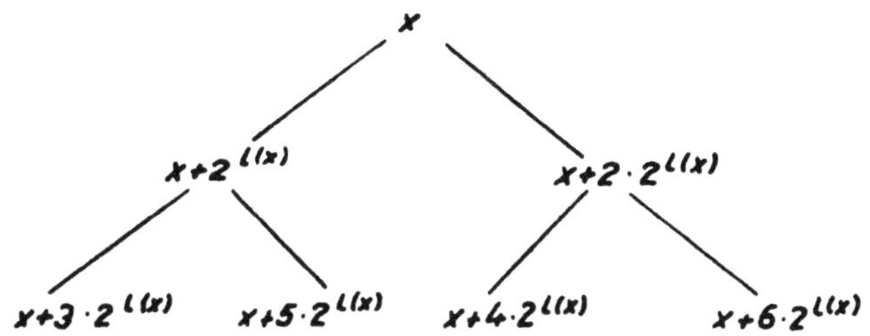

Fig. 4

and S is weakly isotropic with $p(l(x),x) = (2^{l(x)}) \bmod N$.
In a similar manner we have investigated n-ary trees and parallel access to different subtrees. For more details see /21/.
The needed permutations for this tree access are extremly simple and considered in /22/.

References

/1/ Maurer, H. A., Datenstrukturen und Programmierverfahren, Teubner-Verlag, Stuttgart, 1974.

/2/ Edelsbrunner, H., Neue Entwicklungen im Bereich Datenstrukturen, in "Überblick über Informationsverarbeitung" 1983, B. I. Mannheim, S. 55 - 109, (Herausg. H. Maurer).

/3/ Kuck, D. J., Illiac IV software and application programming, IEEE Trans. Comp. C-17, 758 - 770 (1968).

/4/ Budnik, P. and D. K. Kuck, The organization and use of parallel memories. IEEE Trans. Comp. C-20, 1566 - 1569, (1971).

/5/ Wijshoff, H. A. G. and J. v. Leeuwen, The structure of periodic storage schemes for parallel memories, IEEE Trans. Comp. C-34, 501 - 505, (1985).

/6/ Rebel, B. and M. Gössel, On conflictfree parallel memory access. Computers and Artificial Intelligence 2, 395 - 401, (1983).

/7/ Rebel, B. and M. Gössel, Ein paralleler Speicher. ZKI der AdW, Berlin 1982.

/8/ Shapiro, D. H., Theoretical limitations on the use of parallel memories, Ph. D. Thesis, Dept. Comp. Sc. Univ. Illinois, UIUCDS-R-75-776 (1975).

/9/ Wijshoff, H. A. G. and J. v. Leuuwen, Arbitrary versus periodic storage schemes and tesselation of the plane using one type of polyomino. Inf. and Control 62, 1 - 25, (1984).

/10/ Lawrie, D. H., Access and alignment of data in an array processor, IEEE Trans. Comp. C-24, 1148 - 1156, (1975).

/11/ Lawrie, D. H. and R. Vora, The prime memory system for array access. IEEE Trans. Comp. C-31, 435 - 442, (1982).

/12/ Wächter, F., Zur Strukturierung spezieller Permutationsnetzwerke, Diss. A, 1986, ZKI der AdW.

/13/ Kuei, T. Y., Tung, Y. S. and Y. C. Hai, An analysis of a new memory system for conflictfree access. Proc. of the 10-th Int. Conf. Parallel Processing, 318 - 324, (1981).

/14/ Voorhis, D. C. and T. H. Morrin, Memory system for image processing, IEEE Trans. Comp. C-27, 113 - 125, (1978).

/15/ Chor, B., C. E. Leiserson and R. R. Rivest, An application of number theory to the organization of raster graphics memory, Conf. Rec. 23rd Ann. IEEE Symp. Found. Comp. Sci. Chicago, 1982, pp. 92 - 99.

/16/ Gössel, M. and B. Rebel, Parallel memory with recursive address computation, Proc. Parallel Computing 83, ed. Feilmeier, M., Elsevier Sc. Publ. 1984, 515 - 520.

/17/ Shirakawa, H. A., A parallel memory system for image processing, Memoirs of the Research Inst. of Science and Engineering. Ritsumeikan University, Kyoto, 42, 27 - 40, (1983).

/18/ Shirakawa, H. and T. Kumagai, Structure of a three-dimensional access memory system, Memoirs of the Research Inst. of Science and Engineering, Ritsumeikan University, Kyoto 41, 27 - 50, (1982).

/19/ Shirakawa, H., On a parallel memory to access trees. Unpublished manuscript. 1984

/20/ Creutzburg, R., Parallel optimal subtree access with recursively linear memory functions, presented at Parcella '86.

/21/ Rebel, B. and M. Gössel, Adressenberechnungsschaltung, DD-Patentanmeldung, 1985.

/22/ Wächter, F., Structure and application of a permutation network, presented at Parcella '86.

CELLWARE IMPLEMENTATION

T. Legendi 1/

1. Introduction

Based on original research results [1], [2], [3] a family of cellular processors is under development. Smaller - specialized, as for example convolution processors or universal programmable - systems based on conventional elements and specialized - as a sorter system - and universal microprogrammable cellprocessors up to the Megacell Machine, based on new custom designed MOS-LSI circuits form the range. The common basis is the microcell concept - full hardware homogeneity on the level of very small elements, while time-space inhomogeneity in microprogramming ensures the flexibility [4] [5].

This survey lecture introduces to the basic system concepts; cellprogramming methodology; simulation, testing, verification tools and results, cellprogramming languages, application case studies. A comparison against other classes of highly parallel systems will be given. The concrete results in the specialized areas of the cellprocessor project will be shown in some more detail in lectures [6]-[22].

2. Software support tools

Simulation languages - CELLAS, INTERCELLAS - have been implemented for testing cellular algorithms [15], [16].

Cellular microprogramming languages have been designed and implemented [3], [6], [14] with built-in optimization capabilities. A full cellprogramming environment has been implemented [23] for the cellprocessor model [19] including a specialized editor, library system, language extensions and a sophisticated simulation system (allowing both gate level and microinstruction level simulation; its moduls may cooperate with - replace or beeing replaced by - hardware modules).

Cellprogramming environment has been designed for the SPP 2x64K cell prototype and for the Megacell Machine.

1/ Research Group on Theory of Automata, Hungarian Academy of Sciences
H-6720 Szeged, Somogyi u. 7., Hungary

3. Cellgorithms and cellprograms

Cellgorithm methodology has been worked out [2] and refined [4], [5], hundreds of algorithms have been designed and tested on our simulators [25], [28], [7], [9], [10], [13], [17] etc.

Based on the cellgorithms and taking into account the specialities of the concrete cellprocessor architectures methodology (for example for the two state spaces) has been worked out and coding of cellular microprograms and cellprograms [6], [8] has started. On the cellprocessor model and its simulator the testing is under way [19], for the other systems simulation test runs have started.

4. Traditional component based systems

The 256 cell 1000 chip universal microprogrammable cellprocessor model [5], [19] is operational. It shows the principles in working form, gives a solid basis for performance estimation of the LSI prototype (where two chips replace the 500 chips of the model with the equivalent computing power of about ten eight-bit microprocessors).

A traditional component based virtual cellprocessor with 10 MHz transition steps has been designed [26] and a picture processing operator set has been coded and tested [8] for it.
Specialized - convolution - cellular subsystems have been worked out for picture processing systems as for example for the VIDIMET II. analyser.

5. New LSI component based systems

A 16 byte sorter chip is operational now, a sorter machine has been designed and a prototype is to be implemented now.

A 2x64 two state cell universal microprogrammable chip [36] is under testing now. The design of the cellprocessor based on it is finished, the implementation of a 2x64K prototype machine [27], [30] starts now having in mind the modular interconnection of the Megacell Machine.

A somewhat bigger but more powerful 16 state cell based chip [31] has been designed and a pilot version is under implementation. The design of a cellprocessor based on this chip is finished [31].

6. Testing, fault tolerance, WSI implementation

In the present phase we concentrate efforts on testable design and test programs for our chips and subsystems [12].

We pay attention to the application of fault tolerant design principles [1] very adequate to the homogeneous nature of cellprocessors. It is important for both of the (usual, chip based) implementation and for the WSI implementation of cellprocessors [41].

A special WSI cell, WSI packaging [21] and fault tolerant cellprogramming for WSI implementation have been worked out and the first experiments are carried out.

7. Application case studies

Most efforts are concentrated on picture processing where high performance high data rate processing is vitally important [33], [25], [28], [8], [13], [17], [35], [20] etc.

Finite element method has been analysed and cellprogrammed.

General matrix operations, the solution of partial differential equations and of the system of linear equations, large system simulation tasks, process control case studies, digital signal processing including digital filtering have been cellprogrammed.

Geophysical problems are examined now and to be cellprogrammed.

8. Conclusions

In this paper an original research based development project has been summarized. The details are explained in the cited papers including ones in this proceedings, too. These R&D activities have become more and more natural and needed with the advance of the (V)LSI technology and growing user need for superfast processors.

These cellular systems form one competing branch in the rich family of parallel/homogeneous processors [37], [38], [39], [40], [41], [42], [43].

The performance range of these cellular systems will be 100MOPS-10GOPS.

References

[1] Legendi Tamás, Cellprocessors in Computer Architecture, Computational Linguistics and Computer Languages XI /1977/ pp. 147-167.
[2] Legendi Tamás, Programming of Cellular Processors, Informatik Berichte Nr. 7703, Tech. Univ. Braunschweig, pp. 53-66.
[3] Legendi Tamás, TRANSCELL - A Cellular Automata Transition Function Definition and Minimization Language for Cellular Microprogramming, Computational Linguistics and Computer Languages XII /1978/ pp. 55-62.
[4] Legendi Tamás, Cellular Algorithms and their Verification Invited lecture proc. CONPAR'81, Nürnberg, /Händler/, Lecture Notes in Computer Science 111, Springer-Verlag, pp. 169-188.
[5] Legendi Tamás: Cellular Systems. Proceedings of the Workshop PARCELLA'84. Akademie Verlag, Berlin, 1985.
[6]-[22] to be presented at PARCELLA'86
[6] Katona, E.: Assembly level programming of cellular processors
[7] Katona, E.: Two's complement arithmetics and overflow detection in cellular space
[8] Köles, P.: Picture processing on different types of cellular processors
[9] Palágyi, K.: Cellular algorithm for matrix multiplication
[10] Palágyi, K.: Cellular algorithm for binary square-root computation
[11] Tóth, N.: Fault tolerant programming of a two-layer cellular space
[12] Tóth, N.: Testing of cellular arrays
[13] Székely, Z.: A Fast-Fourier-Transformation algorithm for cellular processor
[14] Zádori, L.: A Boolean function optimization algorithm for cellular microprogram generation
[15] Almási, J. - Medvey, M. - Simon, E.: The transition function definition subsystem of the CELLAS 2.1 system
[16] Almási, J. - Medvey, M. - Kovács, I. - Simon, E. - Székely, Z.: The implementation of the CELLAS 2.1 system
[17] Kovács, I.: Cellular programs for statistical methods
[18] Zsótér, A.: A cellprocessor based on 16-state cells
[19] Tóth, J. - Ghymes, B.: Some development aspects of the cellprocessor model
[20] Ghymes, B.: A clustering procedure realized on the cellprocessor based on ISODATA algorithm
[21] Bernáth, L.: Fluid-cooled packages for fault tolerant wafer scale integrated cellprocessor circuits
[22] Tüzkõ, T. - Tóth, J.: Simulation and testing of the SPP chip
[23] Barsi, I.: The Software Environment of the Cellular Processor Model Proceedings of the workshop PARCELLA'84 Akademie Verlag, Berlin, 1985. pp. 97-109.
[24] Katona, E.: A Design Methodology for Complex Cellular Programs, Proceedings of the workshop PARCELLA'84, Akademie Verlag, Berlin, 1985. pp. 117-125.
[25] Vollmar, Legendi /eds./: Cellprocessors and Cellgorithms Report on a common research project. Informatik Skripten No. 1. T.U. Braunschweig, 1981.
[26] Zsótér, A.: Cellprocessors Based on Traditional Components, Proceedings of the workshop PARCELLA'84. Akademie Verlag, Berlin, 1985. pp. 162-166.
[27] Tóth, J.: A 64 kcell LSI Based Cellprocessor Prototype /SPP/ Proceedings of the workshop PARCELLA'84. Akademie Verlag, Berlin, 1985. pp. 154-161.
[28] Vollmar, Legendi /eds./: Cellprocessors and Cellgorithms II. Report on a common research project. Informatik Skripten No. 13. T. U. Braunschweig, 1985.

[29] Legendi, T.: Cellware, Proceedings of the Conference "Parallel Computing'85. W-Berlin, Sept. 1985. North-Holland, 1986. to appear.
[30] Legendi, T. - Tóth, J.: A Full-Custom-LSI-Based Architecture for a Megacell Machine - Proceedings of the Conference "Parallel Computing'85" W-Berlin, Sept., 1985, North-Holland, 1986. to appear.
[31] Zsótér, A.: A 16-State Cellprocessor - Proceedings of the Conference "Parallel Computing'85 W-Berlin, Sept., 1985. North-Holland, 1986. to appear.
[32] Katona, E.: A Programming Language for Cellular Processors - Proceedings of the Conference "Parallel Computing'85" W-Berlin, Sept., 1985, North-Holland. 1986. to appear.
[33] Katona, E.: Cellular Algorithms for Image Convolution - Proceedings of the Conference "Automatische Bildverarbeitung", Berlin, Oct., 1985.
[34] Köles, P.: Picture Processing Algorithms on Large Size Cellular Spaces - Proceedings of the Conference "Automatische Bildverarbeitung" Berlin, Oct., 1985.
[35] Ghymes, B.: Parallel Image Processing by a Cellprocessor. Proceedings of the Conference "Automatische Bildverarbeitung" Berlin, Oct., 1985.
[36] Legendi, T. - Tóth, J. - Zsótér, A.: High performance cellprocessor chips, Proceedings of the conference "Schaltkreisentwurf" Dresden, 1986, T. U. Dresden, pp. 175-180.
[37] Uhr, L.: Algorithm-Structured Computer Arrays and Networks. Academic Press, 1984.
[38] Snyder, L.: Introduction to the Configurable Highly Parallel Computer. Computer, 15, 1, 1982, pp. 47-56.
[39] Batcher, K. E.: Design of a Massively Parallel Processor. IEEE Transaction on Computers, C-29, 9, 1980, pp. 836-840.
[40] Kung, H. T. - Leiserson, C. E.: Algorithms of VLSI Processor Arrays. Symposium on Sparse Matrix Computations, 1978, Proceedings, Knoxville, 1978.
[41] Kung, H. T. - Lam, M. S.: Wafer-Scale Integration and Two-Level Pipelined Implementations of Systolic Arrays. Journal of Parallel and Distributed Computing, 1, 1984, pp. 32-63.
[42] Parkinson, D.: The ICL Distributed Array Processor. Infotech Future Systems Vol. 3, Infotech International, Maidenhead Berkshire, 1977, pp. 389-402.
[43] Fountain, T. J.: The Development of the CLIP7 Image Processing System. Pattern Recognition Letters 1, 1983. pp. 331-339.

A CELLPROCESSOR BASED ON 16-STATE CELLS

A. Zsótér[1/]

1. Introduction

A cellprocessor is a highly parallel computing unit which contains many parallel working identical processing elements called cells. The cellprocessor is not a stand-alone computer but it is a peripheral (back--end processor) of a traditional computing system, which can execute tasks containing inherent parallelism at high speed and in parallel with the host computer [4] [5].

This paper presents a cellprocessor containing 16-state cells, and being implemented with custom-design LSI circuits.

2. The architecture of the cellprocessor

The main structure of the system is shown in Figure 1. The cellprocessor consists of three main parts: cellular space (CS), cellular space control unit (CCU), and input-output system.

The highly parallel computation is performed in the two-dimensional Cellular Space (CS) containing mesh-connected 16-state cells. It is a synchronous system like a cellular automaton. The CS contains 64K cells, and is modularly extensible. The CS is divided into 8x8 blocks of cells. In spite of local connections - teletransport of data is possible between distant blocks [7]. Each block is implemented with a custom-design LSI circuit.

The cells are very simple Boolean processors (fig. 2), which compute their next state upon their own state and on states of their four neighbours. Computing rules (transition functions) are not stored in the cells, but they are broadcast by the CCU to every cell in the form of a microprogram through the command bus. The next state is computed by the block "logic and six working bits", while the present state of the cell is stored in the state-storage. After computing the next state in each cell, there is a close step which writes the next states computed in the block "logic and six working bits" into the state storage simultaneously in the whole cellular space. The 4-bit internal state ensures inhomogeneous operation of cells in the cellular space. E-bit stores result of the comparison between the content of the command-bus and the internal state of the cell.

1/ Attila József University, H-6720 Szeged, Somogyi u. 7. Hungary

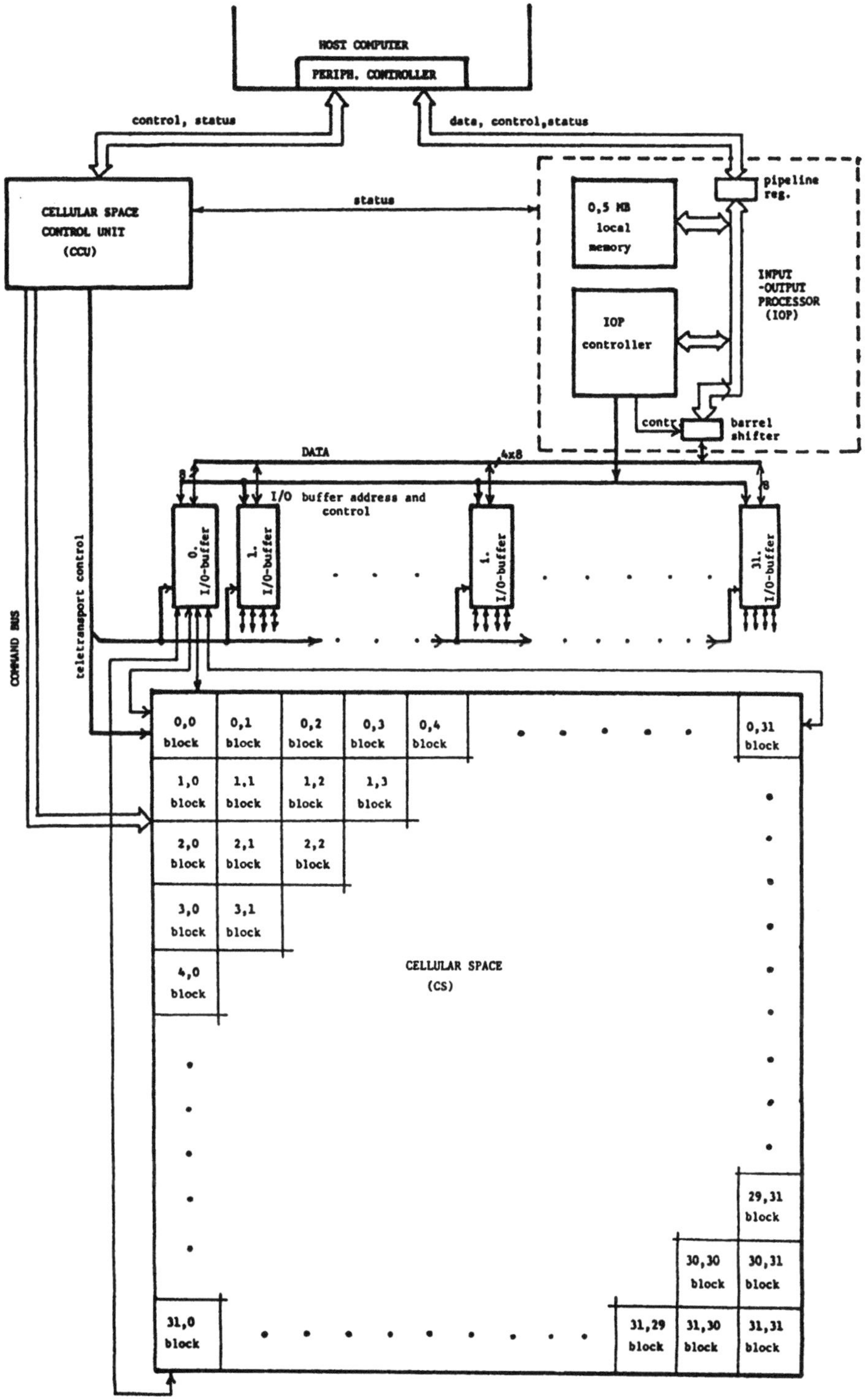

Figure 1. Block diagram of the cellprocessor

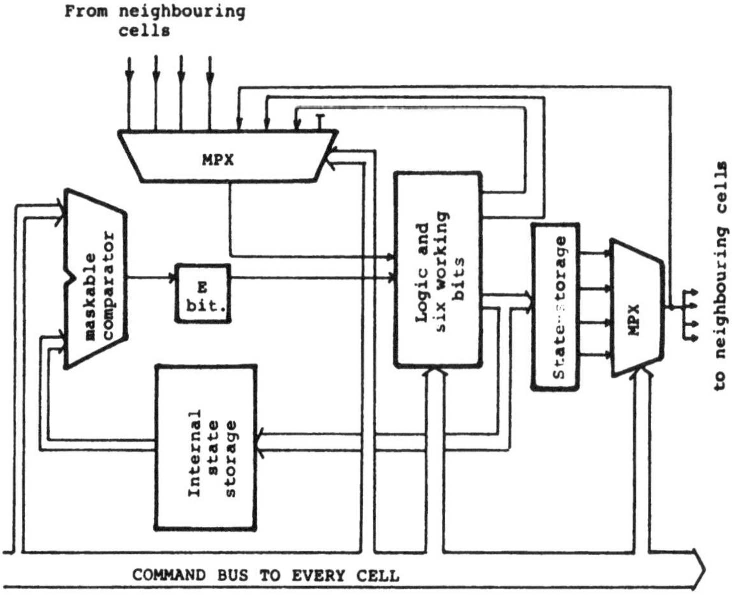

Figure 2. Block diagram of the basic cell

The cellular space control unit is a traditional microprogrammed control unit with a read-write control store. The CCU beside the control of the cellular space interfaces it to the host computer.

While CCU controls the cellular space, input-output processor (IOP) moves data to and from the four edges of the CS (fig. 1.). This is also a microprogrammed control unit having a local memory. The 32 I/O-buffers store input-output data of the CS temporarily.

Because CCU and IOP operate in parallel, the cellular space can work at maximum speed to perform highly parallel computations fast and efficiently.

Both the CS and the input-output system are modularly extensible, so the present cellprocessor can be extended. The homogeneous structure of the system makes design and mass-production easier.

3. Implementation results

The architectural and logic design of the system, as well as layout-design of the full-custom LSI circuit has been made. The fabrication of the LSI chip is under way. This chip, designed for 6 μm depletion - load silicon gate NMOS technology, contains about 18000 devices. Power consumption is about 1W from single +5V power supply.

4. Application possibilities

This system can be used efficiently to solve problems containing inherent parallelism such as matrix-operations, real-time image and signal processing, finite-element analysis, process control etc.

We have developed a cellular space simulation language CELLAS [1] to verify cellular programs and to estimate the computing power of the system. This 16-state cellprocessor is more powerful than the cellprocessor prototype (SPP) [7] because of larger number of states of cells. Convolution with 3x3 window on a 256x256 image with 8-bit pixels can be executed in 3.4 msec, which means 346 MOPS processing rate and real-time image processing. Other parallel nature computations, such as matrix-operations can be executed at a rate of several hundred MOPS depending on the task and on the size of the system.

References

[1] Almási, J., Medvey, M.: The CELLAS 2.1 cellular simulation system. In Cellprocessors and Cellgorithms (Vollmar R. and Legendi T. eds.) Technische Universität Braunschweig, Braunschweig, 1985. 122-132.

[2] Batcher, K. E.: Bit-Serial Parallel Processing Systems. IEEE Transactions on Computers 5(1982), 377-384.

[3] Kung, H. T.: Why Systolic architectures? IEEE Computer 1(1982), 37-46.

[4] Legendi, T.: Cellular Systems. in Proc. of Parcella'84. Akademie-Verlag, Berlin 1985., 90-96.

[5] Legendi, T.: Cellware. in Proc. of "Parallel Computing'85" Conf. North-Holland, 1986.

[6] Snyder, L.: Introduction to the Configurable Highly Parallel (CHiP) Computer. IEEE Computer 1(1982), 47-56.

[7] Tóth, J.: A 64K cell LSI based cellprocessor prototype (SPP). In Proc. of Parcella'84. Akademie-Verlag, Berlin 1985., 154-161.

SIMULATION AND TESTING OF THE SPP CHIP

T. Tűzkő [1] and J. Tóth [1]

1. INTRODUCTION

Increasing percentage of today's LSI and VLSI circuits' testing costs within production cost means demands for new methods and equipments which can reduce testing costs. Homogeneous and regular architectures are also very popular in this respect [1][8].

This paper describes the main steps of testing the SPP chip [6], which can be a basic component of different cellprocessors [5]. Hardware homogeneous /cellular/ structure of this chip offers the advantage of simplified test procedure.

Cellprocessors are some kind of highly parallel computers based on cellular automata principles. In order to facilitate our further discussion, the main features of cellprocessor architecture - first suggested by T. Legendi [5] - are next summarized.

1. A cellprocessor is not a stand-alone computer but is a peripheral device of a traditional computing system. It works under the control of a host computer and executes those tasks which fit to its architecture and capability.

2. A cellprocessor has - beside hardware homogeneity - an inhomogeneous cellular space both in time and space. Inhomogeneity makes programming of the space much easier.

3. Cells are very simple bitprocessors and - beside the local connections - are connected to a common broadcasting bus. This bus is driven by a central unit /CCU/. Transition functions are stored in the CCU in the form of microprogram.

The SPP chip is a full custom-design LSI circuit. It consists of an 8x8 array of cells /henceforth block/ and a switching network. A 6 μm silicon gate NMOS technology is used and the chip is packaged into a 28 pin DIL package.

The cells within a block are mesh-connected and have Neumann-neighbourhood. The basic cell has six different 16 bit microinstructions and the working out of a total /inhomogeneous/ step of the space needs 10 .. 40 microinstructions depending on the complexity of the transition function.

This paper first outlines the whole testing procedure. Then the main resources /logic simulation system and test equipment/ we use are described. Next some problems related to fault modeling are discussed. Then the

[1] József Attila University, Computer Science Department
Szeged, Hungary

basic test pattern generation strategy is summarized and the structure of the test program is detailed.

2. OUTLINE OF THE TEST PROCEDURE

Figure 1. shows the block diagram of the entire test procedure. For functional testing [3] of the chip we can excellently use its own micro-assembly language /SP/P, [4]/ which contains not only microinstructions of the chip, but program organizer instructions /REPEAT-NEXT, GOSUB-RET/ as well. Thus the test appears in the form of a special SP/P microprogram. Data, which are applied to the local inputs of the chip are also involved in the test program. A microassembler compiles the test program from microassembly form to binary form, and the binary sequence obtained can be applied to the chip simulator. The simulator outputs the expected values should be converted into a high level measure-orientated program.

The converted patterns are then ready for compilation into the machine language of the tester. Once compiled, test data are ready for loading into the tester. The tester applies the test patterns to the chip and

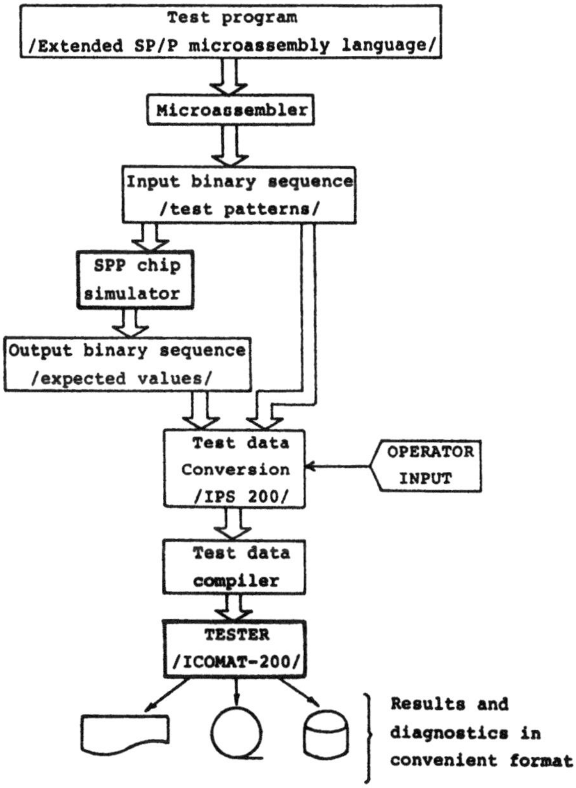

Fig. 1. The test process of the SPP chip

a report which documents the good/bad chips is obtained.

3. SIMULATION OF THE CHIP

The process of design and testing of large-scale integrated circuits demands extensive simulation support, for example logic level simulation, circuit level simulation, fault simulation etc. Here we concentrate on logic simulation.

The simulation system we use supports simulation of hierarchically specified designs. The most important features of the simulation environment are:

- support of a wide range of simulation abstraction levels /system, architecture, register, logic/
- ability to simulate multi-level circuits which contain a combination of abstraction levels during a single simulation
- a single integrated environment which supports all design stages from concept to final verification.

The structure and behaviour of the circuit are described with a netlist language and modelling language, respectively, and are entered separately into the simulation system. The aim of the approach taken in the system is to "generate" a customized simulator for each application.

Unlike most simulators, the system we use has no primitive models. All models are created by the user or extracted from standard model libraries. The advantages of this approach are:

- simulator is technology independent
- models can easily be modified to suit to the application.

The structure of our customized simulator generated by the simulation system excellently fits the architecture of the SPP chip /fig. 2./.

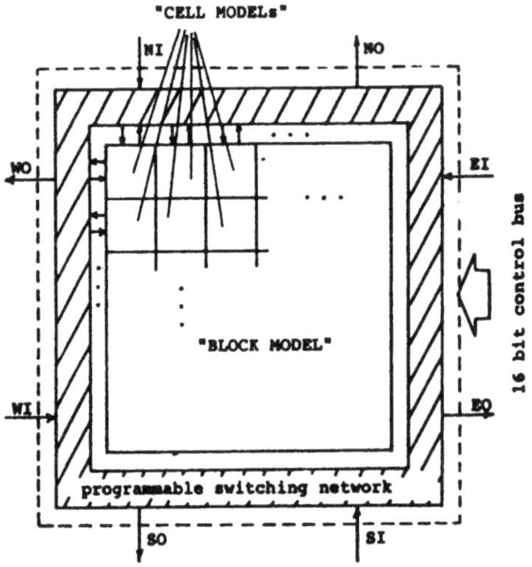

Fig. 2. The structure of the SPP chip simulator

Primiteve elements of the chip simulator are as follows:

- gate elements such as NAND, NOR, INVERTER and COMPLEX GATE elements
- memory elements such as latches
- higher level elements such as multiplexers, registers, shift registers and RAM's.

A "CELL MODEL" contains gate and memory elements, while the "BLOCK MODEL" consists of CELL MODELs only. Higher level elements are used modeling functional elements of the switching network.

4. THE TEST EQUIPMENT USED

A general purpose LSI- VLSI tester /ICOMAT-200; [2]/ is used, which is suitable for measuring DC and functional parameters as well as timing characteristics of large scale integrated circuits. There are two test station units, which can be used in parallel. These are suitable for wafer probe as well as packaged chip testing. There are two kinds of pattern generator in the tester: an algorithmical pattern generator and a unibuffer which stores nonalgorithmical patterns. We use the latter option.

The tester is controlled by a minicomputer. Complex test programs can be described by a high level measure-orientated language /IPS; [2]/. Extended software support is available for creating and processing programs written in IPS, and for making different statistics and documentations.

5. FAULT MODELING

Our aim is to construct a test capable of detecting each detectable single stuck-at fault. Unfortunately we haven't got an ATPG /Automatic Test Pattern Generation/ system. On the other side, manual test pattern generation - based on traditional approaches - would be a very time - consuming work. Thus we proceed as follows:

The problem of test pattern generation is specified by functional level rather than traditional gate-level description of the circuit. Function, in this context means a given task, which can be performed by a hardware element of the chip. For example the block - due to its cellular structure and mainly to its programmability - had several simple functions /shift functions, initialization functions etc./ and test patterns can easily be generated for these functions even manually. This approach is called functional fault modeling.

Then we determine those single stuck-at faults which are not detected by functional test patterns. /Note, that within the block this step should be carried out for one cell only./ These faults can also be detected by additional test patterns. Concerning this point, a simple example will be described in detail later. The fault coverage of the test can easily be expressed in terms of percentage of potential single stuck-at faults.

Some pattern sensitive as well as multiple stuck-at faults can also be detected, but it is difficult to quantify fault coverage for these categories.

6. TEST STRATEGY

The problem of functional level test pattern generation can be decomposed into four subproblems:

1. The function of a hardware element can be looked as a set of mappings. An element of this set is a mapping /for example the shift function of a shift register/ from the set of input data /and present state/ to output data /and next state/. First we have to choose some appropriate elements of the set of input data; these elements will test the given function. Then we have to compute /generate/ the output data /expected patterns/.

2. Most likely, the inputs of the function under test do not represent the input pins of the chip /the primary inputs/. But, because we have access just to the primary inputs, our next subproblem is to manipulate the primary inputs such that the desired stimulus data appears where we really want it.

This process is called backward propagation, since we effectively start with the desired value and propagate it back until we reach the primary inputs.

3. Next we solve the problem of "activating" the function. If execution of that function depends on some conditions, then we have to satisfy those as well.

4. Finally, as the outputs of the function do not necessarily correspond to the chip output pins /called primary outputs/, we have to use forward propagation to make the response observable at a primary output.

For example the chip simulator has the functional model of a shift register which is capable of performing the next operations: parallel load, hold /read/, shift.

If we want to test these operations, our basic approach is as follows:

First we have to decide what values we want to load /hold, shift/, and what the result of this operation should be. Then we determine what we have to apply to the input pins in order to make the desired values appear at the data inputs of the shift register.

Next we determine the conditions that have to be set up in order to make the shift register execute the load /hold, shift/ operation. For our example this requires the LOAD opcode to be present in the microinstruction register.

Finally, we have to make the result of the load operation visible at a chip output in order to compare it with the expected responses.

Activities No. 1., 2., 3., & 4., listed above are realized by an SP/P microprogram.

7. THE TEST PROGRAM

The test program consists of two parts according to the structure of the circuit. First the switching network should be tested. It consists of many different subcircuits, so its test can be realized as it were a conventional /random/ circuit.

Cells - within the block - are tested by the second part of the program. One of the most serious problems here is to control and observe cells inside the block, because long data path have to be formed for backward and forward propagation. Data in a cellular space can be transferred by shift functions, but only at low speed /cell by cell/. In order to reduce time required for testing the block, all the cells are tested in parallel. This means that test data should be pipelined and each cell executes the same microinstructions. Notice, that due to the regular structure of the block the process of parallel testing and pipeline data flow can easily be organized. Essentially the test program of the block is a cellular program.

Next we describe some functional level test pattern generation procedures for the block.

1. A specially arranged matrix is shifted through the block. This matrix is constructed in such a way [7], that each cell takes up all of its possible neighbourhood combinations at least once during the shift process. Some pattern sensitive faults - of shift functions - related to the state of the nearest neighbours can be detected. Due to the pleasant fact that shift function can be carried out in many ways, different parts of the hardware can be tested by shift functions. Moreover, the process of shift function execution is completed by microinstructions which have no effect, if the hardware is correct, but they invert one or more bit positions in the matrix if a fault occurs. A lot of stuck-at faults can be detected by these "inoperative" microinstructions, and they wouldn't be detected by shift functions, only.

2. In this procedure we concentrate on checking the "WRITE" and "READ" functions of the internal state storage within each cell. Notice, that the number of possible internal states in a cell is equal to the number of cells within a block. Thus each cell can be loaded with a different internal state. Then - using a simple algorithm - we can change the internal state of each cell 64 times in such a way, that every cell puts on all of its possible internal states.

During this procedure we can determine the parity of the cells' internal state and only these parity bits should be shifted out per cell in order to check this procedure. We can greatly reduce the number of expected values by this data compression.

Some special kind of pattern sensitive faults - related to the internal state of the cells - can also be detected by this procedure.

3. Finally, an efficient procedure is shown, which tests the initialization function of the block as well as detects stuck-at memory elements /latches/. First, we initialize the block. /This means that each memory element is set to state 0 except those, which enable parallel program execution./ Then a special kind of shift function is executed, which sets a cell to state 1 if and only if one of its neighbours or the cell itself was in state 1 previously. Thus, if a cell remains in state 1 after initialization, its faulty value will propagate in every direction to the four edges of the block and can easily be observed. This shift function is called "1-propagation function". /"0-propagation function" can also be executed if memory elements of the block are all set to state 1 initially./

Notice that propagation function consists of "inoperative microinstructions" only. /They have no effect if the hardware is correct./ This procedure can be completed by other microinstructions of this kind in order to increase its efficiency.

8. CONCLUSION

This paper describes the main steps of simulation and testing of the SPP chip. Due to the facts that this circuit has cellular structure and can be microprogrammed, test pattern generation - based on functional fault modeling - is greatly simplified. Some simple examples are shown to demonstrate the test generation procedure.

The test program obtained is an efficient GO/NOGO test of the chip, concerning detectable single stuck-at faults. A lot of multiple as well as pattern sensitive faults can also be detected.

Currently we are working on programming the test equipment for functional and DC measurements.

Further work involves testing cellular fields which contain hundreds of SPP chips.

LITERATURE

[1] A. D. Friedman: Easily testable Iterative Systems,
IEEE Trans. on Comput. Vol, C-22, No. 12, Dec. 1973 pp. 1061-1064.

[2] ICOMAT-200; Computer Controlled LSI Tester;
Vol. 1-4. MEV, Budapest, 1985.

[3] Jacob A.: Functional Level Test Generation for Complex Digital Systems, Proc. 1981 IEEE Test Conference

[4] E. Katona: The SP/P language /Manuscript/, Research Group on Automata Theory of The Hungarian Academy of Science, Szeged, 1985.

[5] T. Legendi: Cellprocessors in Computer Architecture, Computation Linguistics and Computer Languages XI. 1977. pp. 147-167.

[6] J. Tóth: A 64 Kcell LSI Based Cellprocessor Prototype /SPP/, in Proc. of The II-nd International Workshop on Parallel Processing by Cellular Automata and Arrays, Berlin, G. D. R., 1984

[7] N. Tóth: Testing of the SPP; /Manuscript/, Research Group on Automata Theory of The Hungarian Academy of Science, Szeged, 1986

[8] C. H. Sung: Testable Sequential Cellular Arrays IEEE Trans. on Comput. Vol, C-25, No. 1, Jan. 1976 pp. 11-18.

FLUID-COOLED PACKAGES FOR FAULT-TOLERANT WAFER SCALE INTEGRATED CELLPROCESSOR CIRCUITS

László Bernáth[1/]

Summary

Fault-tolerant cellular architectures facilitate economical manufacturing of wafer scale integrated semiconductor devices even at a relatively restricted microelectronic technology at our disposal. The task of packaging full 3-10 inch wafers is studied. An efficient heat removal from a silicon surface dissipating up to 100 W, realization of 100-400 interconnection points i.e. "leads" are rather challenging engineering problems. Comparisons are made between several types of fluid cooled wafer packages developed by our group. Without going into technical details basic idea and conception of each types are discussed. As a conclusion it is stressed that these new packaging techniques under research combined with the fault-tolerant cellular architectures might contribute to development of a new generation of parallel computers.

Introduction

A full wafer cellular field is expected to offer significant cost and size advantages to future cellprocessor systems, because the whole cellular field of the system (or a major segment of it) is made on one single large size wafer, without cutting the wafer into small chips, as is done traditionally. Obviously, multi-wafer systems can be realized as well. Cellular architectures offer excellent possibilities to design fault tolerant circuits (defects on the wafer must be tolerated in redundancy) at a relatively low refuse-rate. Fault-tolerant architectures and realization of the respective WSI circuits will be discussed in other proceedings of our group. The subject of the present study is giving an outline of our efforts to develop mounting and interconnection techniques, packaging methods for wafer LSI cellular circuits which aim to realize small size compact and low cost electronic equipments.

[1/] Research Group on Theory of Automata Hungarian Academy of Sciences, József Attila University, Szeged, Hungary

Basic considerations

- Three different fluid cooled package construction for small (2"), medium (3"-5") and large- (up to 10") size wafers have been researched and made progress in our laboratory.

- Resultant thermal resistance of each of these devices is to be better than 1 C/W, in cca. 3 meter per second forced air convection.

NOTE: A suitable fluid is applied as coolant to remove heat of great intensity from the safe side of the wafer. Dissipation of a 3 inch WSI circuit is supposed to be as high as 80-100 W as a result of the relatively restricted microelectronic technology at our disposal.

To coole liquid coolant itself forced air convection is applied.

- The number of logical interconnection points i.e. "leads" is to be as many as 160-400.

- In the first stage of our experiments main stress is put on the following problems:

a, to research and test different ways of an effective heat removal from silicon surfaces,

b, to develop proper mounting techniques and constructions for large size wafers taking thermal expansion of the silicon wafer at an operation temperature of 70 ^{o}C and during Au-Si eutectic bond process into consideration,

c, to test reliability of the numerous thermocompressive bonds around the wafer.

Dissipation wafer

A so called dissipation wafer has been developed to simulate thermal behavior of a real WSI circuit. Besides, it makes possible to test reliability of the 160 thermocompressive bonds under heavy duty as well.

This way, we can speed up our research work and cut costs. Experiments with waferpackages can be carried on undependently from the microelectronic realization of the WSI circuit.

In fact, the dissipation wafer is a standard 3 inch wafer with a resistor network on its safe side. A traditional thin-layer patterning technology was applied to produce a multi-layer resist coating which was cut into 80 separated resistor chains by laser beam. Each of the resistor chains ends in two bond pads for power in/out connections.

Resultant heat dissipation of the network varies according to power voltage.

A semiconductor sensor is attached to the top of the wafer to control surface-temperature during operation.

Connection panel

A common part of the three wafer package constructions is a goldened, fine patterned printed board. Its main task is to connect bond-pads of the wafer to the pins of the four flat cable connectors on both ends of the panel. These connectors (with 40 pins each) ensure intercommunication between the wafer and its suroundings.

Wafer package for small size wafers /WSI.P-N4/

Test model for small size (up to 3") wafers is based on traditional conception. Generally, Au-Si eutectic bond is used for semiconductor chips, but it is quite difficult to get a uniform attachment between large surfaces of Si wafer and substrate. Epoxi bond is also unsuitable, because of its poor thermal conductivity and insufficient reliability. A multicoated, metallized (Au) molybdenum sheet was selected as substrate because its thermal expansion coefficient is quite similar to that of Si wafer. A new slide-on eutectic bond technique have been researched to ensure a uniform attachment and good thermal contact between wafer and molybdenum carrier. This mechanically rigid metallic carrier can be fluid-cooled at its bottom side.

Wafer package for medium size wafers /WSI.P-N1/

In case of medium size wafers (3"-5") eutectic bond is also unsuitable because the slightest difference between thermal expansion coefficients of Si and substrate results in casualties of the wafer during the bond process. In test model of the package for wafers of this range soft silicone-rubber bond was applied to ensure an elastic attachment between the wafer and the rigid, massive substrate. Unlike traditional methods, heat removal occures at the safe side of the wafer using a special liquid coolant. The well known heat-pipe principle have been applied in this construction to ensure a very intensive heat transport. Heat pipe designed for this purpose is a closed hollow tube containing a small amount of special fluid that transports heat from wafer to the other end of the tube cooled by forced air convection. The fluid inside the pipe is vaporised. As the vapor spreads through the pipe some of it condenses at the cool-end of the pipe releasing heat to the pipe wall and the forced air convection. The condensed fluid is returned to the bottom of the pipe. To assist this process the pipe has an inner lining of porous material that draws the liquid by capillary action. The energy needed to vaporize a liquid is called the latent heat of vaporization. This is the energy the heat pipe conveys to ensure a very intensive heat transport.

Wafer package for large size wafers /WSI.P-N2/

Wafer package system labelled WSI.P-N2 is suitable to encapsule and coole wafers up to 10". It is based on a quite untraditional conception and involves original ideas as well. Both safe- and bottom side of the wafer contacts directly with a liquid coolant circulated by a miniature pump in closed system. Soft, elastic fixture of the wafer ensures that neither thermal stress nor any loading force affects the wafer. This construction is suitable to achieve a resultant thermal resistance better than 0,5 C^{o}/W in a 3 meter per second forced air convection.

A device like this needs a rather sophisticated technology so it is designed for special applications.

Conclusion

Developments of new mounting, interconnection techniques for WSI circuits are organic part of the cellprocessor project headed by dr. Legendi in Szeged. Both traditional and original, untraditional constructions have been researched and made progress in our laboratory. These efforts might contribute to development of a new generation of parallel computers.

Fluid cooled wafer package

WSI.P-N2

References

[1] Full Wafer Memory Approach /256 kbit/
Nippon Telephone and Telegraph, 1984.
(copy of this publication is available at JATE, Szeged)

[2] True Liquid Cooling of Computers Proceedings of the 1977. June
Dallas, National Computer Conference

[3] IBM 3081, TCM (Thermal Conductive Module)
Héliummal töltött integrált áramkör.
Müszaki Élet, 1983/May

Relevant foreign patents (priority number)

1. SONY Co.: Wafer Construction for single-crystal semiconductor device. /: US 84-574535:/
2. DURROUGHS Co.: Chain configurable polycellular WSI circuit. /:GB 80-8027212:/
3. The Board of Trusties of leland Stanford J. Univ.: Method and means for improved heat removal in compact semiconductors utilizing coolant chambers and microscopic chanels. /:US 81-23407:/
4. WESTINGHOUSE Electric Co.: Assembly heat sink for semiconductor devices /:82-436104:/

ON THE IMPLEMENTATION OF THE CELLAS 2.1 SYSTEM

J. Almási, I. Kovács, M. Medvey
E. Simon, Z. Székely [1)]

CELLAS is a general purpose cellular programming language proposed and defined by T. Legendi [6]. CELLAS 2.1 may be considered as a successor to the original CELLAS. The CELLAS 2.1 System [1], presented at II. International Workshop on Parallel Processing by Cellular Automata and Arrays in Berlin in 1984, has been realized by the authors of this paper. The main goal of the system is the functional simulation of cellular processors proposed by T. Legendi [6]. Structure of the system, some of main data structures and algorithms are mentioned in the paper. Finally some examples illustrate the useful tools of the system.

1. The CELLAS 2.1 System

The CELLAS 2.1 System consists of two main parts:

- transition function definition subsystem,
- cellular space simulator.

Communication between these parts is realised by CELLAS libraries. A member of a library is identified by the name of the member. The user can define his own library on a file or may use common libraries. Common libraries contain generally used functions and programs.

2. Transition function definition subsystem

2.1 Language of the subsystem

The subsystem has a high-level special purpose language. There are three levels in the language. The whole program forms the first level. Definition of some transition functions gives the second level. A program may contain more than one second level block. Description of functions is given on the third level by blocks of terms and/or blocks of microconfiguration terms [5]. A third level block may describe more than one function. They may be indicated at the beginning of the block.

1) Research Group on Theory of Automata
Hungarian Academy of Sciences
H-6720 Szeged, Somogyi u. 7.

Data types of the language are ARITHMETIC, FUNCTION, TEXT, VARIABLE and EXPRESSION. Accessing rules are similar to the rules of the well-known block structure languages. VARIABLE type essentially means an implicit loop-variable. It represents a sequence of values, assigned to it, when it is used in the description of transition functions. EXPRESSION type denotes a formula-variable. Its actual value is an arithmetic expression of ARITHMETIC and/or VARIABLE and/or EXPRESSION type constants and variables. Their usage can be seen in the second example at the end of this paper.

Cell-states may be decomposed into bit groups. It can be done homogeneously for each neighbour or inhomogeneously one by one. Definition of dynamic transition functions is possible. A dynamic transition function specifies the new inner state of the cell. Conversion functions also may be defined for the satisfaction of special demands of displaying in the CELLAS 2.1 simulator.

2.2 Implementation of the subsystem

The compiler of the subsystem's language is discussed later in this paper. The essential part of the subsystem is the table-generator. It makes a transition table with state reduction from the description of a transition function. This kind of transition table was proposed by E. Katona. Let n be the number of neighbours and s be the number of cell-states. Then the table means a data structure $(R_1,\ldots,R_n,T)$. Here R_i $(1 \leq i \leq n)$ is a reduction table of s elements, and it carries out a mapping from $\{0,1,\ldots,s-1\}$ to $\{0,1,\ldots,s-1\}$, where $1 \leq s \leq s$ holds. It gives a reduced state to all possible states of the i-th neighbour. States, which are equivalent from the view-point of the transition function, are mapped to the same reduced state. T gives the value of the new state by the formula $T(\sum_{i=1}^{n} r_i \times \prod_{j=i+1}^{n} s_j)$ when neighbours have the reduced states $r_1,\ldots,r_n$. To avoid this complicated computation the reduced states multiplied by $\prod_{j=i+1}^{n} s_j$ are written into table R_i. In this way the new state can be computed by the formula $T(\sum_{i=1}^{n} R_i(a_i))$, where $a_i \in \{0,1,\ldots,s-1\}$ $(1 \leq i \leq n)$ are the states of neighbours. This method uses n+1 indexing and n-1 addition operations to compute a new state.

3. Cellular space simulator

3.1 Summary and some tools of the language

To simulate a cellprocessor we may define one or more fields [1]. A field is a two-dimensional array of cells.

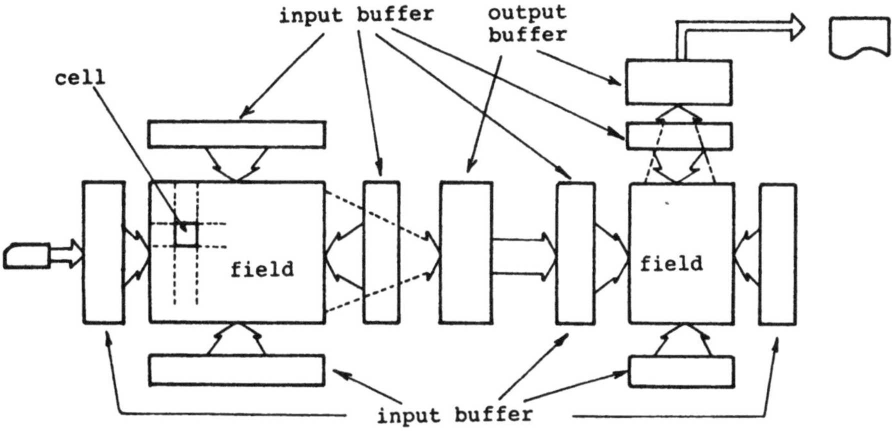

Fig. 1. Fields, buffers and cells

One input and one output buffer can be connected to each side of a field to ensure communication with the outside world. A cell has five state components: external, internal, neighbour, conversion-external and conversion-internal states. Transition functions are assigned to internal states and neighbourhoods are assigned to neighbour states. These assignments may be different in two fields. The possibility of the space inhomogeneity of neighbourhood ensures a generalized teletransport feature [7].

Conversion functions are used at displaying. They are assigned to conversion-internal states. A conversion function maps the external and/or internal states of a cell to a string considered the conversion-external state of the cell. This tool provides a method to follow moving of valuable data and to distinguish them from data having other or no meaning.

General and special purpose cellular structures (Processing Elements) may be defined with variable parameters and can be stored in common and/or private CELLAS libraries with the associated functions and initial configurations. These PEs can be used in a lot of cellular programs [4].

User defined subsystems may be linked to the simulator to satisfy special demands. These subsystems can be activated from a CELLAS 2.1 program with actual parameters.

Error handling of the simulator may be modified in execution time according to the user's claims.

3.2 Implementation of the simulator

The simulator consists of a compiler and an interpreter. The compiler translates the instructions to an inner code and calls the interpreter to execute them one by one. Parameters of instructions are in postfix form after compilation. At first they are prepared to a common form for all interpreting routines. The structure of the interpreter follows the structure of the language.

The implementation of the simulator required about 8 man-years of work. The compiler is discussed later. The hand-written interpreter is about 15000 source lines coded in FORTRAN. The simulator uses nearly one megabyte storage on a RIAD-1055M computer.

3.2.1 Algorithm of the state transition computation

Following actions are taken for the fields which are pointed out:

a) - state transition in external and conversion-external state spaces,
   - assignment modifications (transition functions and neighbourhoods),
   - output buffer manipulations.

b) - input buffer manipulations,
   - displaying.

c) - other actions between global state transitions, claimed by the user.

This method ensures the possibility of data transmission between cells of two different fields without any delay.

The average state transition of one cell is 5 msec.

4. The compilers

4.1 The HLP/SZ system

Helsinki Language Processor is a compiler writing system developed at the University of Helsinki. The first Hungarian version is implemented at the Research Group on Theory of Automata of the Hungarian Academy of Sciences [2]. The system called HLP/SZ has been running on a CDC computer. Its implementation language is SIMULA 67 which means that the whole system is written in SIMULA language. Generated compilers are made in two different languages: SIMULA 67 and FORTRAN. The system consists of modules for lexical syntactic and semantic processing of programming languages. Code generation is performed during the syntax analysis or the final traversal of the attributed parse tree. Innovative developments in the system include an algorithm for generating efficient lexical scanners (from the lexical metadescription), automatic generation of error recovery routines for an LALR(1) parser, and optimized attribute evaluation mechanisms on the base of an attribute grammar. HLP/SZ has been used in the research on the theory and design of programming languages and compilers. First realistic application of the system was to generate two different compilers for the CELLAS 2.1 System.

4.2 Compiler of the transition function definition subsystem

The subsystem is an independent part of the whole CELLAS 2.1 System. Therefore it has own programming language. The main conception of define language objects is similar to the block structure. So thus, one of the most important tasks of the compiler is to check legal occurences of language objects. Static semantics of the language is defined by using attribute grammar. The used metalanguage is the HLP/SZ. It should be noted that the metadescription consists of about 170 context-free productions and 30 different attributes. The generated compiler has nearly 15000 FORTRAN source lines.

4.3 Compiler of CELLAS 2.1 simulator

The compiler of the CELLAS 2.1 simulator was designed and implemented for a RIAD-1055M computer and it has been running as an integrated part of the whole simulation system. Definition of the language was written in HLP/SZ metalanguage and the first several experimental compilers generated in SIMULA 67 language on a CDC computer. It was easy to modify the original language because of its static semantics is given by an attribute grammar. Final version of the compiler has been generated on a CDC computer in FORTRAN and the compiler was transported to a RIAD-1055M computer. The attribute grammar consists of about 250 context-free productions with at least 100 nonterminals and nearly 60 semantical attributes. The generated compiler is about 25000 source lines without syntactic error recovery informations.

5. Examples

5.1 Simulation of a three-dimensional cellular space using generalized teletransport

The problem is solved by mapping of plane sections of the three-dimensional space into a two-dimensional cellular field. The method can be seen in Fig. 2. Numbers around the cells give the serial numbers of neighbours in the case of three-dimensional von Neumann neighbourhood. The associated CELLAS 2.1 program is omitted due to lack of space.

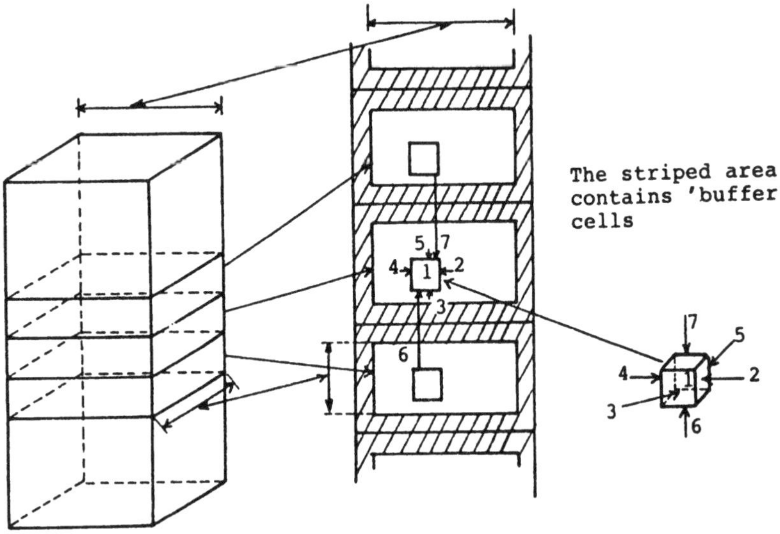

Fig. 2.

5.2 Definition of a transition function

Let's consider the multiplication of binary numbers by a bit-sequential multiplier using 16-state cells. It gets two k-bit operands and computes their product on 2xk bits. The operands move one against another having 'thinned format' (there are zeros inserted between the bits). For details see [3]. A cell is decomposed into four bits. Micro-configuration term of the transition function is as follows:

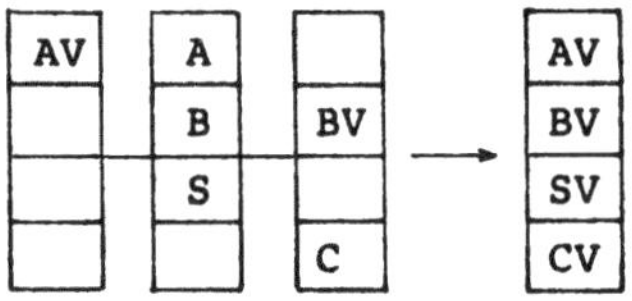

where [CV,SV]=S+C+AxB
(as a 2-bit binary number)

This transition function can be written in the transition function definition language as follows:

```
DCL VARIABLE A,AV,B,BV,C,S; STATE 15; CELL [4,3,2,1];
BEGIN; DEF FUNCTION MULTIPLIER; CELL ,,,,[4,3,<1,2>],;
  A:=<0,1>; AV:=A; B:=A; BV:=A; C:=A; S:=A;
  DCL EXPRESSION CVSV; CVSV:- S+C+AxB;
  MICRO (1,3);
    TERM [AV,,,], [A,B,S,]     ,[,BV,,C],
         $       , [AV,BV,CVSV],$
  ENDM;
END;
```

5.3 Usage of a conversion function

In the case of the multiplier mentioned above a very attractive display scheme can be reached by using a conversion function (Fig. 3). The definition of the function and the CELLAS 2.1 program is also omitted.

```
. . . . . . 1 . 1 . 0 . 0
1 . 1 . 0 . 1 . . . . . .
. . 0 0 1 1 0 0 0 1 . . .
. . . . . . . C . . . . .
```

Fig. 3. Display of the multiplication 5x13 before the computation of the last partial product

References:

[1] Almási, J., M. Medvey: The CELLAS 2.1 Cellular Simulation System Cellprocessors and Cellgorithms II., Informatik Skripten No. 13., T. U. Braunschweig, September 1985, pp. 122-132.

[2] Gyimóthy, T., E. Simon, Á. Makay: An Implementation of the HLP Acta Cybernetica, Tom. 6, Fasc. 3, 1983, pp. 315-327.

[3] Katona, E.: Binary Addition and Multiplication in Cellular Space Acta Cybernetica, Tom. 5, Fasc. 4, 1982, pp. 457-464.

[4] Katona, E.: A Design Methodology for Complex Cellular Programs Parcella'84, Akademie-Verlag, Berlin, 1985, pp. 117-125.

[5] Legendi, T.: A 2D Transition Function Definition Language for a Subsystem of the CELLAS Cellular Processor Simulation Language Computational Linguistics and Computer Languages XIII., 1979, pp. 169-194.

[6] Legendi, T.: Cellprocessors in Computer Architecture Computational Linguistics and Computer Languages XI., 1976, pp. 147-167.

[7] Tóth, J.: A 64K Cell LSI Based Cellprocessor Prototype /SPP/ Parcella'84, Akademie-Verlag, Berlin, 1985, pp. 154-161.

A BOOLEAN FUNCTION OPTIMIZATION FOR CELLULAR MICROPROGRAM GENERATION

Zádori László [1)]

1. INTRODUCTION

A cellular processor architecture, called SPP [1], has been developed by the Research Group of Automata Theory in Szeged. This architecture contains a cellular array where each cell has an external state $\in\{0,1\}$ and an internal state $\in\{0,1\}^6$. So every cell transition function is a Boolean function $f: A_1 \times A_2 \times A_3 \times A_4 \times A \times B \rightarrow A$, where A, A_1, A_2, A_3, A_4 are the external state sets of the cell and its four neighbours, respectively and B is the set of its internal states. In the cellular space every function is executed by a microprogram that is a sequence of microcommands. Each cell has a storage bit. Every microcommand can change the value of the storage bit depending on the neighbourhood and the state of the cell. More exactly every microcommand is of the form (H,g) where H is a subcube of $A_1 \times A_2 \times A_3 \times A_4 \times B$ and g is a Boolean function with one variable depending on the external state of the cell. If a cell has a neighbourhood state $(a_1, a_2, a_3, a_4, b) \in H$ then the value of its storage bit changes according to the function g. After the execution of the microprogram the value of storage bit will be the new external state of the cell.

It is important to describe f by a short microprogram because the run time of the cellularprogram is proportional to the length of the microprogram i.e. to the number of microcommands. We will give a heuristic algorithm to find a near optimum solution. On the basis of this algorithm a program was developed producing quite optimum microprograms in practice. This program inputs a function f given by formulas and yields a microprogram of f as an output. We note, that our algorithm described here starts from a table of f.

2. DEFINITION AND FORMULATION OF THE PROBLEM

Let $\underline{2} = \{0,1\}$. Let n, m, k be nonnegative integers, $n + m \geq k$. Let a partial Boolean function $f: H(\subseteq \underline{2}^{n+m}) \rightarrow \underline{2}^k$ be given. A subcube of $\underline{2}^n$ is a direct product $A_0 \times \ldots \times A_{n-1}$, $\emptyset \neq A_i \subseteq \underline{2}$, $0 \leq i \leq n-1$.

A subcube $A_0 \times \ldots \times A_{n-1}$ will be denoted by $[a_0, a_1, \ldots, a_{n-1}]$ where

---

1) József Attila University
Computer Science Department, Szeged, Hungary

$$a_i = \begin{cases} 0 \text{ if } A_i = \{0\} \\ 1 \text{ if } A_i = \{1\} \\ * \text{ if } A_i = \{0,1\}. \end{cases}$$

We call a pair (A,g) coloured subcube, briefly c-subcube if A is a subcube of $\underline{2}^n$ and g is a function g: $\underline{2}^m \to \underline{2}^k$. A c-subcube $(A_1 \times \dots \times A_{n-1}, g)$ will be denoted $[a_0,\dots,a_{n-1},g]$ where a_i is defined above, $0 \le i \le n-1$. Note that for SPP n = 10, m = 1, k = 1. We say, a function f: $H(\subseteq \underline{2}^{n+m}) \to \underline{2}^k$ is represented by a sequence of c-subcubes if for every vector x = $= (x_0,\dots,x_{n+m-1}) \in H$ we have $f(x_0,\dots,x_{n+m-1}) = g(x_n,\dots,x_{n+m-1})$ where g is the colour of the last c-subcube covering x. We assume throughout that m and k are fixed.

Our aim is to find one of the shortest sequences of c-subcubes representing any given function f. To give an algorithm that takes it in time bounded by a polynomial of 2^n - if it is possible - is hard [1)]. That is why it is reasonable to look for heuristic algorithms that can be applied in practice that is they yield near optimum solutions. Further on such an algorithm will be shown.

3. THE ALGORITHM

We create a $2^n \times (n+1)$ matrix in the following way. We fill in the i-th row of the matrix, $0 \le i \le 2^n-1$, with a vector whose first n components are binary digits of $i = \sum_{j=0}^{n-1} i_j 2^j$, $i_j \in \{0,1\}$ and its last component is either a function g: $2^m \to 2^k$ where $g(x_0,\dots,x_{m-1}) = f(i_{n-1},\dots,i_0,x_0,\dots,x_{m-1})$ for every $(i_{n-1},\dots,i_0,x_0,\dots,x_{m-1}) \in H$ or $\emptyset$ according to that there is or not a vector $(i_{n-1},\dots,i_0,j_0,\dots,j_{m-1}) \in H$, respectively. For simplicity we assume that H is nonempty and f is defined either everywhere or nowhere on the sets $\{(y_0,\dots,y_{n-1},x_0,\dots,x_{m-1}) | x_j \in \underline{2}, 0 \le j \le m-1\}$, $y_0,\dots,y_{n-1} \in \underline{2}$. So the rows of the obtained matrix are unique. The obtained matrix is called the reduced table of f. The set of its rows is denoted by RT. Observe, in RT the elements different from $(y_0,\dots,y_{n-1},\emptyset)$, $y_0,\dots,y_{n-1} \in \underline{2}$, can be considered c-subcubes where the cubes are single points of $\underline{2}^n$. Thus, the sequence of c-subcubes relating to the rows of the reduced table of f represents the function f. Let x = $= (x_0,\dots,x_{n-1}) \in \underline{2}^n$ and let the colour of x be the function g if $(x_0,\dots,x_{n-1},g) \in$ RT, provided that there exists such a function g, otherwise the colour of x is undefined.

We will need the following definitions. Let C be the set of the colours given by RT and $B \subseteq C$. Consider all the elements of $\underline{2}^n$ that have

---

1) It can be shown that the problem having the values of f as an input is in NP but it is not known to be NP complet.

colours in B. Denote the least subcube containing the former elements of $\underline{2}^n$ by S(B). We say B generates S(B) and S(B) is called a subcube generated by B. A subset of $\underline{2}^n$ will be called one-coloured if on one hand it contains an element coloured by g on the other hand its every coloured element has the colour g.

The first part of our algorithm is based on the following two notices.

1) If we have such a subcube S of $\underline{2}^n$ that $\underline{2}^n \setminus S$ is one-coloured then we can put the c-subcube [*,...,*,g] as the first member of the desired sequence where g is the colour of $\underline{2}^n \setminus S$. Then we have to deal with only a less task corresponding to the subcube S.

2) We can assume that the c-subcubes of the desired sequence correspond to maximum one-coloured subcubes.

The first part of the algorithm works on the set RT. In each step it can change the colours of elements of RT, more exactly it can cancel certain colours. During the first part of the algorithm we build a sequence describing f in reversed order.

Let a stack be given with depth n+1. In the j-th step of the first part of the algorithm V_j will be a subcube at the top of the stack and Z_j will be the set of rows of a reduced table created for the j-th step. Now the first part of the algorithm is the following.

Step 0. $V_0 = \underline{2}^n$
$Z_0 = RT$

Step j(j ≥ 1). Let us observe whether V_j is one-coloured.

a) If V_j is one-coloured then V_j and its colour determine a member of the desired sequence. Then V_j will be taken out of the stack. If the stack is empty we are ready, the procedure stops. Otherwise we determine Z_{j+1} that is obtained cancelling the colours of elements of V_j in Z_j. Then j = j+1.

b) If the colour of every element of V_j is undefined, then V_j will be taken out of the stack. If the stack is empty the procedure is stopped. Otherwise $Z_{j+1} = Z_j$ and j = j+1.

c) If there exist two elements of V_j having different colours than we look for a maximum set of colours B that B is a subset of the colours of V_j and $S(B) \subsetneq V_j$. If there exists such a set then S(B) is put into the stack and j = j + 1. Otherwise we choose a maximum one-coloured subcube $S \subset 2^n$ in the following way. Let S be a maximum subcube coloured by c such that there exists a c coloured element of $S \wedge V_j$ as well as the number of elements of V_j having the colour c is minimum among colours occuring in V_j. A member of the desired sequence is determined by S and its colour. Then Z_{j+1} will be obtained cancelling the colours of elements of S in Z_j and then j = j + 1.

Notice during the first part of the algorithm every subcube of $\underline{2}^n$ appears in the stack or in the obtained sequence at most once and the execution time of the cases a, b, and c, are bounded by a polynomial of 2^n. Thus, this part of the algorithm is polynomial.

Executing the first part of the algorithm we can obtain a sequence of c-subcubes in that certain redundancies can occure. Let $(A_0,a_0)\ldots,$ $\ldots,(A_t,a_t)$ be the obtained sequence in normal order.

We have two possibilities to stop redundancies. Let $B_j = A_j \setminus (\bigcup_{l=j+1}^{t} A_l)$, $0 \le j \le t$.

1./ Assume $0 \le i_1,\ldots,i_s < i$, $\bigcup_{j=1}^{s} B_{ij} \supseteq B_i$ and $a_{i1} = \ldots = a_{is} = a_i$. In this case A_i can be cancelled.

2./ Let $0 \le i < j \le t$, $(A_i,a_i) = [b_0,\ldots,b_h,\ldots,b_{n-1},b]$ and $(A_j,a_j) = [b_0,\ldots,\overline{b}_h,\ldots,b_{n-1},b]$ where $b_h = 1$ and $\overline{b}_h = 0$ or $b_h = 0$ and $\overline{b}_h = 1$. We create a set H_i and H_j in the following manner. Let $H_i^0 = \{A_i\}$ and $H_j^0 = \{A_j\}$. Define recursively the following sets

$H_i^{v+1} = \{A_l \mid i \le \ell \le j$ and there exists $A_s \in H_i^v$ that $s < \ell$, $a_s \ne a_\ell$ and $A_s \cap B_\ell = \emptyset\}$

$H_j^{v+1} = \{A_l \mid i \le \ell \le j$ and there exists $A_s \in H_j^v$ that $s > \ell$, $a_s \ne a_\ell$ and $A_s \cap B_\ell \ne \emptyset\}$.

Now let $H_i = \bigcup_{v=0}^{j-i} H_i^v$ and $H_j = \bigcup_{v=0}^{j-i} H_j^v$. If $H_i \cap H_j = \emptyset$ we can put the elements of H_j immediately before A_i in original order. Then (A_i,a_i) and (A_j,a_j) can be reduced.

The second part of the algorithm uses the previous two possibilities. First starting from the last element of the sequence we execute a procedure using possibility 1) and getting on forward in the sequence. Then - at most t times - we execute a procedure corresponding to possibility 2). Both possibilities have time bounded by a polynomial of 2^n. So the second part of the algorithm is polynomial.

Observe that after executing the second part of the algorithm the redundancies described above are stopped. In practice it can be applied simpler procedures based on possibility 1) and 2).

REFERENCE

[1] J. Tóth: A 64 Kcell LSI Based Cellprocessor Prototype /SPP/, in Proc. of The II-nd International Workshop on Parallel Processing by Cellular Automata and Arrays, Berlin, G. D. R., 1984.

ASSEMBLY-LEVEL PROGRAMMING OF CELLULAR PROCESSORS

Endre Katona[1)]

Abstract. We can agree that cell transition functions of a microprogrammed cellular processor form the same level of programming as machine instructions of a conventional computer, because both of them are replaced by microprograms in the course of execution. That is why we say "assembly-level programming" of a cellular processor if transition functions are described in a given language, the compiler of which can generate an optimal microprogram to each transition function.

In this paper cellular assembly languages will be characterized in general, and a cellular assembly program will be given as example for the Cellprocessor Prototype [6] solving multiplication of Boolean matrixes.

1. INTRODUCTION

A cellular processor [4] contains an nxm array of microprogrammed Boolean processors, called cells, which are connected according to the von Neumann neighborhood. Each cell has an s-bit state register and executes a state transition function $f: A^5 \to A$ where $A=\{0,1,\dots,2^s-1\}$, in any time-step. Such a transition function is computed by executing a certain sequence of microinstructions broadcast by a central control unit (CCU) to each cell. Thus a time-step involves several micro-steps.

A cellular processor ensures time-space inhomogeneity of transition functions. Inhomogeneity in time means that CCU can send different microprograms in consecutive time-steps. Inhomogeneity in space is solved by internal states. Each cell has a q-bit internal state register loaded initially, and cells with different internal states may execute different transition functions in the same time-step. In other words, a transition function $f: A^5 \times B \to A$ is executed where $B=\{0,1,\dots,2^q-1\}$ is the set of internal states.

Note that Cellprocessor Prototype, called SPP [6], contains two layers of cells each consisting of 256x256 cells with s=1 and q=6, but internal states are common for the two layers. Transition functions are of type $f: A^5 \times B \to A \times B$, that is, internal states also can be changed.

To make cellular processors more flexible, homogeneous local neighborhood of cells can be changed by a switching network, called tele-

1) Research Group on Automata Theory
Hungarian Academy of Sciences
Somogyi u. 7, H-6720 Szeged, Hungary

transport, ensuring almost arbitrary interconnection pattern for 8x8 blocks of cells. That is, homogeneous topology is used inside of blocks but inhomogeneous topology can be applied between blocks.

Cellular processors must contain a high-speed I/O processor performing data transmission between a local memory and the border cells of the array. I/O processor is driven by a separate microprogram called I/O program.

It is clear that we need special languages to program a cellular processor. Three levels of languages can be distinguished:

- Microassembly language. Such a language ensures direct use of microinstructions of a given cellular processor.
- Cellular assembly language. At this level of programming transition functions can be defined and microprograms are generated by the compiler [7].
- Cellular graph language (CELLGRAPH, see [2]). Cellular programs are considered as networks of processing elements, and only the interconnection structure of PEs have to be described in the language.

CELLGRAPH programs can be translated into cellular assembly ones while cellular assembly programs into microassembly ones. CELLGRAPH language is convenient and machine-independent, but its compiler works with low efficiency in general: the cellular microprogram, generated from a cellular assembly program, is redundant in most cases. On the other hand, an optimal microprogram can be generated from a cellular assembly program, because each cellprocessor architecture has its own cellular assembly language ensuring almost maximum utilization of hardware abilities.

Note that an interesting assembly-level cellular language has been defined in [5] which is independent of the hardware architecture but it does not give satisfactory support for efficient programming.

2. CELLULAR ASSEMBLY LANGUAGES

Assembly-level programming of a cellular processor means the description of following subjects:

- initial configuration of internal and external states of cells;
- topology of the array (teletransport paths);
- definition of transition functions and their distribution "in time and space";
- input-output management.

These four subjects correspond to four components of a cellular assembly language. Each component has its own instruction set and the components are translated separately. First two components are translated into initial loader programs with data files to be loaded. Translation of third and fourth components results in a CCU-microprogram and I/O-microprogram, respectively.

Further on we try to characterize cellular assembly languages by showing typical examples of instructions from each language component. To understand these instruction examples we have to explain that syntactical structures $(a_1,\ldots,a_n)$ and $((a_1,b_1),\ldots,(a_n,b_n))$ mean n-component vectors the elements of which are scalars and pairs, respectively. Consecutive vector elements can be described in a compact way: (2,3,4,5,6)=(2:6), (10,12,14,16,18)=(10:18:2). Operation signs **, ++, etc. denote special vector operations. For any further detail see [3].

1. Initial configuration description. Example:
CONF (#E1), ((1,1),(1,2),(1,5)),(0,0,1);
This instruction specifies that first external bits (see E1) of cells (1,1), (1,2) and (1,5) should be set initially to 0, 0, 1, respectively. The whole initial configuration can be described by a sequence of CONF (and other) instructions.

2. Topology description. Example:
PATH (5,5,#E), (5,10,#W);
This instruction specifies that eastern edge of block (5,5) is connected to western edge of block (5,10). The whole teletransport network can be given by a sequence of PATH instructions. We can see that a PATH instruction specifies only the endpoints of a teletransport path; path generation is made automatically by the compiler.

3. Transition function description. Transition functions can be defined by formulas in a certain sublanguage, and their distribution may be given by FUNASGN instructions. Example:
FUNASGN (5), (F1,F2,F3);
This instruction specifies that cells with internal state 5 execute a time-varying sequence of transition functions F1,F2,F3,F1,F2,F3,... .

4. Input-output description. Example:
DCLARRAY VECT(200), 1, #INP;
INPUT VECT, (3), 25, 2;
First instruction declares the array VECT of 200 elements stored in the local memory. Each element consists of 1 byte. #INP means that VECT is loaded initially into the local memory by the host computer. Second instruction specifies that elements of VECT should be transferred to the I/O buffer number 3 (which is connected to some border cells of the array). Transmission starts in the 25-th step and continues in every second step.

Instructions for the compiler. These instructions make the programming easier and more flexible by controlling the compilation process. For instance, parameter variables can be declared and used in any instruction of the language. Their value can be set by assignment instructions. Example: DCLPAR X; X=5; These instructions are executed by the compiler.

To avoid iterative repetition of instructions in the program, "cycles" can be used as follows:

FOR $I=(i_1,\dots,i_n)$;

instructions;

END;

Such a "cycle" means for the compiler to repeat the instructions in the "cycle" for any $I=i_1,\dots,i_n$.

3. AN EXAMPLE: MULTIPLICATION OF BOOLEAN MATRIXES

In [1] a cellular algorithm has been given for Boolean matrix multiplication applying cells with 3-bit state registers. This algorithm is modified here for SPP, the cells of which have only one external state-bit.

Let A and B be Boolean matrixes of sizes nxp and pxm, respectively. Product C=A·B can be computed by an nxm cellular array: matrix A is shifted from left to right, B is shifted from up to down throughout the array (fig.1). Matrix elements follow each other with one cell gap. In this way elements of A and B can go through the array using the only external state-bit. Elements of C are computed in the first internal state-bits of cells.

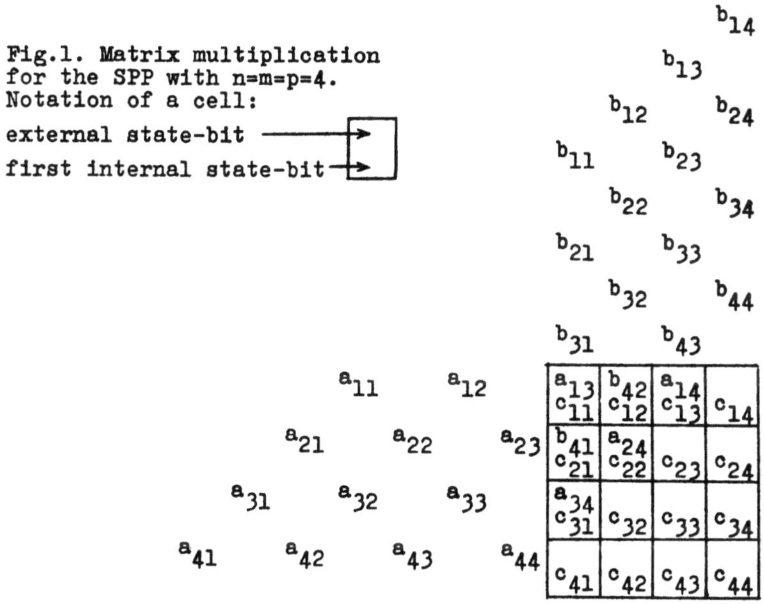

Fig.1. Matrix multiplication for the SPP with n=m=p=4. Notation of a cell:

A chess-board inhomogeneity is needed in the array where white cells shift the elements of A to the right and black cells execute the transition function f_M (fig.2). It is clear that a black-white exchange is necessary in each step to ensure continuous movement of data according to fig.1.

When matrix C has been computed, then transition function f_T (fig.2) should be executed by each cell and C can be shifted out of the cellular array.

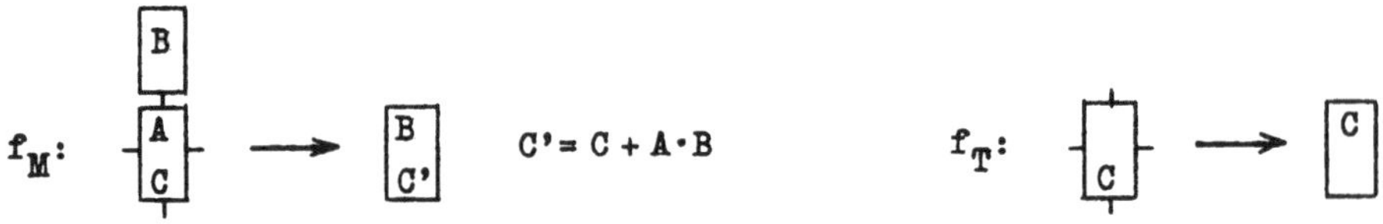

Fig.2. Transition functions

Further on we have to solve the I/O problem. Suppose that matrixes A and B are stored in the local memory in a compressed way: 8 elements are stored in one byte, that is, A and B are (n/8)xp and px(m/8) arrays of bytes, respectively. To produce the slanting format of data (fig.1) we need converter elements each of them transforms a stream of bytes (fig.3).

As a consequence, only a 248x248 matrix multiplier array can be embedded into the 256x256 array of SPP (fig.4) and the time-space inhomogeneous transition function distribution of fig.5 should be used.

Fig.3. A byte converter element consisting of 8x8 cells. x and y denote different internal states to demonstrate inhomogeneity.

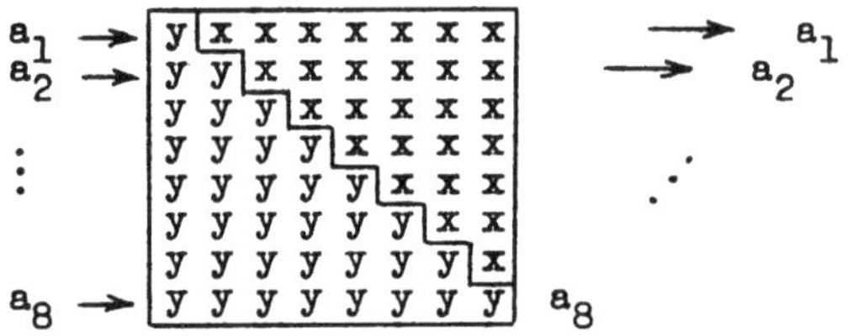

Fig.4. Partition of the 256x256 cellular array. Numbers in parentheses mean the internal states used in different segments.

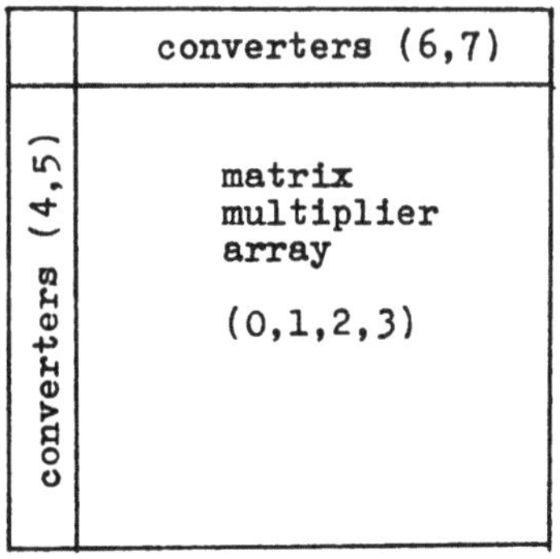

Fig.5. Transition function distribution (t=0,1, 2,...). Arrows denote shift functions.

time \ internal states	0,1	2,3	4	5	6	7
2t+1	→	f_M	→	→	↓	I
2t+2	f_M	→	→	I	↓	↓

Cellular assembly program of the Boolean matrix multiplier is given below. To simplify the program only one layer of cells is used. (Remember that SPP contains two layers of cells, see section 1.) The other layer could compute another matrix multiplication at the same time.

We can see that instructions of the four language components are used in a mixed way; they will be separated by the compiler.

```
DCLARRAY A(31,248), 1, #IN;
DCLARRAY B(248,31), 1, #IN;
DCLARRAY C(248,31), 1, #OUT;
```

A, B and C are 248x248 Boolean matrixes stored in compressed form

```
RDF FM, 20;
RDF FT, 20;
```

Transition functions are defined in a separate sublanguage. These instructions read in their tables.

```
DCLPAR TRIANG1(36,2), TRIANG2(36,2);
FOR I=(0:7);
  TRIANG1 = TRIANG1 JOIN (I)**(0:I);
  TRIANG2 = TRIANG2 JOIN (I:7)**(I);
END;
```

Auxiliary vectors TRIANG1, TRIANG2 are constructed to describe the inhomogeneity of converters.

```
FILL (#I2), (9:255:2), (8:255:2), 1;
FILL (#I2), (8:255:2), (9:255:2), 1;
FOR I=(8:248:8);
  CONF (#I1), ((I,0))++TRIANG1, (1);
  CONF (#I1), ((0,I))++TRIANG2, (1);
END;
FILL (#I3), (8:255), (0:7), 1;
FILL (#I3,#I2), (0:7), (8:255), 11B;
```

initial configuration description

```
DO 3*248+256;
  FUNASGN (0,1), (#R,FM);
  FUNASGN (2,3), (FM,#R);
  FUNASGN (4), (#R);
  FUNASGN (5), (#R,#ID);
  FUNASGN (6), (#D);
  FUNASGN (7), (#ID,#D);
  FOR I=(1,31);
    INPUT A((I,1),(0,1),248), (I), 1+8*(I-1), 2;
    INPUT B((1,I),(1,0),248), (I), 2+8*(I-1), 2;
  END;
DEND;
```

A structure "DO n; specification DEND;" means that n transition steps should be executed according to the given specification.

1. matrix multiplication.

```
DO 1;
  FUNASGN (0:3), (FT);
DEND;
```

2. Transition step with function f_T.

```
DO 248;
  FUNASGN (0:3), (#D);
  FOR I=(1:31);
    OUTPUT C((1,I),(1,0),248), (I), 1, 1;
  END;
DEND;
```

3. Elements of C are shifted out of the cellular array.

Note that correct syntax of the language would require different types of parentheses. In the above example we have used "(" and ")" in any case. Detailed description of the language is given in [3].

REFERENCES

[1] Katona, E.: Cellular algorithms for binary matrix operations. Proceedings of CONPAR 81, Lecture Notes in Computer Science 111, pp. 203-216, 1981.

[2] Katona, E.: A programming language for cellular processors. Proceedings of "Parallel Computing'85", Berlin (West), 1986.

[3] Katona E.: Cellular assembly language for Cellprocessor Prototype. Manuscript in Hungarian, 1985.

[4] Legendi, T.: Cellprocessors in computer architecture. Computational Linguistics and Computer Languages XI, 1977, pp.147-167.

[5] Seutter, F.: CEPROL - Eine Zellulare Programmierspache. Proceedings of Third Braunschweig Cellular Meeting, Informatik-Skripten 8, T.U. Braunschweig, 1984.

[6] Tóth, J.: A 64K cell LSI based cellprocessor prototype. Proceedings of PARCELLA'84, Akademie-Verlag Berlin, 1985, pp.154-161.

[7] Zádori, L.: A Boolean function optimization algorithm for generation of cellular microprograms. Submitted to PARCELLA'86.

FAULT TOLERANT PROGRAMMING OF A TWO-LAYER CELLULAR ARRAY

Nándor Tóth [1)]

1. INTRODUCTION

Fault tolerance occurs at many levels in sequential and parallel computer systems. Several approaches to the design of fault tolerant arrays of processors have appeared in the literature. Some of these approaches [1], [6] use redundant switching mechanism in each processor element /or cell/. A second group of approaches [5], [8] employ redundant switches between the processor elements routing around the faulty cells and connecting the good ones. Kung [3] uses delay registers in the cell and redundant tracks in the channel between cells. These previous works apply additional hardware to solve the problem. H. Nishio and Y. Kobuchi [7] study fault tolerant cellular spaces and use the well-known triple modular redundancy avoiding the effect of errors. Gross [2] applies this idea for L-processors which is a conception of cellular processor suggested by T. Legendi [4].

In this paper we study a special cellular array which is a mathematical model of the Cellprocessor Prototype [9]. A new method is proposed using time and state redundancy to avoid the effect of faulty cells. We show that a cellular program using only the upper layer of a two-layer cellular array can be simulated by another cellular program which uses both layers, providing that the faulty cells are separated.

2. DEFINITIONS

<u>A two-dimensional cellular array (CA)</u> is a six-tuple (C, C_I, A, B, N, Φ), where

$C = \{c_{11}, c_{12}, \ldots, c_{1n}, \ldots, c_{n1}, \ldots, c_{nn}\}$ - is the set of cells

$C_I = \{c_{01}, \ldots, c_{0n}, c_{1,n+1}, \ldots, c_{n,n+1}, c_{n+1,n}, \ldots, c_{n+1,1}, c_{n0}, \ldots, c_{10}\}$ - is the set of input cells, C is bounded by C_I [see Fig. 1]

$A = \{0, 1, \ldots, s_a\}$ - is the finite set of external states

$B = \{0, 1, \ldots, s_b\}$ - is the finite set of internal states

$N : C \to (C \cup C_I)^5$ - is the neighbourhood function, where

$$N(c_{ij}) = (c_{ij}, c_{i,j+1}, c_{i+1,j}, c_{i,j-1}, c_{i-1,j})$$

$\Phi = \{f \mid f : A^5 \times B \to A \times B\}$ - is the set of transition functions

---

1) Research Group on Automata Theory
Hungarian Academy of Sciences
Somogyi u. 7., H-6720 Szeged, Hungary

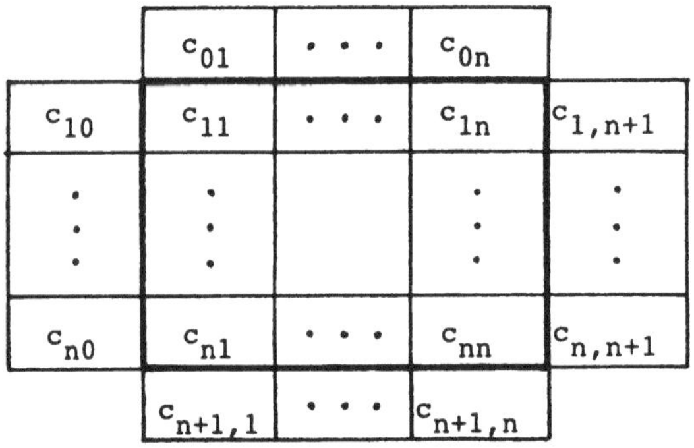

Fig. 1. Cells and input cells

<u>A configuration of CA</u> is defined as a global /external/ state of CA and denoted by a mapping κ: $C \to A$. $\kappa(C) = (a_{11},\ldots,a_{nn})$, where $\kappa(c_{ij}) = a_{ij}$, $1 \le i,j \le n$. The set of all configurations is denoted by K. The CA works as usual: at time t the CA has an arbitrary configuration. From t to t+1 each cell changes its states synchronously by its transition function which depends on the external states of its neighbours and on its own internal state.

Let $\bar{f} = (f_{11},\ldots,f_{nn})$ be a vector over Φ, where f_{ij} is the transition function of c_{ij}. <u>F: K → K</u> is called a <u>global transition</u> induced by $\bar{f}$, if for arbitrary $(a_{11},\ldots,a_{nn})$ configuration of CA

$$F(a_{11},\ldots,a_{nn}) = (a'_{11},\ldots,a'_{nn}) \text{ , where}$$

$$a'_{ij} = P_1^2(f_{ij}(a_{ij},a_{i,j+1},a_{i+1,j},a_{i,j-1},a_{i-1,j},b_{ij})) \text{ , } 1 \le i,j \le n$$

/$P_1^2(x_1x_2) = x_1$, denotes the first projection/

A <u>T-step program of CA</u> is defined as a mapping P: $C \to \Phi^T$.

Let c be a cell of C. $P(c) = (f_c^1,f_c^2,\ldots,f_c^T)$ is a T-component vector over Φ, where f_c^i is the transition function of c in the i-th step $(1 \le i \le T)$.

A <u>run of P</u>, (denoted by ϕ) is a sequence $\kappa_0,\kappa_1,\ldots,\kappa_T$ of configurations, where κ_0 is an initial configuration and $\kappa_{i+1} = F_p^{i+1}(\kappa_i)$, $0 \le i \le T-1$ where $F_p = (F_p^1,F_p^2,\ldots,F_p^T)$ a sequence of global transitions induced by P. /F_p^i is induced by $\bar{f}^i = (f^i_{c_{11}},f^i_{c_{12}},\ldots,f^i_{c_{nn}})$.

Simulation

Let P and P' be two cellular programs of CA. <u>P' simulates P in n-slow</u> if and only if there exists a mapping G: K → K such that for any run $\kappa_0,\ldots,\kappa_T$ of P there exists a run $\kappa'_0,\ldots,\kappa'_{n\cdot T}$ of P' that the following diagram is commutative

$$\begin{array}{ccc} \kappa_i & \xrightarrow{\quad F_p^{i+1} \quad} & \kappa_{i+1} \\ G \downarrow & & \downarrow G \\ \kappa'_{n\cdot i} & \xrightarrow{F_{p'}^{ni+1} \circ F_{p'}^{ni+2} \circ \dots \circ F_{p'}^{n(i+1)}} & \kappa'_{n(i+1)} \end{array}$$

<u>A two-layer cellular array</u> is a two-dimensional cellular array, where $A = \{0,1\}$ and every $c \in C$ has two external state registers as it is shown in figure 2.

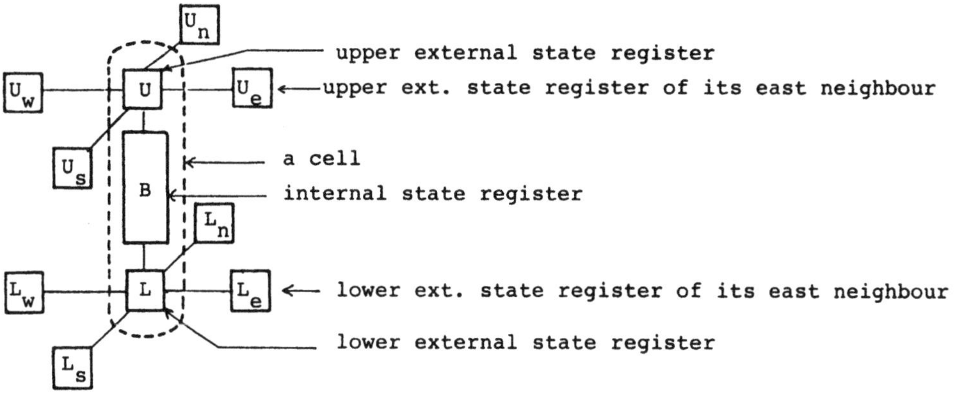

Fig. 2. A cell of the two-layer CA

A configuration of two-layer CA is defined as a global state of external registers and denoted by a mapping $\kappa: C \to A \times A$, where $\kappa(c_{ij}) = (a_{ij}^1, a_{ij}^2)$

a_{ij}^1 - state of upper register /U/

a_{ij}^2 - state of lower register /L/

Upper registers form the upper layer and lower registers form the lower layer. Both layers work as a two-dimensional CA one by one as usual: From time t to time t+1 each cell changes its states by two transition functions (f,g), where f and g are the transition function of the upper layer and lower layer, respectively. These functions are defined as follows:

$$f,g\colon A^6 \times B \to A \times B$$
$$f\colon U \times U_e \times U_s \times U_w \times U_n \times L \times B \to U \times B$$
$$g\colon L \times L_e \times L_s \times L_w \times L_n \times U \times B \to L \times B$$

<u>Faulty cell, separated faulty cells</u>

A <u>cell is faulty</u> if its next state differs from the expected one. In physical systems it is appeared as errors in the circuitry such as broken wires or nonfunctional transistors. We don't make a distinction between different kinds of errors. C is divided into two subsets as good cells and faulty cells.

Some <u>faulty cells are (n,m)-separated</u> if there exists a rectangle of cells with n rows and m columns, bounded with good cells and this rectangle contains the faulty cells (see Fig. 3.)

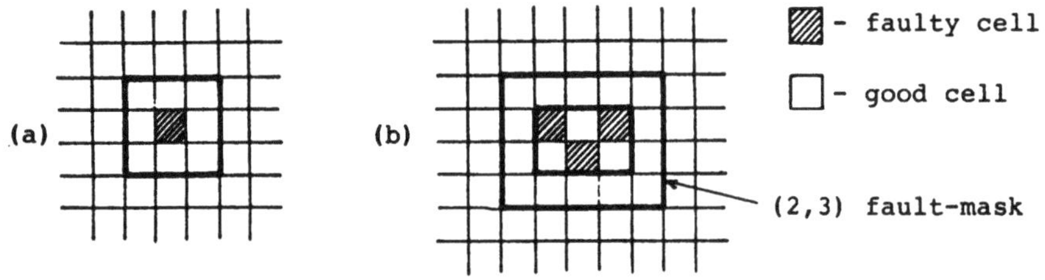

Fig. 3. (a) (1,1)-separated faulty cell,
(b) (2,3)-separated faulty cells

The rectangle with n+2 rows and m+2 columns containing the boundary good cells is called <u>(n,m)-fault-mask</u>.

A <u>path</u> is a sequence $c_0, c_1, \ldots, c_m$ of cells such that c_i is a neighbour of c_{i-1}, $1 \leq i \leq m$.

3. THE FAULT TOLERANT PROGRAMMING METHOD

If a cellular program P of two-layer CA, uses only the upper layer then every cell changes only its upper and internal states. The state of its lower register is unchanged during the time of any run of P. Let P be a program using only the upper layer (every cell is good). Our aim is to show that P can be simulated by another cellular program, P' using both layers (some cells are faulty).

Let c_0 be a faulty cell. In the simulation we replace the upper state register of c_0 by the lower state register of a good cell c_1. The upper states of $N(c_0)$ are necessary to calculate the next upper state of c_0 in P. Thus these states must be contained in the lower states of $N(c_1)$ or/and in the internal state of c_1 when c_1 calculates its lower state in P' which corresponds to the upper state of c_0. Similarly the lower state of c_1 is necessary to calculate the next upper states of $N(c_0)$ in P'. Therefore, we need some paths /routing around the faulty cell/ from $N(c_0)$ to $N(c_1)$ and from c_1 to $N(c_0)$ flowing these necessary state information. This "data transport" is necessary before every global transition of P' corresponding to a global transition P, because the cells of $N(c_0)$ calculate their states in P' like in P (except c_0).

How can we choose c_1^2? We would like the number of global transitions required by data transport to be minimum. This number depends on the length of the data paths. Thus let c_1 be one of the boundary cells of c_0.

We assume that all of good cells can be correctly initialized (loading of initial configuration) and the input-output arrangement of a cellular program (writing input data into the input cells and reading output data out of the boundary cells of C in several steps) does not have an effect on simulation. Then we have the following result, if there are only single defects in the cellular array.

<u>THEOREM 1.</u> If every faulty cell can be covered by disjoint (1,1)-fault-masks then an arbitrary cellular program, P using only the upper layer can be simulated in 4-slow by another cellular program, P' using both layers.

<u>PROOF</u>. Let P be an arbitrary T-step program using only the upper layer and ϕ an arbitrary run of P. We denote the t-th configuration of ϕ by κ_t, where $\kappa_t(c_i) = (a_i,0), \forall c_i \in C$.

G /see the definition of simulation/ is defined as follows,

$$G(\kappa(c_i)) = \begin{cases} (a_i,a_j) \text{ if } c_i \text{ replaces the faulty cell, } c_j \\ \text{undefined if } c_i \text{ is faulty} \\ (a_i,o) = \kappa(c_i) \text{ if } c_i \text{ is good but does not replace and} \\ \qquad\qquad \text{faulty cell} \end{cases}$$

Let c_o be a faulty cell and we choose c_1 to replace c_0 (see Fig. 4.). /We regard only one fault-mask but the others behave similarly - they are disjoint./ Now, we give a sequence of global transitions, F_1, F_2, F_3, F_4^{t+1} which satisfies the following equation.

$$\text{(1)} \qquad G(F_P^{t+1}(\kappa_t)) = \\ = F_4^{t+1}(F_3(F_2(F_1(G(\kappa_t)))))$$

Fig. 4. An (1,1)-fault-mask

Let f_{c_i} be the transition function of c_i in F_P^{t+1}. Then the transition function of c_i in F_4^{t+1} is defined as follows

$$\begin{cases} (f_{c_i}, f_{c_j}) \quad \text{if } c_i \text{ replaces the faulty cell } c_j \\ \text{undefined if } c_i \text{ is faulty} \\ (f_{c_i}, g_0) \text{ if } c_i \text{ is good but does not replace any faulty} \\ \qquad \text{cell } /g_0 = \text{constant 0 function}/ \end{cases}$$

F_1, F_2 and F_3 are the global transitions of data transport. These global transitions are illustrated in figure 5.

The transition functions of cells outside the fault-masks are (f_I,g_0) in F_1, F_2 and F_3, where f_I denotes the identity function and g_0 denotes the constant 0 function.

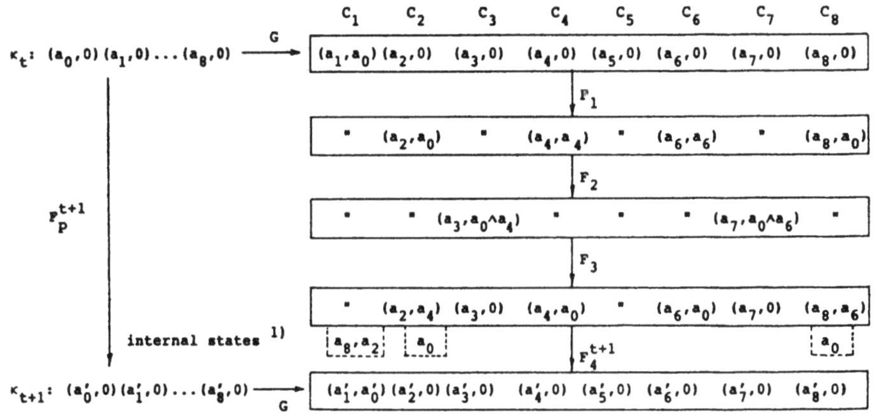

Fig. 5. F_1, F_2, F_3 in fault-masks /states denoted by " are unchanged/

Similarly, F_4^t can be given to F_p^t, $0 \leq t \leq T-1$. Thus there exist P' such that

$$F_{P'} = (F_1, F_2, F_3, F_4^1, F_1, F_2, F_3, F_4^2, \ldots, F_1, F_2, F_3, F_4^T)$$

and

$$G(F_P^{i+1}(\kappa_i)) = F_4^{i+1}(F_3(F_2(F_1(G(\kappa_i))))), \quad \forall i \; 0 \leq i \leq T-1. \qquad \square$$

This programming method can also be applied, if there are clustered defects in the cellular array. In the following theorem /see below/ we have a suprising result concerning time redundancy. To avoid the effect of a 2x2 clustered defect we need less time redundancy than it is necessary for a simple defect.

THEOREM 2. If every faulty cell can be covered by disjoint (2,2)-fault-masks then an arbitrary cellular program, P using only the upper layer can be simulated in 3-slow by another cellular program, P' using both layers.

Proof. We regard only one fault-mask. G, P, ϕ, κ_t are defined similarly as in Theorem 1. We assume that c_0, c_1, c_2, c_3 are faulty c_0, c_1, c_2, c_3 are replaced by c_4, c_7, c_{10}, c_{13} respectively /see Fig. 6./. We give a sequence of global transitions, F_1, F_2, F_3^t for any F_p^t. F_3^t is defined similarly as F_4^t in Theorem 1. F_1 and F_2 /the global transitions of data transport/ are illustrated in figure 7.

---

1) a_8, a_2 are loaded into the internal state register of c_1 and a_0 is loaded into the internal state register of c_2 and c_8 because it is necessary to calculate the next states.

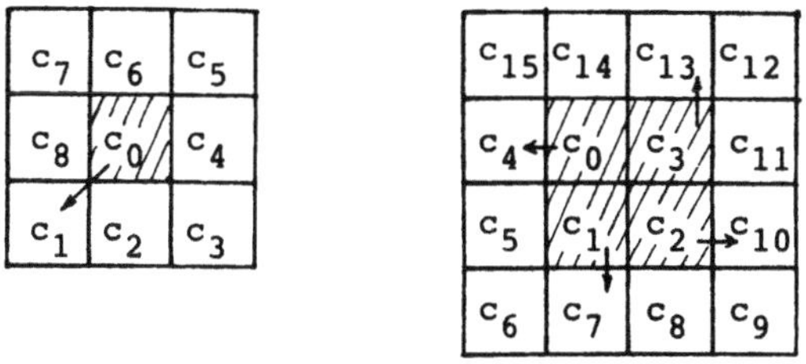

Fig. 6. A (2,2)-fault-mask

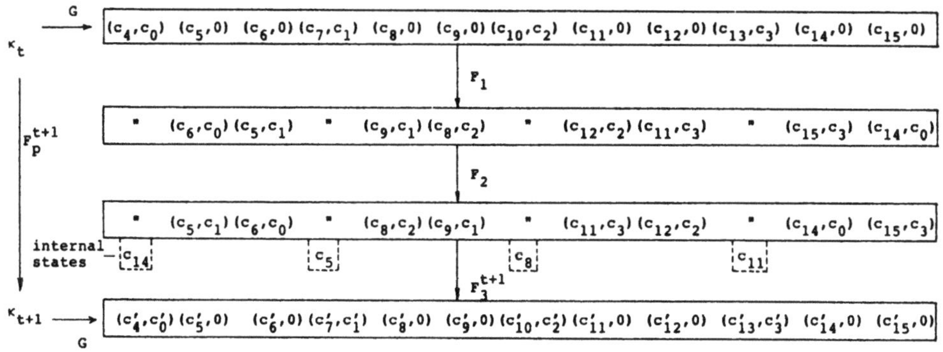

Fig. 7. F_1, F_2 in fault-masks

The transition functions of cells outside the fault-masks are (f_I, g_0) in F_1 and F_2.

Thus P' is given as follows,

$$F_{P'} = (F_1, F_2, F_3^1, F_1, F_2, F_3^2, \ldots, F_1, F_2, F_3^T) \text{ and}$$

$$G(F_p^{i+1}(\kappa_i)) = F_3^{i+1}(F_2(F_1(G(\kappa_i)))) \;, \forall i \quad 0 \le i \le T-1 \qquad \square$$

4. CONCLUDING REMARKS

This paper has introduced a method for the fault tolerant programming of cellular arrays. It is based on the following idea: a faulty cell can be replaced by a good cell if it has enough redundant states. This solution inquires time redundancy, because it increases the number of time-steps of cellular programs. Time redundancy can be decreased by some hardware support and in this way the method can be applied to create a fault tolerant procedure for wafer-scale integrated cellular arrays under implementation and for the two-layer Cellprocessor Prototype.

Literature

[1] R. C. Aubusson and I. Catt: Wafer-scale integration - A fault tolerant procedure.
IEEE J. Solid-State Circuits, SC-13(1978), 339-344.

[2] S. R. Gross: On fault tolerant L-processors
Acta Cybernetica, 5(1981), 377-387.

[3] H. T. Kung and Monica S. Lam: Wafer-scale integration and two-level pipelined implementation of systolic arrays
Journal of comp. and distrib. comp., 1(1984), 32-63.

[4] T. Legendi: Cellprocessor in computer architecture.
Computational Linguis. and Comp. Languages, 11(1977), 147-167.

[5] F. T. Leighton and C. E. Leiserson: Wafer-scale integration of systolic arrays.
IEEE Trans. Comput. C-34(1985), 448-461.

[6] F. B. Manning: An approache to highly integrated, computer-maintained cellular array.
IEEE Trans. Comput. C-26(1977), 536-552.

[7] H. Nishio and Y. Kobuchi: Fault tolerant cellular spaces.
Journal of comp. and syst. sci. 11(1975), 150-170.

[8] A. L. Rosenberg: The Diagenes approach to testable fault-tolerant arrays of processors.
IEEE Trans. Comput. C-23(1983), 902-910.

[9] J. Tóth: A 64 Kcell LSI based Cellprocessor Prototype. Proceedings of the Workshop "Parallel Processing by Cellular Automata and Arrays", (1984), 154-161.

A CLUSTERING PROCEDURE ON THE CELLPROCESSOR BASED ON ISODATA ALGORITHM

Balázs Ghymes[1)]

ABSTRACT

The ISODATA clustering procedure is a well known and largely used tool in classification techniques in image processing. However the running time of the ISODATA algorithm is rather long on a traditional computer. In this paper we describe a speedup possibility by the computation of the criterion function, intra-class variance and the inter-class separability distance realized on the cellprocessor.

INTRODUCTION

The clustering procedure realizing a sort of classification without subject is based on the features of the patterns, that is, the similar clusters will be drawn together, and the different ones will be separated. Generally the clustering procedure is used to evaluate multispectral earth images. In this case the patterns are the pixel-vectors of the image, which contain the intensity values of the corresponding spectral band. Since an earth image contain a great amount of datas (10 million pixels per image) it is necessary that the clustering algorithm should be fast and efficient.

In our method certain part of the algorithm is computed on the cellprocessor which is attached to the host machine. In this configuration the host machine starts special tasks running on the cellprocessor to compute that part of the algorithm which would be very time-consuming on the host machine.

There are several clustering methods mentioned in image processing literature, particularly the classical iterative methods and the histogram methods. Becasue of their importance, here we deal only with the iterative methods. The main task is to partitioning the pattern-set X containing the pixels into disjointed subsets. Each subset represents a cluster. After the initial partitioning the patterns have to be reclassified in each iterative step. A so called criterion function is ordered to each iterative step in order to reflect the goodness of the clustering. This procedure must be repeated until the difference of two values of the criterion function belonging to two successive step is under a given

1) József Attila University Computer Science Department
Somogyi u. 7., H-6720 Szeged, Hungary

threshold. There are several examples for the criterion function, e.g. [1]:

$$J_i = \sum_{\underline{x} \in X_i} \| \underline{x} - \underline{m}_i \|^2 \tag{1}$$

where X_i is the ith subset and $\| . \|$ means normalization. The cluster mean $\underline{m}_i$ is:

$$\underline{m}_i = \frac{1}{n_i} \sum_{\underline{x} \in X_i} \underline{x} \tag{2}$$

where n_i is the number of patterns belonging to X_i. Then the total criterion function is:

$$J_e = \sum_{i=1}^{c} J_i \tag{3}$$

where c is the number of the clusters.

THE ISODATA ALGORITHM

Before showing the ISODATA algorithm we must note that during the algorithm the number of the clusters must be modified, too. There are two measures, the intra-class variance and the inter-class separability distance to permit the modification. If the intra-class variance is too small, the cluster must be deleted, and if it is too large, the cluster must be split. If the inter-class separability distance is too small between two clusters, they must be lumped together.

The algorithm is the following [2]:

1.) Fix an arbitrary initial partitioning and compute J_e and $\underline{m}_i$-s ($i=1,\dots,c$). A cluster is represented by its center $\underline{m}_i$.
2.) For each pattern reclassify them into that cluster which is the closest.
3.) Compute the new J_e' and $\underline{m}_i'$-s. If $|J_e' - J_e| > T$ then goto step 2. (T is the given threshold.)
4.) Compute the intra-class variance σ_i^2 for each cluster where

$$\sigma_i^2 = \sum_{k=1}^{r} \sigma_{i,k}^2 = \sum_{k=1}^{r} \frac{1}{n_i} \sum_{j=1}^{n_i} (x_{j,k} - m_{i,k})^2 \tag{4}$$

and r is the dimension-number of the pattern-vector. If σ_i^2 is too small, the cluster will be deleted, and if it is too large, the cluster will be split, then goto step 2.
5.) Compute the inter-class separability distance between two cluster by

$$d(C_i,C_j) = \sum_{k=1}^{r} \frac{(m_{i,k}-m_{j,k})^2}{\sigma_{i,k}^2 \sigma_{j,k}^2} \qquad i \neq j \tag{5}$$

If the separability distance is too small, the two clusters will be lumped together, then goto step 2.

6.) Stop.

IMPLEMENTATION ON THE CELLPROCESSOR

In the previous section we can see that it is necessary to compute J_e and $\underline{m}_i$-s after each iterative step which, at the same time, is very time-consuming. When these measures, i.e. the criterion function, the intra-class variance and the inter-class separability distance is computed on the cellprocessor, the algorithm becomes faster. Here we show only the structure of the cellular space corresponding to the cellprogram, further information can be found in [3] and [4]. We can compute the mean of each cluster $\underline{m}_i$ by the following structure:

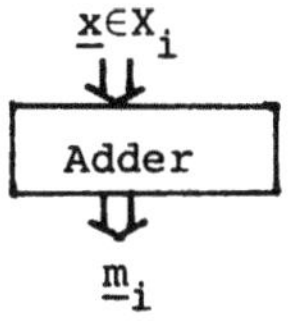

and the criterion function of the ith cluster J_i:

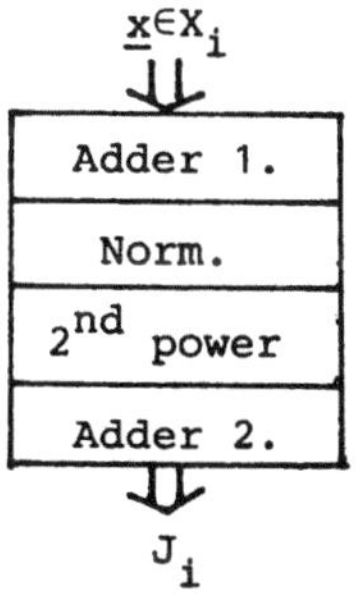

Adder 1. subtracts from each pattern-vector $\underline{x}$ the mean of the ith cluster $\underline{m}_i$. To calculate the intra-class variance the following structure can be used:

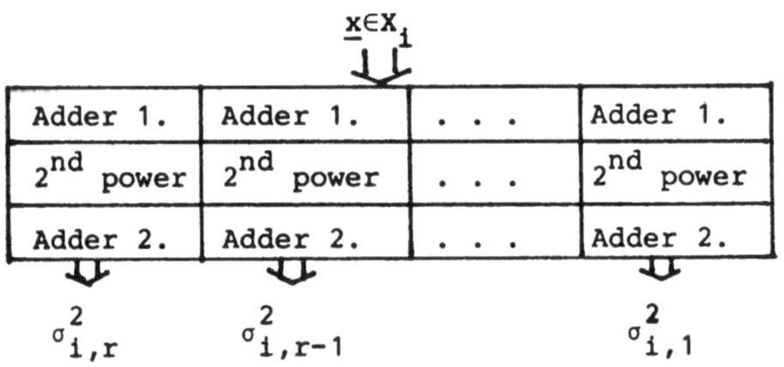

and to calculate the inter-class separability distance:

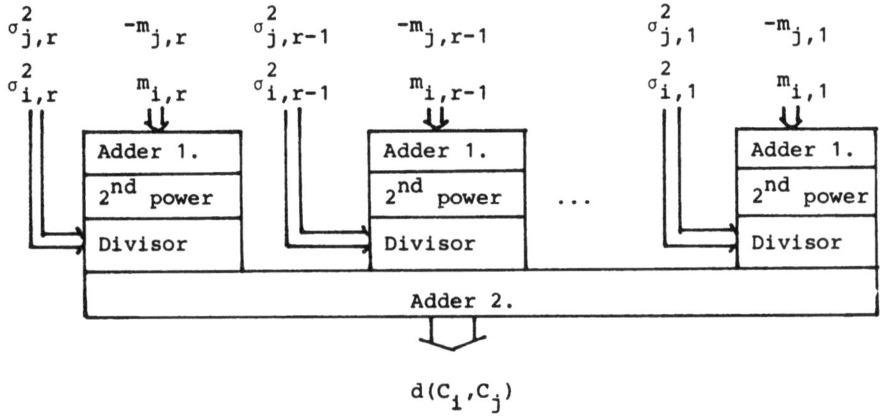

By this structure the adder 2. computes the sum of its input datas.

CONCLUSION

The ISODATA algorithm shown in the previous sections is faster and its power of computation is greater than that of the traditional one. It is an important result, as using a great amount of datas the clustering procedure is a computation-demanding task. With this algorithm it's possible to create such an interactive clustering method, where the evaluation of multispectral earth images is within an acceptable time interval.

REFERENCES

[1] R.O. Duda - P.E. Hart: Pattern Classification and Scene Analysis John Wile & Sons, 1973.

[2] H. Do-Tu - M. Installé: A Fast Clustering Procedure Based on ISODATA Algorithm with Application to Remote Sensing. Proc. of the 4th International Joint Conf. on Pattern Recognition. Kyoto, 1978. pp 326-328.

[3] E. Katona: Binary Addition and Multiplication in Cellular Space Cellprocessors and Cellgorithms.Ed. by R.. Vollmar and T. Legendi No. 1. Braunschweig, 1981.
[4] E. Katona: Cellular Algorithms for Fixed Point Vector- and Matrix-Multiplication.Proc. of the Conf. Programming Systems' 81, pp 262-280., in Hungarian

PICTURE PROCESSING ON DIFFERENT TYPES OF CELLULAR PROCESSORS

Peter Köles[1)]

1. Introduction

There are different types of cellular processor architectures under design and realization. They differ from each other in the type of the cells, the size of the cellular space, the input-output possibilities and so on. Therefore a given task needs different solution methods on different architectures.

This paper compares the cellprocessors as well as their programming techniques in case of picture processing which seems to be the most important application area. The comparison is carried out by showing the cellular picture processing techniques suitable for the individual architectures. Different cellprograms of a given task are also sketched for the architectures.

2. Cellprocessor architectures

All cellprocessor architectures [9] consist of three main parts (Fig. 1.) such as the cellular space, the cellular space control unit (CCU) and the input-output processor (IOP).

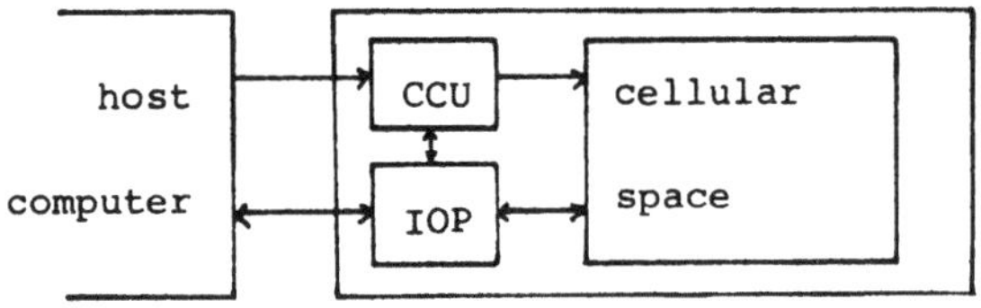

Fig. 1. Cellprocessor architecture

The cellular space is a rectangular cell-matrix, its cells have maximum 16 states. In the cellular net the von Neumann neighbourhood is assumed. CCU controls the cellular space, broadcasts microinstructions to the cells. IOP controls input-output transmission between the cellular space and host computer.

Cellprocessor architectures have further abilities to be flexible the most important ones are: inhomogeneity in time and in space [9].

1) Research Group on Automata Theory of Hungarian Academy of Sciences, H-6720 Szeged, Somogyi u. 7., Hungary

There are three different types of cellprocessor architectures under design and fabrication, namely the cellprocessor based on traditional components (ROLL) [14], the cellular processor prototype (SPP) [13] and a 16-state cellprocessor (TT) [15]. From the point of view of cellular programming main differences of architectures are recited below.

(i) The size of the cellular space of the first architecture is 15x16, but the other two architectures have a cellular space of size 256x256. These large cellular spaces are divided into blocks (one block is integrated into one chip). Blocks are connected by a switching network, so any interconnection structure may be realized. The way between two non-neighbouring blocks is called a teletransport path. Teletransport paths are programmable.

(ii) Cells of architectures ROLL and SPP are two-state cells with five or six internal state bits, respectively. All the six internal bits of SPP and only one internal bit of ROLL may be handled dynamically. (Dynamic internal bits can be written during a computation, therefore they may be used to extend storing and computing capacity of the cells.) The cellular space of SPP is a so-called two-layer cellspace. The two layers work alternately step by step. TT cells have four internal and external bits, as well.

(iii) ROLL works by stored transition functions (one step is one clocktime) but in the case of SPP and TT transition functions are broadcast to the cells as a sequence of microinstructions.

(iv) Because of the small cellular space ROLL can offer more hardwired input-output possibilities than the others.

3. Picture processing solution methods on different architectures

Pixels may be represented in two different ways in the cellular space. A pixel may take place in one cell or in more cells. In the latter case one cell usually stores only one bit of a pixel. Further we consider this latter case.

There are three different methods for picture processing, namely two-, one-, zero-dimensional (2D, 1D, 0D) processing (Fig. 2.). Names come from the size of the cellular space which is needed for a cellular algorithm. For example, in case of 2D processing both sizes of the cellular space are proportional to both sizes of the picture to be processed. In 0D case the size of the cellular space is independent of the size of the picture [1].

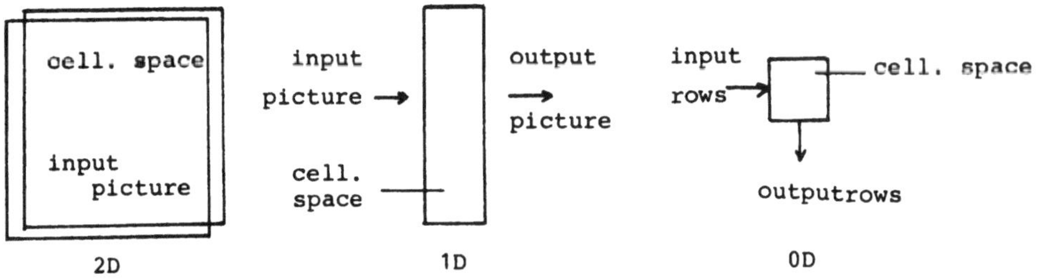

Fig. 2. 2D, 1D, 0D processing

For picture processing algorithms there is a classification considering the input and output data structures and interrelationship between them, because these features essentially influence the cellular computing methods [6]. The importance of the classification lays with the fact, that problems of a given class can usually be solved by similar cellular solution methods. Therefore for a picture processing problem it is enough to consider its class and from the general cellular solution methods of this class we can easily create a suitable cellular algorithm.

To create a concrete cellprogram for a concrete architecture we must consider the concrete size of cellular space, the type of the cells and the special abilities of architectures. ([3] shows the way from cellular algorithms to cellular programs.) A general solution method (further base algorithm) supposes an ideal cellular space with the most suitable cells and input-output management. In most cases the base algorithm must be transformed to the concrete architectures.

3.1. 2D solutions

Because of the small cellular space 2D solution is omitted in case of architecture ROLL except the very special case of binary pictures of size 15x16 or similar size.

In case of SPP and TT (a part of) the picture is initially loaded into the cellular space (Fig. 3.), where "empty" columns preclude overflows. For local (window) operations the neighbouring pixels must be overlapped each other so that all pixels will be available to the computing. The vertical neighbouring pixels are available by von Neumann neighbourhood. To reach overlapping of horizontal neighbours we can use teletransport paths or simple shift transition functions.

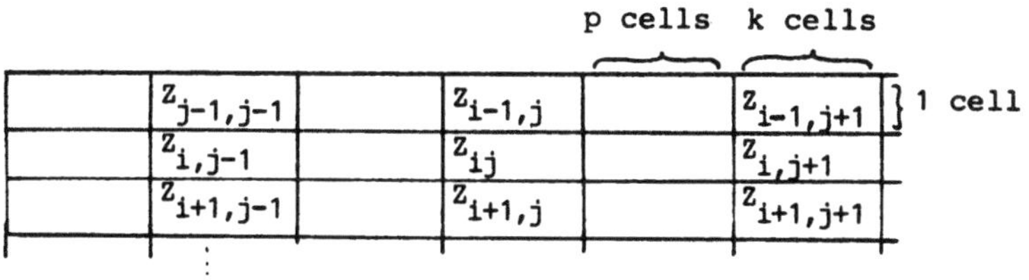

Fig. 3. Initial configuration of 2D processing

TT cells usually have enough external bits to store the bits of pixels and to count new values. In case of SPP computation may be performed on one or more internal bits while the only one external bit stores a bit of a pixel. The second layer of cellspace may also be used for the realization of the algorithm.

3.2. 1D solutions

The small size of ROLL cellular space limits the possible solutions. It is imaginable to use ROLL for simple bit-serial algorithms by partitioning of the picture, but obviously they cannot give so powerful solutions.

In case of larger cellular spaces (SPP, TT) input pictures are being passed through the cellular space while output pictures are computed continuously. The rectangular cellular space may be divided into one-dimensional processing stripes (Fig. 4.). Each of them can compute a certain part of a complex computation. Therefore more transformations may be performed on a picture without overhead.

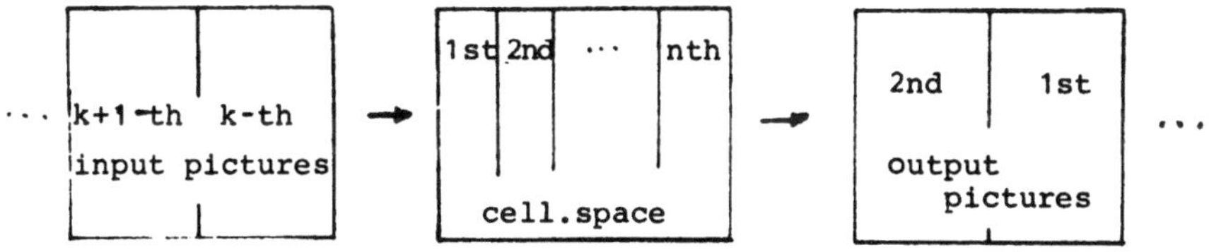

Fig. 4. Pipe-line 1D solution

If the size of the pictures or the 1D solution needs longer processing stripe than the length of one side of the available cellular space, we can rearrange the rectangular cellular space into a virtual long stripe shaped cellular space by teletransport paths (Fig. 5.) [7]. To combine methods shown in Fig. 4. and Fig. 5. is also possible.

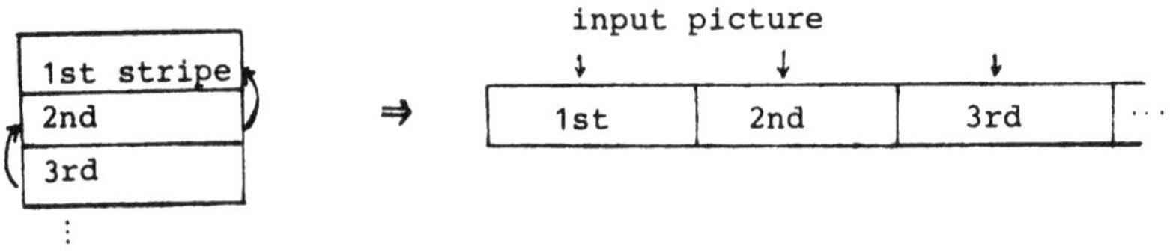

Fig. 5. Virtual long stripe cellspace

3.3. 0D solutions

It is the most suitable solution for the architecture ROLL. The most of picture processing cellular programs of ROLL are 0D solutions. The advantages of 0D processing elements (PEs) lay in the fact that on one hand they can be arbitrarily small and on the other hand they are very fast, because of they receive input pixels needed for a computation in the best format and order.

From 0D PEs we can form 1D processing stripes for large cellular spaces (Fig. 6.) by teletransport [7]. To transfer the necessary data of PEs is a bit complicated in this case.

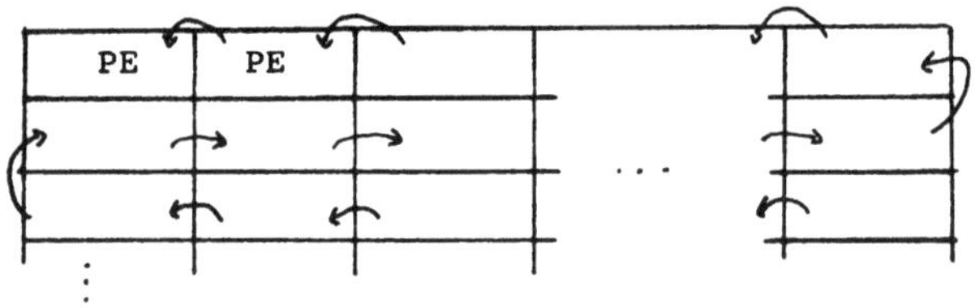

Fig. 6. 1D stripe from 0D processing elements

4. Cellprograms on different architectures

In this section an example is introduced. A 0D base algorithm for convolution type algorithms is given [2]. From this cellular algorithm cellular programs are created for each architecture. All the phases of procedures are not detailed here, only the basic principles of the cellular program creation. The example also shows the general programming methods and techniques of the different architectures.

Let $A=(a_{ij})$ be an nxn picture and let $C=(c_{uv})$ be an mxm mask where each element c_{uv} is a fixed coefficient. Convolution of picture A with mask C results a picture $B=(b_{ij})$ defined as follows:

$$b_{ij}=\sum_{u=1}^{m}\sum_{v=1}^{m} c_{uv}\cdot a_{i+u-1,j+v-1}.$$

Such a picture transformation can be computed by a 0D PE shown in Fig. 7. (Arrows mean data flows inside the PE.)

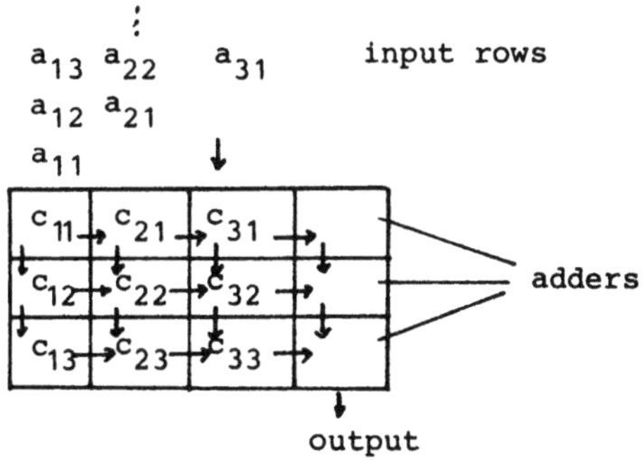

Fig. 7. 0D PE for convolution (m=3)

c_{uv} is a multiplier element, where input pixels are multiplied by the stored element of the given mask. Its internal structure is shown in Fig. 8.

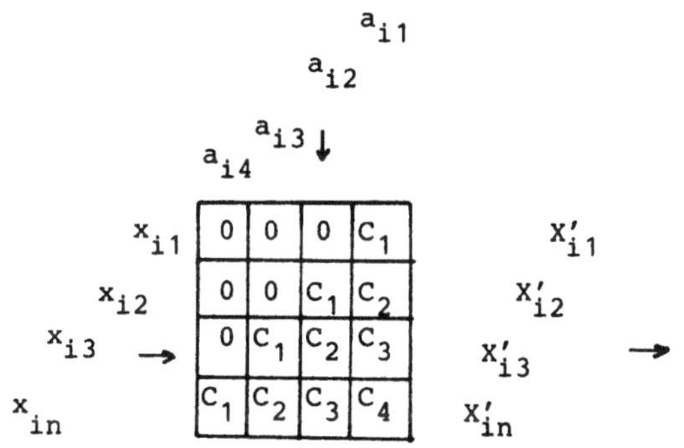

Fig. 8. Constant multiplier (Data are 4 bit long)

The multiplier can perform the operation X'=x+ac. Its local transition function (described by so-called microconfiguration term [10]):

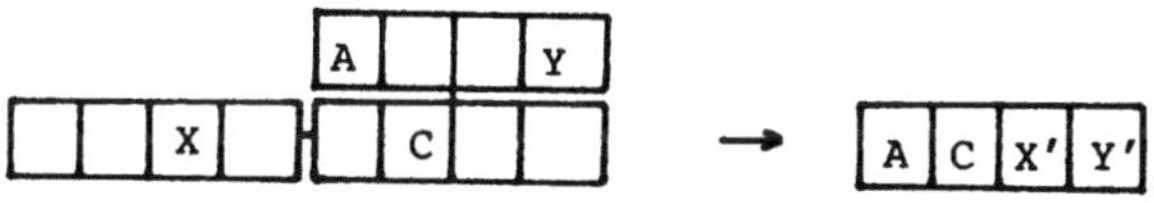

where [Y'X'](as a two-bits binary number):=X+Y+A·C

Notice, that the multiplier receives input and gives output in every step. It is easy to see, that PE of Fig. 7. can compute the image B row by row, one element b_{ij} is produced in any time-step.

This base algorithm is applicable for architecture TT without any transformation. A 1D processing stripe is formed from 64 PEs by teletransport paths. (Fig. 6.) For the cellprogram the elimination of redundant data transmission (neighbouring PEs need almost the same rows) as well as synchronisation of PEs are necessary.

In case of SPP basic principle is the same shown in Fig. 7. One 16-state cell is replaced by only one SPP cell. Data flow is reduced by thinning of data. (One data per two steps.) Two steps are necessary to perform the transition function of the base algorithm. All the two layers and two dynamic internal bits are also used. Bits A and Y move in the first layer, X moves in the second layer. One of the dynamic internal bits stores the bit C, the second internal bit is used for the computation X'. Communication between the two layers is realized by this second internal bit.

In the cellular space of ROLL only one multiplier can be realized. This multiplier must replace the nine multipliers of the base algorithm.

Consider the sketch of Fig. 8. Let us see, that all the bits of a_i are multiplied by the bits c_1 of a coefficient. In next step a_i is multiplied by the bits c_2 of the same coefficient, while next pixel a_{i+1} is multiplied by the bits c_1. If bits c_1 are exchanged for the bits c_1 of the next coefficient in this step, the pixel a_{i+1} is multiplicated by these bits of the second coefficient. So changing the bits of coefficients of the mask before every pixel, the nine multiplication of the mask can be performed in one multiplier one after the other. (Of course, bits of coefficients must be coded into the transition functions.) Because of cells of ROLL are not so "clever" than cells of SPP one step of the base algorithm requires six steps on the architecture ROLL, but the number of cells is the same in both cases. Therefore the computation of one pixel b_{ij} takes 54 steps (but one step is one clocktime here). The details of concrete realization is omitted here, because of its sophisticated solution.

5. Conclusions

For picture processing problems a wide set of cellular algorithms and general solution methods are at our disposal to develop cellular programs for the cellprocessors. Programming of cellprocessors is flexible, there are 0D solutions for small cellular spaces but large cellular spaces may be restructured into the most appropriate form by software devices. Many picture processing cellular programs have been developed for each architecture. It has been found that all the architectures are suitable for picture processing but different architectures require different solution methods, of course.

Architectures SPP and TT are similar in the sense, that each one has a relatively large cellular space therefore cellular solution methods for them are also similar. Because of the smaller storing capacity of SPP cells PEs may be larger and the computation may be a bit more complicated on this architecture. However the circuit of SPP cells and chips are less complicated. They may be realized by current available hardware technology in Hungary.

6. References

[1] Katona, E.: Computation of window operations by cellular processors. Proc. Methoden und Algorithmen der digitalen Bildverarbeitung, T.U. Dresden, 1985. pp. 17-25.

[2] Katona, E.: Cellular algorithms for image convolution. Proc. Automatische Bildverarbeitung, Kammer der Technik of GDR, 1985.

[3] Köles, P.: From cellular algorithms to cellular programs. Proc. PARCELLA'84, Akademie Verlag, 1985. pp. 126-132.

[4] Köles, P.: Digital picture processing by cellprocessor. Computers and Artificial Intelligence, Vol. 2, No. 4, 1983. pp. 331-339.

[5] Köles, P.: Cellular algorithms for picture processing. Proc. Methoden und Algorithmen der digitalen Bildverarbeitung, T.U. Dresden, 1985. pp. 36-46.

[6] Köles, P., Katona, E.: Cellular solution methods for different classes of picture processing algorithms. Proc. Parallel Computing '85, North-Holland, 1986.

[7] Köles, P.: Picture processing algorithms on large size cellular spaces. Proc. Automatische Bildverarbeitung, Kammer der Technik of GDR, 1985.

[8] Kung, H.T., Song, S.W.: A systolic 2-D convolution chip. Non conventional computers and image processing: algorithms and programs. L. Uhr (ed), Academic Press, 1981.

[9] Legendi, T.: Cellprocessors in computer architecture. Computational Linguistics and Computer Languages 11, 1977, pp. 147-167.

[10] Legendi, T.: A 2D transition function definiton language for a subsystem of the CELLAS cellular programming simulation language. Computational Linguistics and Computer Languages 13, 1979. pp. 169-194.

[11] Pratt, W.K.: Digital Image Processing. J. Whiley and Sons, 1978.

[12] Rosenfeld, A.: Parallel algorithms for image analysis. Techn. Report TR-1180, Univ. of Maryland, 1982.

[13] Tóth, J.: A 64 kcell LSI based cellprocessor prototype (SPP). Proc. PARCELLA'84, Akademie Verlag, 1985. pp. 154-161.

[14] Zsótér, A.: Cellprocessors based on traditional components. Proc. PARCELLA'84, Akademie Verlag, 1985. pp. 162-166.

[15] Zsótér, A., Legendi, T.: A 16-state cellprocessor. Proc. Parallel Computing'85, North-Holland, 1986.

CELLULAR ALGORITHM FOR MATRIX MULTIPLICATION

Kálmán Palágyi[1/]

A cellular processor [2] is a special device for highly parallel processing, where computations are performed by a regular array of elementary Boolean processors /cells/.

Several parallel algorithms have been constructed for matrix multiplication [1], [4], [6], [7] involving word-level parallelism. In this paper a bit-level parallel algorithm is given for matrix multiplication. This algorithm is realized as a cellular program for a given universal--purpose cellular processor called Cellprocessor Prototype /SPP/ [8], but it is also suitable for special-purpose hardware realization.

1. Characteristics of Cellprocessor Prototype

The cellular space of Cellprocessor Prototype is a 256x256 array of von Neumann neighbourhood cells and has two layers. Each cell contains two external state-bits /for the two layers/ and six internal state-bits which are common for the two layers. The structure of a cell can be seen in Fig. 1.

The two layers work on a chopped mode. Cells in upper layer work with a transition function

$$f: U \times U_e \times U_s \times U_w \times U_n \times I_1 \times I_2 \times I_3 \times I_4 \times I_5 \times I_6 \to U \times I_1 \times I_2 \times I_3 \times I_4 \times I_5 \times I_6$$

while cells in lower layer work with

$$g: L \times L_e \times L_s \times L_w \times L_n \times I_1 \times I_2 \times I_3 \times I_4 \times I_5 \times I_6 \to L \times I_1 \times I_2 \times I_3 \times I_4 \times I_5 \times I_6$$

/each component corresponds to the set {0,1}/.

A transition step consists of two sub-steps while a pair of functions (f,g) is executed. During this time both external state-bits change their states, the internal state-bits may be changed twice.

An 8x8 array of cells is called a block. Blocks are not connected to form a von Neumann neighbourhood space but they are connected by a programmable switching network. Usually two neighbouring blocks are connected according to the von Neumann neighbourhood but it is possible to jump over a block. A way which connects non-neighbouring blocks is called a teletransport path. Teletransport paths are very useful because remote /software/ PE-s can be connected and the input-output processor can communicate with internal PE-s.

Detailed description of the Cellprocessor Prototype is omitted here.

1/ Attila József University, Computer Science Department, Somogyi u. 7. H-6720 Szeged, Hungary

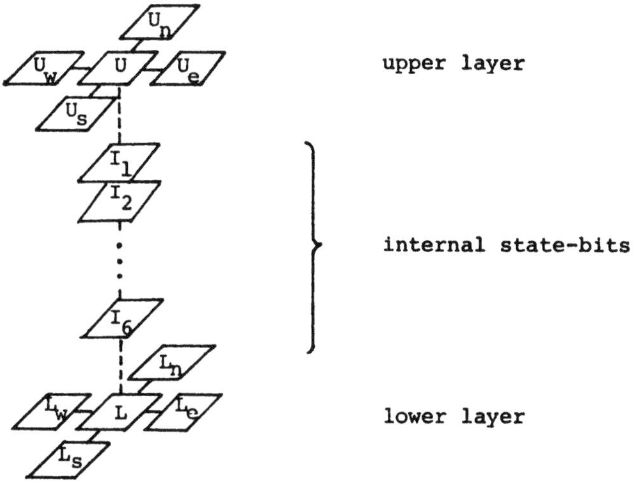

Fig. 1. The structure of a cell which consists of the bits $U, I_1, I_2, \ldots, I_6, L$. /The other bits belong to the neighbouring cells./

2. A "macrocell" algorithm for matrix multiplication

Let $A=[a_{ij}]$ be an $n_1 x n_2$ matrix, and let $B=[b_{ij}]$ be an $n_2 x n_3$ matrix. The task is to compute the product matrix $C=[c_{ij}]=A \cdot B$ of size $n_1 x n_3$, where $c_{ij} = \sum_{k=1}^{n_2} a_{ij} \cdot b_{kj}$. The task can be computed by a processor array shown in Fig. 2.

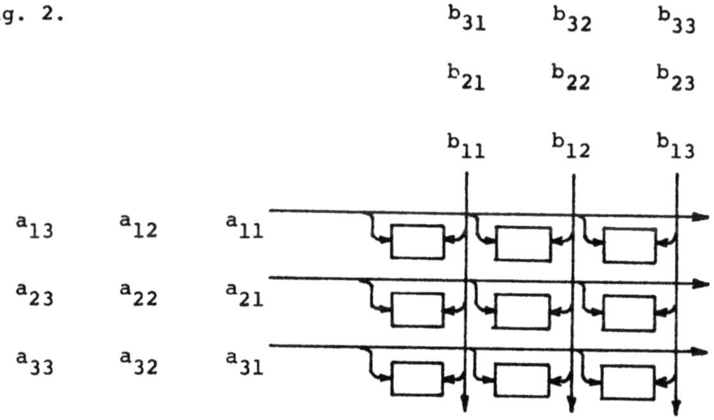

Fig.2. Sketch of a matrix multiplier array for $n_1=n_2=n_3=3$.

An elementary processor is a complete vector mutiplier /inner--product-step processor/. Element c_{ij} is computed by the processor (i,j). Fig. 3 defines the computation performed by a processor in any time-step. Note that a similar array is applied for matrix multiplication by E. Katona [4].

Fig. 3. Computation performed by a vector multiplier element, where $c'=c+a\cdot b$.

It is easy to see that the processor array of Fig. 2 can compute the product C after n_2 steps.

Matrix multiplier algorithm sketched in Fig. 2 can be called a *macro-cell algorithm*, because each cell in the array performs complete arithmetic operations /addition and multiplication of binary numbers/. Further on we show that internal structure of each macrocell may also be a cellular structure where elementary cells perform bit-level operations /microcells/. If each macrocell is replaced by the corresponding microcell network, a regular array of microcells is gained resulting a microcell algorithm for matrix multiplication.

3. A "microcell" algorithm for vector multiplication

Let $\underline{a}=(a_1,\dots,a_n)$ and $\underline{b}=(b_1,\dots,b_n)$ be two n-dimensional vectors, where operands a_i,b_i are binary numbers of k bits. The task is to compute the inner product $c=\underline{a}\cdot\underline{b}=\sum_{i=1}^{n} a_i\cdot b_i$, where c is a binary number of 2k-1 bits.

In this section a cellular algorithm will be presented solving the signed vector multiplication. This algorithm is based on a cellular unsigned vector multiplier, which will be described at first.

Our unsigned vector multiplier requires 3x(2k-1) array of 2-state cells /one-layer algorithm/, which is based on the cellular algorithm for unsigned vector multiplication [3]. Operands a_i,b_i are moved in the first and the third cell-rows with the "thinned" format of Fig. 4 /between the digits zeros are inserted/. The middle cell-row works as an adder. Partial products are generated in an overlapped manner, and each is created on the appropriate position. Vectors $\underline{a}$ and $\underline{b}$ move step by step one against the other in such a form. The bits of a_i will meet the bits of b_i and the inserted zero digits of b_{i-1} and b_{i+1}.

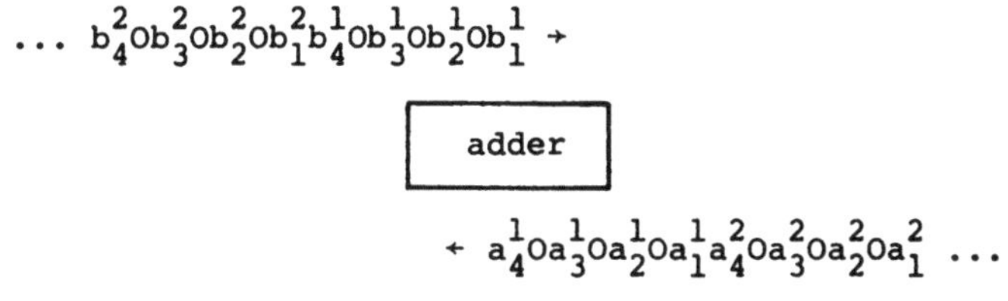

Fig. 4. Cellular algorithm for unsigned vector multiplication, where operands $a_i=[a_4^i a_3^i a_2^i a_1^i]$, $b_i=[b_4^i b_3^i b_2^i b_1^i]$ are unsigned binary numbers of 4 digits.

The three rows of the cellular unsigned vector multiplier have different transition functions, which may be defined together as follows:

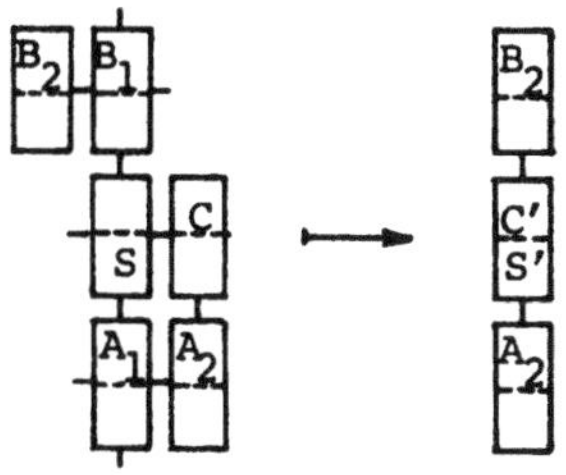

shift right

addition, where $2C'+S'=S+C+A_1 \cdot B_1$

shift left

/Upper bit of a cell is external state bit, while the lower bit is an internal one./

The inner product will be computed in the sum bits "S".

If at t=0 the configuration of Fig. 4 is assumed, then at t=2k-1 all the partial products of $a_1 \cdot b_1, \ldots,$ at t=n(2k-1) all the partial products of $a_n \cdot b_n$ are generated. It is easy to see that at t=n(2k-1)+1 the rightmost k cells of the adder have zero carry bits. To compute the complete inner product further k steps are needed, thus the whole vector multiplication process requires n(2k-1)+k steps.

The above algorithm uses only one of the layers of Cellprocessor Prototype. The other layer will be used for solving the signed vector multiplication.

The cellular signed vector multiplier uses the lower layer for control. The upper layer generates and sums the partial products. Control bits are moved in the lower layer of the first and the third cell-rows with the input operands /Fig. 5 /. Control bits "1" are moved with signs of operands and the inserted zero digits.

Signed multiplication is based on the following method [5]. The product $z=x \cdot y$ - where $x=[x_4x_3x_2x_1]$, $y=[y_4y_3y_2y_1]$ and $z=[z_7 \ldots z_1]$ are two's complement binary numbers - may be defined as follows:

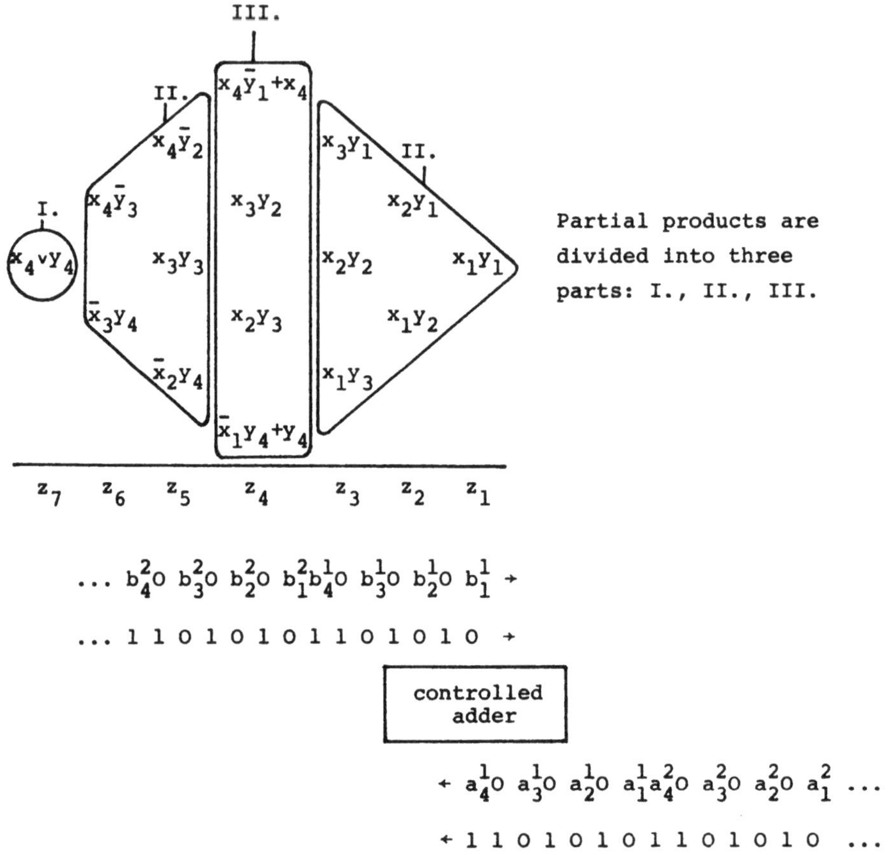

Fig. 5. Two-layer cellular signed vector multiplier, where operands $a_i=[a_4^i a_3^i a_2^i a_1^i]$, $b_i=[b_4^i b_3^i b_2^i b_1^i]$ are two's complement binary numbers of 4 digits.

24	24	24	. . .	24	24	24	24	. . .	24	
0	8	8	. . .	8	16	8	8	. . .	8	26
25	25	25	. . .	25	25	25	25	. . .	25	25
k					k					

Fig. 6. The initial configuration of internal states.

Three internal state bits - sum bit S and control signal $J=2J_2+J_1$ - are used by the adder cell-row. The three rows of the multiplier have different transition functions, which may be defined together as follows:

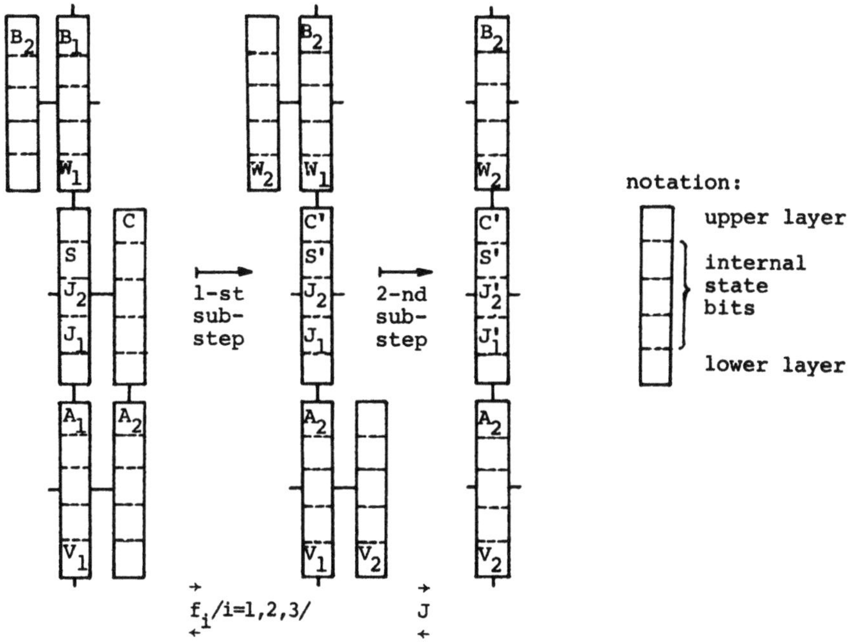

where:

J: $J'_2=W_2$, $J'_1=V_2$

/This function is assigned to each cell of adder cell-row./

$$f_1:\quad 2C'+S'=S+C+\begin{cases} A_1\cdot B_1 & \text{if } J=0,1,2 \\ A_1\vee B_1 & \text{if } J=3 \end{cases}$$

/This function generates the partial product of part I., it is assigned to 0-7 internal states./

$$f_2:\quad 2C'+S'=S+C+\begin{cases} A_1\cdot B_1 & \text{if } J=0,3 \\ A_1\cdot \bar{B}_1 & \text{if } J=1 \\ \bar{A}_1\cdot B_1 & \text{if } J=2 \end{cases}$$

/This function generates the partial products of part II., it is assigned to 8-15 internal states./

$$f_3:\quad 2C'+S'=S+C+\begin{cases} A_1\cdot B_1 & \text{if } J=0,3 \\ A_1\cdot \bar{B}_1+A_1 & \text{if } J=1 \quad /\le 3 \text{ because } C=0/ \\ \bar{A}_1\cdot B_1+B_1 & \text{if } J=2 \quad /\le 3 \text{ because } C\wedge\bar{A}_1=0/ \end{cases}$$

/This function generates the partial products of part III., it is assigned to 16-23 internal states./

The transition function of internal state 26 is the identity. Each cell has zero external state in initial configuration.

It is easy to see that the content of the adder cell-row is increased only by the necessary partial products.

4. A "microcell" algorithm for matrix multiplication

The internal structure of a vector multiplier element of section 2 is a 4x2k array of microcells, where k is divisible by 8 /Fig. 7/, thus k/4 blocks of Cellprocessor Prototype contain two vector multipliers /Fig. 8/.

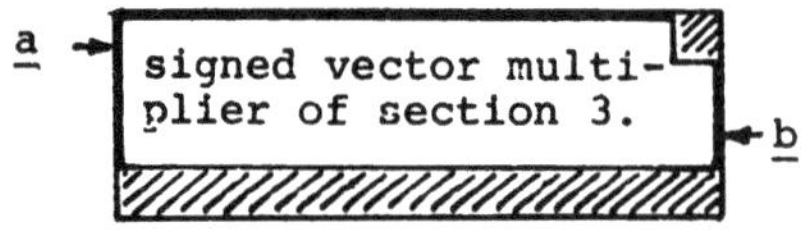

Fig. 7. The internal structure of a macrocell.

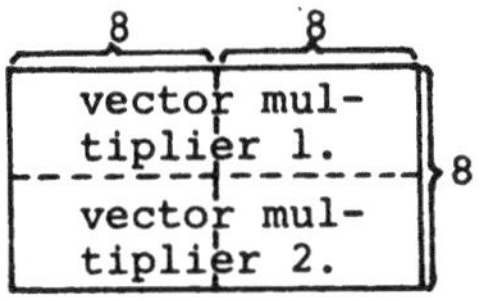

Fig. 8. Vector multipliers in the cellular space of Cellprocessor Prototype in the case k=8.

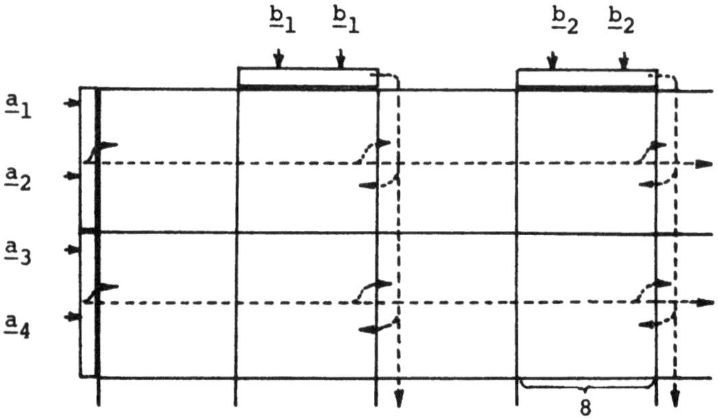

Fig. 9. Teletransport paths of matrix multiplier in the case k=8, where $\underline{a}_i$ is the i-th row of A and $\underline{b}_j$ is the j-th column of B.

The whole matrix multiplication requires $(n_2+1)(2k-1)$ steps.

5. Remarks

(i) The planned Cellprocessor Prototype contains a 256x256 cellular array, while a vector multiplier PE covers a 4x2k array of cells. This fact implies that 64x(128/k) vector multiplier PE-s can be embedded into the cellular space /$n_1 \le 64$, $n_3 \le 128/k$/.

(ii) If $n_1 > 64$ or $n_3 > 128/k$ then matrix A and B should be divided shown in Fig. 10.

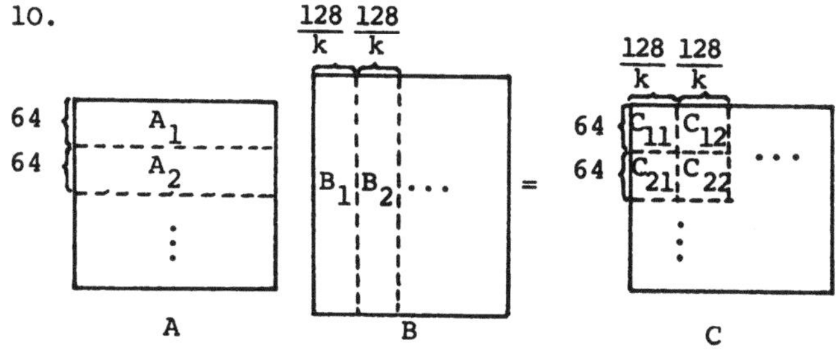

Fig. 10. Multiplication of large matrixes.

It is clear that for any i and j $C_{ij} = A_i \cdot B_j$ holds. Partial products $A_i \cdot B_j$ may be computed using the cellprocessor and the matrix C will be received from the submatrixes $C_{11}, C_{12}, \dots$. This method has been proposed by E. Katona [4] for multiplication of large matrixes.

(iii) There is no overflow-detection in the cellular vector multiplier of section 3. To provent overflow, longer word-length should be used. If for any i,j $-2^r \le a_{ij}, b_{ij} \le 2^r$ holds then a word-length $k \ge r + \frac{1}{2}\log_2 n + 2$ should be chosen to avoid overflow.

References

[1] Huang, K.H. and Abraham J.A.: Efficient Parallel Algorithms for Processor Arrays. Proc. of the 1982. Int. Conf. on Parallel Processing, pp. 271-279.

[2] Legendi, T.: Cellprocessors in computer architecture, Computational Linguistics and Computer Languages v. XI, pp. 147-167, 1977.

[3] Katona, E.: Cellular algorithms for fixed point vector- and matrix multiplication. Proceedings of the Conference Programming Systems'81, pp. 262-280, in Hungarian.

[4] Katona, E.: Cellular algorithms for binary matrix operations. Proceedings of the Conference CONPAR'81, Lecture Notes in Computer Science 111, pp. 203-216.

[5] Katona, E.: Two's complement binary addition and multiplication, manuscript in Hungarian.

[6] Kung, H.T.: The structure of parallel algorithms. Advances in Computers, v. 19, Academic Press, New-York, 1980. pp. 65-112.

[7] Moraga, C.: VLSI: Algorithms and Realizations Case studies. Forschungsbericht Nr. 176, Universität Dortmund, 1984.

[8] Tóth, J.: A 64K cell LSI based Cellprocessor Prototype (SPP). Proceedings of the Conference PARCELLA'84, pp. 154-161.

A FAST FOURIER TRANSFORMATION ALGORITHM FOR CELLULAR PROCESSOR

Zoltán Székely[1)]

Abstract

One of the most important algorithms, which can be realized in parallel way is the FFT algorithm suggested by Cooley and Tukey.

We have developed a realization of that algorithm for our special cellular architecture. This architecture has a special block structure, and a switching network is offered ensuring almost arbitrary interconnection pattern for blocks. Using this ability of the cellprocessor the usual "butterfly network" can be embedded directly into the cellular array. In this way the main problem we had to solve was the realization of a single butterfly element.

Another problem is that our processor is too small for a usual size FFT. However, the FFT algorithm has a fairly good possibility to partition it based on the regularity of its network.

1. Fast Fourier Transformation

Fourier-transform of a discrete function f, given in the points $f_i=f(x_i)$ $(0\le i<N)$, is the discrete function F defined by

$$F_k=\frac{1}{N}\cdot\sum_{i=0}^{N-1} f_i\cdot e^{-\frac{2\pi jik}{N}} \qquad (0\le k<N),$$

when j denotes the imaginary unit. (F can be complex even if f is real.) So the discrete Fourier transformation (DFT) is a linear transformation of the complex N-dimensional vectorspace determined by the matrix $\Phi=(\varphi_{ik})_{N\times N}$, where $\varphi_{ik}=e^{-\frac{2\pi jik}{N}}$, such that

$$\underline{F}=\frac{1}{N}\cdot\Phi\underline{f}$$

holds for the vectors $\underline{f}^T=(f_0,\dots,f_{N-1})$ and $\underline{F}^T=(F_0,\dots,F_{N-1})$ ($\underline{X}^T$ denotes the transposed of the column-vector $\underline{X}$).

Fast Fourier Transformation (FFT) is a speed decimation procedure of DFT based on a 2-power number of points developed by Cooley and Tukey [2]. The substance of that procedure is a reduction of the decimation redundancies occuring in the above-mentioned multiplication by the help of a

1) József Attila University, Computer Science Department, H-6720 Szeged, Somogyi u. 7., Hungary

special decimation network (shuffle-exchange network). This procedure has a good possibility to execute it in parallel way too [1, 3].

The most commonly used versions of the FFT are the "Decimation in Frequency" (DIF) and the "Decimation in Time" (DIT) algorithms (see e.g. in [9]). In these algorithms the components of the input vector "go through" a so-called butterfly-network and we get the components of the output vector, as a result. The butterfly-network consists of butterlies having two input and two output points. Fig. 1. shows the butterfly-operations of the DIF and DIT algorithms.

Fig.1. a) the butterfly of DIF b) the butterfly of DIT

A standard butterfly-network based on N=16 points is shown in Fig. 2. Left and right constants in butterflies belong to the DIF and DIT algorithms respectively. The constants are denoted shortly by u instead of $e^{-\frac{2\pi j u}{16}}$ $(0 \leq u < 7)$.

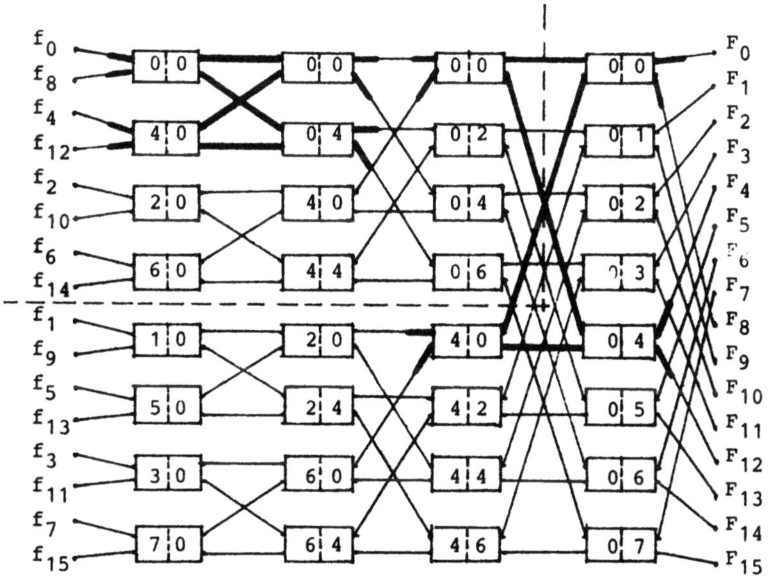

Fig. 2. Butterfly-network for N=16

2. Partition of FFT-algorithms

Our partition method is based on the network shown in Fig. 2. Only DIF-type FFT will be examined in the sequel, but the method can be applied for DIT-algorithm too.

We shall use the following notation: Let M be a power of 2. An Mx(log M+1) size network Q of butterflies is called M-butterfly, if the k'th element of its i'th row is connected with the i'th and i_k^{*}'th element only from the k+1'th column of the network, when i_k^* is a binary number having the same digits as i except the k'th one (from right), i.e. $i_k^* = i_\ell \ldots \bar{i}_k \ldots i_1$ if $i = i_\ell \ldots i_k \ldots i_1$ ($\bar{x}$ is the negation of x). E.g. Fig. 3. shows an 1-butterfly (single), a 2-butterfly, and a 4-butterfly.

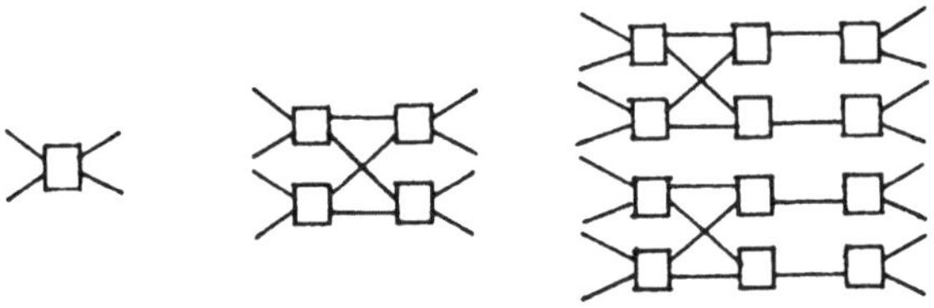

Fig. 3. a) single butterfly b) 2-butterfly c) 4-butterfly

Note that an N-point FFT can be executed by an N/2-butterfly.

The concretization C of an M-butterfly Q is an exact determination of the distribution of the weight-factors in Q. That can be given with an Mx(log M+1) size complex matrix. We say that a (C-concrete) M-buterfly Q generates the output vector $\underline{F}$ from the input vector $\underline{f}$, if giving $\underline{f}$ to the left edge of the network of Q as an input and "going through" it from the left to the right (and executing the butterfly-operations from one step to the other), we get the vector $\underline{F}$ as an output. ($\underline{f}$ and $\underline{F}$ are 2M-dimensional vectors).

We shall prove that an arbitrary M-butterfly Q can be built from L-butterflies, if L is a power of 2 and less than M.

First we present the following statement: There exists a number K≥M for L, such that for an arbitrary C-concrete K-butterfly R and for a (2K-dimensional) input vector $\underline{f}$ it is possible to give a number m, concretizations $C_1, \ldots, C_m$ of L-butterflies and a sequence $\underline{f}_1, \ldots, \underline{f}_m$ of (2L-dimensional) input vectors, such that the following states hold:

(i) an arbitrary component of $\underline{f}_i$ is a component of $\underline{f}$ or $\underline{F}_k$ (k<i), when $\underline{F}_k$ is the output vector generated from the input vector $\underline{f}_k$ by the C_k-concrete L-butterfly P_k, and

(ii) an arbitrary component of the output vector $\underline{F}$ generated from the input vector $\underline{f}$ by R is a component of $\underline{F}_k$ for some k ($1 \le k \le m$).

Consider the case of L=2 and K=16. From Fig. 2. we can realize that a 16-butterfly can be obtained by help of suitable applications of 2-butterflies: use 4-times 2-butterflies similar to the one denoted by thicklines in the first and second column of the network, 4-times 2-butterflies similar to the one denoted by thicklines in 3'th and 4'th column and get the 16-butterfly, as a result.

Note that if the length of a K-butterfly R (log K+1) is v-times greater than the length of an L-butterfly P (log L+1) (v=1,2,...), then similarly to the above description we can form v items of log L+1-wide columns in R and applying P K/L-times in each column, we get the network of R. (If $L=2^u$ then according to the above condition $K=2^{uv+v-1}$ and $m=K/L\cdot v$.) We omit the correct proof because of lack of space, but it can be constructed easily. As $K(v)\to\infty$ if $v\to\infty$, we have an integer v such that $K\geq M$, and our statement is completed.

As to the general case, note, that if we delete K-M rows ($K\geq M$) from the bottom of R and delete as many columns from the right side of R as it remains log M+1 pieces of that only, then we get Q. It means, that applying the above-described process to Q and breaking it off in the appropriate step (even in the middle of executing P), we obtain the network of Q. (E.g. in Fig. 2. the part marked with dotted line shows how to obtain a 4-butterfly Q from a 2-butterfly P with cutting of the process to build an 8-butterfly K.)

3. The cellprocessor architecture

The cellular space consists of blocks with 8x8 cells in each one. Cells in a block are connected to each other with von Neumann neighbourhood. A cell has an external state from the set {0,...,15}, and an internal state from {0,...,31}. The transition function $f_{t,b}$ works in the t'th transition step on the cells having the internal state b.

Each of the 4 edges (east, south, west and nord) of a block has an edge-buffer, which consists of 4x8 bits and is connected to the edge of the block regularly (Fig. 4.). These buffers play important role at data--transmission between the blocks, as follows.

Consider a given edge Z of a given block B. In each transition step we map a triple (B_i,Z_i,b_i) ($1\leq b_i\leq 4$, $1\leq i\leq 4$) to the pair (B,Z). B_i, Z_i and b_i denote a block, an edge and a bit-selector, respectively. According to that map the b_i'th bit of the k'th cell of the edge Z_i of the block B_i will be written into the i'th bit of the k'th pseudocell of the edge-buffer belonging to the edge Z of the block B before the transition step

($1 \leq k \leq 8$, $1 \leq i \leq 4$), after that the transition is executed as the suitable neighbours of the cells of B were in the edge-buffer. (For details see [6, 7].) Basically the processor maps the von Neumann-neighbourhood to each block. (E.g. if Z="east", then $B_i = B'$, where B' is the eastern "neighbour-block" of B, Z_i="west" and $b_i = i$, $1 \leq i \leq 4$.) The other maps are called teletransports. Such a map can be given with a teletransport scheme, as shown in Fig. 5. (Here the block B_2 is a "Neumann-neighbour on the 2nd bit" and is not denoted.)

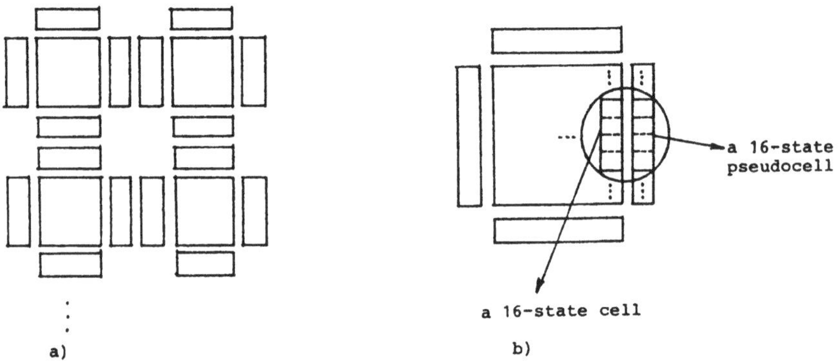

Fig. 4. The block-structure with the edge-buffers

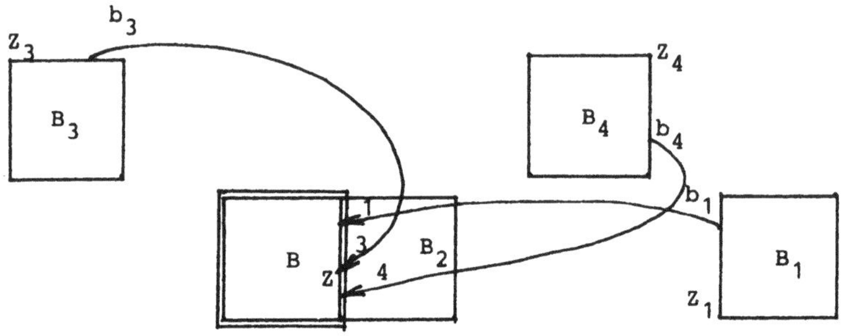

Fig. 5. Teletransport scheme belonging to the pair (B,Z)

4. Realization of the butterfly-network

We made a realization of the FFT DIF-algorithm. Input data are supposed with 8 bits. A complex operand is represented as a pair of real numbers with 32 bits (the binary point is between the 16'th and 17'th digits). The graph of the butterfly-operation is shown in Fig. 6. It is presented with data-flow technique (see in [5]). The input and the output vectors of the single butterfly are $(x,y)=(x_1+j\cdot x_2, y_1+j\cdot y_2)$ and

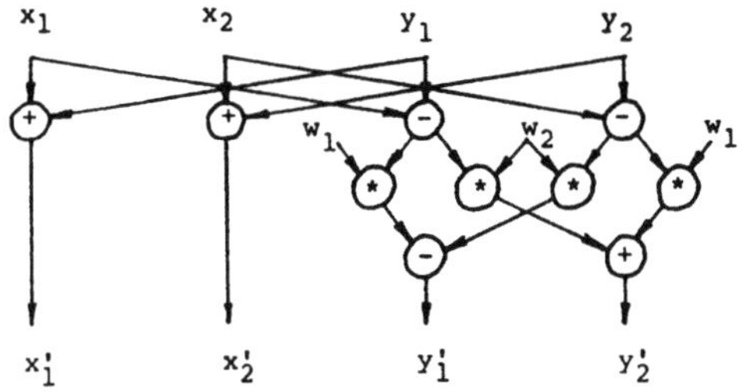

Fig. 6. The graph of the DIF-butterfly

$(x',y')=(x_1'+j\cdot x_2', y_1'+j\cdot y_2')$ respectively.

We embedded the graph into the cellular space synchronously, i.e. the first (least) digits of the input data enter the structure symultaneously and the first digits of the output data leave it symultaneously too. So the butterfly has a constant time-cycle, which coincides with the length of the operands, i.e. with 32. (See Fig. 7.)

Our butterfly needs 4 blocks of cells. The main parts of the structure are the 4 multipliers. One of them multiplies a 32 bit real number and a 16 bit real constant using 3x10+2 cells. The characterizing constants are written to the multipliers. The i/o cells of the multipliers are marked with "*". These ones receive the input digits in each step on the 4'th "bit-channel" and send the output digits on the 3'rd one 17 steps later.

The additive units are involved in the data-channel of the butterfly, which uses 24 central cells of it. This channel receives the input data, organizes the data-synchronization to the multipliers and performs the additive operations. (The carry-save adders and substractors are marked with rectangles, their sum-bits with ".".) x_1, x_2, y_1, y_2 present the input points of the structure and x_1', x_2', y_1', y_2' the output points of it.

The graph has two short branches, so we need a delay-network to satisfy the synchronization. It is solved by teletransport from the points "o" to the points "•". The numbers in Fig. 7. mean the used internal states. If we omitted to write a number in a cell, then 0 internal state supposed with identical transition function there. (The number of used internal states is 25.)

The data-transmission between butterflies is also solved with teletransport. Its structure was discussed in part 2. The applied teletransport scheme is presented by Fig. 8.

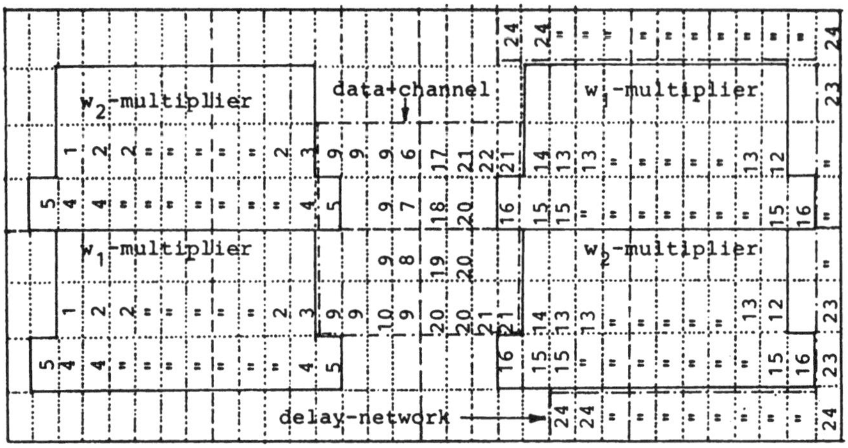

a) A cell is represented by [ ] in a) and c)

and by [ ] in b).

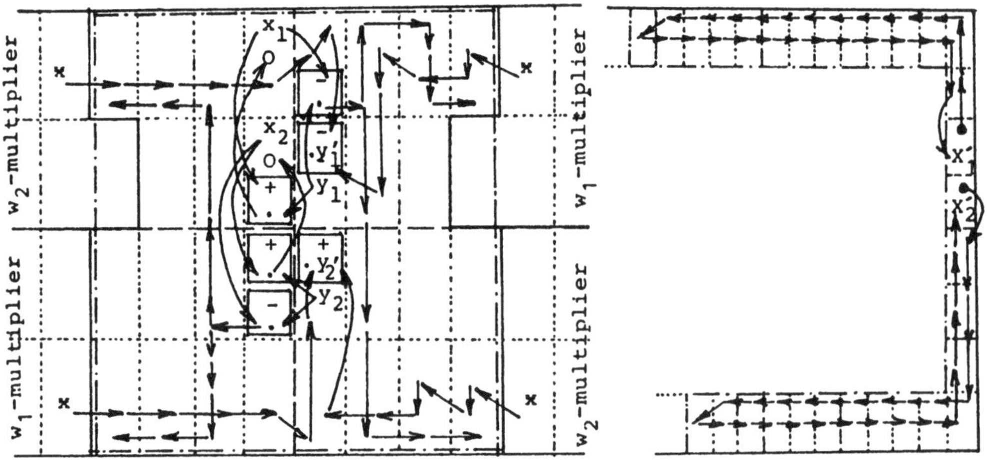

b) c)

Fig. 7. a) The cellular butterfly-structure
b) The data-channel and
c) the delay-network in detail

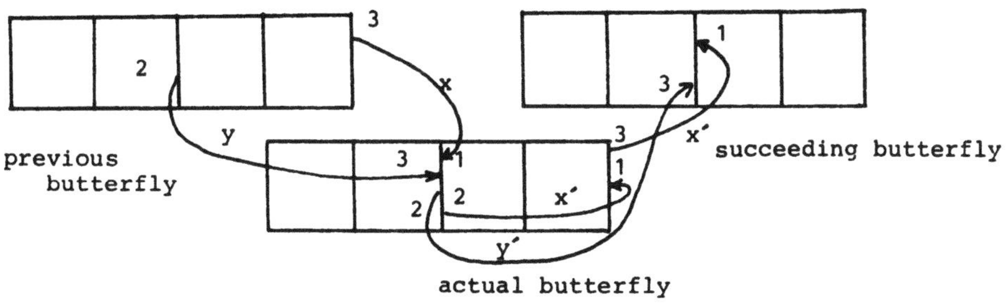

Fig. 8. The teletransport scheme of the cell-butterfly

5. Concluding remarks

As our cellprocessor has a 256x256 size cellular space, we can place in it a 32-butterfly and execute a 64-point FFT only simultaneously. The partition method, however, yields a possibility to execute larger FFT-s too.

Our butterfly structure can be applied in pipeline. In this case we do not need alwasy change the constants occuring in the multipliers. (Similar pipeline algorithm see in [4].) This condition holds at two-dimensional FFT, which can be traced back to sequences of one-dimensional ones [8]. Thus our algorithm can be fairly effective in picture processing.

References

[1] Bergland, G.D., A parallel implementation of the Fast Fourier Transform Algorithm, IEEE Transactions on Comp., vol. c-21, No. 4, 1972., pp. 366-370.
[2] Cooley, J.W. and Tukey, J.W., An algorithm for the machine calculation of complex Fourier Series, Math. Comput., vol. 19, pp. 297-301. Apr. 1965.
[3] Corinthios, J.C. and Smith, K.C. and Yen, J.L., A parallel Radix-4 Fast Fourier Transform computer, IEEE Transactions on Comp., vol. c-24, No. 1, 1975, pp. 80-92.
[4] Groginsky, H.L. and Works, G.A., A pipeline Fast Fourier Transform, IEEE Transactions on Comp., vol. c-19., No. 11, 1970, pp. 1015-1019.
[5] Katona, E., A design methodology for complex cellular programs, Proc. of the conference "PARCELLA'84", pp. 117-125, 1985.
[6] Legendi, T., Cellprocessors in computer architecture, Comput. Linguistics and Comput. Languages, 11. 1977. pp. 147-167.
[7] Legendi, T. and Zsótér, A., A 16-state cellprocessor, Proc. of the conference "Parallel Computing'85".
[8] Mueller, P.T., Siegel, L.J. and Siegel, H.J., Parallel algorithms for the two-dimensional FFT, Int. Conf. on Pattern Recognition 1980, Proc. pp. 497-502, 1980.
[9] Weiss, H.-P., Fast Fourier Transforms in cellular automata, Cellprocessors and Cellgorithms, pp. 236-254, Braunschweig, 1981.

A FAULT DETECTION METHOD IN PARTIALLY UTILIZED CELLULAR (SYSTOLIC) ARRAYS

Hermann Hellwagner 1) 2)

1. Introduction

Recently, problems like wafer-scale integration, fault-tolerance and reconfiguration of systolic architectures became subject of intensive research, e.g. in [4,7,9]. In this context, one of the most important problems and a basic requirement for any reconfiguration strategy is an efficient fault detection and fault location scheme. As it becomes feasible to integrate large systolic arrays on a single VLSI chip, the simple approach to isolate each cell from the rest of the system and perform tests on it could become obsolete in the future. As a consequence, methods of fault diagnosis exploiting the systolic nature of the system under test have been proposed [1,8]. Although these methods are powerful in that they are able to *locate* all faulty processors - provided they satisfy certain constraints - they are expensive in terms of hardware or time overhead, respectively, for diagnosis. Apparently little work has been done, however, on simple and "cheap", yet powerful and fast (parallel) fault *detection* mechanisms for systolic structures.

In this paper we present a method of fault detection in systolic arrays in which on each clock tick only half the cells are utilized. Partially utilized systolic systems of this kind are the result of certain design techniques [5,6]. Marrying this design methodology with ideas of fault diagnosis in cellular automata [2], we obtain a simple fault detection scheme for the above-mentioned class of systolic structures. The diagnosis is proposed to be applied to the array whenever it is utilized not more than by half. Thus, the array is occasionally tested for faults, without interfering with its normal operation. Only if a fault is detected due to our cheap strategy, a more expensive and sophisticated technique may be invoked to locate faulty cells and reconfigure the array.

Section 2 of the paper briefly reviews the two "sources" and sketches the basic principles of our fault detection method. In section 3 two quite distinct examples will illustrate our approach. In section 4 a general procedure to design a fault detection strategy for a given systolic array is described, and in section 5 concluding remarks are given.

The style of our presentation is quite informal. More formal treatment to obtain more precise results is subject of future research. We hope that, despite our verbal discussion, the reader can properly realize the features of our method.

2. The Operation Duplication Method

The proposed fault detection method which is called Operation Duplication Method (ODM) is a combination of two previous results:

(1) Harao/Noguchi [2] construct cellular automata with error detection capability.
Consider, for example, a 2D lattice structure. In a cellular automata which simulates the given machine and is capable of detecting errors, each cell's function (which we call "primary cell func-

1) Systems Theory and Information Engineering, University of Linz, A - 4040 Linz / Austria
2) This work was supported in part by Siemens Corporation, Research Laboratories Munich, ZTI, under project STI-DFT.

tion") is duplicated by the "secondary function" of its left neighbour (and the cell's secondary function itself duplicates the primary function of its right neighbour). Before each state transition, each cell's "primary state" is compared with the "secondary state" of its left neighbour (the duplicating cell). In case of a mismatch an error signal is set which subsequently propagates. Under certain conditions (two misoperating cells must not be horizontally adjacent), any errors of the cell information (memory elements), local function (logical circuits) and detection function (detection circuits) can be detected.

(2) Leiserson [5,6] proposes a design methodology and a theoretical framework to convert semisystolic systems (which constitute his design space) into purely systolic systems (implementation space). The main advantage of this approach is that a synchronous system can be conveniently designed with rippling logic describing global communication (in particular broadcasting), and then converted to a systolic implementation in which the effect of global communication is achieved by multiple local communications. In addition, the performance of the systolic system is better for sufficiently large systems because the clock period of the semisystolic system is longer in order to allow signals ripple down the array. As a consequence of this design and transformation procedure, the state of each transformed cell goes through an extra delay thus forming an "active" and an "idle" portion of the state. Therefore, just every other processor in the transformed system does useful work. Two clock periods are required in the new system to simulate one in the old system. But as the two stages of the cell states form two "equivalence classes" of computation in the new system, two independent jobs may share the array to double throughput. For an example, the reader is referred to the Systolic Priority Queue of the next section.

Arrays designed according to Leiserson's methodology represent a suitable framework for embedding Harao/Noguchi's approach in workable computational devices. To realize operation duplication and thus to enable fault detection, the second task in one of Leiserson's arrays has to be a copy of the first one such that on each clock tick pairs of adjacent cells perform identical operations. Within each such pair (P_{i-1},P_i), the processor closer to the host, P_{i-1}, works on the secondary (duplicating) job and duplicates the primary function of its neighbour P_i. (In this context, the host is defined as the device receiving the *resulting* data stream, and is denoted by P_0.) On the next clock tick, processor P_{i-1} compares its new state with that of P_i in order to check P_{i-1}'s and P_i's previous computations. If the states do not match, one of the two cells or one of the local communication lines is faulty, and a fault signal is set by P_{i-1} which is propagated towards the host on subsequent clock ticks without alteration. If the states are the same, no fault has occurred during the previous clock period. P_{i-1} then performs its normal (now primary) operation and is duplicated by P_{i-2}, whereas P_i works on the secondary job in order to duplicate P_{i+1}'s operation.

Due to the ODM, each cell periodically switches between duplicating and duplicated mode of operation; on every other clock tick, that is, whenever a cell is working on the primary job, its operation is duplicated and is checked at the beginning of the next clock cycle.
By virtue of this duplicate-and-compare feature, the array is capable of detecting faults which have induced an error in the currently active task. The hardware and time overhead for this fault detection scheme is small. Each processor has to be extended by a comparator logic and a test register required to hold the duplicated cell's state before comparison, and the clock period has to be elongated by the duration required for state comparison.

More details of the ODM will be worked out in the next sections.

3. Examples

We present two quite distinct examples to deepen the reader's insight into the method:

(1) 1D Systolic Priority Queue (SPQ) [5]

We consider a 1D systolic array of n identical processors $P_1, ..., P_n$ implementing in hardware a real-time priority queue, a data structure in which items from a given set (in our case, integers) are kept sorted according to some criterion (in our case, in ascending order) and which is capable of inserting an item into the proper place and delivering the first (in our case, smallest) item in constant time.

Leiserson has presented a semisystolic design with broadcasting for this device. Queue items are kept sorted left-to-right in the array with each processor containing one item. (Initially, each cell contains an item ∞ which is larger than all other items from the set.) The host talks to the left end of the array where the minimum is kept. In order to insert an item *i* into this semisystolic priority queue (SSPQ), the host broadcasts the command INSERT(*i*) to all the cells. Each cell compares *i* with the item it contains; those processors with larger items shift their data to the right, and the broadcast item drops into the proper cell. To remove the minimum element of the SSPQ, the host broadcasts EXTRACTMIN, and all processors shift their data left with the minimum being delivered to the host. Both operations can be implemented within one clock cycle.
We restrict ourselves to these operations although several kinds of DELETE operations may be provided, too, e.g., the deletion of the smallest element greater than the broadcast item or the deletion of an item if it is present. Both DELETE operations do not introduce difficulties for fault detection though they require a priority broadcast [5] to be performed.

A cell's operation during a clock cycle may be specified more precisely using a pseudocode notation; the corresponding block diagram of the cell is shown in Fig. 1a):

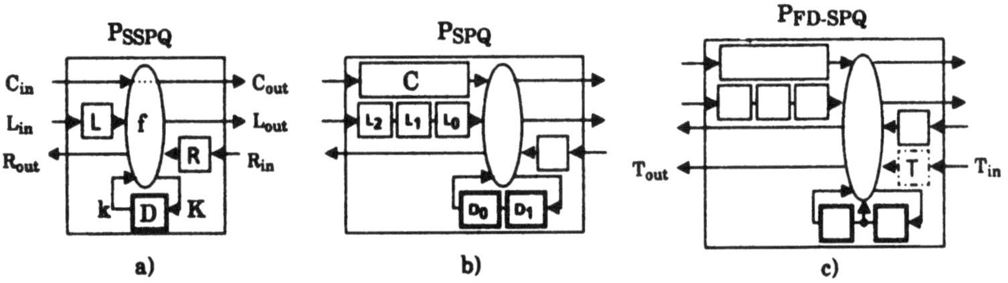

Fig. 1: Block diagram of a processor of: a) SSPQ, b) SPQ, c) FD-SPQ.

1. Let command ripple down the array (implements instruction broadcast).

   $C_{out} := C_{in}$.

2. Load registers with values on (input) lines.

   $L := L_{in}$. -- Input from left neighbour.
   $R := R_{in}$. -- Input from right neighbour.
   $D := K$. -- Cell item (key) goes through one delay.

3. Establish actual key for new operation. If present, input from one of the neighbours determines present key.

   k := D. -- k ... present key.
   if L ≠ nil then k := L.
   if R ≠ nil then k := R.

4a. If C_{in} = INS(i), INSERT operation is performed (by the combinational logic f).

```
INSERT(i):
  if i < k
    then L_out := k; K := i.     -- Shift item to the right; receive new item.
    else L_out := nil; K := k.   -- K ... next key.
  R_out := nil.
```

4b. If C_{in} = EXMIN, EXTRACTMIN operation is performed.

```
EXTRACTMIN:
  R_out := k.                    -- Shift item left.
  K := nil.                      -- Receive new item on the next clock tick.
  L_out := nil.
```

Using Leiserson's tools [5], the broadcast can be eliminated, and the SSPQ is converted to a purely systolic system whose response time is two clock cycles. Fig. 1b) is the block diagram of a cell of the resulting SPQ. Extra registers have been introduced such that the cell state (cell item) goes through one, the input from the left neighbour goes through two additional delays, and the rippling of instructions down the command line is prohibited by a command register. The combinational logic and the right-to-left data path (towards the host) is unchanged. Leiserson has shown that in such a converted system all inputs to a cell arrive at exactly the right instant. Taking into consideration the additional delays, a description of the cell operation corresponding to the above specification may be easily derived. Unfortunately, due to space limitations, we are not able to discuss the construction and operation of the SSPQ and the SPQ in more detail. The reader may verify, however, that the arrays based on the cells of Fig. 1 are operational, and that a second, completely independent data stream may be interlocked into the first one in the SPQ.

We now construct the corresponding fault detecting SPQ (FD-SPQ). Fig. 1c) shows the structure of a cell of FD-SPQ. To allow comparison, each processor is equipped with a test register required to receive the right neighbour's item for comparison or, if a fault has been detected, to transfer an error signal towards the host on the test data path. Fig. 2 illustrates the activities of a 4-cell FD-SPQ executing an INSERT and a subsequent EXTRACTMIN operation. The contents of the registers are shown after having been loaded according to step 2 of the cell operation. The secondary (duplicating) job is printed in ***boldface***. On even-numbered clock ticks even-numbered processors duplicate their right neighbours' operation; results are compared on the next clock tick. A corresponding statement holds for odd-numbered processors and odd-numbered clock cycles.

More formally, the operation of a cell P_s, $s = 1, ..., n-1$, in clock cycle t, $t = 0, 1, ..., t_{max}$, may be specified by the following pseudocode sequence:

```
Load registers (including test register T).
if (t-s) mod 2 = 0                                  -- t ... number of clock cycle; s ... cell number
  then Perform normal operation; T_out := nil.      -- Duplicating cell.
  else if T = error or T ≠ D_1                      -- Duplicated cell; compares results of
        then T_out := error.                        -- previous clock cycle (t-1) when it was
        else Perform normal operation; T_out := K.  -- a duplicating cell itself.
```

Special measures must be taken for the boundary processors. The cell most distant from the host, P_n, need not duplicate any other processor. Therefore, it does not have the "test equipment" mentioned above, and its operation reduces to:

```
Load registers and perform normal operation.
if (t-n) mod 2 = 0              -- n ... processor number.
  then T_out := nil.
  else T_out := K.
```

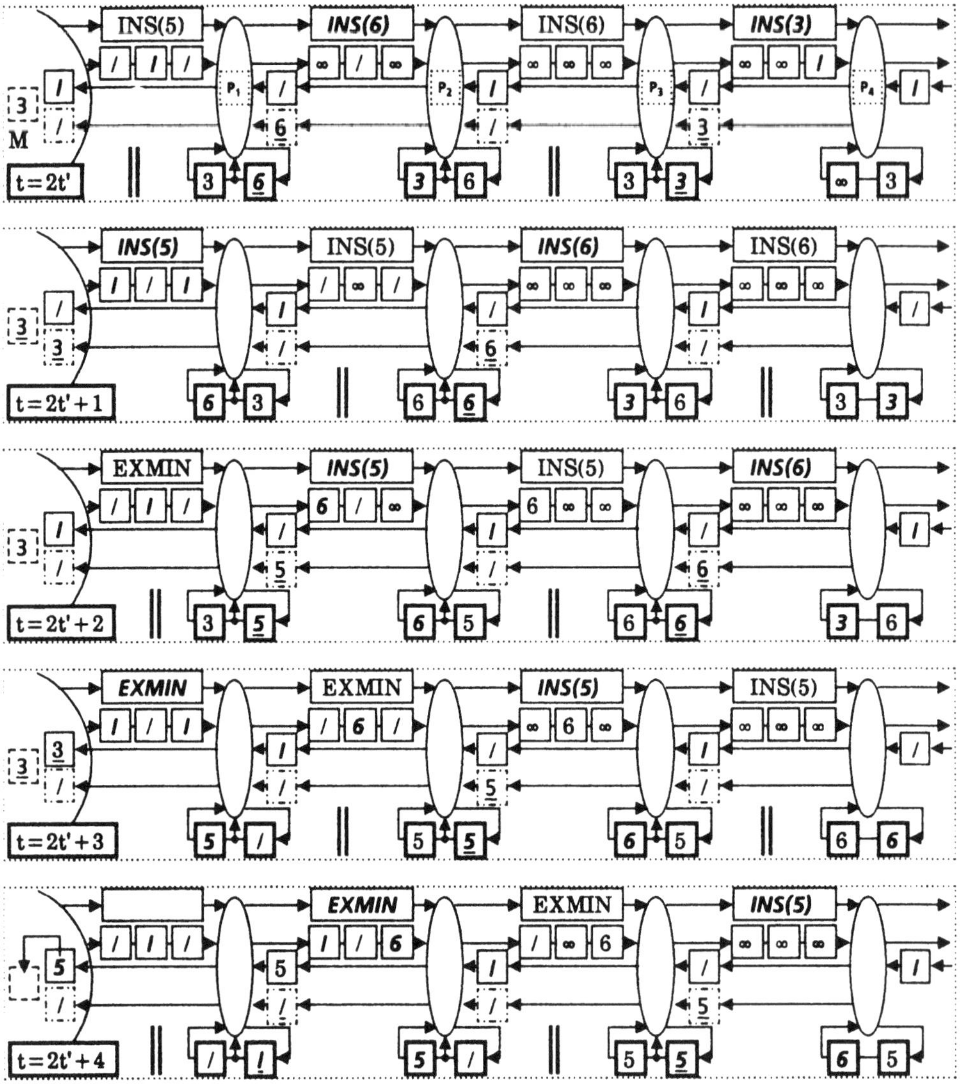

|| indicates that adjacent cells perform identical operations.
Underlined items are compared to check previous computations.
Fig. 2: Sequence of operations of a 4-cell FD-SPQ executing INSERT and EXTRACTMIN.

The host's operation must be extended such that it duplicates the primary operation of its neighbouring cell P_1; that is, the host or the array controller, respectively, must simulate P_1's left neighbour and compare the results thus making it possible to detect faults in the first cell, too. Equivalently, a special "test cell" could be provided to perform this task. This cell would be activated in a distinguished test mode only and would work on the duplicating job only.

In our example, however, the host simulates P_1's left neighbour. For this sake, an additional register M is provided to hold the current minimum element of the queue which resides in cell P_1. Whenever the host inserts a new minimum into the primary data stream, the old minimum is inserted into the secondary data stream one clock tick later, and the new minimum is stored in register M. (Besides simple duplication of data and commands, this is the only measures that have to be taken to enable operation duplication.) To detect faults in P_1, the host compares the outcomes of P_1 with the contents of the minimum register M. After an INSERT operation, the host is transferred P_1's primary item via the test (T-) data path (see, e.g., clock cycle $t=2t'+1$ in Fig. 2). Due to an EXTRACTMIN, however, the minimum is delivered regularly in the result register R ($t=2t'+3$). In this case, the host receives the new minimum of the FD-SPQ one clock tick later ($t=2t'+4$) from the duplicating task.

A functional fault is a basic feature of our fault detection scheme. A cell is defined as faulty if either the combinational logic f produces an incorrect computation result which deviates from the expected result or some of the registers D, L, R and T, which are to hold queue items, do not hold and transfer items correctly. One of the data paths corresponding to these registers is said to be faulty if it changes an item during data transmission. The command lines and registers of the FD-SPQ are assumed to be fault-free because some faults in these components could go undetected since they do not transfer or hold queue items, on the comparison of which fault detection is based.
The FD-SPQ is able to detect any modelled fault *iff* the fault has caused the faulty component to behave erroneously and to induce an error in the currently manipulated data stream. Although permanent faults are considered in the fault model, some transient faults may be detected, too.

(2) 1D Systolic Matrix-Vector Multiplication Array (SMVMA) [5]

Our second array will turn out to be very well-suited to the ODM because its flow of data is so straightforward. Consider the problem of multiplying a $n \times n$ matrix $A=[a_{ij}]$ with a n-column vector $\mathbf{x}=[x_1\ x_2\ \ldots\ x_n]^T$. The elements of the product vector $y=[y_1\ y_2\ \ldots\ y_n]^T$, $y=A\mathbf{x}$, can be computed by the following recurrencies:

$$y_i^{(1)}=0 \qquad i,k=1,2,\ldots,n$$

$$y_i^{(k+1)}=y_i^{(k)}+a_{ik}x_k \qquad \text{(inner-product step)}$$

$$y_i=y_i^{(n+1)}.$$

The well-known 1D systolic array [5] consisting of 2n-1 inner-product-step processors can be adopted to compute the matrix-vector product. As long as just one matrix-vector multiplication is active in the array, only every other cell is doing useful work at any given time, with its neighbours being idle, just as is the case with systolic systems produced by Leiserson's transformation tools. In addition, the data flow is very regular in that, as soon as an input element has entered the array, it is "pumped" down the line of processors without changing its direction, as, for example, the queue items in the SPQ do.

For these reasons, it is easy to realize the ODM in this SMVMA. All the data streams have to be duplicated and "shifted left" one processor; in other words, they are arranged in such a manner that each processor working on the primary task and its left neighbour are supplied identical input data. Fig. 3 depicts the global arrangement of data for a SMVMA with $n=3$, where the duplicating data streams are again shown in ***boldface***. The figure also shows that an additional "duplication processor" P_0 is introduced in order to duplicate the originally leftmost processor P_1. A "host" is omitted in this figure since it is of no importance for the array's operation - it is unable to submit instructions to the array, and it merely must receive the product vector y.

The amount of "test equipment" required for comparison is minimal. A processor P_i duplicating the operation of its neighbour P_{i+1} in clock cycle t simply saves the computational result of cycle t, say $y_j^{(k)}$, in an additional register for comparison in the next clock cycle. On clock tick $t+1$, P_i

should receive exactly the same result, $y_j^{(k)}$, from P_{i+1} via the y-data path. Comparison of these values in P_i before its actual operation confirms P_i's and P_{i+1}'s error-free computations or, in case of a mismatch, makes evident an error in processors P_i or P_{i+1} or on the y-data path, respectively.

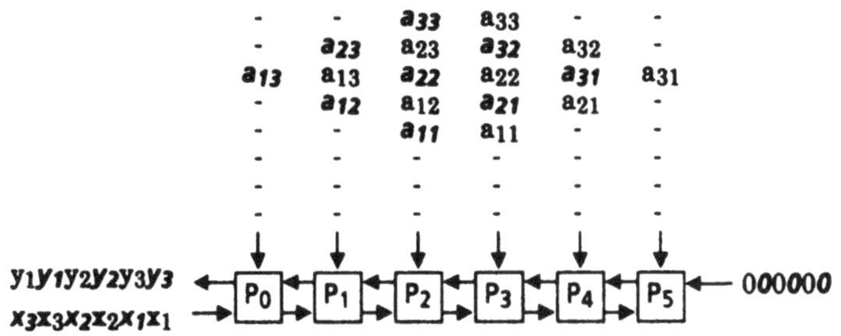

Fig. 3: Fault-detecting 6-processor matrix-vector multiplication array (n = 3).

Like in the FD-SPQ, the fault model comprises functional faults in any component which is to hold, transmit or manipulate data from the y-data stream ("result" data). That is, faults in the combinational logic and in y-data registers of a processor and on the y-data path can be detected, whereas x- and A-data paths and registers are assumed to be fault-free.

More details of fault detection in the SMVMA and a comparison with a similar method [1] have been reported in [3].

4. Designing a Fault-Detecting Systolic Array

Summing up the main features of our method, we propose a general procedure to design a fault detecting systolic array for a given problem. The design strategy comprises six steps:

(1) Construct a partially utilized systolic system which solves the given problem.

In order to find such an initial design, either Leiserson's design and conversion methodology can be applied, as was demonstrated by the SPQ example, or an intuitive design can be adopted which is characterized by a simple and regular data flow, as was the case with the SMVMA.

(2) Interlock a secondary (duplicating) job such that operation duplication is established.

In some arrays, e.g., in the SMVMA, it is sufficient to merely duplicate the input data of the primary job and provide it as input to the secondary task. In other cases, however, this may not suffice. Consider, for example, the SPQ of the previous section. Simply providing a one-to-one copy of the primary job as the secondary job would result in each cell's secondary operation duplicating its own primary operation one clock tick later. Obviously, if the cell has a permanent fault, it might induce identical errors in both data streams which could remain undetected. Hence, the aim of this design step is to make *pairs* of processors behave identically in a *single* clock cycle.

(3) Provide test equipment and extend cell operation to perform comparison.

For comparison, individual cells must be equipped with comparator logic and additional registers. An additional "test" data path must be provided in arrays in which the cells' computational results are not communicated towards the host, anyway, but can travel away from the host, too.

The overall design rule of this step is that the flow of results to be compared or the flow of error signals, respectively, must be oriented towards the host.

(4) Differentiate between inner and boundary processors'operation.

Inner processors usually make no difficulties. For the boundary processors, however, special measures have to be taken such that they fit in well with operation duplication and fault detection in the rest of the system. In general, the cell(s) most distant from the host need not duplicate any other processor(s). As a consequence, compare operations may be skipped, and test equipment may be omitted. The more difficult problem is to have duplicated the primary function of the cell(s) next to the host. Our examples have shown two alternatives to solve this problem - to adapt the operation of the host or the array controller, respectively, such that a duplicating cell is simulated, or to actually establish a distinguished "test" cell for this task.

(5) Distinguish normal operation mode and test mode.

It may prove useful to distinguish these two modes of operation. Whenever the computational load on the array is heavy, that is, two independent jobs are processed by the system, no attempt is being made to detect faults - in fact, there is even no possibility to do that since all the cells are busy. But as soon as just one task is active in the system, there is redundant space to make use of the ODM to diagnose the array, and test mode is entered. The major goal of this step is to design the actions the array controller is expected to take in order to switch the system from normal operation mode to test mode, and vice versa. These activities include, but are not restricted to: setting up the secondary (duplicating) job, initializing idle cells to guarantee proper duplication of the currently active task, activating the test cell (if present) and the test equipment and enabling comparisons, and making the controller receive and evaluate test results.

(6) Determine the fault detection capability of the resulting array.

Obviously, only those faults can be detected which induce an error in the *result* data stream. Here, a result element is defined as an item being manipulated upon (and not merely utilized) by the cells' combinational logic and forming the basis of comparisons. In our examples, queue items in the SPQ and elements of the y-data stream in the SMVMA are result elements. We can state, therefore, that in general any fault in a component which is to hold, transmit or manipulate result elements, is detectable. Additional faults may be detectable in particular cases.

5. Conclusion

We have proposed a fault detection scheme for partially utilized systolic arrays based on the fact that idle cells can be used to duplicate the active cells' operation. The method has been shown to be well-suited to arrays produced as the result of a certain design methodology [5]. In addition, any array being utilized not more than by half and exhibiting regular flow of data can be augmented such that it is able to detect faults during operation.
It is evident that the method is especially well-suited to completely homogeneous arrays. As a subject of future research, we shall attempt to extend the method to arrays with more than one cell type. As already mentioned above, a major effort will also be devoted to treat the topics more formally and to obtain more precise results.

References

[1] Y. H. CHOI, S.H. HAN, M. MALEK
"Fault Diagnosis of Reconfigurable Systolic Arrays"
Proc. ICCD' 84, Oct. 1984, pp. 451 - 455; IEEE Computer Society Press

[2] M. HARAO, S. NOGUCHI
"Fault Tolerant Cellular Automata"
Journal of Computer and System Sciences 11, 1975, pp. 171 - 185

[3] H. HELLWAGNER
"Die Prüfproblematik in systolischen (zellularen) Architekturen"
Proc. 19. Fachkolloqium Informationstechnik/1. Tagung Schaltkreisentwurf, Dresden/DDR
Jan. 1986, Vol. 2, pp. 214 - 220

[4] T. LEIGHTON, C.E. LEISERSON
"Wafer-Scale Integration of Systolic Arrays"
IEEE Trans. Computers, Vol. C-34, No. 5, May 1985, pp. 448 - 461

[5] C.E. LEISERSON
Area-Efficient VLSI Computation
Ph. D. Thesis, Oct. 1981
Dept. of Computer Science, Carnegie-Mellon-University, Pittsburgh, Pennsylvania, USA

[6] C.E. LEISERSON, J.B. SAXE
"Optimizing Synchronous Systems"
Proc. 22nd Ann. Symp. on Foundations of Computer Science, Oct. 1981, pp. 23 - 36
IEEE Computer Society Press

[7] A.L. ROSENBERG
"The Diogenes Approach to Testable Fault-Tolerant Arrays of Processors"
IEEE Trans. Computers, Vol. C-32, No. 10, Oct. 1983, pp. 902 - 910

[8] A.K. SOMANI, V.K. AGARWAL
"System Level Diagnosis in Systolic Systems"
Proc. ICCD' 84, Oct. 1984, pp. 445 - 450; IEEE Computer Society Press

[9] S. YALAMANCHILI, J.K. AGGARWAL
"Reconfiguration Strategies for Parallel Architectures"
IEEE COMPUTER, Dec. 1985, pp. 44 - 61

ON THE SYNTHESIS OF SYSTOLIC ALGORITHMS AND ARRAYS

Nikolay Petkov Turkedjiev[1)]

1. INTRODUCTION. SYNTHESIS OF REALIZATION STRUCTURES IN THE DIGITAL SIGNAL PROCESSING AND THE THEORY OF CELLULAR SYSTEMS.

The digital signal processing is conserned with the following kinds of mappings /1/:

input digital signal $\underline{x}$: $T \to X$ (T - time scale, X - input alphabet)

output digital signal $\underline{y}$: $T \to Y$ (Y - output alphabet)

$\underline{x} \in \underline{X}$, $\underline{y} \in \underline{Y}$ ($\underline{X}$, $\underline{Y}$ - the sets of all input and output signals)

system mapping $S: \underline{X} \to \underline{Y}$ (S - casual).

A system mapping can be specified in different ways, e.g. in time-, frequency- or z-domain /2/. A very important representation is the one by means of recurrent equations in the time domain:

$$y(t) = f(y(t-1), y(t-2) \ldots y(t-m), x(t), x(t-1) \ldots x(t-n)) \; , \qquad (1.1)$$

because it can give insights into how the mapping can efficiently be realized - the structure in Fig. 1.1 is the hardware counterpart of the expression (1.1).

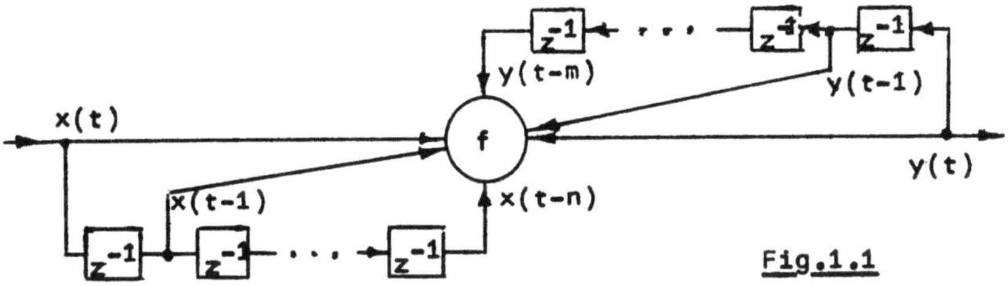

Fig.1.1

An essential progress in the synthesis of digital signal processing structures has been achieved, because efficient means (z-Transformation) are available for transforming a given system mapping in the form (1.1). More of that, a given set of linear recurrent equations of the type (1.1) can be transformed into another one by means of arithmetic transformations on h(z), $y(z) = h(z)x(z)$, in z-domain and, in that way, one can get different realization structures /2/.

This approach has been generalized for systems with space-time structure /3/. The mappings conserned are:

space-time input signal $\dot{\underline{x}}$: $R \times T \to X$, $\dot{\underline{x}} \in \dot{\underline{X}}$,

space-time output signal $\dot{\underline{y}}$: $R \times T \to Y$, $\dot{\underline{y}} \in \dot{\underline{Y}}$,

system mapping $S : \dot{\underline{X}} - \dot{\underline{Y}}$,

and the equations corresponding to (1.1) are recurrent in space and time. By means of the multi-dimentional z-transformation, a given set of such space-time recurrent equations can be transformed in another

1) Technische Universität Dresden, Sektion Informationstechnik, 8027 Dresden, Mommsenstr. 13, DDR

one and in that way different realization structures can be obtained for the same linear system mapping.

Fig. 1.2 shows the synthesis methodology in the theory of the linear space-time invariant systems. Principally, it is a methodology to generate space-time recurrent equations representation of a given system mapping.

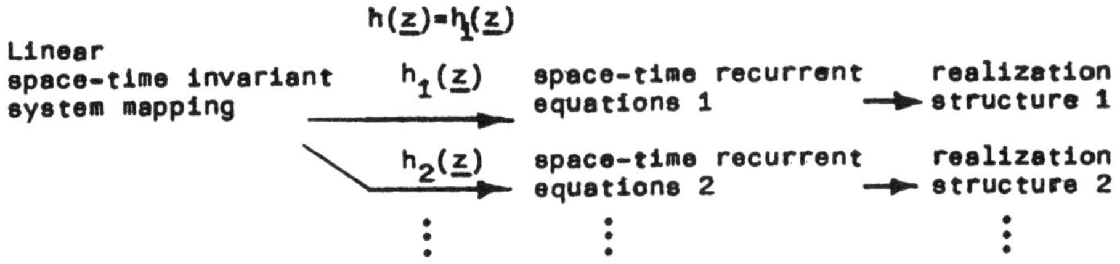

Fig.1.2

This approach can be extended for general computation problems by creating tools for formulating a given computational problem in terms of space-time recurrent equations. The concept of an algorithm expressed by means of a functional graph or a set of recurrent equations plays an important intermediate role in that process. By means of a task allocation function $\hat{r}$ and a task scheduling function $\hat{t}$ an algorithm, functional graph or a set of recurrent equations respectively, can be turned into a set of space-time recurrent equations and, in that way, embedded in a realization structure (Fig. 1.3).

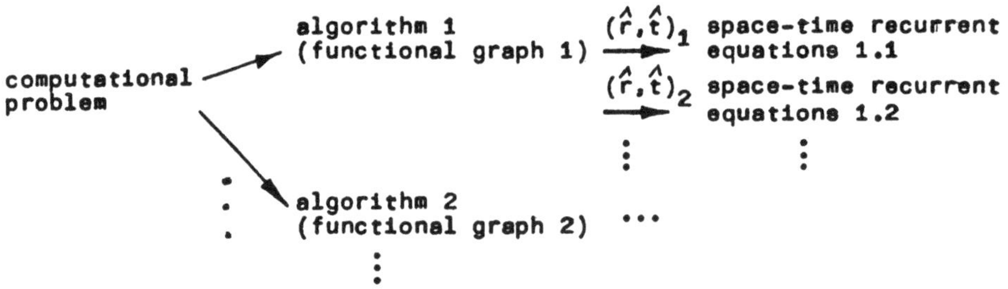

Fig.1.3

Space-time equations with a certain regular structure can be realized in regular realization structures, the so called systolic arrays /4/, which hold a great potential for VLSI-implementation. The synthesis procedure in Fig. 1.3 is more general than that used in the theory of the linear space-time invariant systems but less mechanical. In order to make it a practical tool for the creation of systolic arrays, a certain discipline must be introduced by specifying the kind of algorithms and transformations $(\hat{r},\hat{t})$ at the intermediate levels of the system design. In this paper, two classes of algorithms suitable for systolic implementation as well as the corresponding transformations $(\hat{r},\hat{t})$ are specified. The theorems given are design procedures at the same time.

2. THEORETICAL FRAMEWORK /5/

2.1 FUNCTIONAL GRAPH

A functional graph $\underline{G}_f = (K_f, \underline{Z}_f)$ is a directed graph (Fig.2.1.1) with the following properties:

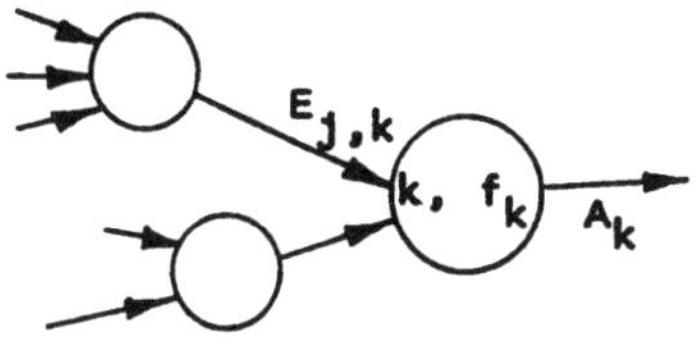

Fig. 2.1.1

1) Every node k has a single output A_k and all arcs starting in k beginn from the output A_k.
2) Every node k has a limitted number of inputs $E_{j,k}$, $j \in J$, and only one arc ends in each input.
3) The arc set $\underline{Z}_f$ consists of arcs beginning in node outputs and ending in node inputs. Open arcs are also alowed.

$$\underline{Z}_f = \left\{ (A_{k'}, E_{j,k}) /\ k, k' \in K_f \cup \emptyset,\ k' \neq k,\ j \in J \right\} \quad (J \text{ - a finite set})$$

4) A function is attached to each node by means of the mapping

$$f: K_f \rightarrow F\ ,\quad F \equiv \left\{ f_i / f_i: X^{n_i} \rightarrow Y,\ n_i \in \{1, 2, \ldots |J|\} \right\}\ ,$$

so that $f_k: X^{d_k} \rightarrow Y$, $k \in K_f$, where d_k is the inner degree of node k (Fig. 2.1.2).

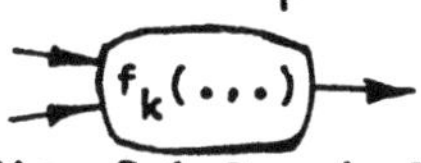

Fig. 2.1.2 - $d_k = 3$

2.2. ALGORITHM

Input data $\hat{x}$ is a mapping $\hat{x}: M_E \rightarrow X$, $M_E \subset J \times K_f$ (M_E - the set of the node input indices), $\hat{x} \in \hat{X}$ ($\hat{X}$ - the set of all input data combinations).
External input data is a mapping $\hat{x}_{\bar{A}}: M_{\bar{A}E} \rightarrow X$, $M_{\bar{A}E} \subset M_E \subset J \times K_f$, ($M_{\bar{A}E}$ - the set of all node input indices, in which nodes open arcs end), $\hat{x}_{\bar{A}} \in \hat{X}_{\bar{A}}$.
Output data $\hat{y}$ is a mapping $\hat{y}: K_f \rightarrow Y$, $\hat{y} \in \hat{Y}$.
External output data $\hat{y}_{\bar{A}}$ is a mapping $\hat{y}_{\bar{A}}: M_{\bar{A}A} \rightarrow Y$, $M_{\bar{A}A} \subset K_f$, ($M_{\bar{A}A}$ - the set of all node output indices in which nodes open arcs beginn), $\hat{y}_{\bar{A}} \in \hat{Y}_{\bar{A}}$.
The mappings above attach an element of X and Y to each input, output respectively. In the following is asumed $X \equiv Y$.
The following set of recurrent equations can be constructed for the functional graph $\underline{G}_f$:

$$\left| \begin{array}{ll} \hat{y}_{\bar{A}}(k) = \hat{y}(k) & \text{for } k \in M_{\bar{A}A} \\ \hat{y}(k) = f_k(\hat{x}(j_1,k), \hat{x}(j_2,k) \ldots \hat{x}(j_{d_k},k))\ , & k \in K_f\ , \\ \hat{x}(j,k) = \hat{y}(k') & \text{for } (j,k) \in M_E \setminus M_{\bar{A}E} \text{ and } (A_{k'}, E_{j,k}) \in \underline{Z}_f \\ \hat{x}(j,k) = \hat{x}_{\bar{A}}(j,k) & \text{for } (j,k) \in M_{\bar{A}E} \end{array} \right. \qquad (2.2.1)$$

and a functional graph $\underline{G}_f$ can be given for each such a set.
The set (2.2.1.) can be considered to be a system of equations for the transformation of certain external input data $\hat{x}_{\bar{A}}$ inexternal output data $\hat{y}_{\bar{A}}$, where $\hat{x}$ and $\hat{y}$ are intermediate variables. In that way the algabraic structure $(\underline{G}_f, \hat{X}, \hat{Y}, \hat{X}_{\bar{A}}, \hat{Y}_{\bar{A}})$ specifies a mapping from $\hat{X}_{\bar{A}}$ in $\hat{Y}_{\bar{A}}$. The algebraic structure $\mathcal{A} \equiv (\underline{G}_f, \hat{X}, \hat{Y}, \hat{X}_{\bar{A}}, \hat{Y}_{\bar{A}})$ is called an algorithm, if the set (2.2.1) can be solved effectively by simple substitutions of the intermediate variables $\hat{x}$ and $\hat{y}$ in the equations for

$\hat{Y}_{\bar{A}}$. In that case we write $\mathcal{A} : \hat{X}_{\bar{A}} \rightarrow \hat{Y}_{\bar{A}}$.

2.3. REALIZABILITY OF FUNCTIONAL GRAPHS

The condition that ($\underline{G}_f$, $\hat{X}$, $\hat{Y}$, $\hat{X}_{\bar{A}}$, $\hat{Y}_{\bar{A}}$) represents an algorithm can be formulated and effectively varified by means of the notion of realisability of a functional graph.

A functional graph $\underline{G}_f$ is called to be realisable , if a mapping pair $(\hat{r},\hat{t})$ exists, such that:

1) The mapping $(\hat{r},\hat{t})$: $K_f \rightarrow R\times T$ is injective. R is a finite set called processor location set. T is a descrete time scale and a limitted number of elements of T falls in every time period of a given length.
2) $(A_{k_1}, E_{j,k_2}) \in \underline{Z}_f \Rightarrow \hat{t}(k_1) < \hat{t}(k_2)$.

$\hat{r}$ is called task allocation function and $\hat{t}$ task scheduling function. The definition given reflects the necessities of a physical realization. Exact conditions on the structure of realizable functional graphs are given in /5/. These conditions allow to set the order of the substitution in the solution of (2.2.1).

3. DESIGN OF REALIZATION STRUCTURES, SYSTOLIC ARRAYS.

3.1. TRANSFORMING A SET OF RECURRENT EQUATIONS IN A SET OF SPACE-TIME RECURRENT EQUATIONS

If R is considered to be the cellular space of a system, then the input and output data can be transformed in the corresponding system theoretical mappings:

Space-time input signal $\dot{\underline{x}}$: $\mathcal{M}_E \rightarrow X, \mathcal{M}_E = \{(j,\hat{r}(k),\hat{t}(k)/(j,k)\in M_E\}$

$\dot{\underline{x}}(j,r,t) := \hat{x}(j,k)$, $(j,k)\in M_E$, $r = \hat{r}(k)$, $t = \hat{t}(k)$, $\dot{\underline{x}} \in \dot{\underline{X}}$.

Similarly are defined external space-time input signal $\dot{\underline{x}}_{\bar{A}}$, space-time output signal $\dot{\underline{y}}$, and external space-time output signal $\dot{\underline{y}}_{\bar{A}}$.

The recurrent equations (2.2.1) are transformed into the space-time recurrent equations

$$
\begin{cases}
\dot{\underline{y}}_{\bar{A}}(r,t) = \dot{\underline{y}}(r,t) , \quad (r,t)\in\mathcal{M}_{\bar{A}A}\subset R\times T & (3.1.1)\\
\dot{\underline{y}}(r,t) = f_{r,t}(\dot{\underline{x}}(j_1,r,t),\dot{\underline{x}}(j_2,r,t)\ldots\dot{\underline{x}}(j_{d_{r,t}},r,t)) , \quad (r,t)\in\mathcal{M}_A\subset R\times T\\
\dot{\underline{x}}(j,r,t) = \dot{\underline{x}}_{\bar{A}}(j,r,t) , \quad (j,r,t)\in\mathcal{M}_{\bar{A}E}\subset J\times R\times T\\
\dot{\underline{x}}(j,r,t) = \dot{\underline{y}}(r',t') , \quad (j,r,t)\in\mathcal{M}_E\setminus\mathcal{M}_{\bar{A}E} , \ r'=\hat{r}(k'), \ t'=\hat{t}(k'), \ r=\hat{r}(k),\\
\qquad t = \hat{t}(k), \ (A_{k'}, E_{j,k}) \in \underline{Z}_f
\end{cases}
$$

(3.1.1) specifies a casual system mapping S: $\dot{\underline{X}}_{\bar{A}} \rightarrow \dot{\underline{Y}}_{\bar{A}}$, if $\underline{G}_f$ is a functional graph.

3.2 SYNCHRONOUS REALIZATION STRUCTURES

Let $(\hat{r},\hat{t}^s)$ be an injective mapping from K_f in $R\times\mathbb{Z}$ so that

$\exists(\hat{r},\hat{t})$: $\hat{t}(k)\in [\hat{t}^s(k),\hat{t}^s(k)+1)$ for $\forall$ $k\in K_f$ and $(\hat{r},\hat{t})$ is a mapping pair with the properties 1-2 from 2.3. $\hat{t}^s$ specifies a clock period $[\hat{t}^s(k),\hat{t}^s(k)+1)$ in which the computation task of node k is executed and in that period the processor $P_{\hat{r}(k)}$ has no other computation task to fulfil. In that way, $(\hat{r},\hat{t}^{s})$ specifies a synchronous hardware realization. It can be shown that such a mapping pair exists for every realizable functional graph. The opposite statement is in general false /5/. In the following we are conserned with such (synchronous) mapping pairs only. In /5/ is given a general realization scheme for such realization mapping pairs and arbitrary realizable graphs. A communication network $O(|R|^2)$ is necessary for the realization of arbitrary functional graph arcs. That scheme is not acceptable in the case $|R| \gg 1$ which is interesting for VLSI implementation, because it is gouverned by the communication network.

3.3. SPECIAL REALIZATION STRUCTURES. SYSTOLIC ARRAYS.

Certain realization structures, the so called systolic arrays /4/, do not require such a complex communication network and hold a great potential for VLSI implementation.

A hardware realization structure is called a systolic array /5/, if

1) The processors are regularly positioned, $R = \left\{ (i,\underline{z})/i \in I, \underline{z} \in \mathbb{R}^n, \underline{z} = \sum_{i=1}^{n} c_i \underline{e}^{*(i)} \right\}$, and the processors $P_{i,\underline{z}}$ and $P_{i,\underline{z}'}$ execute the same function $f_{i,\underline{z}} = f_{i,\underline{z}'}$ during all clock periods. The processores are positioned in processor cells with coordinates $\underline{z}$ and i marks the different processors in one cell. All cells have the same structure.
2) The processor connections do not depend on the position of the cell: Input $E_{j,i,\underline{z}}$ of processor $P_{i,\underline{z}}$ becomes input data units from the processor output $A_{\hat{i},\underline{z}'}$ of $P_{\hat{i},\underline{z}'}$ through a chain of $n^{(j,i)}$ delay elements, where $\hat{i} = \hat{i}(i,j)$, $\underline{z}' = \underline{z} - \underline{a}^{(j,i)}$, $\underline{a}^{(j,i)} = \sum_{l=1}^{n} a_l^{(j,i)} \underline{e}^{*(l)}$, $a_l^{(j,i)} \in \mathbb{Z}$, $n^{(j,i)} \in \mathbb{N} \cup 0$. A processor can possibly become external input data units in certain clock periods.
3) There is at least one pipeline cell connection. A connection is called to be a pipeline cell connection, if
   a) $\underline{a}^{(j,i)} \neq 0$ (i.e. $\underline{a}^{(j,i)}$ specifies a connection between different cells,
   b) $n^{(j,i)} \neq 0$ (a pipeline connection, i.e. not a direct connection, but a connection through a number of delay elements),

A processor array is called to be full-systolic, if all connections between different cells are pipelined.

Only special kind of algorithms can be embedded in systolic arrays. We refer to these as to systolic algorithms.

4. CLASSES OF SYSTOLIC ALGORITHMS

The nodes of a functional graph can be combined in groups, which are called clusters, if they form clusters in RxT under a certain mapping pair $(\hat{r},\hat{t})$ called a cluster realization /5/. Functional graphs constituting of identical clusters are called to be cluster-homogeneous graphs. A necessary condition for a functional graph to be embedded in a systotolic array is that it is a cluster-homogeneous graph or can be extended to such a one.

4.1. CLUSTER-HOMOGENEOUS FUNCTIONAL GRAPHS WITH CLUSTER-INDEPENDENT DATA DEPENDENCIES

Theorem 4.1.: Let $\underline{G}_f$ be a realizable functional graph, so that:

1) $K_f \subset I \times \mathbb{Z}^n$, I - a finite set, ($k = (i,\underline{c})$, $i \in I$, $\underline{c} \in \mathbb{Z}^n$, $\underline{c}$ marks a cluster and i a certain node in that cluster) and
$$\exists \underline{e} \in \mathbb{Z}^n: \left| \underline{c} - \frac{\underline{c}.\underline{e}}{e^2}\underline{e} \right| \leq C,\ C \in \mathbb{N}$$

2) The arcs of $\underline{G}_f$, i.e. the so called data dependencies, are independent of the position $\underline{c}$ of the cluster in $\mathbb{Z}^n$:
$(A_{i',\underline{c}'}, E_{j,i,\underline{c}}) \in \underline{Z}_f \Rightarrow \underline{c}' = \underline{c} - \underline{d}^{(j,i)}$, $i' = \hat{i}'(i,j)$, $\hat{i}': I \times J \to I$, and $\underline{d}^{(j,i)}.\underline{e} \geq 0$.

3) The functional graph is cluster-homogeneous: $\forall (i,\underline{c}),(i,\underline{c}') \in K_f: f_{i,\underline{c}} = f_{i,\underline{c}'}$

The functional graph with the properties 1-3 can be embedded in a systolic array.

Proof: Let us consider the processor location set
$$R^{(n)} = \{ (i,\underline{z})/\ i \in I, \underline{z} \in \mathbb{R}^n,\ \underline{z} = \underline{c} - (\underline{c}.\underline{e}/e^2)\underline{e},\ (i,\underline{c}) \in K_f \}$$
and specify the function of the processor $P_{i,\underline{z}}$ by $f_{i,\underline{z}} = f_{i,\underline{c}}$.
It can be shown that $R^{(n)}$ is finite.

Let the processor output $A_{i',\underline{z}'}$ be connected with the processor input $E_{j,i,\underline{z}}$, $i' = \hat{i}'(i,j)$, $\underline{z}' = \underline{z} - (\underline{d}^{(j,i)} - (\underline{d}^{(j,i)}.\underline{e}/e^2)\underline{e})$ through a chain of $\underline{d}^{(j,i)}.\underline{e}$ delay elements.

The relations above specify a processor array for which the properties 1 and 2 from 3.3. become evident, if we introduce the denotions $\underline{e}^{*(l)} = \underline{e}^{(l)} - (\underline{e}^{(l)}.\underline{e}/e^2)\underline{e}$, where $\underline{e}^{(l)}$, $l = 1...n$, are the unit basis vectors, $\underline{a}^{(j,i)} = \underline{d}^{(j,i)} - (\underline{d}^{(j,i)}.\underline{e}/e^2)\underline{e}$, $n^{(j,i)} = \underline{d}^{(j,i)}.\underline{e}$.

It is always possible to achieve by means of a linear injective transformation in $\mathbb{Z}^n$ that for at least one data dependence vector $\underline{d}^{(j,i)}$ holds:
$$\underline{d}^{(j,i)}.\underline{e} \neq 0 \quad \text{and} \quad \underline{d}^{(j,i)} - (\underline{d}^{(j,i)}.\underline{e}/e^2)\underline{e} \neq 0,$$
so that property 3. from 3.3. can also be satisfied. In particular applications the upper procedure is applied to as many data dependency vectors as possible, in order to get a full-systolic array or a systolic array with a desired structure and properties /6/. The case $n > 3$ can be transformed in a case $n \leq 3$ by means of a similar linear injective transformation of the coordinates of the processors. The properties of the systolic array are retained by the linearity of the transformation. The functional graph $\underline{G}_f$ is embedded in the processor array specified above by means of a task allocation function $\hat{r}(i,\underline{c}) = (i,\underline{c}-(\underline{c}.\underline{e}/e^2)\underline{e})$ and a task scheduling function $\hat{t}^s(i,\underline{c}) = \underline{c}.\underline{e}$.
Details can be found in /5/.

Example: 1-D-convolution $y_i = \sum_{j=0}^{2} a_j x_{i-j}$.

The algorithm used is expressed in terms of its functional graph (Fig. 4.1.1). The nodes in Fig.4.1.1.a) are clusters and the structure of one cluster is shown in Fig. 4.1.1.b). The external input and output data is given in Fig. 4.1.1.a).

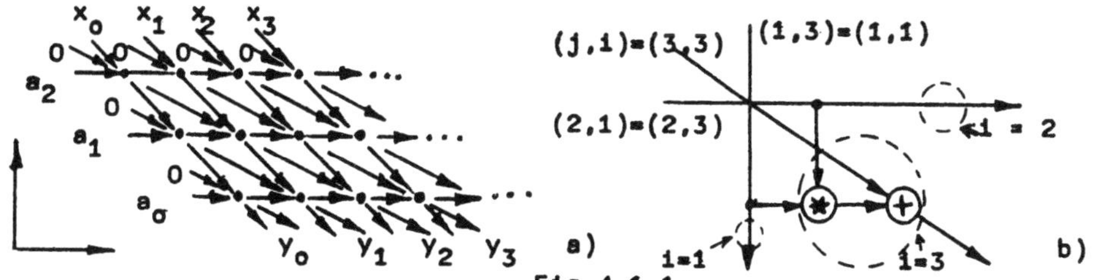

Fig.4.1.1

The data dependency vectors for that graph are

$$\underline{d}^{(3,3)} = (2,-1)\ ,\quad \underline{d}^{(2,3)} = (1,0)\ ,\quad \underline{d}^{(1,3)} = (1,-1)\ .$$

For $\underline{e} = (1,0)$, the systolic array in Fig. 4.1.2 results from the procedure of theorem 4.1.

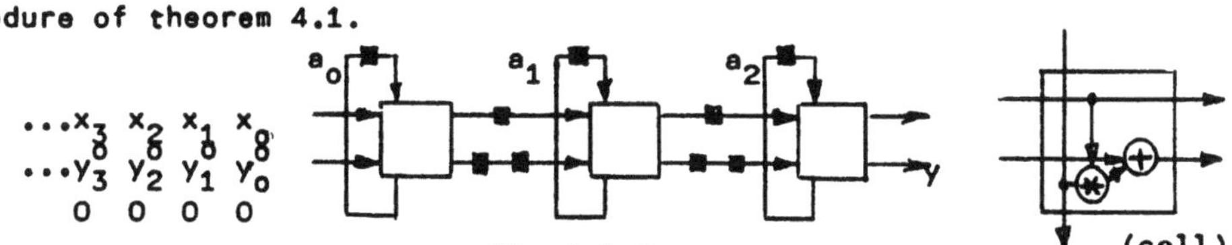

Fig.4.1.2

4.2. CLUSTER-HOMOGENEOUS FUNCTIONAL GRAPHS WITH TREE STRUCTURE OF THE CLUSTER GRAPH

Theorem 4.2: Let $\underline{G}_f$ be a cluster-homogeneous functional graph and its cluster graph $\mathcal{G} = (\underline{K}, \underline{\mathcal{Z}})$, $\underline{K} = \{K_i\}$, $\underline{\mathcal{Z}} = \{(A_{K_i}^{(cl)}, E_{l,K_{i'}}^{(cl)}) \,/\, K_i, K_{i'} \in \underline{K},\ i \neq i',\ \exists\, (A_k, E_{j,i,k'}) \in \underline{Z}_f\ ,\ k \in K_i,\ k' \in K_{i'},\ l \in \{1 \ldots L\},\ l = \hat{l}(i,j),\ \hat{l}: I \times J \to \{1 \ldots L\}\}$ has at tree structure, i.e. the undirected graph $\mathcal{G}$ has no cycles. (K_i, $i \in I$, are clusters in $\underline{G}_f$ and $\underline{K}$ is the set of all clusters. $A_{K_i}^{(cl)}$ and $E_{l,K_{i'}}^{(cl)}$ denote cluster inputs, outputs respectively. l denotes different cluster inputs.

$\underline{G}_f$ can be extended to a functional graph $\underline{G}_f'$ which can be embedded in a systolic array.

Proof: Let $\underline{\mathcal{G}}^{(l)}$ be a cluster graph which is obtained after the removal of the arcs ending in the cluster inputs with index l. $\underline{\mathcal{G}}^{(l)}$ consists of number of connected graphs $\underline{\mathcal{G}}_{c_l}^{(l)}$, $c_l \in \mathbb{Z}$, $\bigcup_{\forall c_l} \underline{\mathcal{G}}_{c_l}^{(l)} = \underline{\mathcal{G}}^{(l)}$.

It can be shown that, because of the tree structure, the set $\underline{K}_{c_1}^{(1)} \cap \underline{K}_{c_2}^{(2)} \cap \ldots \cap K_{c_L}^{(L)}$ for any combination $(c_1, c_2, \ldots c_L)$ is empty or has a single element, a certain cluster. An injective mapping $\underline{c}: \underline{K} \to \mathbb{Z}^L$ is specified by means of $\underline{c}(K_i) = (c_1, c_2, \ldots c_L) \Leftrightarrow K_i \in K_{c_1}^{(1)} \cap K_{c_2}^{(2)} \cap \ldots \cap K_{c_L}^{(L)}$.

It can be shown that for every arc holds

$$\exists\, (A_{K_1}^{(cl)}, E_{l,K_2}^{(cl)}) \in \underline{\mathcal{Z}} \Rightarrow c_m(K_1) = c_m(K_2),\ m \neq l,\ c_l(K_1) \neq c_l(K_2).$$

It can also be shown that the connected graphs can be enummerated so that $c_l(K_1) < c_l(K_2)$ above. Because of the tree structure follows also

$$\neg\exists\, K_i \in \underline{K}\ ,\ K_i \neq K_1\ ,\ K_2 \,\Big|\, \begin{array}{l} c_m(K_1) = c_m(K_i) = c_m(K_2)\ ,\ m \neq l, \\ c_l(K_1) < c_l(K_i) < c_l(K_2) \end{array}$$

It follows from the relations above that the arcs of $\mathcal{G}$ lie along the coordinate axes of $\mathbb{Z}^n$ and do not cross nodes. The arcs with length greater than one can then be replaced by additional nodes and arcs with length one. Additional external input data is specified for the additional nodes, so that the ordinary input data is output without changes at these nodes. It can be shown that the new cluster graph $\mathcal{G}'$ represents the same computation as $\mathcal{G}$. On the other hand, theorem 4.1 holds for it.

Example: Computation of a polynom $P_7(x) = \sum_{i=0}^{7} a_i x^i$
The cluster graph with the external input and output data is shown in Fig. 4.2.1.a), and the structure of a cluster in Fig. 4.2.1b).

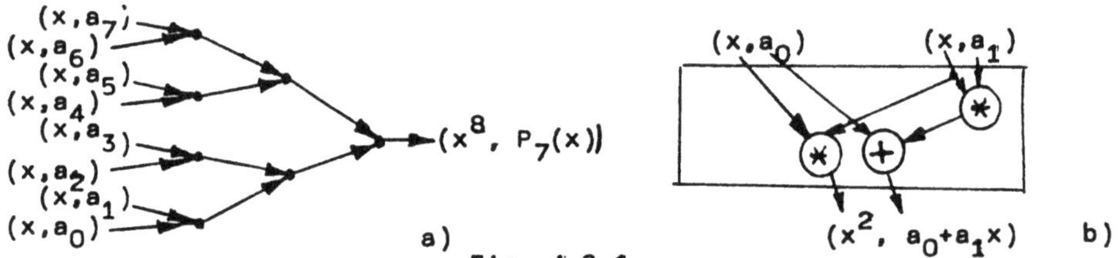

Fig. 4.2.1

By means of the procedure developped in theorem 4.2 the cluster graph is embedded in $\mathbb{Z}^2$ (Fig.4.2.2.a). This cluster graph is extended then to the cluster graph in Fig. 4.2.2.b) and external input data is specified for the additional nodes.

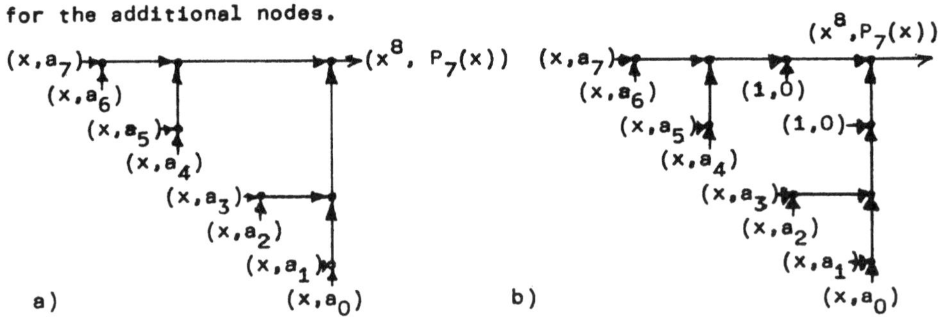

Fig. 4.2.2

REFERENCES:

/1/ Wunsch, G.: Systemtheorie. AVG, Leipzig 1975.
/2/ Rabiner, L.R., and Gold, B.: Theory and application of digital signal processing. Prentice-Hall Inc., Englewood Cliffs 1975.
/3/ Wunsch, G.: Zellulare Systeme. Akademie-Verlag, Berlin 1977.
/4/ Kung, H. T.: Why systolic architectures. IEEE Computer 15 (1981) 1, pp.37-46.
/5/ Petkov-Turkedjiev, N.: Beitrag zur Synthese systoliscer Algorithmen und Prozessorfelder. Dissertation A, TU Dresden, 1986.
/6/ Moldovan, D. I.: On the design of algorithms for VLSI systolic arrays. Proc. IEEE 71 (1983).

ANALYSIS OF SOME MIGRATION PROCESSES IN A 2-DIMENSIONAL CELLULAR SPACE

P. Zamperoni[1]

1. A model of the migration process

Among the several morphogenetic processes, which can be simulated by aid of 2-dimensional cellular automata, migration processes provide useful models for investigating a number of biological, physical and sociological phenomena involving the reaggregation and self-organization of cellular entities unter the control of local transition functions. Such processes are characterized by the following features:

- No births or deaths of cells occur; the initial cell population distribution, described by the probabilities of occurrence p_0 , p_1 ... p_{k-1} of the k cell classes, does not change from one iteration to the next.
- The evolution process consists of local migrations, in which neighbouring cells of different classes swap their places. In other words, the cell mobility is assumed to amount to one lattice unity per iteration.
- Local migrations take place under the control of a quantity, called here the "degree of affinity", in the sense that migrations aim at maximizing the local degree of affinity between the actual cell and its 4- or 8-neighbours.

In order to compy with the requirement of physical compatibility between the single swaps, which can take place only one after the other, the migration process must be simulated in the sequential processing mode. A feature of sequential processing is that the result depends upon the scanning sequence of the cellular space. Therefore in this investigation a random-scan option has been provided beside the conventional line-by-line scanning sequence.

Before going into further details, let us give an outline of the migration model and of the parameters that influence this process. We consider a 2-dimensional cellular space containing k types of cells S_0 , S_1 ... S_{k-1} , which can be also considered as states assumed by the cellular units. The initial configuration is, within the scope of this work, a random cellular field with probability of occurrence p_i $(i=0...k-1;\ 0 \leqslant p_i \leqslant 1)$ for the class S_i. Further, we define a set of affinity coefficients a_{ij} between the classes S_i and S_j , obeying to the following restrictions, for $i,j = 0...k-1$:

$$a_{ij} = f(\,|i-j|\,) \tag{1}$$

and

$$0 < a_{ij} = a_{ji} \leqslant 1 = a_{ii} \quad \forall\, i,j \tag{2}$$

It follows that the distance

$$d_{ij} = k(1 - a_{ij}) \tag{3}$$

between two classes S_i and S_j has metrical properties. Particular attention has been devoted to the linear coefficient set:

$$a_{ij} = 1 - \frac{|i-j|}{k} \tag{4}$$

---

1) Institut für Nachrichtentechnik, Technische Universität, Schleinitzstraße 23
D - 33 Braunschweig (BRD)

The total affinity A_0 between a cell P_0 and its 8-neighbourhood of cells $P_1 \dots P_8$ is defined as:

$$
\begin{matrix} P_1 & P_2 & P_3 \\ P_4 & P_0 & P_5 \\ P_6 & P_7 & P_8 \end{matrix}
$$

$$A_0 = \sum_{0}^{8}{}_n \, a_{ij}(0,n) \tag{5}$$

where $a_{ij}(0,n)$ is the affinity coefficient between the class S_i of cell P_0 and S_j of cell P_n (n=0..8). Swapping the cells P_0 and P_m (m=1...8) one obtains a new value A_m of the total affinity:

$$A_m = \sum_{0}^{8}{}_n \, a_{ij}(m,n) \tag{6}$$

Now the cell P_q to be actually exchanged with P_0 is the one for which:

$$A_q = \max \left\{ A_m \right\} \quad \text{for } m = 0 \dots 8 \tag{7}$$

The migration process has been simulated within this frame, with the aim of determining experimentally the self-organization patterns arising as the cellular field evolves, generation after generation.

The general problem of "sorting out" in mixed cell populations has been treated by R. Rosen /1/, who introduced the concept of "affinity" between cell classes, and followed an approach based upon the maximization of the global affinity over the whole cellular field. According to /1/, absolutely stable patterns are characterized by an absolute affinity maximum; however, such patterns are seldom reachable, starting from an arbitrary initial configuration, and having a limited cell mobility, as in our case. As shown in /1/, the theoretical a-priori investigation of absolutely stable patterns requires to evaluate separately $\binom{u}{k}$ possible independent expressions of the total affinity, with $u = \frac{k(k+1)}{2}$ unknown quantities (the number of edges between cells of given class pairs) and k relations between them. For k=2 one obtains $\binom{3}{2} = 3$, but already for k=3, $\binom{6}{3} = 20$, and this approach becomes too cumbersome. In our case, for k=4, $\binom{10}{4} = 210$ constitutes a prohibitive amount of independent global affinity expressions to be maximized in order to find all the possible solutions. Nevertheless, some intuitive considerations about sufficient global stability conditions may be helpful for explaining the experimental results to be exposed in section 2. The following considerations are restricted to a migration process with k=3, an initial distribution given by the quantities p_0, p_1 and p_2, and the distance function $d_{ij} = |i - j|$. Taking, without loss of generality,

$$p_0 \geqslant \frac{1}{3} \quad ; \quad p_0 \geqslant p_1 \geqslant p_2 \tag{8}$$

it can be intuitively realized that the configurations a) (stripes) and b) ("onion") of a field of NxN cells, as shown on Fig.1, are both globally stable. The global distances D_a and D_b for the configurations a) and b) are respectively:

$$D_a = 2N \cdot d_{01} \tag{9}$$

$$D_b = 4(n_0 + n_1) \cdot d_{01} \tag{10}$$

a) is more stable than b) if $D_b > D_a$ i.e. if:

$$2\left(\sqrt{p_0 + p_1} + \sqrt{p_0}\right) > 1 \tag{11}$$

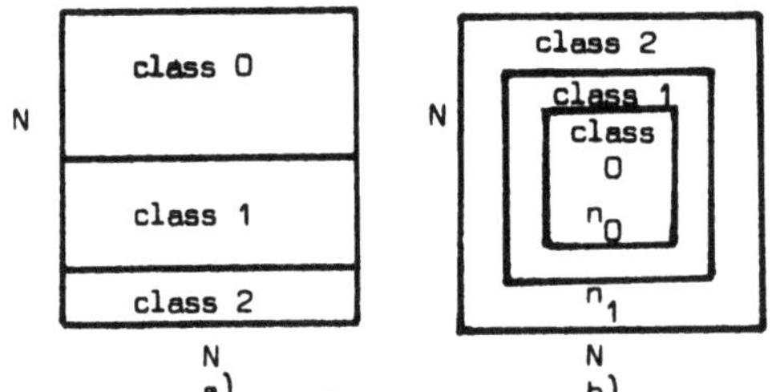

Fig. 1

Under the condition (8), (11) is always fulfilled.
On the other hand, removing the condition (8) the patterns of Fig. 1 can be interpreted as potentially stable local patterns of sparsely distributed classes S_0 and S_1, embedded into a background of S_2-cells. Restricting ourselves to the particular case of the "onion" pattern b), with $n_1 = n_0 + 2$, and defining (one-cell layer of S_1-cells around a S_0-core):

$$\frac{p_1}{p_0} = \frac{2(n_1 + n_0)}{n_0^2} = q \qquad (12)$$

the condition (11) is met if:

$$p_0 > \frac{1}{4(2 + q + 2\sqrt{1 + q})} = T_0 \qquad (13)$$

If p_0 does not exceed the threshold T_0, and p_1 the threshold $T_1 = q \cdot T_0$, sparse "onion" patterns may become absolutely more stable than the corresponding stripes-patterns.
Table I below gives some values of the above-mentioned thresholds for $n_0 = 1$ to 5 cells.

n_0	q	T_0	T_1
1	8	0,0156	0,125
2	3	0,0277	0,083
3	1,78	0,035	0,062
4	1,25	0,04	0,05
5	0,96	0,043	0,0416

Table I

The experimental results, some of which are reported in section 2, confirm the trend shown by Table I: sparse cell populations tend to nest into each other, depending upon their relative frequencies, and all of them nest into the dominant cell class.

All the limitations affecting theoretical a-priori estimation methods for the evolution of migration processes suggest that experimental simulation is indispensable in order to sensibly improve our knowledge of this process. In the following section are exposed some experimental results obtained within the scope of this work.

2. Experimental results

Synthetically generated initial configurations with values of k ranging from 3 to 8, and with several class distributions, have been used, as for instance:

I) $p_i = \frac{1}{k} \quad \forall i = 0...k-1$ equally distributed classes
II) $k = 3$; $p_i = (0,6 , 0,3 , 0,1)$
III) $k = 3$; $p_i = (0,7 , 0,15 , 0,15)$.
IV) $k = 4$ $p_i = (0,33 , 0,17 , 0,17 , 0,33)$
V) $k = 4$ $p_i = (0,5 , 0,25 , 0,13 , 0,12)$

Further, periodic "onion" patterns, consisting of k concentric and homogeneous one-cell layers, with $d_{ij} = 1$ between neighbouring cell layers of the classes S_i and S_j, have been investigated. The size of the cellular field is 32x60 = 1920 cells.
For assessing the rate of convergence of the whole field towards stable patterns, the evolution has been followed for about 100 generations, and the percentage M_t of "moving" cells in the course of the t-th iteration has been registered.
A quite general result, which has been observed, is that after a few hundreds of iterations the migration process is mostly far from having reached a stable state. With typical initial values of $M_1 = 0,5$, M_{100} sinks to about 0,25 for configurations of type I), and to about 0,15 for the types II) and III), featuring an unequal class distribution.
A further quite general remark is that the shape of the homogeneous regions emerging from the self-organization process is not sensibly influenced by the scanning sequence.

In what follows, random scanning will be assumed, unless otherwise indicated. Computing the affinity only in the 4-neighbourhood of the central cell (i.e. neglecting P_1, P_3, P_6 and P_8 in (5) and (6)) favours the formation of laminar regions instead of convex blobs.

Let us now take a closer look at the evolution of some initial configurations with equally distributed classes. Fig. 2 shows some stages in the evolution taking place with the linear affinity coefficient set (4), and visualizes the influence of the neighbourhood type, as outlined above. The tendency to converge toward the "stronger" stable configuration of Fig. 1a is clearly visible. Because of the limited cell mobility, a locally stable multiple-stripes pattern establishes itself before the absolutely stable configuration of Fig. 1a can be reached. Substantially the same final state is attained starting from a 4-class random initial configuration (see Fig. 3), or from a regular pattern (see Fig. 4), both with equally distributed classes.
Substituting the linear affinity coefficients of (4) with a free chosen set $F = \{a_0, a_1 \dots a_s \dots a_{k-1}\}$, with $a_s = a_{ij}$, $s = |i - j|$, some interesting variants of the evolution process can be observed. Taking, for instance, $F = \{1, 0{,}01, 0{,}01\}$ the affinity between cells of the same class is enhanced as against the between-class affinities. This causes the formation of compact and rather convex blobs instead of stripes, as shown on Fig. 5. On the other hand, if the between-class affinity sensibly exceeds the self-affinity, those cell classes, for which other cells have the highest affinity, tend to arrange themselves as a protective layer between blobs of the other classes, as shown in the example of Fig. 6. Here, assuming the affinity set $F = \{0{,}5, 1, 0{,}01\}$, the cells of class S_1 (-) play this role.

Let us observe now what happens with sparsely distributed cell populations, for instance with cell class frequencies of: $p_0 = 0{,}7$, $p_1 = p_2 = 0{,}15$ (see Fig. 7). Irrespective of the chosen affinity coefficient set, the sparse cell classes S_1 and S_2 are expelled from the bulk of the dominant class, and organize themselves into laminar or convex regions, depending upon the affinity coefficients, in the fashion described previously in connection with the equally distributed cellular field. Inclusions of S_0-blobs in the S_1-S_2 domain are possible, but not the converse.

Experiments performed with a higher number of classes (k = 8) did not bring substantially new points of view in the assessment of the simulation results. Some examples are given in Fig. 8 and Fig. 9, where the symbols for the additional classes S_4 to S_7, not considered up to now, are explained in the caption of Fig. 8. Fig. 8 illustrates the evolution of an equally distributed field with linear affinity coefficients, after the 100th generation. The cells' tendency to organize themselves into the laminar stable state conflicts against the poor mobility due to the increased number of cell classes, causing them to settle to the second-best stable configuration, characterized by convex blobs. In Fig. 9, where the "hetherophile" affinity coefficient set $F = \{0{,}01, 0{,}04, 0{,}09, 0{,}16, 0{,}25, 0{,}36, 0{,}49, 0{,}64\}$ has been used, an interesting phenomenon can be observed. Because of the quadratic growth rate of a_{ij} as a function of $|i - j|$, the global affinity attains a maximum when as many cells as possible of the following class pairs: S_0("space") and S_7("8"); S_1("-") and S_6("X"); S_2("I") and S_5("*"); S_3("O") and

S_4("+"), in the given priority order, become direct neighbours. As shown on Fig. 9, the cellular field organizes itself in this sense, by filtering out different sub-fields, each constituted by a mixture of cells of only one of those class pairs.

3. Conclusion

The examples reported above give only a very limited insight into the variety of experimental results recorded up to now. A more detailed evaluation of these results must now be undertaken, in order to be able to formulate a complex of systematic rules for describing the evolution of a migration process. However, as the degree of complexity grows rapidly for increasing number of classes, it is not expected to attain results of such compactness and generality as for the two-class case (/1/, /2/).

References:

/1/ Rosen, R.: Foundations of mathematical biology, Vol.II - Cellular Systems. Academic Press, New York 1972.

/2/ Wolf, G., Gössel, M.: Stable configurations of linear and generalized linear binary cellular automats. Z. elektr. Inform.- u. Energietechnik, Vol. 11 (1981), N.1 p.1-12.

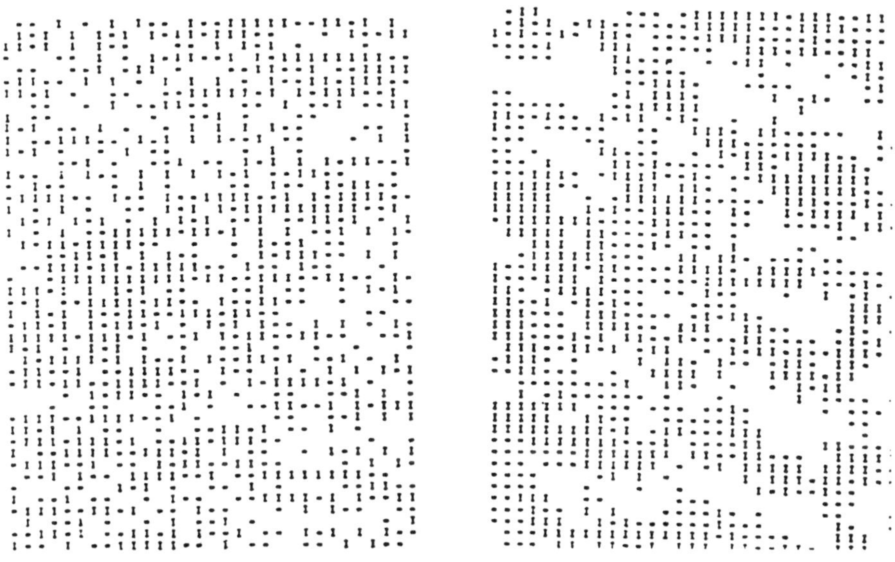

a) b)

Fig. 2: Three stages in the evolution of a random configuration with equally distributed classes and linear affinity coefficients. k = 3 classes
Symbols for all the following figures:
"blank" = cell class S_0
" - " = " " S_1
" I " = " " S_2
" O " = " " S_3 (only in Fig. 3,4,8,9)
a) Initial configuration b) 10th generation
c) 100th generation, 8-neighbours affinity } (next page)
d) 100th generation, 4-neighbours affinity }

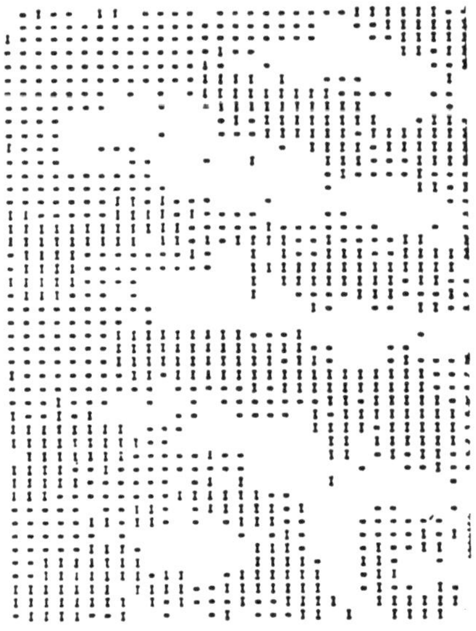

Fig. 2c

Fig. 2d

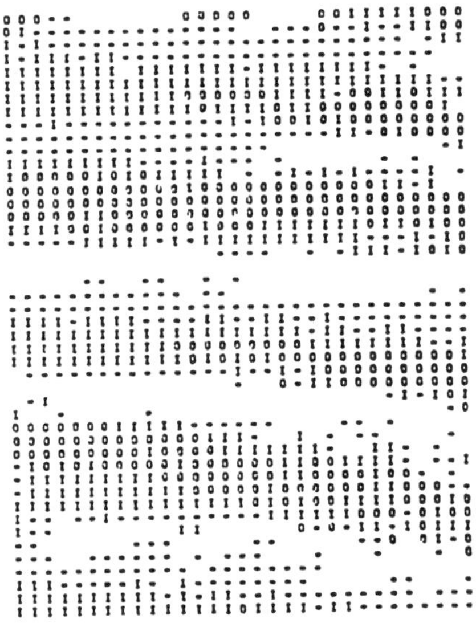

Fig. 3 100th generation, starting from a 4-class equally distributed initial random configuration, with linear affinity coefficients and 4-neighbours affinity

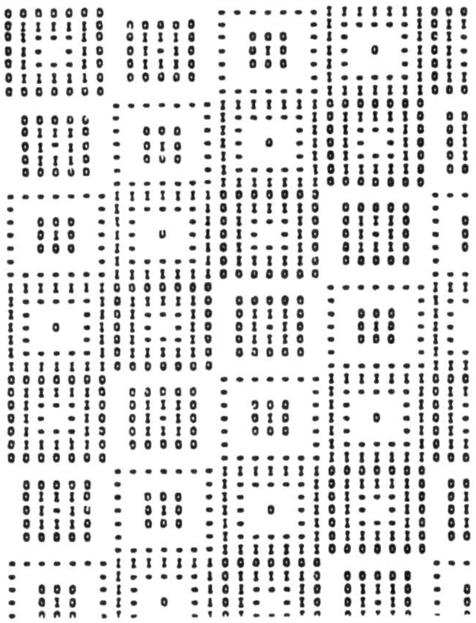

a)

Fig. 4
a) Initial configuration with a 4-class regular pattern and equally distributed classes.
b) 100th generation; linear affinity coefficients and 4-neighbours affinity

(next page)

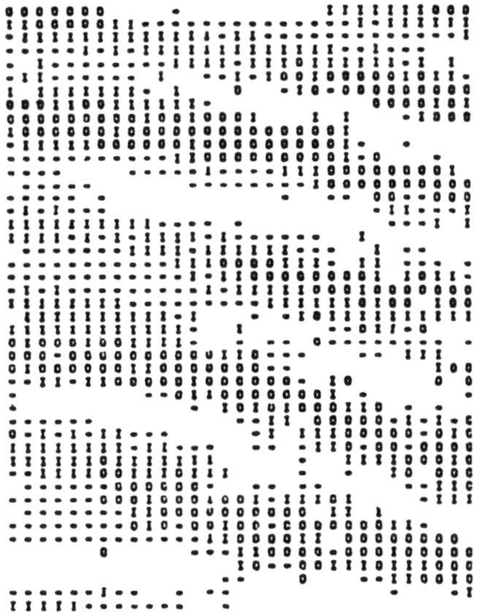

Fig. 4b

Fig. 5 100th generation.

Equally distributed initial configuration with 3 classes.
Affinity coeficient set:
$\{1 , 0{,}01 , 0{,}01\}$
4-neighbours affinity

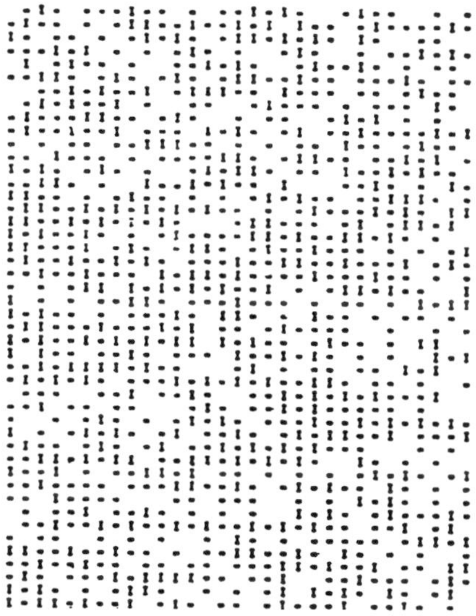

Fig. 6 100th generation

Random initial configuration with 3 classes, $p_0 = p_2 = 0{,}25$, $p_1 = 0{,}5$
Affinity coefficient set: $\{0{,}5 , 1 , 0{,}01\}$
4-neighbour affinity

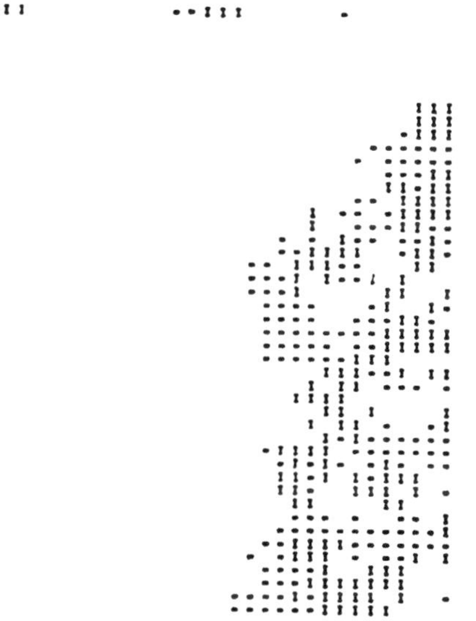

Fig. 7 100th generation

Sparsely distributed random cell population with 3 classes; $p_0 = 0{,}7$, $p_1 = p_2 = 0{,}15$. Affinity coefficient set: $\{1 , 0{,}01 , 0{,}01\}$
8-neighbour affinity

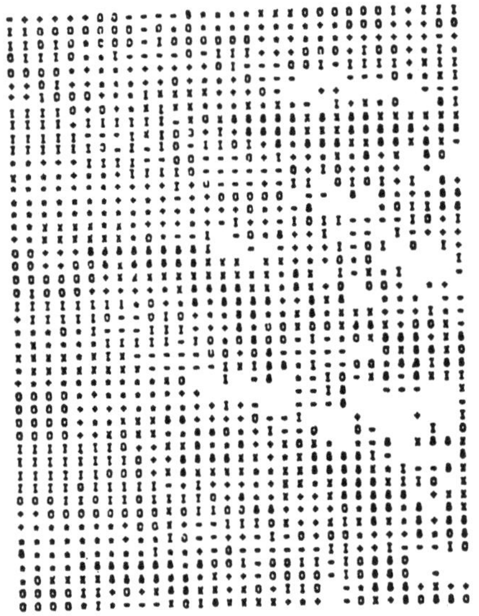

Fig. 8 100th generation

Equally distributed initial random configuration with 8 classes, linear affinity coefficients and 4-neighbour affinity.

Symbols used for the classes S_4 to S_7 (see also the caption of Fig. 2):

" + " = cell class S_4

" # " = " " S_5

" X " = " " S_6

" 8 " = " " S_7

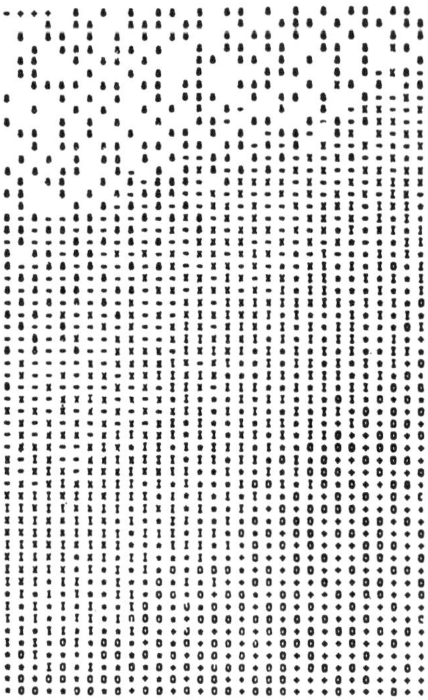

Fig. 9 100th generation

Equally distributed initial random configuration with 8 classes.
Affinity coefficient set: {0,01 , 0,04 0,09 , 0,16 , 0,25 , 0,36 , 0,49 , 0,64}
4-neighbour affinity
Symbols as in Fig. 8.

Parallel Algorithms in Image Processing and Computer Graphics

V. Kovalevsky, N. Luth
Berlin, ZKI

Abstract

Parallel algorithms for computing functions of large neighborhoods, for boundary tracing and geometrical transformations by means of the image processing system ROBOTRON A6472 are presented. The run time of the algorithms as well the efficiency of using the hardware are estimated.

1. Introduction

The most procedures used in image processing and computer graphics may be performed in shorter time when using parallel processors. The ways of "parallelizing" algorithms are different for different algorithm classes. In the simplest case an image must be transformed in such a way that the output gray value $G_o(x,y)$ at a pixel $p(x,y)$ be a function of the input gray value $G_i(x,y)$ at the corresponding pixel or a function of some input gray values in a close neighborhood of $p(x,y)$. In such a case the problem may be simply subdivided into n independent problems each being solved by a separate processor of a parallel processor array.

Much more sophisticated and interesting are the problems in which the output $G_o(x,y)$ is a "global" function of the input image, i.e. it depends upon the values $G_i(x\ ,y\ )$ at pixels $p(x\ ,y\ )$ being far away from $p(x,y)$. The problems of this kind which we have considered in our investigation may be classified into the following three classes:

C1. Computing associative functions of predefined large neighborhoods by hierarchically decomposing the neighborhood into smaller and smaller subsets. A typical example is the computation of the arithmetic mean over all squares of $2^n \times 2^n$ pixels with n from 1 to 8.

C2. Computing functions of sequences of pixels, the sequences being dependent on the image content, e.g. parallel tracing of all boundaries in the image.

C3. Computing geometrically transformed images by reducing various transformations to translations by steps of the length 2^k.

The authors have implemented the solutions of the problems on the Image Processing System ROBOTRON A6472 [1]. It contains 4 to 8 image memory units of 512x512 bytes each and three pipe-line processors of the type SIMD (single instruction for multiple data). The processors work with video rate in such a way that each processor may perform during every TV-frame (40 ms) up to 18x512x512 elementary byte operations on the pixels of the input memory units. Besides that up to 3N elementary operations with N being the number of the input image memory units may be performed by the memory control unit: each memory unit may be read with a preset $(\Delta x,\Delta y)$ and a magnification m thus performing the coordinate transformation

$$x_{out} = (x_{inp} - \Delta x)/m$$
$$y_{out} = (y_{inp} - \Delta y)/m.$$

The result is written into an output memory unit. The operation sequence is specified by a program before starting a frame. Feeding the operation sequence into the processors takes another 40 ms. The sequence is one and the same for all 512^2 pixels of the output image and is performed in 40 + 40 = 80 ms. Thus the maximum operation speed of the system containing 8 image memory units may be reached if 5 memory units are read with different coordinate transformations and all possible processor operations are used the results being written into the 3 remaining memory units. The total number of operations performed during one frame is then

$$NF = 512^2(3x8 + 3x18) = 512^2 x78 = 20.4 \cdot 10^6 .$$

It takes 80 ms time and thus the maximum speed is

$$S_{max} = 512^2 x78/(80 \cdot 10^{-3}) = 256\ 10^6 \text{ op/s}.$$

If only 4 image memory units are used these values are $NF=66 \cdot 512^2 = 17 \cdot 10^6$ and $S_{max} = 216 \cdot 10^6$ respectively.

It is easy to see that the function of the system is pseudo-parallel: the result of all operations performed by one pipe-line processor during a frame is exactly the same as that of implementing simultaneously 512x512 slow processors each realizing one and the same short program consisting of up to 4x4+18=34 byte operations applied to pixels of up to 4 input images. From the point of view of a programmer the system may be regarded as three arrays each containing 512x512 slow processors. The processors are working synchronously and all of them complete their operation sequence during the time of a frame, i.e. during 80 ms. The program controlling the arrays consists of subroutine calls each call feeding simultaneously up to three different operation sequences into the three arrays and starting a frame run. The time complexity of an algorithm is exactly specified by the number F of frame runs necessary to solve the corresponding problem.

The blocks which a processor consists of are rather specific: some of them perform an input transformation by a look-up table, some other compute the histogram of the output image etc. Hence it is hardly possible to realize an expedient algorithm which is using all processor blocks during all the frames. Thus only a fraction of all the possible processor operations is being realized during the most frames and therefore only a fraction of the maximum speed S_{max} may be reached. This fraction characterizes the efficiency of the parallelization of an algorithm when being implemented on the A6472 system. We call it the efficiency and define it as being equal to

$$E_{ff} = N_{op}/(NF \cdot F)$$

with N_{op} being the total number of computer operations necessary to solve the same problem by a convential computer supposed that the image is located in the memory. The efficient speed of the system is equal to $S_e = S_{max} E_{ff}$.

We are presenting here some algorithms developed for the solution of various problems from the above three classes by the A6472 system. For every algorithm its time complexity, the actual run time and the efficiency of its pseudo-parallel implementation by means of the said system is reported.

2. Computations in Predefined Large Neighborhoods

This class of problems includes the computation of various functions of many arguments which functions may be represented as a superposition of functions of one variable and of certain functions of two variables. The first ones being realized by the look-up tables are restricted in their input and output range by the word length of 10 bits. The functions of two variables are the addition, substraction and all 16 logical functions of two binary variables applied to every bit of the word separately.

Consider a typical problem of this class, namely computing the arithmetic mean in every LxL fragment with $L=2^n$:

$$\forall x,y \in [0,511] \quad M(x,y) = L^{-2} \sum_{i,j=-W}^{(W-1)} \sum I(x+i, y+j)$$

with w=L/2. The addition at the right hand side is modulo 512. The values of M(x,y) must be computed for all 512^2 pixels of the output image. The idea of the algorithm consists in computing first the mean of a 2x2 neighborhood, then the mean of four such neighborhoods etc until the wanted $2^n \times 2^n$ size is reached. Each time the gray values of four pixels $p(x-\Delta x_1, y-\Delta y_1)$, $p(x-\Delta x_2, y-\Delta y_2)$, $p(x-\Delta x_3, y-\Delta y_3)$, $p(x-\Delta x_4, y-\Delta y_4)$ are added up and divided by 4. The translations $x-\Delta x_i$ and $y-\Delta y_i$ are realized by reading the image memory units with different presets. The hardware realization does not permit to read one and the same memory unit with different presets. Therefore four copies of an image are needed. The program solving the problem consists of the following frame runs:

f1: Make three copies I_2, I_3, I_4 of the input image I_1;

f2: $I_5(x,y)=I_6(x,y)=I_7(x,y)=I_8(x,y)=1/4 \sum_{i=1}^{4} I_i(x-\Delta x_i, y-\Delta y_i)$;

f3: $I_1(x,y)=I_2(x,y)=I_3(x,y)=I_4(x,y)=1/4 \sum_{i=5}^{8} I_i(x-\Delta x_i, y-\Delta y_i)$;

f4: ...

The procedures f2 and f3 must be repeated while doubling the values of Δx_i and Δy_i each time until the wanted neighborhodd size is reached. The initial values are such that f2 produces the mean for a 2x2 neighborhood and f3 for a 4x4 one. It is easy to see that the number of the frame runs necessary to achieve the neighborhood size of LxL is equal to $F=1+\log_2 L$. During this time $3 \times 512^2 \log_2 L$ additions, $512^2 \cdot \log_2 L$ divisions by 4 and $8 \times 512^2 \cdot \log_2 L$ coordinate additions are performed. Hence the total number of necessary operations is:

$$N_{op} = 512^2(3+1+8) \cdot \log_2 L = 12 \cdot 512^2 \log_2 L.$$

The efficiency E_{ff} of using the A6472 hardware for the arithmetic mean problem with L=256 is:

$$E_{ff} = N_{op}/(NF \cdot F) =$$

$$= 12 \times 512^2 \times \log_2 L/(78 \times 512^2 \cdot (1+\log_2 L)) = 0.14$$

with $F=1+\log_2 L$ being the number of the frame runs. The efficiency is only 14%. Nevertheless the speed is still rather high: the averaging in every 256x256 neighborhood is completed in 1+8=9 frame runs, i.e. in t=0.72 seconds. In the case when the system has less than 8 image memory units or some of the units must be reserved to store the original image and spme other images the speed is something lower. E.g. when using only 3 memory units $4 \cdot \log_2 L$ frame runs are needed which makes for L=256 t=2.6 seconds. Since the number of the necessary operations remains the same the efficiency becomes almost four times less:

$$E_{ff} = 12 \times 512^2 \cdot \log_2 L / (66 \times 512^2 \cdot 4 \cdot \log_2 L) = 0.045 = 4.5\%.$$

It should be noted that the described algorithm may obviously be used also for neighborhoods of $3^n \times 3^n$ pixels.

The arithmetic mean may be efficiently used to suppress noise in images. Its smoothing properties may be made still better by applying it repeatedly to the smoothed image. Really, the arithmetic mean in every quadratic neighborhood is obviously a convolution of the input image with a "rectangular" kernel being equal to $1/L^2$ inside the LxL neighborhood and to zero outside it. It is well-known that the convolution is assosiative and the convolution of many rectangular functions is a good approximation of the gaussian function. Thus when applying the arithmetic mean procedure again and again to the resulting image a good approximation to the convolution with the gaussian kernel may be achieved. Practically it is sufficient to repeat the mean procedure 3 times. Figure 1 shows the experimental impulse response of a threefold arithmetic mean with L=16 (the crosses) as compared with the closest ideal gaussian curve (the solid line). The general case of repeated filtering has been analysed in [2].

Another practically important problem of the class C1 is that of computing the minimum and maximum gray value in a $m^n \times m^n$ neighborhood of every pixel with m=2 or m=3. This problem belongs to the class C1 since the minimum or maximum of two values may be reduced to calculating the sign of their difference and to using the sign as a logical variable controlling the choice of one of the given values. All the necessary functions of one or two variables are realizable by the A6472 processor. The minimum (maximum) of more than two variables may be obviously represented as the superposition of minima (maxima) of two variables:

$$\min(v_1, v_2, v_3, v_4) = \min(\min(v_1, v_2), \min(v_3, v_4))$$

and so on. The time complexity of the algorithm implemented with 5 image memory units is equal to $4 \cdot \log_2 L$ frame runs which corresponds under L=256 to 2.6 seconds. The number of the necessary operations N_{op} and the efficiency E_{ff} are:

$$N_{op} = 8 \cdot 512^2 \cdot 2 \cdot \log_2 L,$$

$$E_{ff} = 8 \cdot 512^2 \cdot 2 \cdot \log_2 L \,/ (78 \cdot 512^2 \cdot 4 \cdot \log_2 L) = 0.05.$$

A rather more complicated problem is the calculation of the arithmetic mean over the intersection of the gliding neighborhood with a predefined region in the given image. This procedure is of great importance for smoothing noisy images at locations which are near the boundary of two regions of rather different mean gray values. The difficulty of this problem consists in that the number of summands is no more a known constant but rather a variable which may vary from 1 to L^2. Hence a division by a variable must be realized inspite of this operation is not implemented in the hardware. Another difficulty consists in the necessity of calculating the sum of many variables which sum cannot be represented by one byte. Hence two image memory units must be used: one for the least significant and the other for the most significant byte of the sum. The processing of the carries must be programmed. The division was realized as the subtraction of logarithms the latter being produced by a look-up table. The roundig errors reach up to 2 gray levels from 256 which is acceptable in many applications. The time complexity of the algorithm using only 4 image memory units is $9+10 \cdot \log_2 L$ frame runs which corresponds to 3.2 seconds with L=8.

3. Computation on Digital Curves

The problem class C2 includes computations of various functions of many arguments which are distributed along a digital curve in a raster image. The arguments compose an ordered sequence, however their location relative to the output pixel is not predetermined as it was the case for the class C1. In the case of C2 the location depends upon the orientation and the shape of the given curve. A typical example of a problem of C2 is that of measuring the length of labeled connected curve segments. Consider a collection of digital curves in a raster image, e.g. the boundaries of some uniformly colored regions of two or more colors. The curve elements possesing a predefined feature (e.g. high curvature) are labeled. Let S be the set of all labeled curve elements. We shall call a connected component of S a labeled curve segment or shortly a segment. Assume that all branching points are not labeled and hence a segment never contains branching points. The problem consists in assigning to every labeled curve element $\bar{r}=(x,y)$ an integer value $L(\bar{r})$ which is equal to the lengh of the segment containing $\bar{r}$. The length of a segment is defined as the number of its elements.

The idea of the parallel algorithm is as follows. The curves are supposed to be directed. E.g. region boundaries may be regarded as directed in such a way that the region having the greater color label lies to the right of the direction. For every $\bar{r}$ its distances $DB(\bar{r})$ to the begin of the segment and the distance $DE(\bar{r})$ to its end are computed and added. Both distances are computed simultaneously in iterations. Consider the distance $DE(\bar{r})$. At first the values of $DE(\bar{r})$ are set to zero for all $\bar{r}$. During the (i+1)th iteration a new value $DE_{i+1}(\bar{r})$ is computed:

$$DE_{i+1}(r) = \begin{cases} DE_i(\bar{r}+\bar{d}(ID(\bar{r}))+1 & \text{if } \bar{r} \text{ is labeled,} \\ 0 & \text{otherwise.} \end{cases}$$

The value $ID(\bar{r})$ is the Freeman code of the direction from $\bar{r}$ to the next curve element. The vector $\bar{d}(ID)$ is the coordinate difference between the next curve element and $\bar{r}$.The translation $\bar{r}+\bar{d}(ID)$ is realized by means of reading an image by the preset $\bar{d}(ID')$ with a fixed preset direction ID'. Since the necessary presets are different for different pixels $\bar{r}$ the whole image must be first labeled by the labels $ID(\bar{r})$. If there are K copies of the image $DE_i(\bar{r})$ then K different values of ID may be realized in parallel during one frame run: the values of $DE_i(\bar{r}+\bar{d}(ID\ ))$ obtained by the corresponding preset of $DE_i(\bar{r})$ are increased by 1 and written into the output image $DE_{i+1}(\bar{r})$ only for those pixels whose direction code $ID(\bar{r})$ is equal to the actual preset direction ID .

In the case of tracing boundary segments of a binary image containing no skeletons (only full regions as defined by Pavlidis [3]) four directions are sufficient. When using 7 memory units 2 frame runs per each step along the boundary are sufficient. The computation of the direction code $ID(\bar{r})$ may be performed in a single run. Thus the time complexity is equal to 1 + 2 L frame runs. In the case of "multicolored" regions, i.e. those labeled by more than two labels, and no restrictions on the topology (such as that of full regions) 2 runs are necessary for the computation of $ID(\bar{r})$ and 5 runs per each step for the tracing. Thus the time complexity in this case is 2+5 L frame runs. An economic assembler program solving the same problem contains 35 operations per pixel for the computation of the direction codes and for searching for the labeled segments. Moreover it contains 20 operations per segment element for the tracing. Thus the necessary number of the operations N_{op} is:

$$N_{op} = 35 \cdot 512^2 + 20 \cdot NB$$

with NB being the total number of the labeled boundary elements. The efficiency E_{ff} is:

$$E_{ff} = N_{op}/(NF \cdot F) = (35 \cdot 512^2 + 20 \cdot NB\ )/(78 \cdot 512^2 (2+5 \cdot L_{max})) =$$

$$= (0.47+0.27 \cdot C)/(2+5\ L_{max})$$

with $C=NB/512^2$ being the fraction of the labeled boundary elements in the whole image of 512^2 pixels. Under C=0.1 and $L_{max}=10$ the efficiency is E =0.9% and the effective speed is

$$S_e = S_{max} E_{ff} = 256 \cdot 10^6 \cdot 0.009 = 2.3 \cdot 10^6 \text{ op/s}$$

which in spite of the low efficiency is still higher than the speed of a common mini-computer.

The same idea was successfully used to compute the chords in the boundaries. The chords were represented as vectors whose components were coded by 4 bits each. Thus the components were in the range from -8 to 7. Two chords were computed for every boundary point: one running in the direction of the boundary and the other in the opposite direction. By means of these chords the curvature at every point of the boundaries was estimated as the curvature of the circle running through the three end points of the chords (Figure 3). It is easy to see that the radius of the circle equals $R = |AC| / (2 \cdot \sin\gamma)$ and the curvature CR is the inverse value of R. Denoting the components of the chord AB by x_1, y_1 and those of BC by x_2, y_2 and using the vector product of the chords to get $\sin\gamma$ one obtains:

$$CR = \frac{2 \cdot |x_1 y_2 - x_2 y_1|}{\sqrt{x_1^2 + y_1^2}\ \sqrt{x_2^2 + y_2^2}\ \sqrt{(x_2 - x_1)^2 + (y_2 - y_1)^2}} . \qquad (1)$$

The range of the curvature value obtained by our algorithm corresponds to the radii from 4 to 64 pixels. The precision is about ±10%. It is stipulated by the small code length used for the chord components. The time complexity of the chord computation is 40 frame runs (3.2 seconds), that of the curvature computation by (1) is only 7 runs! The total run time of the program is 6 seconds. Because of using only 4 memory units the size of the image was reduced to 256^2 pixels. When using at least 5 memory units the size may be made 512^2 without increasing the run time.

The ideas presented in this section may be used for computing additive functionals along all paths in a tree when moving from the leaves to the root.

4. Geometrical Transformations by means of 2 -Translations

The idea to perform geometrical transformations on the A6472 system by means of translations is due to Wilhelmi [1]. His suggestion is as follows.

Any geometrical transformation of a raster image may be performed by translating each pixel with its gray value to another location in the raster. For each pixel $\bar{r}$ of the input image I the translation of $\bar{r}$ must be encoded at the same location $\bar{r}$ in another image memory wich we shall call the translation table T. Then the gray value in the output image O is defined by

$$O(\bar{r} + T(\bar{r})) = I(\bar{r}) .$$

If the set of different translation vectors consists of NT vectors then all necessary translations may be performed during NT frame runs. In the ith run the input image I is being read with a preset $\bar{t}$ and all gray values $I(\bar{r} - \bar{t})$ are translated to the output pixel $O(\bar{r})$ if $T(\bar{r} - \bar{t})$ is equal to $\bar{t}$:

$$O^{(i)}(\bar{r}) = O^{(i-1)}(\bar{r}) .\text{OR}. I(\bar{r} - \bar{t}) .\text{AND}. (T(\bar{r} - \bar{t}) .\text{EQ}. \bar{t}) .$$

This technique is a universal one but unfortunately it is very slow since in the worst case NT may be as large as 256^2.

Our improvement of the technique consists in dissolving a one-dimensional translation by a distance x into a set of translations by some smaller distances equal to 2^k with $k = 0, 1, 2, \ldots$ A pixel $\bar{r}$ is being translated by the distance 2^k if and only if the kth bit of the binary representation of x is equal to 1. When using this technique a difficulty arises consisting in the possible overlapping of values being translating from different locations to one and the same. Therefore the applications are at present limited to those cases in which no overlapping takes place.

Anotner improvement consists in accelerating the computation of tne translation table T by using certain regularities in its structure. The techniques are different in different particular cases. In all cases described below in Table 1 we were able to compute the table T for an image of 512x512 pixels in less than 0.6 seconds by means of a rather slow computer K 1620 having no floating point processing capability.

Table 1 represents the obtained results for rotating an image by an arbitrary angle, reflecting an image against an axis and sampling every second pixel with the aim of compressing a 512x512 image to a 256x256 one.

Table 1

Procedure	Nop	Frames	Eff %	Speed Mop	Time sec
Rotation k·90 (4 m)	$4 \cdot 512^2$	43	0.14	0.3	3.7
Rotation k·90 (8 m)	$4 \cdot 512^2$	23	0.22	0.5	2.1
Rotation arb. (4 m)	$8 \cdot 512^2$	60	0.20	0.4	6.0
Rotation arb. (8 m)	$8 \cdot 512^2$	32	0.34	0.9	3.2
Reflection (4 m)	$4 \cdot 512^2$	25	0.24	0.5	2.3
Reflection (8 m)	$4 \cdot 512^2$	12	0.42	1.1	1.3
Compression (4 m)	$5 \cdot 256^2$	39	0.05	0.1	3.4
Compression (8 m)	$5 \cdot 256^2$	22	0.07	0.2	2.1

Here "4 m" and "8 m" denote the usage of 4 or 8 memory units respectively, the effective speed is in millions of operations per second.

As one may see the efficiency of using the hardware for geometric transformations is essentially lower as for the smoothing (14% for the arithmetic mean). Nevertheless the average speed remains rather high: about $0.5 \cdot 10^6$ operations per second.

5. Conclusion

The presented examples are demonstrating a set of parallel image processing algorithms which are implemented on the pseudo-parallel SIMD system ROBOTRON A6472 and may also be implemented on other parallel image processing hardware. In many cases a very high average speed of computations (e.g. $34 \cdot 10^6$ operations per second for the arithmetic mean) has been achieved. However in all cases the hardware of the rather specialized system A6472 is being used rather inefficiently: in the best case only 14% of the total number of the possible operations are used. This knowledge may be useful for the development of the future parallel image processing systems.

References

1. Kempe V., Rebel B., Wilhelmi W.: The Interactive Image Processing Console A6471, Proceedings of the 6th International Conference on Patternn Recognition , p. 607, 1982.

2. Eichhorn, E., Kovalevski, W., Saedler, J., Wilhelmi, W.: Algorithmen auf dem Displayprozessor K2067, Bild und Ton, May 1986 (to be published).

3. Pavlidis, T.: Algorithms for Graphics and Image Processing, Computer Science Press, Rockville, p. 150, 1982.

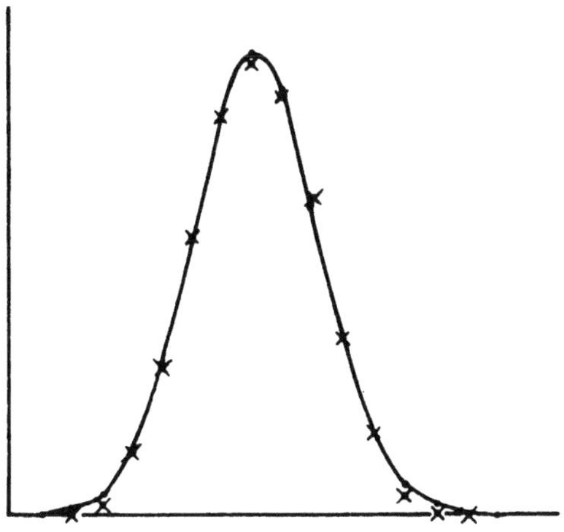

Figure 1. Experimental impulse response of the threefold arithmetic mean with L=16 (the crosses) as compared with the closest Gaussian curve (the solid line)

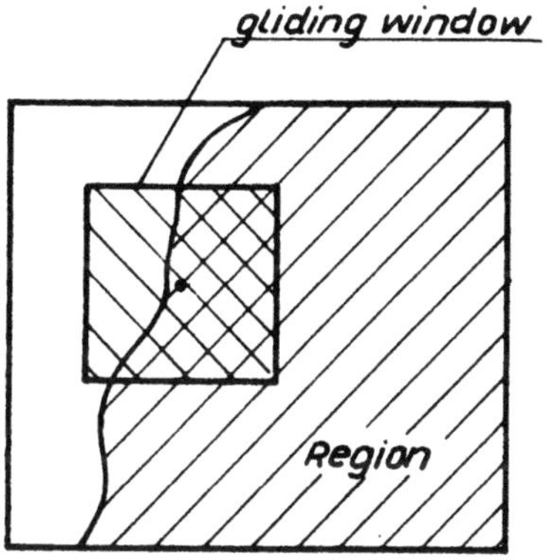

Figure 2. To the calculation of the arithmetic mean over the intersection of a gliding window with a predefined region

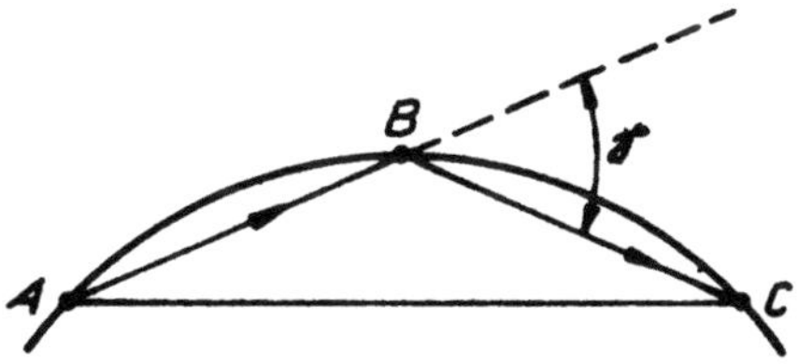

Figure 3. To the estimation of the curvature of the boundaries (see text)

VLSI-FRIENDLY PROCESSOR DESIGNS FOR MACHINE VISION SYSTEMS

K. Fritzsch, G. Schwarze
Central Institute of Cybernetics and Information Processing
of the Academy of Sciences of the GDR (ZKI)
Kurstrasse 33, Berlin
DDR-1080

Abstract:
Three kinds of parallelism are of importance in image recognition for preprocessing, feature extraction and pattern matching, from which different architectures have been derived. Solutions for preprocessing and pattern matching are presented which can be effectively implemented in VLSI.

1. Introduction

For extracting information from visual scenes segment- or contour-oriented approaches may be used. Considerable progress has been achieved already in designing efficient processor architectures for detecting edges or contours in images and identifying them with real ones in the scene mapped onto the image plane. The parallelism inherent to most of imagé processing steps leads in a straightforward manner to parallelism in the processor design and in this line to a high repetition rate on a single chip or to multi-usable IC's for a single processor.

Analyzing the processing steps in machine vision systems mainly three types of parallelism may be found:
- local operations in the raster-grid representation may be parallelized,
- extraction of features can be performed in parallel,
- parallelism in matching models of objects, sets of local features etc. with their possible instances in the actual image.

In the following some results concerning the first and third type of parallelism are reported. The second type seems of lower importance. Nevertheless, the computation of some morphometrical features as area moments of different degree are suited for VLSI implementation as shown by Andersson/1/.

2. Preprocessing of gray-tone images

In the case of using local operations in image processing it seems appropriate to distinguish between parallelism at the 'entire image' level (for instance: CLIP4-processor) and at the 'processing window' level. The second case is commonly combined with pipeline-processing (for instance: CYTO III-computer). For the latter case we will give an example for an efficient high performance structure.

The base for this structure is the microprogrammable specialized processor GIPP (GRAYSCALE IMAGE PREPROCESSOR), developed at ZKI /2/.

The processor GIPP works in a parallel manner inside a 3x3-window and has the following properties:

- The number N of clock pulses for the evaluation of the new gray value of central point is independent from the type of image processing function and the gray level distribution inside the window.
- The number N of the clock pulses is only dependent from gray levels NGL of the designed image processing system ($N = \log_2 NGL$).
- The GIPP generates at every clock pulse one bit of the new central point value (typical: 100ns/clock pulse).
- The GIPP has a high repetition rate of internal substructures. That is the premise for an optimal realization in a semi-custom chip.
- Image processing functions controlled by microprogramms are for instance:
  - .mask operations as thinning, thickening, restoration, directional median
  - .sorting operations as rank-filter, including median, max- and min-operations
  - .table-lookup-operations as data compression by Freeman- chain coding, combined with node coding,
  - .image algebra operations (in the sense of Serra and Sternberg) as dilatation, erosion, opening, closing, convex hull, medial axis transform et.al.
  - .extraction of texture features: generation of various structuring elements.

The mentioned properties, especially the synchronous processing modus, are advantageous for developing various structures with a multiplicity of GIPPs, without producing severe control problems. A practicable solution with a wide application field is given in fig.1. This example shows a structure with m=2 parallel pipelines and n GIPPs in each pipeline ($m > 2$ is possible). In the programmable interconnection networks IN(i) (see fig.2) may be implemented simple arithmetic (add, subtract), logical (and, or) and shift operations, for instance

$E1 = I1 - I2$	$E1 = I1 \cap I2$	$E1 = I1$
$E2 = 0$	$E2 = I1 \cup I2$	$E2 = I2$

In fig.3 three concrete examples are shown for the programming of substructures of the described complex structure for some image processing operations. Such substructures may be combined to structures for complete tasks.

a) Edge-detection by the range-filter /3/:
   GRADIENT = RANGE(9,5) = RANK(9) - RANK(5)
b) Detection of imperfections of a stripe pattern by using the closing operation of the image algebra: IMAGE=(IMAGE $\oplus$ MASK) $\ominus$ MASK
   ($\oplus \triangleq$ dilatation, $\ominus \triangleq$ erosion)
c) Detection of crossing points in a line pattern using the eroding operation parallelly with two different masks M1 and M2.

The principle of parallel pipelines with a multiplicity of GIPP-processors differs from other known image processing systems and has advantages based on its great flexibility for a wide class of image processing tasks, short processing time and a reasonable cost/performance ratio. The high repitition rate of the same kind of processors and interconnection networks in the described image processing system make the VLSI-realization economically feasible.

3. Pattern matching in contour images

Contour images may be divided into linear strings of local features. The string may be generated by interpreting the local features along a contour as the string elements (fig. 4). Another possibility is choosing one or some prominent local features as a kind of pivot element /4/ and listing the local features in a neighborhood of the pivot element in a circular manner (arranging them in dependence of the angle between the locus of the feature and a given straight line as in fig. 5). The recognition is performed by matching the resulting string against a prototype string previously generated by teaching or modelling. The classical methodology for string matching is delivered by dynamic programming.

The distance between two strings is estimated by evaluating all sequences of permitted transformations from one to the another. In the present case deletion, insertion, substitution, and exchanging two neighboring elements together with the corresponding costs are given. The distance δ_{ij} is represented by the costs of matching two partial strings of length i and j resp.

$$\delta_{i\,j} = \min\Big\{\delta_{i\,j-1} + D(b_j),\ \delta_{i-1\,j} + I(a_i),\ \delta_{i-1\,j-1} + S(a_i, b_j),\ \delta_{i-2\,j-2} + C(a_{i-1}a_i)\Big\}. \qquad (1)$$

I, D and S are costs for inserting, deleting and substituting elements. C are the costs for exchanging two neighboring elements, if $a_{i-1}a_i = b_j b_{j-1}$.

Liu and Fu /5/ have proposed a processor array for solving the task of dynamic programming according to (1), but without the exchange term. This term is of importance in image matching tasks. Little variations in the locus of pivot features may result in an exchange of neighboring features in circular arrangements.

Also with the exchange term the corresponding processor array is rectangular with I rows and J columns according to the number of elements in both strings. But in the actual calculation five rows at the same time with additional interconnections between neighbor processor elements may be sufficient as shown in fig. 6.

Taking into account that the processors of each row are needed only for a limited time the number of rows may be reduced to three (fig. 7). An array of J identical processor elements each in 3 rows connected by busses is proposed for implementing the dynamic programming algorithm.

The structure of a single processor element has been derived from the demands for storing and buffering the string elements, for estimating and storing intermediate and minimum distances and for access to the bus, to the neighbor elements and to the cost function table. The array may be used also for other string matching tasks in speech recognition, information retrieval and text-processing with typing-error capability.

References:

/1/ Andersson, R.L.: Real-Time Gray-Scale Video Processing Using a Moment-Generating Chip. IEEE J. of Robotics and Automation, Vol. RA-1, No. 2 June 1985, pp. 79-84

/2/ Roesler, U., G. Schwarze, T. L. Chung: Lokale Bildoperatoren zur Manipulation von Grauwertobjekten und ihre Implementierung durch den Prozessor GIPP. Journal of Information Processing and Cybernetics EIK 21(1985) 7/8, 343-354

/3/ Bailey, D. G., R. M. Hodgson: Range-filters: local-intensity subrange filters and their properties. Image Vision and Computing, Vol. 3, No. 3, August 1985, pp. 99-110

/4/ Kiesewetter, H.: Private communication

/5/ Liu, H.-H. and K. S. Fu: VLSI arrays for minimum distance classifications. In: Fu, K. S. (ed.): VLSI for pattern recognition and image processing. Springer, Berlin 1984

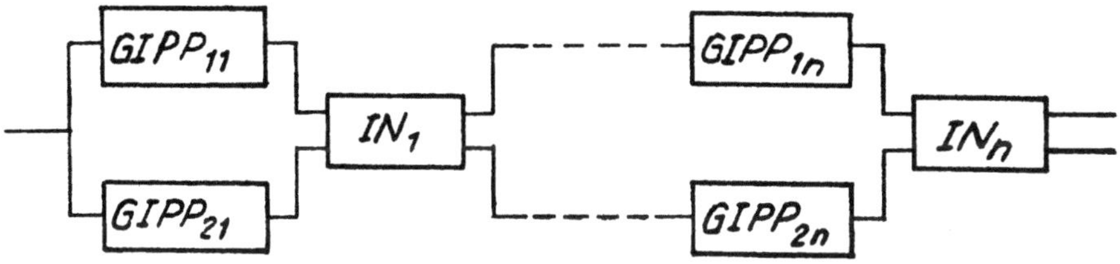

Fig. 1 Structure with m=2 pipelines and n GIPPs in each pipeline

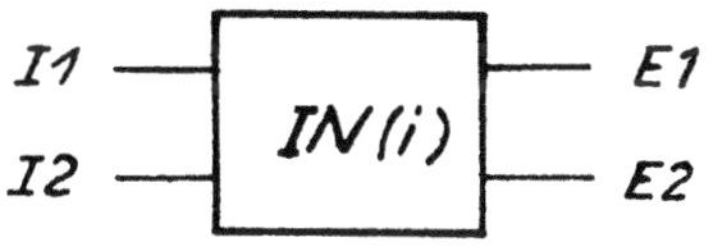

Fig. 2 Interconnection network IN(i)

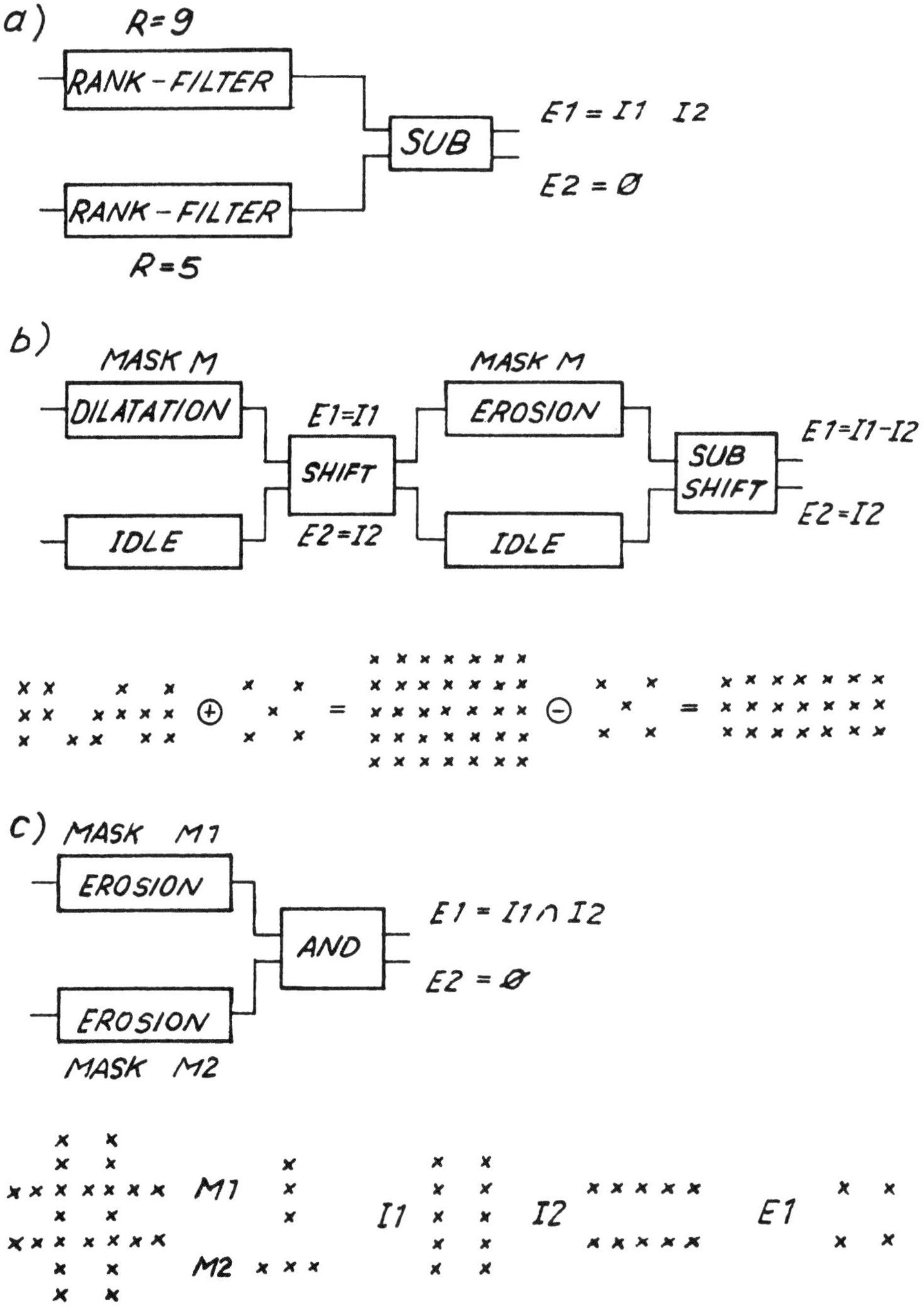

Fig. 3 Examples with substructures

Fig. 4 Contour and corresponding string of feature elements

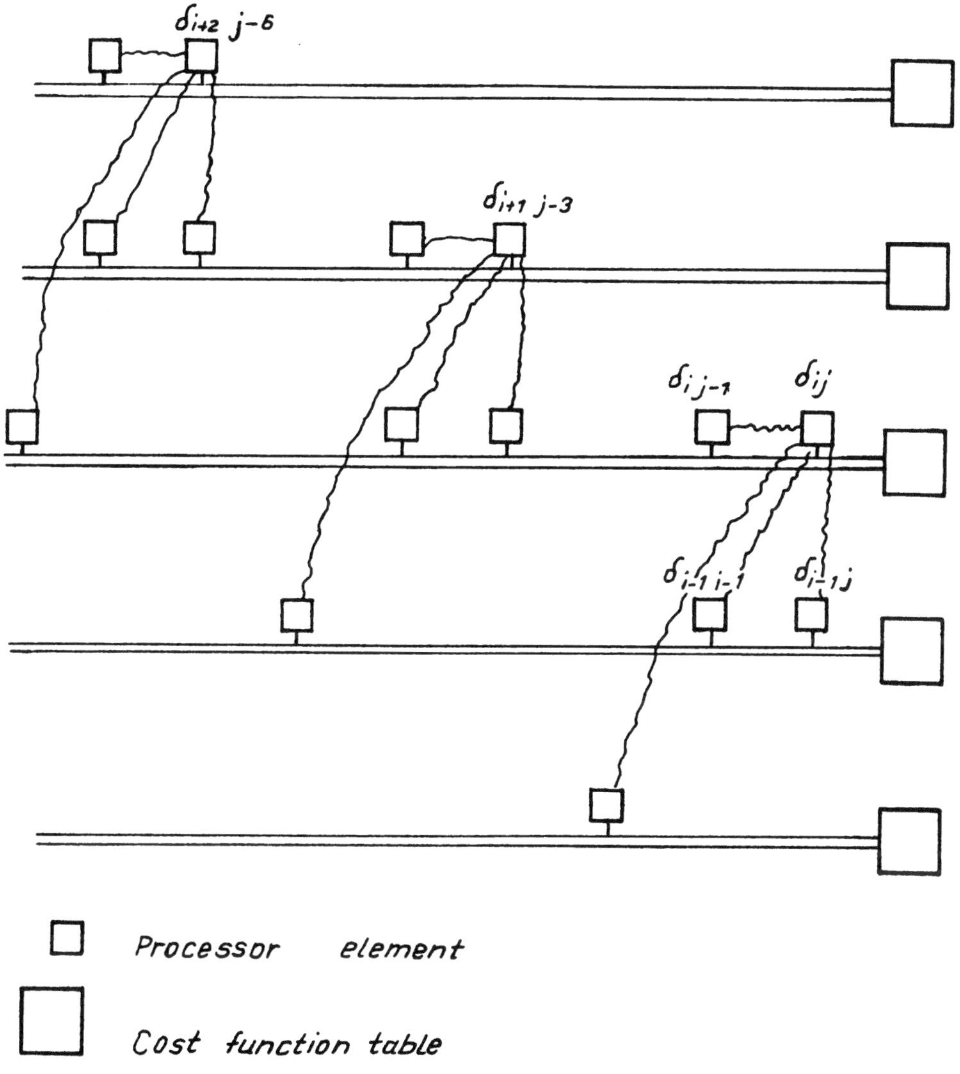

Fig. 6 Access pattern for parallely solving eq. (1)

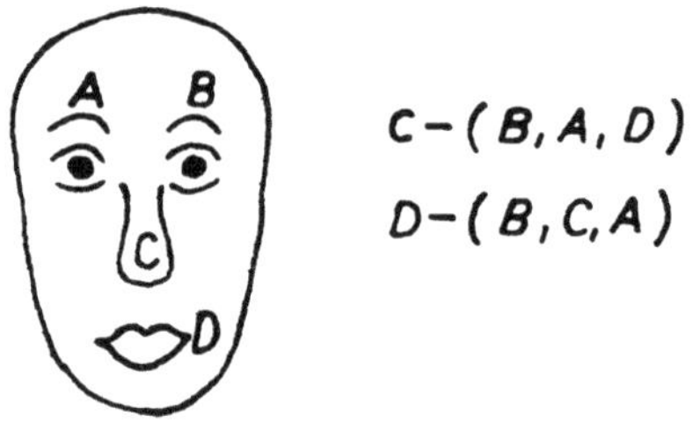

Fig. 5 Circular arrangement of local features around C and D as pivot features

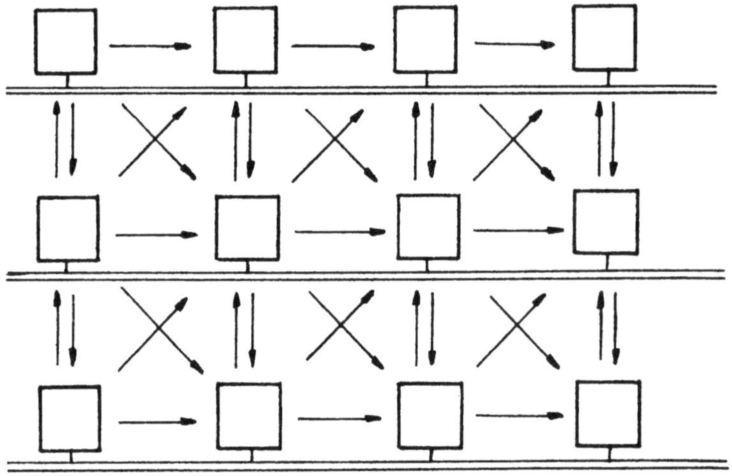

Fig. 7 Signal flow in the processor array

BITEXACT SYMMETRIC SCALING IN RASTERS

H.. Kiesewetter, N. Eichhorn

Academy of Sciences of the GDR
Central Institute
for Cybernetics and Information Processes
GDR 1086 Berlin, Kurstrasse 33

Let us introduce the following operator notation for scaling:

(1) $S(T) \bullet X = T \cdot X$

There is no problem of scaling in continuous spaces. Operator multiplication ● on the left-hand side is simply achieved by real multiplication * on the right-hand side. If an interval of length L with respect to X has to be scaled onto an interval of length K, then we take

(2) $T = K/L$

Scaling in continuous spaces is additive

(3) $S(T) \bullet (X1+X2) = S(T) \bullet X1 + S(T) \bullet X2$

and homogeneous

(4) $T = (F \cdot K)/(F \cdot L) = K/L \qquad (F > 0)$

In raster spaces, however, we have a principal limitation for scaling, because one pixel cannot be divided into parts. As a consequence, arbitrary ratios, general additivity and homogeneity cannot be achieved and therefore, constructing of scaling operators in raster spaces becomes a problem.

We consider 'raster intervals' of the following form:

(5) $0, 1, .. \quad L \quad$ for X

$0, 1, .. \quad K \quad$ for $S(K/L) \bullet X$

$0 \leq K \leq L$

It must be noticed, that a raster interval of length L consists of L+1 discrete pixels.
Scaling in raster spaces is usually based on some embedding and digitization scheme (/1/). The commonly applied scaling operator takes the form

(6) $S(K/L) \bullet X = ENT((K/L) \cdot X + 0.5)$,

where arithmetic operations on the right-hand side are performed as real operations with appropiate accuracy and ENT(R) denotes the integral part of R.
This operator has the following properties:

(7) $S(K/L) \bullet 0 = 0$

(8) $S(K/L) \bullet L = K$

(9) $S(L/L) \bullet X = X$

(10) $S(K/L) \bullet X = S(X/L) \bullet K$

The formula

$$(11) \qquad S(K/L)^{\bullet}(L-X) \;+\; S(K/L)^{\bullet}X \;=\; K$$

representing superposition of scalings, implies a contradiction for even values of L at the 'mid pixel' $X = L/2$, since the relation

$$(11') \qquad 2 * S(K/L)^{\bullet}(L/2) \;=\; K$$

cannot be fulfilled for odd values of K. To avoid this contradiction, we shall restrict lengths L to the values

$$(12) \qquad L(N) \;=\; 2^{**}N - 1 \qquad\qquad N = 1,\ 2,.$$

for the rest of this paper and write simply $L = L(N)$ for fixed values of N.
Condition (12) is important for scaling in rasters.
It provides a 'full raster' X ($0 \leq X \leq L(N)$) of all pixels, admitting a N-placed binary representation, as well as an appropiate class of ratios

$$K/L(N) \quad \text{for } 0 \leq K \leq L(N)$$

Binary representations of X and K will be given by the formulas

$$(13) \qquad X \;=\; \sum_{M=1}^{N} B(M)^{\bullet}X * 2^{**}(M-1)$$

$$(14) \qquad K \;=\; \sum_{I=1}^{N} B(I)^{\bullet}K * 2^{**}(I-1)$$

Here again we apply operator notation, but now with respect to the 'bit functionals' $B(M)^{\bullet}X$ resp. $B(I)^{\bullet}K$.
Taking into account condition (12), identity (11) is valid too for the common scaling operator.
Now let us state two properties, which provide some kind of additivity and homogeneity for scaling in rasters. These properties will be related to a 'double raster'

$$0 \leq X \leq L(N+1)\ ,$$

its left 'subraster'

$$0 \leq X \leq L(N)$$

and its right 'subraster'

$$L(N) + 1 \leq X \leq L(N+1)$$

It must be mentioned, that condition (12) implies the relation

$$(12') \qquad L(N+1) = 2*L(N) + 1$$

Additivity of raster scaling:

$$(15) \qquad S(K/L(N+1))^{\bullet}(L(N)+1+X) =$$

$$S(K/L(N+1))^{\bullet}(L(N)+1) \;+\; S(K/L(N+1))^{\bullet}X$$

Homogeneity of raster scaling:

$$(16) \qquad S(K/L(N))^{\bullet}X = S((2*K)/L(N+1))^{\bullet}X$$

$$= S((2*K+1)/L(N+1))^{\bullet}X$$

Relations (15) and (16) should hold for $0 \leq X \leq L(N)$. The common scaling operator doesn't fulfill neither (15) nor (16). In order to understand the reason for its failure, we analyze its differential behaviour by means of the 'differential operators'

$$(17) \qquad D(K)\bullet X \; = \; S(K/L)\bullet X - S((K-1)/L)\bullet X$$

By summation we get

$$(18) \qquad S(K/L)\bullet X \; = \; \sum_{J=1}^{K} D(J)\bullet X$$

The differential operators represent bit functionals too. Each term of the sum (18) should contribute a constant number of pixels. From (9) and

$$(18') \qquad \sum_{J=1}^{L} D(J)\bullet X \; = \; X$$

we deduce this constant number to be

$$(19) \qquad |D(J)\bullet X| \; = \; (L+1)/2$$

This equation is valid for the common scaling operator as illustrated in table 1 for L = 15. But this table also reveals remarkable deviations from symmetry within each subraster. These deviations don't occur for N = 1,2,3.

	0	1	2	3	4	5	6	7	8	9	A	B	C	D	E	F
B(1) ●X		•		•		•		•		•		•		•		•
B(2) ●X			•	•			•	•			•	•			•	•
B(3) ●X					•	•	•	•					•	•	•	•
B(4) ●X									•	•	•	•	•	•	•	•
	•	•	•	•	•	•	•	•	•	•	•	•	•	•	•	•
D(1) ●X									•	•	•	•	•	•	•	•
D(2) ●X					•	•	•	•					•	•	•	•
D(3) ●X				•					•	•	•	•		•	•	•
D(4) ●X			•				•	•			•	•	•		•	•
D(5) ●X						•			•	•		•	•	•	•	•
D(6) ●X					•			•		•	•		•	•	•	•
D(7) ●X							•		•		•	•	•	•	•	•
D(8) ●X		•		•		•		•		•		•		•		•
D(9) ●X							•		•		•	•	•	•	•	•
D(10)●X					•			•		•	•		•	•	•	•
D(11)●X						•			•	•		•	•	•	•	•
D(12)●X			•				•	•			•	•	•		•	•
D(13)●X				•					•	•	•	•		•	•	•
D(14)●X					•	•	•	•					•	•	•	•
D(15)●X									•	•	•	•	•	•	•	•

Table 1. Differential behaviour of the common scaling operator

In order to construct a scaling operator of high symmetry, we start with the following differential scheme (cf. table 2 for N = 4):

$$(20) \qquad D(2^{**}(M-1)+J^{*}2^{**}M)\bullet X \; = \; B(N+1-M)\bullet X$$

for M = 1,2,.. N and J = 0,1,..

	0	1	2	3	4	5	6	7	8	9	A	B	C	D	E	F
$B(1)\bullet X$		•		•		•		•		•		•		•		•
$B(2)\bullet X$			•	•			•	•			•	•			•	•
$B(3)\bullet X$					•	•	•	•					•	•	•	•
$B(4)\bullet X$									•	•	•	•	•	•	•	•
	•	•	•	•	•	•	•	•	•	•	•	•	•	•	•	•
$D(1)\bullet X$									•	•	•	•	•	•	•	•
$D(2)\bullet X$					•	•	•	•					•	•	•	•
$D(3)\bullet X$									•	•	•	•	•	•	•	•
$D(4)\bullet X$			•	•			•	•			•	•			•	•
$D(5)\bullet X$									•	•	•	•	•	•	•	•
$D(6)\bullet X$					•	•	•	•					•	•	•	•
$D(7)\bullet X$									•	•	•	•	•	•	•	•
$D(8)\bullet X$		•		•		•		•		•		•		•		•
$D(9)\bullet X$									•	•	•	•	•	•	•	•
$D(10)\bullet X$					•	•	•	•					•	•	•	•
$D(11)\bullet X$									•	•	•	•	•	•	•	•
$D(12)\bullet X$			•	•			•	•			•	•			•	•
$D(13)\bullet X$									•	•	•	•	•	•	•	•
$D(14)\bullet X$					•	•	•	•					•	•	•	•
$D(15)\bullet X$									•	•	•	•	•	•	•	•

Table 2. Differential behaviour of the symmetric scaling operator

Adding of differential operators according to (18) results in the following formulas for the symmetric scaling operator:

(21) $P(1)\bullet K = B(N)\bullet K$

$$P(M)\bullet K = B(N+1-M)\bullet K + \sum_{I=1}^{M-1} P(I)\bullet K$$

$M = 2,3,. \quad N$

(22) $$S(K/L)\bullet X = \sum_{M=1}^{N} P(M)\bullet K * B(M)\bullet X$$

This operator fulfills properties (7), (8), (9), (10), (11), (15), (16) and (19).

The 'rest operator' will be defined by

(23) $R(K/L)\bullet X = (K/L)*X - S(K/L)\bullet X$

In the case of symmetric raster scaling we get an explicit formula for the rest operator. It is based on cyclic permutations modulo N of the bit functionals.

(24) $B(I-N) = B(I)$

We define 'variation functionals'

(25) $V(I)\bullet K = B(I-1)\bullet K - B(I)\bullet K$

and 'variation operators'

(26) $$U(M)\bullet K = \sum_{J=1}^{N} V(J+1-M)\bullet K * 2**(J-1)$$

cyclically modulo N. Then we get (cf. appendix):

(27) $$R(K/L)\bullet X = \sum_{M=1}^{N} U(M)\bullet K * B(M)\bullet X$$

Table 3 illustrates the application of the cyclic notation for N = 4.

K	B(4)	B(3)	B(2)	B(1)	V(4)	V(3)	V(2)	V(1)	U(1)	U(2)	U(3)	U(4)
0	0	0	0	0	0	0	0	0	0	0	0	0
1	0	0	0	1	0	0	1	-1	1	2	4	-7
2	0	0	1	0	0	1	-1	0	2	4	-7	1
3	0	0	1	1	0	1	0	-1	3	6	-3	-6
4	0	1	0	0	1	-1	0	0	4	-7	1	2
5	0	1	0	1	1	-1	1	-1	5	-5	5	-5
6	0	1	1	0	1	0	-1	0	6	-3	-6	3
7	0	1	1	1	1	0	0	-1	7	-1	-2	-4
8	1	0	0	0	-1	0	0	1	-7	1	2	4
9	1	0	0	1	-1	0	1	0	-6	3	6	-3
10	1	0	1	0	-1	1	-1	1	-5	5	-5	5
11	1	0	1	1	-1	1	0	0	-4	7	-1	-2
12	1	1	0	0	0	-1	0	1	-3	-6	3	6
13	1	1	0	1	0	-1	1	0	-2	-4	7	-1
14	1	1	1	0	0	0	-1	1	-1	-2	-4	7
15	1	1	1	1	0	0	0	0	0	0	0	0

Table 3. Variation cycles for the rest operator

There are five variation cycles, represented by

V(4)	V(3)	V(2)	V(1)	U(1)	U(2)	U(3)	U(4)
0	0	0	0	0	0	0	0
0	0	1	-1	1	2	4	-7
0	1	0	-1	3	6	-3	-6
1	-1	1	-1	5	-5	5	-5
1	0	0	-1	7	-1	-2	-4

and producing the rest operators

$$R(0/15)^{\bullet}X = 0$$

$$R(1/15)^{\bullet}X = 1/15*(1*B(1)+2*B(2)+4*B(3)-7*B(4))^{\bullet}X$$

$$R(3/15)^{\bullet}X = 1/15*(3*B(1)+6*B(2)-3*B(3)-6*B(4))^{\bullet}X$$

$$R(5/15)^{\bullet}X = 1/15*(5*B(1)-5*B(2)+5*B(3)-5*B(4))^{\bullet}X$$

$$R(7/15)^{\bullet}X = 1/15*(7*B(1)-1*B(2)-2*B(3)-4*B(4))^{\bullet}X$$

The following properties of the rest operator $R(K/L)^{\bullet}X$ can be deduced from the corresponding properties of the scaling operator $S(K/L)^{\bullet}X$ and of $(K/L)*X$ for $0 \le X \le L(N)$ and $0 \le K \le L(N)$:

(28) $R(K/L)^{\bullet}0 = 0$

(29) $R(K/L)^{\bullet}L = 0$

(30) $R(L/L)^{\bullet}X = 0$

(31) $R(K/L)^{\bullet}(L-X) + R(K/L)^{\bullet}X = 0$

(32) $$R(K/L(N+1))\bullet(L(N)+1+X) =$$

$$R(K/L(N+1))\bullet(L(N)+1) + R(K/L(N+1))\bullet X$$

(33) $$R((2*K)/L(N+1))\bullet X =$$

$$R(K/L(N))\bullet X - (K/L(N+1)) * (X/L(N))$$

(34) $$R((2*K+1)/L(N+1))\bullet X =$$

$$R(K/L(N))\bullet X + X/L(N+1) - (K/L(N+1)) * (X/L(N))$$

Let

(35) $$AR(K/L) = \max_{0 \le X \le L} |R(K/L)\bullet X|$$

be the maximum absolute rest value with respect to X and

(36) $$AD(L) = \max_{\substack{0 \le X \le L \\ 0 \le K \le L}} |R(K/L)\bullet X|$$

the maximum absolute deviation with respect to X and K.
For L and K fixed the rest operator takes its maximum absolute value, if

(37) $$B(M)\bullet X = 1 \quad \text{for } U(M)\bullet K > 0$$
resp. $$B(M)\bullet X = 0 \quad \text{for } U(M)\bullet K \le 0$$

Because of (26') this is true for

(38) $$X(K/L) = \sum_{M=1}^{N} B(N+1-M)\bullet(L-K) * 2**(M-1)$$

and proves the relation

(39) $$AR(K/L) = \left(\sum_{M=1}^{N} |U(M)\bullet K| \right)/2$$

The worst variation cycles are

(40) | | | |
|---|---|---|
| | 1 -1 1 -1 ... 1 -1 | for even N |
| resp. | 0 1 -1 1 -1 ... 1 -1 | for odd N |

That means maximum absolute deviation is assumed at

(41) $$K = L(N)/3 \quad \text{for even } N$$
resp. $$K = (L(N)-1)/6 \quad \text{for odd } N$$

and takes the values

(42) $$AD(L(N)) = N/6 \quad \text{for even } N$$
resp. $$AD(L(N)) = N/6 - (1+2/L(N))/18 \quad \text{for odd } N$$

Let us denote the maximum relative deviation by

(43) $$RD(L) = \max_{\substack{0 \le X \le L \\ 0 \le K \le L}} |(K/L)*X - S(K/L)\bullet X| /L$$

Taking into account

(12") $$N = ld(1+L)$$ (dual logarithm)

we deduce for symmetric raster scaling from (42)

$$(44) \qquad RD(L) \leq ld(1+L)/(6 \cdot L)$$

The corresponding formula for common raster scaling is simply

$$(45) \qquad RD(L) \leq 1/(2 \cdot L)$$

This is by definition the best possible digitization scheme for $(K/L) \cdot X$.
Symmetric raster scaling can only be achieved with increasing deviation.

Summary:

Analyzing the differential behaviour a symmetric scaling operator has been derived. It is operating on full rasters of length $2^{N}-1$ and fulfills special rules of additivity and homogeneity. Deviations from continuous scaling are calculated by means of cycles of variation operators. Explicit formulas are given for the rest operator, the maximum deviation and the scaling at which it is assumed. The result promisses to give interesting ideas for the solution of some geometric problems of raster spaces, such as linear and bilinear interpolation, rotation and zooming.

Literature:

/1/ T.A. Anderson , C.E. Kim :
Representation of digital line segments and their preimages
Computer Vision, Graphics, and Image Processing 30, 279-288 (1985)

Appendix: Proof of the rest operator formula (26)

Rearranging the double sum for $K \cdot X$ according to (13) and (14) we get

$$
\begin{aligned}
K \cdot X = \; & \sum_{J=1}^{N-1} 2^{(J-1)} \cdot \sum_{M=1}^{J} B(J+1-M) \bullet K \cdot B(M) \bullet X \\
+ \; & 2^{(N-1)} \cdot \sum_{M=1}^{N} B(N+1-M) \bullet K \cdot B(M) \bullet X \\
+ \; 2^{N} \cdot & \sum_{J=1}^{N-1} 2^{(J-1)} \cdot \sum_{M=J+1}^{N} B(N+J+1-M) \bullet K \cdot B(M) \bullet X
\end{aligned}
$$

This is just the well-known shifting rule for multiplication.
Adding and subtracting the term

$$\sum_{J=1}^{N-1} 2^{(J-1)} \cdot \sum_{M=J+1}^{N} B(N+J+1-M) \bullet K \cdot B(M) \bullet X$$

and applying the cyclic notation (24) we arrive at the formula

$$
\begin{aligned}
K \cdot X = \; & L \cdot \sum_{J=1}^{N-1} 2^{(J-1)} \cdot \sum_{M=J+1}^{N} B(N+J+1-M) \bullet K \cdot B(M) \bullet X \\
+ \; & \sum_{J=1}^{N} 2^{(J-1)} \cdot \sum_{M=1}^{N} B(J+1-M) \bullet K \cdot B(M) \bullet X
\end{aligned}
$$

Now we change the order of summation in both terms.

$$K^{*}X = L^{*}\sum_{M=2}^{N}\left(\sum_{J=2}^{M} B(N+J-M)^{\bullet}K * 2^{**}(J-2)\right) * B(M)^{\bullet}X + \sum_{M=1}^{N}\left(\sum_{J=1}^{N} B(J+1-M)^{\bullet}K * 2^{**}(J-1)\right) * B(M)^{\bullet}X$$

The second term shows already the cyclic operators

(46) $$Q(M)^{\bullet}K = \sum_{J=1}^{N} B(J+1-M)^{\bullet}K * 2^{**}(J-1)$$

fulfilling the identity

(47) $$2 * Q(M)^{\bullet}K = L * B(N+1-M)^{\bullet}K + Q(M+1)^{\bullet}K$$

Introducing this leads to the final result, since the operators $P(M)^{\bullet}K$ may equally be defined by the formula

(21') $$P(M)^{\bullet}K = B(N+1-M)^{\bullet}K + \sum_{J=2}^{M} B(N+J-M)^{\bullet}K * 2^{**}(J-2)$$

and the variation operators $U(M)^{\bullet}K$ by

(26') $$U(M)^{\bullet}K = Q(M+1)^{\bullet}K - Q(M)^{\bullet}K = Q(M)^{\bullet}K - L * B(N+1-M)^{\bullet}K$$

MMS 16-A MULTI-MICROPROCESSOR SYSTEM OF THE GDR

Georg Kinnemann

Central Institute of Cybernetics and Information Processes
GDR - 1086 Berlin, Kurstraße 33

Introduction

The MMS 16 is a module system on the base of 16-bit microprocessors. It has been developed by a team of several companies including Academy of Sciences of the GDR. The system is intended

- for personal computers
- for industrial control systems and
- as OEM product

and includes moduls with U 8001 CPU, with K 1810 WM 86 CPU and an assortment of memory and I/O boards.

The base of the Multi-Microprocessor System is the Microprocessor System Bus I (8-bit and 16-bit data) of IEC Sub-Committee 47 B (Special implementation of Multibus I). Up to 16 processors are able to operate on this parallel line bus. Parallel and serial arbitration are possible.

Multi-Microprocessor System MMS 16

/1/ offers an overview of MMS 16 moduls. The system includes two processor boards comprising K 1810 WM 86 CPU developed and produced by U.S.S.R. This CPU contains four 16-bit general purpose registers, two 16-bit pointer registers, two 16-bit index registers and four 16-bit segment registers allowing extended addressing to a memory space up to 1 Mbyte. The processor boards are composed of CPU, interrupt controller, interval timer, communication interface, 16 KByte EPROM, 4 KByte RAM and bus interface circuitry.

The third processor board includes U 8001 CPU developed and produced by the GDR. This CPU is compatible to Zilog's Z8001 /2/. In addition to the components of K 1810 WM 86 processor board the U 8001 CPU board comprises powerful U 8010 memory managment unit for addressing to a memory space up to 16 Mbyte.

Fig. 1 presents the general system architecture of the Multi-Microprocessor System MMS16. All processor boards are linked by the parallel system bus. For communication between several processors via the system bus common accessible memories are necessary. Global memories and dual-port memories are available in MMS16. The advantage of dual-port memory is that the bus load is decreased because transmission of one message needs only one access to the system bus.

Exchange of messages is provided by interprocessor communication software (ICS) /3/ running under BOS 1810 realtime operating system

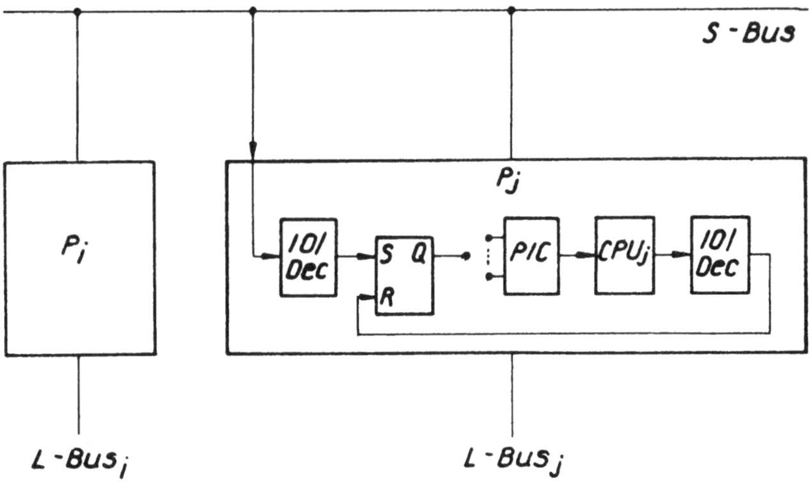

Fig. 3: I/O-mapped interrupt between processors

munication Software (ICS) are implemented only for K 1810 WM 86 based processor boards.

Workplace Computer robotron A 7100 /1/

First application of Multi-Microprocessor System MMS16 is A 7100 Workplace Computer developed and produced by robotron company. Scheme of this computer is shown in Fig. 4. It includes following moduls:

- processor board comprising K 1810 WM 86 CPU
- 128 Kbyte dual-port memory
- 512 Kbyte dynamic RAM
- monochrome display for 80x25 characters or 640x400 pixels graphic resolution
- 2x500 KByte mini floppy disk unit
- optional SCP 1700 operating system (compatible with CP/M 86) or BOS 1810 operating system (compatible with RMx86)

Robot Control system

First application of MMS16 in our institute will be a robot control system. Today this system illustrated in the upper part of Fig. 5 is under development. The core of this robot control system consists of processor boards comprising K 1810 WM 86 CPU. Robot programming and control system is based on realtime operating system BOS 1810 and interprocessor communication software ICS. Furthermore robot control system includes a number of joint control processors JCP /4/. One JCP is intended for control of one robot joint and comprises following function elements:

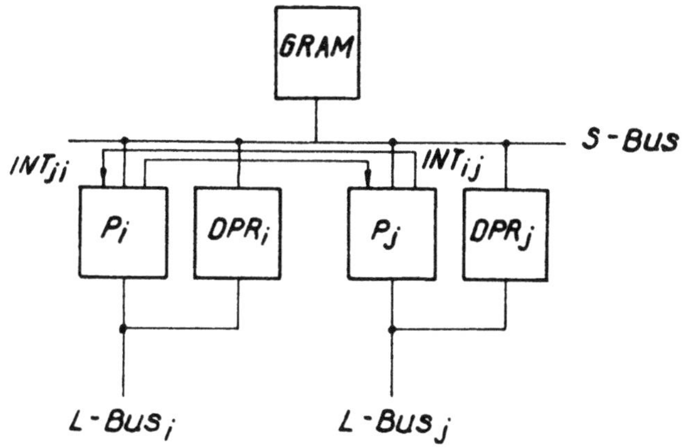

Fig. 1: General system architecture of MMS 16

(compatible to RMX 86). Two one-directional channels between each pair of processors support transmission of messages from transmitting processor to receiving processor. Internally messages are queued into static FIFO-ring buffer. That means that there are two special situations: full and empty buffers. These special situations are signalled by means of interrupts via system bus.

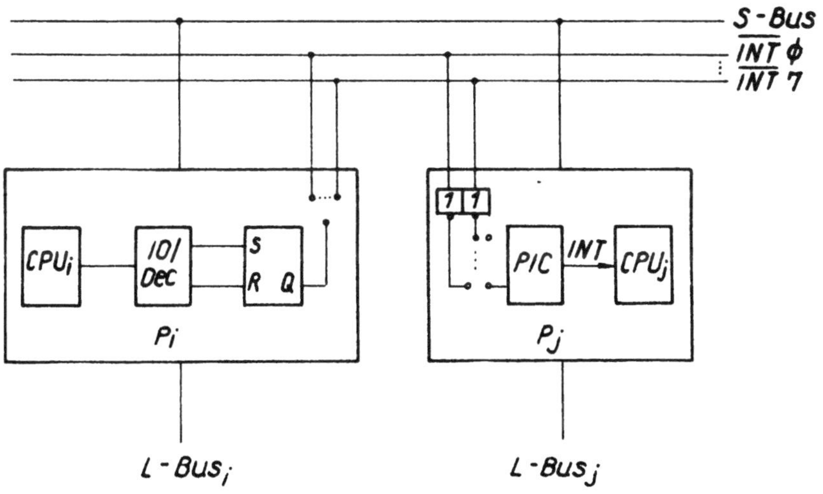

Fig. 2: Flag interrupt between processors

Fig. 2 and 3 present two possibilities for sending interrupts from one processor to another: flag interrupt and I/O-mapped interrupt. For implementation of multi-microprocessor systems consisting of many processors the use of I/O-mapped interrupt is better because no interrupt lines are occupied. The BOS 1810 operating system and Interprocessor Com-

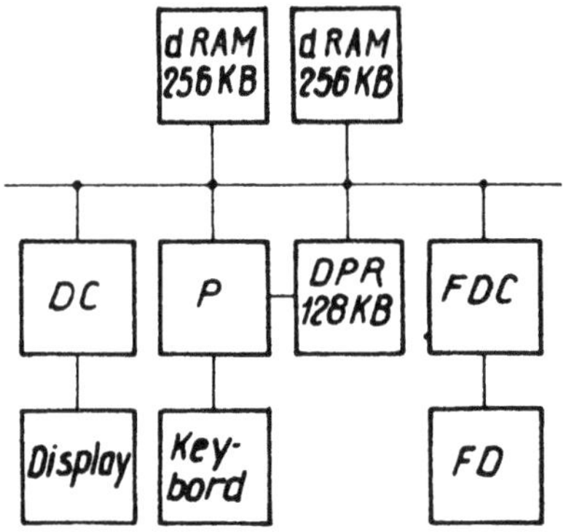

Fig. 4: Scheme of A 7100 Workplace Computer

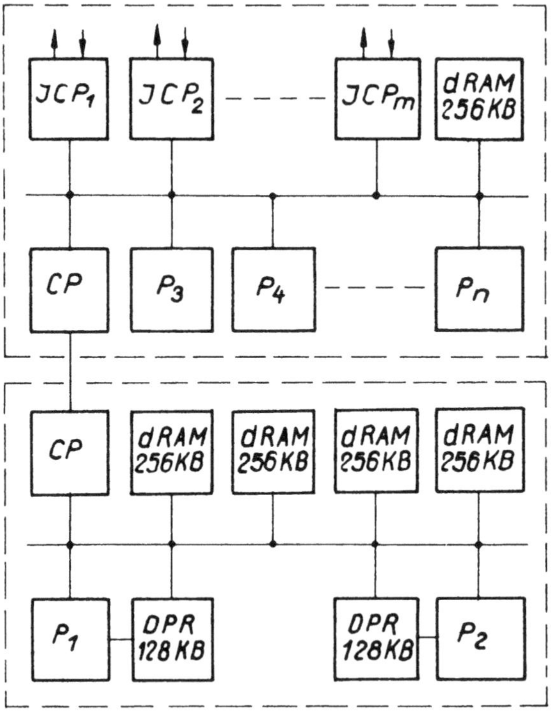

Fig. 5: Robot control system and LISP workplace computer

- U 881 single-chip microcomputer including central processing unit with a powerful instruction set, 124 general-purpose registers, 16 control registers and 4 I/O port registers
- 2 KByte dual-port RAM for communication between K 1810 WM 86 processor boards and single-chip microcomputer
- control circuitry for connecting with robot

LISP workplace computer

Second application of MMS16 in our institute will be a workplace computer intended for artificial intelligence applications. The scheme of this computer is shown in the lower part of Fig. 5. The system includes two processor boards comprising U 8001 CPU. The first processor board is intended for communication to a personal computer including display, keybord and floppy disk as well as for garbage collection. The second processor board is used for implementation of a LISP interpreter. Cell memory of LISP system has a memory space of 1MByte and is provided by means of four dynamic memory moduls. For communication between LISP workplace computer and robot control system a special communication processor CP is under development now.

Conclusion

The paper shows that MMS16 is a powerful 16-bit multi-microprocessor system including several CPU systems. Implementations of easy single-processor systems (such as workplace computers) up to powerful multi-microprocessor systems (such as industrial control systems and LISP workplace computers) are possible.

References

/1/ Junge, Keller; Das Mikrorechnermodulsystem 16 und sein Einsatz im Arbeitsplatzcomputer robotron A 7100; Neue Technik im Büro, 29 (1985) 3, p. 81-87

/2/ Meinecke; 16-bit-Mikroprozessor U 8000, radio fernsehen elektronik 34 (1985) 11 und 12, p. 687-691 and 760-763

/3/ Despang, Vack, Petrov, Djambazov; Multiprocessor Hardware and Operating System for Process Control Applications, Proceedings of the III. Bilateral Meeting GDR-Italy, Berlin, 1985 February 19th-21st, p. 294-302

/4/ Mädiger, Jaap, Positioniermodul mit U 881 für Industrieroboter; Proceedings of 8. Wissenschaftlich-technische Konferenz "Elektronische Automatisierungssysteme" 19.-20. Dezember 1985 in Berlin, p. 32-34

DECENTRALIZED DIAGNOSIS IN REGULAR STRUCTURED MULTIPROCESSOR SYSTEMS

Andreas Stopp
Central Institute of Cybernetics and Information Processes
Berlin, GDR

1. Introduction

Fault tolerance in order to achieve reliability and availability in regulary structured multiprocessor systems bases on structural redundancy which allows dynamic redundancy. The components of dynamic redundancy are:

- system level diagnosis
- reconfiguration

The system level diagnosis consists of two parts:

- self-diagnosis of each node
- neighbourhood diagnosis

The diagnosis algorithm depends on network structure, fault assumption and intended diagnosability.

Decentralized structures need decentralized diagnosis,central observers for diagnosis are unreliable.

A configuration is described by a graph G with a set of nodes V (processor nodes) and a set of edges E (links). A bus may be represented by a set of links.

Faulty elements may be both nodes as well as edges.

2. Regular structured multiprocessor systems for large networks

These decentralized structures differ by

- communication by buses or links
- the law of network structures and their parameters and restrictions
- width (w) (number of nodes per bus)
- dimension (D)
- number of nodes (N)
- number of links or buses

Examples of connection structures for large systems are listed in table 1. Some structures have been briefly described in /2/.

The following additional facts are interesting for local decentralized diagnosis:

- number of ports per node
- number of direct neighbours of a node

Name	Number of nodes	Number of links (L) or buses (B)	Number of ports per node	Number of direct neighbours
Near-Neighbour-Mesh (NNM)	$N=W^D$	$L=DxN$	2D	2D
Binary-n-Cube (BnC)	$N=2^D$	$L=DxN/2$	D	D
Cube-Connected-Cycle (CCC)	$N=Dx2^D$	$L=3xDx2^{D-1}$	3	3
Spanning-Bus-Hypercube (SBH)	$N=W^D$	$B=W^{D-1}xD$	D	D (W-1)
Dual-Bus-Hypercube (DBH)	$N=W^D$	$B=W^{D-1}x2$	2	2 (W-1)

Table 1: Examples of connection structures for large networks

3. Local decentralized diagnosis in large systems

Global decentralized diagnosis in large systems leads to an increasing overhead. In order to reduce the diagnosis overhead principles of local decentralized diagnosis and global fault registration are suggested. Therefore it is proposed to describe the configuration by a law and a fault list for each node. We consider the relations of configurations (see fig. 1).

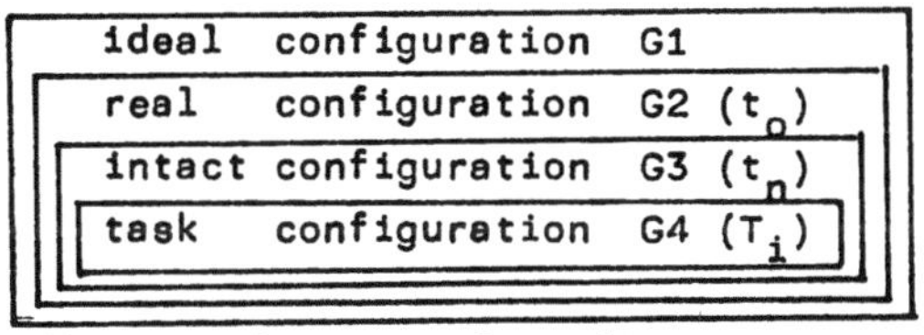

Fig. 1: Relations of configurations

- The ideal configuration G1 is the intended complete configuration described by the law of the structure.
- The real configuration G2(t_o) is the initial noncomplete configuration. The missing elements are non-existent or faulty after production and are treated like normal faults although no recovery is possible. The difference of elements has to be small. G2 is described by the law of G1 and the list of "faulty" elements at the time to.
- The intact configuration G3 (t_n) is described by the law of G1 and the list of faulty elements at the time t_n.
- The task configuration G4 (T_i) is the requested configuration in order to realize the task T_i.

The relation of the described configurations is:

$$G1 \supset G2 \supset G3 \supset G4$$

The diagnosis has to locate all faulty elements and to determine G3. The reconfiguration has to place G4 in G3.

4. Self-diagnosis of a node

The node consists of the communication processor, the task processor(s) and the private and common resources of both.

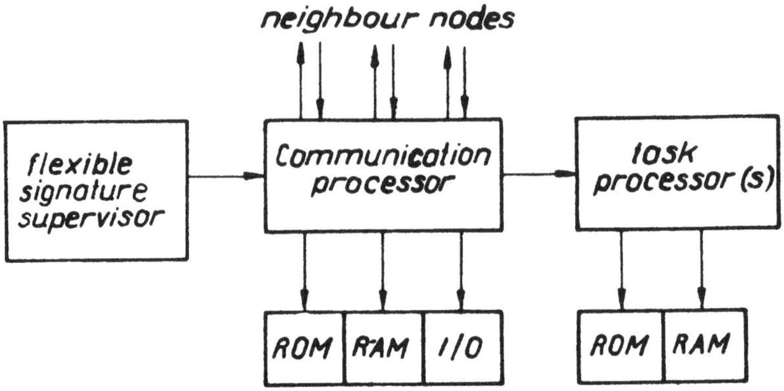

Fig.2: Test-scheme of a node

The communication processor is responsible for receiving, relaying and sending messages and it leads the diagnosis (self-diagnosis inside and neighbourhood diagnosis outside the node).

The assumption for the diagnosis is, that a faulty node will be switched off the system. It doesn't send messages, this will be realized by self-test supported by the flexible signature supervisor (FSS).

The result of the selfdiagnosis is:

$s_j=0$ v_j is defect ⟶ v_j switches off
$=1$ v_j is intact

It is desirable to improve the reliability and to speed up the switching off the faulty node by all available or additional checking mechanisms (i.e. selfchecking checkers, supervisor circuits, built-in test-techniques, ECC's, SEC-DEC-circuits etc.). Strong demands simplify the system level diagnosis.

5. Neighbourhood diagnosis

Neighbourhood diagnosis consists of cyclic testphase and event-dependent diagnosis phase.

5.1 Testphase

Each intact node v_i sends its testresults s_i to all direct neighbours v_j after the cyclic self-diagnosis of each node.

Each intact node v_i receives the testresults s_j of each intact direct neighbour v_j and fills in the testvector $S(i, t_n)$ at that time t_n.

$s_j=1$ if v_j is intact — was announced by v_j
$=0$ if v_j is defect — is assumed by v_i after testtime-intervall (may be supported by status or interrupt)

It is suitable for structures with buses to use a DxW testmatrix $S(i,t_n)$.

If the testvector is complete or the testtime is over, then the comparison of the present testvector $S(i, t_n)$ of v_i with the last testvector $S(i, t_{n-1})$ of v_i follows.
If $S(i, t_n) = S(i, t_{n-1})$ then
the testphase is finished in node v_i at the time t_n.

If both vectors differ the diagnoses phase will be started independent of the reason being a fault event or a fault removal.
If transient faults should be treated, the testvector $S(i, t_{n-2})$ must be included in the comparison.

5.2 Diagnosisphase

The diagnosis starts after detection of state alteration of the testvector. The diagnosis has to detect and to locate reliably the fault events or fault removals. The effort depends on the desired reliability and diagnosability.

- Analysis of the testvector
  All fault events or fault removals of the direct neighbourhood may be detected by testvector analysis in each intact node v_i to be faulty, suspect or repaired with uncertainty by only one node.
- Confirmation and localization of detected events
  . A link may be analyzed by both its intact nodes
  . A bus may be analyzed by all its intact nodes
  . A node may be analyzed by all its intact direct neighbournodes

  If a bus or a link is suspect the observer node can communicate with the other intact node(s) on alternative paths to confirm the suspect event.

  If a node is suspect the observernode can communicate with all direct intact neighbours of the suspect node on alternative paths to comfirm the suspect event.

  Some different ways of diagnosis are proposed:

  - fault-event-independent algorithm
    . Diagnosis by local fault-induced adjacency matrices
  - fault-event-dependent algorithm
    . Diagnosis by fault-dependent routing
    . Diagnosis by directed local broadcasting

6. Diagnosis by local fault-induced adjacency matrices

A global adjacency matrix is used in /1/ for smaller systems with global view of each node. Here is proposed diagnosis by local adjacency matrices. A local diagnosis graph G5 (v_i) described by its local adjacency matrix $A(v_i)$ exists for each node. The local graph comprises preferably all direct neighbours and all edges to the neighbour nodes and at least one closed path from node v_i to node v_i for each edge of v_i.

The local fault induced adjacency matrix originates from the local limited transmission of the testvectors of each node.

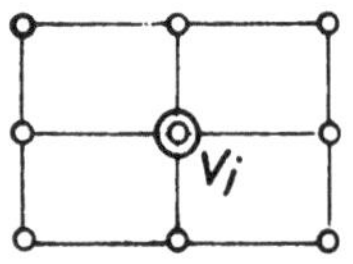

Fig. 3: Example for a local diagnosis graph of v_i (NNM, D=2)

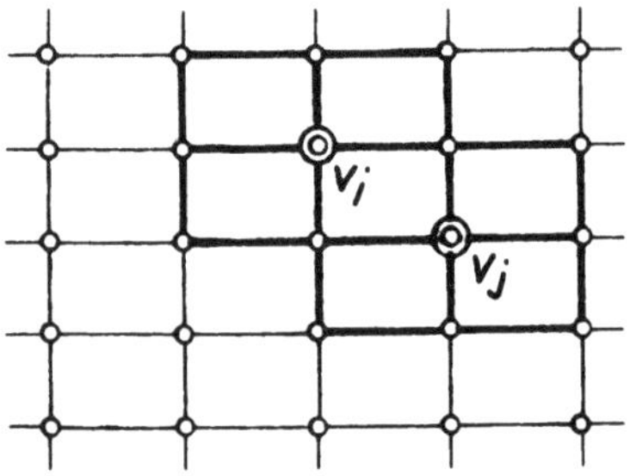

Fig. 4: Example of two local diagnosis graphs of v_i and v_j in a larger structure (NNM, D=2)

Each node posesses an own individual local adjacency matrix therefore the node v_i has to choose the common elements of the testvectors received from the intact adjacent neighbours in order to complete the matrix (directly from direct neighbours or indirectly from indirect neighbours via other indirect and direct neighbours).

When the local fault-induced adjacency matrix of v_i is complete, v_i analyses the matrix and determinates the faulty elements.

This algorithm is especially suitable for structures with links.

7. Diagnosis by fault-dependent routing

A minimal diagnosis graph represents a path that realizes communication to an alternative intact node on a shortest alternative way.

A minimal dynamic diagnosis graph represents a path that realizes communication to an alternative intact node and which varies according to the local fault state. It is a minimal, an alternative minimal (i.e. permutation of the dimension sequence) or a longer alternative path which is determined by analysing the fault state of the concerned nodes and edges.

8. Diagnosis by directed local broadcast

The directed local broadcast is especially proposed for structures with buses.

Directed local broadcast is stepwise, complete or partial bus broadcast started by the observernode via a set of chosen buses in order to speed up the parallel message routing to the set of destination nodes and in order to limit the diagnosis in space.

The set of destination nodes is the set of neighbour nodes of the suspect node (see fig 5) or suspect edge (see fig 6). These relations are known by the law of the structure. The local broadcast algorithm differs for suspect nodes and edges and is determined by the law of the structure, the address of the observernode and the address of the suspect object.

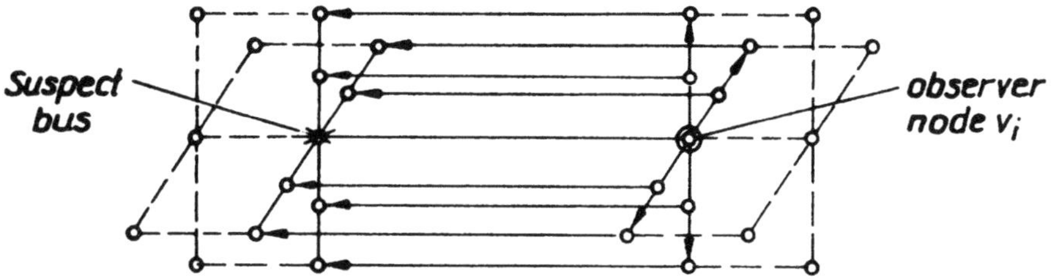

Fig.5: Example for directed local broadcast concerning a suspect node (SBH; D=3)

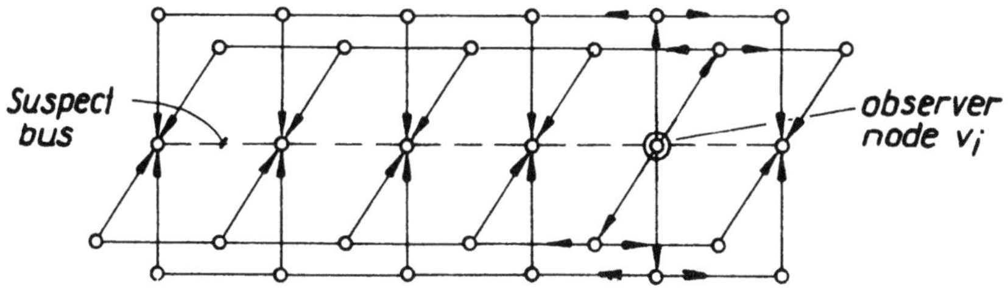

Fig.6: Example for directed local broadcast concerning a suspect bus (SBH; D=3)

The diagnosis is a dynamic decentralized process. This means, that an unknown set of direct neighbours of the suspect object (dynamic set of observernodes) start the diagnosis independently and asynchronously.

The first node of the local broadcast space receiving the required number of independent equal messages starts the global fault registration.

9. Global fault registration

The first node which has diagnosed the event starts the global registration by global broadcast to all nodes of the system and breaks off the diagnosis of this event.

After broadcast request each node checks whether the event is already known (limitation of broadcast). Each node adds the broadcasted fault events and deletes the broadcasted fault removals in its fault list.

The fault lists of all intact nodes have to be equal. The consistency may be checked by neighbourhood test.

Summary

Decentralized multimicroprocessor systems require decentralized diagnosis.

In this paper principles for decentralized diagnosis in large systems with regular structure are proposed. The system level diagnosis consists of local decentralized diagnosis and global fault registration.

Each node knows the law of the regular structure and the fault list.

The aim is to speed up the diagnosis by dynamic decentralized principles with sufficient diagnosability and thereby to diminish the diagnosis overhead.

The local decentralized diagnosis consists of selfdiagnosis and neighbourhood diagnosis.

The assumption for selfdiagnosis is, that a faulty node will be switched off the system. This is supported by a hardware redundancy unit in each node, called flexible signature supervisor.

The neighbourhood diagnosis is an addition of cyclic test and event diagnosis. Different principles of diagnosis

- by local fault-induced adjacency matrices
- by fault-dependent routing
- by directed local broadcast

are shown.

The global fault registration is realized by global broadcast.

References

/1/ Maehle, E.: Fehlertolerantes Verhalten in Multiprozessoren - Untersuchungen zur Diagnose und Rekonfiguration
Diss. Erlangen 1982

/2/ Wittie, L.D.: Communication Structures for Large Networks of Microcomputers
IEEE Trans. on Computers 4/81 S. 264-273

/3/ Lala, P.K.: Fault-Tolerant and Fault-Testable Hardware Design
Prentice-Hall London 1985

STRUCTURE AND APPLICATION OF A PERMUTATION NETWORK

F. Wächter[1)]

1. Parallel memory with permutation network

The development of special processors for digital signal processing with an architecture adapted to the favoured algorithms also demands special memories. To get fast signal processing these memories have to be organized in parallel together with a special permutation network. Fig. 1 shows the structure of such a memory whose conception was developed in the ZKI /1/. It consists of N memory moduls M_i, N address processors A_i to compute the addresses of the accesses to the memory moduls and a permutation network PNW which adapts the turn of the dates fetched from the memory moduls to the format of access (window), wherein N is a prime number.

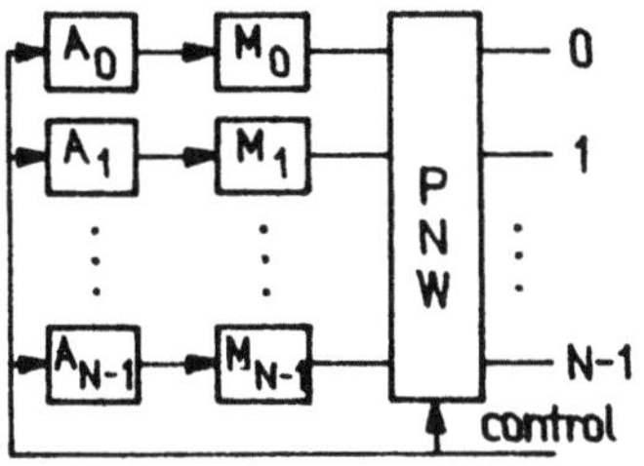

Fig.1 structure of a parallel memory

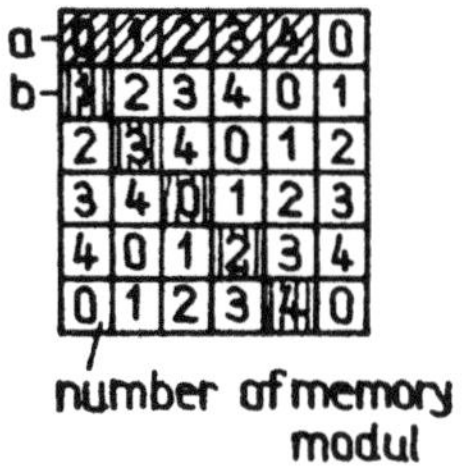

Fig.2 linear windows of access, N=5

2. Applications of the parallel memory

In the memory the access with connected and unconnected linear windows is possible. Fig.2 shows two of such windows for N=5. Linear windows are used to solve problems of image processing /1/, of matrix operations /2/ and of parts of speech recognition /3/. Fig.3 gives an example for the accesses to the elements of a matrix at a matrix-vector multiplication in a systolic array.

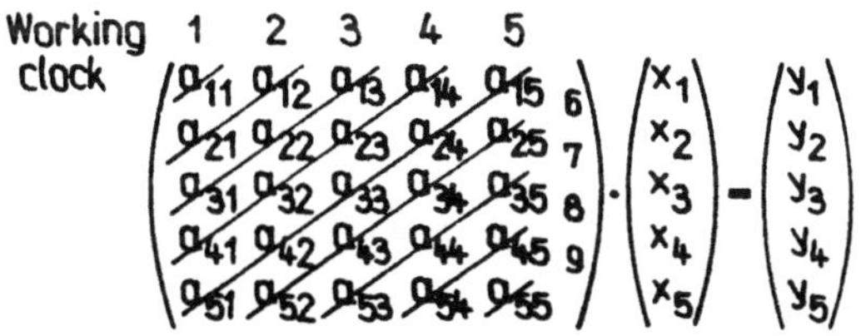

Fig.3 accesses to matrix elements for multiplication in a systolic array

1) AdW der DDR, Zentralinstitut für Kybernetik und Informationsprozesse, IT Dresden, 8027 Dresden, Zeunerstr. 36

The permutation needed for the access with linear windows can be described with

$$P(S,F) = \begin{pmatrix} S & S+F & S+2F & \dots & S+(N-1)F \\ 0 & 1 & 2 & & N-1 \end{pmatrix} \tag{1}$$

wherein S is the number of the memory modul in which the first element of the window is stored, F is the distance of the elements of the window. The operation in (1) have to be done modulo N. This permutation controlled by S and F changes the turn of the dates fetched from the memory moduls so, that the dates of the i-th element of the window appear at the i-th output line of the PNW. The parameters of the windows in fig.2 are a) S=0, F=1 and b) S=1, F=2.

Further using a memory like fig.1 the parallel access to the nodes of parts of trees is possible /4/. In /4/ the numbers of the sons of a node x are $x + M^k \cdot i$, $i=1,\dots,M$. The dates of node x are stored in memory module $M_{x \bmod N}$. The first element of the window is the node x_0. The permutation needed has the same form as (1). The parameters are $S=x_0 \bmod N$, $F=M^k \bmod N$, wherein k is $\log_M x_0$ rounded off to the nearest integer. Fig.4 shows such a tree with M=2 and two accesses for N=5 with $x_0=0$ and $x_0=1$.

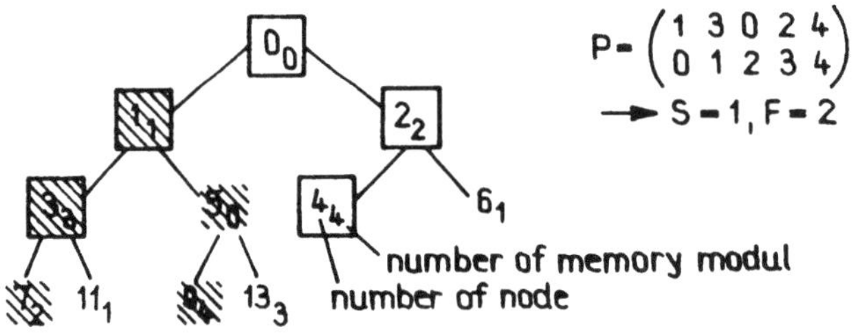

Fig.4 accesses to parts of a tree, a) $x_0=0$:□ , b) $x_0=1$: ▨
and permutation for b)

3. Structure of the permutation network

A PNW to realize the permutation P can be structured in levels of single switches /1,5/. The control signals of the levels are c_i, c_j' of the decompositions

$$(-S) \bmod N = \sum_{i=0}^{n-1} c_i 2^i, \quad (F^{-1}) \bmod N = \prod_{j=0}^{m-1} r^{2^j \cdot c_j'} \bmod N, \quad c_i, c_j' \in \{0,1\} \tag{2}$$

wherein r is a primitive root of N, $n=\lceil \mathrm{ld} N \rceil$, $m=\lceil \mathrm{ld}(N-1) \rceil$ with $\lceil \mathrm{ld} x \rceil$ is equal $\log_2 x$ rounded up to the nearest integer. Fig.5 shows an example of such a PNW with N=5 and a switch control for the parameters S=1, F=2, wherein r=3 is used.

For great values of N such PNWs need a high wiring amount. The wiring can be optimized by using algorithms of placement and routing and by using special switches /6/. There is a further possibility to optimize the wiring founded on a decomposition in the form of

$$(-S) \bmod N = \sum_{i=0}^{n-1} c_i a_i \bmod N \,, \quad (F^{-1}) \bmod N = \prod_{j=0}^{m-1} p_j^{c'_j} \bmod N \,. \tag{3}$$

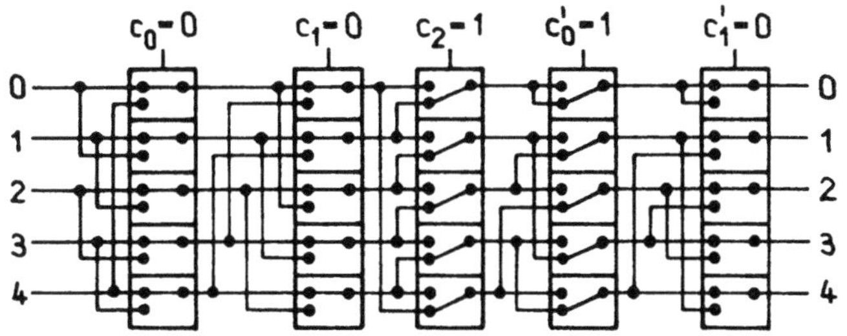

Fig.5 PNW for N=5 with control for S=1, F=2

The base elements a_i, p_j are chosen so, that with (3) all values up to N-1 can be generated. In (2) is $a_i=2^i$ and $p_j=r^{2^j} \bmod N$. By selecting bases (a_i), (p_j) the wiring can be optimized.
Computations of bases show, that there can be bases with paires of equal elements,for instance $(a_i)=(1,2,4,4)$ for N=11. In this case the wiring amount can be decreased if the levels with the elements of a pair are placed neighbouring and both levels have the same placement of switches. A further criterion of the selection of the base (p_j) is the order of the elements in the multiplicative group R of residual classes modulo N. Comparing the properties of cyclic finite groups and the description of a permutation as a product of disjoint cycles it can be shown that at a determined turn of the elements of the subgroup generated by the element p_i and its cosets in R are equal the cycles of the permutation $P' : x \rightarrow x \cdot p_j \bmod N$. If the order of p_j is m_j, the permutation P' has $(N-1)/m_j$ cycles with m_j elements. For instance with N=13, $p_j=3$, $m_j=3$ P' has the cycles (1,3,9), (2,6,5),(4,12,10), (8, 11,7). If the switches of a cycle will be placed neighbouring, a wiring with maximum m_j tracks and short wiring length is possible in the level with the element p_j. That means, base elements with a low order in R allow a good wiring. By neighbouring placement of levels with elements p_i, p_j with $m_i=k \cdot m_j$ a placement of switches is possible with maximum tracks for both levels of m_i+m_j. This placement can be done because the group generated by p_j is a subgroup of the group generated by p_i. Fig.6 shows the multiplicative levels of a PNW for N=13 with an optimized placement in the discussed way The optimization by selecting bases which allow a good wiring was used to optimize a design of a PNW for N=17 /6/.

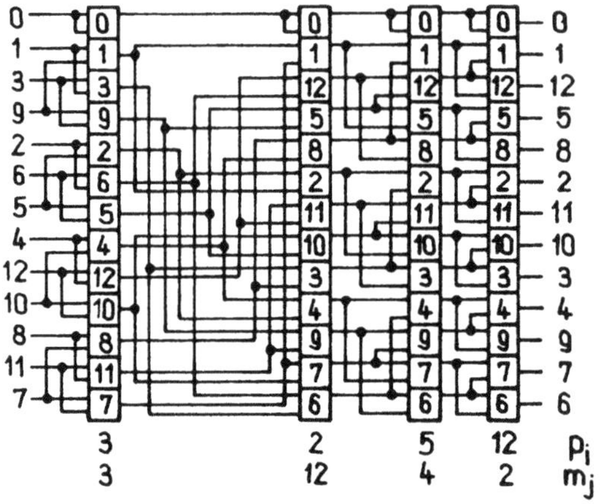

Fig.6 part of a PNW for N=13 with optimized placement

Ref.

/1/ Rebel,B., Gössel,M.: Ein paralleler Speicher. AdW der DDR, ZKI,Berlin 1982

/2/ Kung,H., Leiserson,G.: Systolic apparatus for matrix computations. US-PS 4,493,048

/3/ Frison,P., Quinton,P.: An integrated systolic machine for speech recognition. Proc.Int.Workshop on Parallel Processing and VLSI, Amalfi 1984,175-186, North-Holland Comp.

/4/ Rebel,B., Gössel,M.: Adressenberechnungsschaltung, Patentschrift, 1985

/5/ Pöschel,R. et al: Ein dekomponiertes Permutationsnetzwerk für einen parallelen Bildspeicher. Proc. INFO 84,Bd.5,840-844, Dresden 1984

/6/ Wächter,F.: Zur Strukturierung spezieller Permutationsnetzwerke. AdW der DDR, ZKI-Inf. 2/85

PARALLEL OPTIMAL SUBTREE ACCESS WITH RECURSIVELY LINEAR MEMORY FUNCTIONS

Reiner Creutzburg

Academy of Sciences of the G.D.R.
Central Institute for Cybernetics and
Information Processes
Kurstr. 33, P.O.Box 1298
DDR - 1086 Berlin

Abstract In this paper parallel access to subtrees of trees is investigated. Thereby the module assignment function is supposed to be recursively linear /9/. The results of SHIRAKAWA /8/ till now valid for binary trees are generalized to q-ary trees. Moreover it is shown that the minimal numbers of memory modules necessary for conflictfree subtree access is smaller than the numbers obtained by SHIRAKAWA.

1. Introduction

A lot of research work has been done in designing parallel memories to access arrays /1-7/. Trees are another important data structure in computer science /8-10/. In this note we describe an organization of a parallel memory with a recursively linear module assignment function to access trees. We use the terminology given in /10/ to describe a tree. Consider a labelled q-ary tree such that the immediate successors of x are qx+1, qx+2,...,qx+q, and the label of the root is 0. The level of a node is defined by initially letting the root be at level 1. The level of every other node is one more than the level of its immediate predecessor. The height of a tree is defined to be the maximum level of any node in the tree.
Parallel access to trees means the access to all the $(q^t-1)/(q-1)$ nodes of a complete q-ary subtree of height t with an arbitrary node x as root, as shown in figure 1.

2. Special recursively linear module assignment functions

A module assignment function S is a mapping from the set of the labels of a complete q-ary tree to the N memory modules. We denote the set of indices of memory modules by $\widetilde{N} = \{0,1,\dots,N-1\}$.
A special recursively linear module assignment function $\underline{S}$ for binary trees was introduced in /8/ by the following recurrence equations

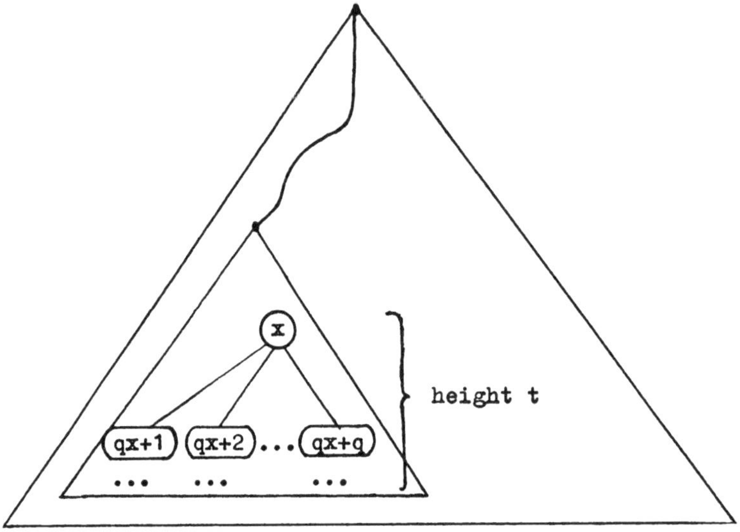

Fig. 1 Labelled complete q-ary subtree of height t

$$\left.\begin{aligned} \underline{S}(0) &\equiv 0 \\ \underline{S}(2x+1) &\equiv a\,\underline{S}(x)+1 \\ \underline{S}(2x+2) &\equiv a\,\underline{S}(x)+2 \end{aligned}\right\} \bmod N, \qquad (1)$$

where a is an integer with $0<a<N$.

In order to generalize the results of /8/ to the case of q-ary trees ($q \geq 1$) we investigate in this chapter the special recursively linear module assignment function S with

$$\left.\begin{aligned} S(0) &\equiv 0 \\ S(qx+1) &\equiv a\,S(x)+1 \\ S(qx+2) &\equiv a\,S(x)+2 \\ &\vdots \\ S(qx+q) &\equiv a\,S(x)+q \end{aligned}\right\} \bmod N, \qquad (2)$$

where a is an integer with $0<a<N$.

For the detailed definition of the terms given in this chapter the reader is refered to /9/.

A number-theoretic consideration of the parameters a and N of (1) for the case of binary subtree access leads to the following generalization of the results given in /8/.

Theorem: A parallel conflictfree access to all the $(q^t-1)/(q-1)$ nodes of an arbitrary complete q-ary subtree of height t of a q-ary tree with a special recursively linear module assignment function S according to (2) is possible, if the number of memory modules N in (2) is equal to

$$N = q^{t-2}(q(t-1)+1)$$

and if the parameter a in (2) satisfies the condition

$$a \equiv \begin{cases} 1 \bmod q+1 & \text{in the case } t=2, \\ \left.\begin{array}{l} 0 \bmod q \\ 1 \bmod 2q+1 \end{array}\right\} & \text{in the case } t=3, \\ \left.\begin{array}{l} 2 \bmod q^{t-2} \\ 1 \bmod q(t-1)+1 \end{array}\right\} & \text{in the case } t>3. \end{cases} \tag{4}$$

We give here the proof for the case $t=3$ only. The general case can be proved quite similar and the case $t=2$ is trivial.

Let us take the special recursively linear module assignment function S modulo $N_1 = q^{t-2}$ and modulo $N_2 = q(t-1)+1$, respectively

$$S \bmod q \; ; \quad S \bmod q(t-1)+1.$$

The numbers N_1 and N_2 are the two factors of N in (3). Clearly, these factors N_1 and N_2 are relative prime for every $q \geq 1$ and $t \geq 2$. From elementary number theory it is known that two integers are congruent modulo N ($N = N_1 N_2$ and $\gcd(N_1, N_2) = 1$) if and only if they are congruent modulo N_1 and N_2, respectively. Therefore we obtain a conflict in the subtree access of the special recursively linear module assignment function (2) if and only if two nodes x and x' of a q-ary subtree have the same values $S(x)$ and $S(x')$ modulo N_1 and modulo N_2, respectively

$$S(x) \equiv S(x') \bmod N_1 \; ; \quad S(x) \equiv S(x') \bmod N_2 .$$

The next figure 2 shows that this is impossible under condition (4) for subtrees of height 3. We consider for example the circled nodes that have the value 1 mod q in the upper part of figure 2. They are located in the lower left corner of every subtree of height 2. The relating nodes in the lower part of figure 2 are also circled and have the values $S(x)+1$, $S(x)+2$, $S(x)+3, \ldots$, $S(x)+q+1$, respectively. Therefore no conflicts can occur. For the other nodes the same consideration gives similar results.

The table 1 lists a lot of special cases concerning parallel subtree access that can be derived from our theorem. Note that also the ratios of needed numbers of memory modules and accessed nodes are given. The results of SHIRAKAWA are underlined in table 1.

<u>Example.</u> From the theorem follows that the parallel conflictfree access to the 21 nodes of an arbitrary complete subquadtree of height $t=3$ is possible with $N=36$ memory modules. The special recursively linear module assignment function S is

$$\left.\begin{array}{l} S(0) \equiv 0 \\ S(4x+1) \equiv 28\, S(x) + 1 \\ S(4x+2) \equiv 28\, S(x) + 2 \\ S(4x+3) \equiv 28\, S(x) + 3 \\ S(4x+4) \equiv 28\, S(x) + 4 \end{array}\right\} \bmod 36. \tag{5}$$

From (5) we obtain the following periodic table form of S:

S(x)	0	1	2	3	4	5	6	7	8	9	10	11	12	13	14	15	16	17
S(4x+1)	1	29	21	13	5	33	25	17	9	1	29	21	13	5	33	25	17	9
S(4x+2)	2	30	22	14	6	34	26	18	10	2	30	22	14	6	34	26	18	10
S(4x+3)	3	31	23	15	7	35	27	19	11	3	31	23	15	7	35	27	19	11
S(4x+4)	4	32	24	16	8	0	28	20	12	4	32	24	16	8	0	28	20	12

S(x)	18	19	20	21	22	23	24	25	26	27	28	29	30	31	32	33	34	35
S(4x+1)	1	29	21	13	5	33	25	17	9	1	29	21	13	5	33	25	17	9
S(4x+2)	2	30	22	14	6	34	26	18	10	2	30	22	14	6	34	26	18	10
S(4x+3)	3	31	23	15	7	35	27	19	11	3	31	23	15	7	35	27	19	11
S(4x+4)	4	32	24	16	8	0	28	20	12	4	32	24	16	8	0	28	20	12

It is interesting to note that the 31 nodes of an arbitrary binary subtree of height $t=5$ can be accessed with $N=72$ memory modules, but the 31 nodes of an arbitrary complete 5-ary subtree of height $t=3$ can be accessed with only $N=55$ memory modules. This means that a storage in "breadth" is more efficient than a storage in "depth" in general.

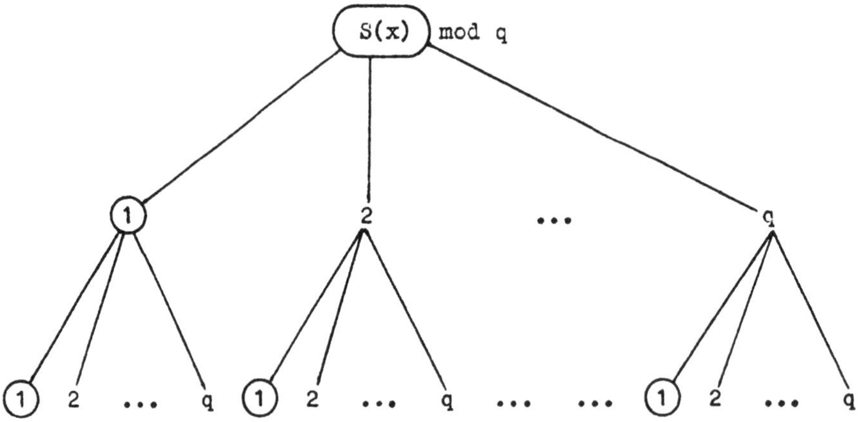

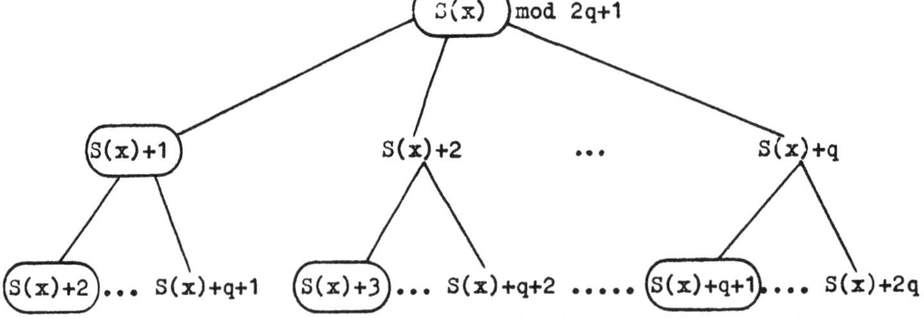

Fig. 2 Complete q-ary subtree of height $t=3$ in the special recursively linear module assignment function taken modulo $N_1=q$ and modulo $N_2=2q+1$

Table 1. List of necessary memory module numbers for parallel, recursively linear complete q-ary subtree access of height t (listed are the number of nodes, the number of memory modules and the ratio of the numbers of memory modules and nodes)

height t	1-ary tree	binary tree	ternary tree	quad-tree	5-ary tree	6-ary tree	7-ary tree	oct-tree
2	2 nodes 1,0 2 memories	3 nodes 1,0 3 memories	4 nodes 1,0 4 memories	5 nodes 1,0 5 memories	6 nodes 1,0 6 memories	7 nodes 1,0 7 memories	8 nodes 1,0 8 memories	9 nodes 1,0 9 memories
3	3 nodes 1,0 3 memories	7 nodes 1,42 10 memories	13 nodes 1,61 21 memories	21 nodes 1,71 36 memories	31 nodes 1,77 55 memories	43 nodes 1,81 78 memories	57 nodes 1,84 105 memories	73 nodes 1,86 136 memories
4	4 nodes 1,0 4 memories	15 nodes 1,87 28 memories	40 nodes 2,25 90 memories	85 nodes 2,44 208 memories	156 nodes 2,56 400 memories	259 nodes 2,64 684 memories	400 nodes 2,69 1078 memories	594 nodes 2,70 1600 memories
5	5 nodes 1,0 5 memories	31 nodes 2,32 72 memories	121 nodes 2,90 351 memories	341 nodes 3,19 1088 memories	...	...	...	...
6	6 nodes 1,0 6 memories	63 nodes 2,79 176 memories	364 nodes 3,56 1296 memories	...	...	...	...	...
7	7 nodes 1,0 7 memories	127 nodes 3,27 416 memories	...	...	...	...	...	...

3. General recursively linear module assignment functions

In order to further minimize the number of needed memory modules N for parallel subtree access we introduce the following general recursively linear module assignment function S with

$$\left.\begin{aligned} S(0) &\equiv 0 \\ S(qx+1) &\equiv a_1\, S(x) + b_1 \\ S(qx+2) &\equiv a_2\, S(x) + b_2 \\ &\;\;\vdots \\ S(qx+q) &\equiv a_q\, S(x) + b_q \end{aligned}\right\} \bmod N, \tag{6}$$

where the a_i and b_i are integers with $0 < a_i < N$ and $0 < b_i < N$ $(i=1,\dots,q)$.

With this general recursively linear module assignment function (6) we obtained the following two results for subtree access :

1) The 7 nodes of an arbitrary complete binary subtree of height 3 can be accessed in parallel using (6) with $N=10$ memory modules and $N=10$ is the minimum number. In this case the same results occured for the special and general recursively linear module assignment functions (1), (2) and (6), respectively. We have for example:

$$\left.\begin{aligned} S(0) &\equiv 0 \\ S(2x+1) &\equiv 6\, S(x) + 1 \\ S(2x+2) &\equiv 6\, S(x) + 2 \end{aligned}\right\} \bmod 10. \tag{7}$$

A periodic table form of S is:

S(x)	0	1	2	3	4	5	6	7	8	9
S(2x+1)	1	7	3	9	5	1	7	3	9	5
S(2x+2)	2	8	4	0	6	2	8	4	0	6 .

2) The 15 nodes of an arbitrary complete subtree of height $t=4$ can be accessed in parallel using (6) with $N=20$ memory modules instead of the 28 needed memory modules according to (2) and $N=20$ is the minimum number. This means a reduction of hardware amount of about 30 per cent. We obtained the general recursively linear module assignment function S with

$$\left.\begin{aligned} S(0) &\equiv 0 \\ S(2x+1) &\equiv 13\, S(x) + 1 \\ S(2x+2) &\equiv 17\, S(x) + 7 \end{aligned}\right\} \bmod 20$$

and the following table form of S:

S(x)	0	1	2	3	4	5	6	7	8	9	10	11	12	13	14	15	16	17	18	19
S(2x+1)	1	14	7	0	13	6	19	12	5	18	11	4	17	10	3	16	9	2	15	8
S(2x+2)	7	4	1	18	15	12	9	6	3	0	17	14	11	8	5	2	19	16	13	10.

4. Final remarks

As a final result we present in the following table and in figure 3 a nonlinear module assignment function for binary subtree access of height $t=3$ that needs only $N=9$ memory modules:

S(x)	0	1	2	3	4	5	6	7	8
S(2x+1)	1	3	5	5	7	7	0	0	1
S(2x+2)	2	4	6	6	8	8	4	3	2 .

It is proved in /9/ that N=9 is the minimum number in this case. With the help of a simple computer program we have shown that there does not exist a recursively linear module assignment function for $N < 10$.

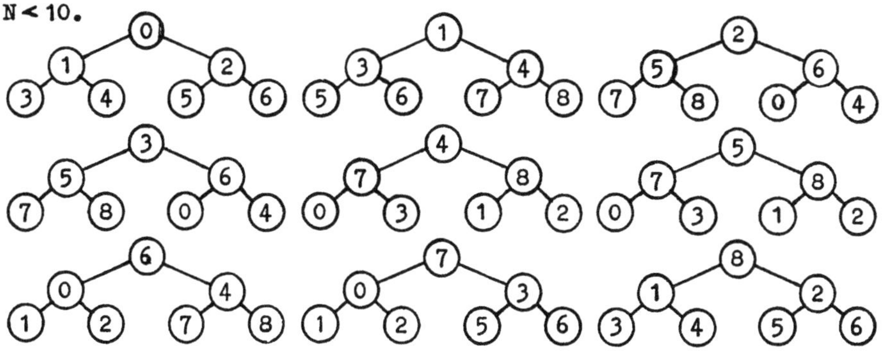

Fig. 3 Illustration of an optimal module assignment function for parallel conflictfree access to complete binary subtrees of height t=3 with N=9 memory modules

The author would like to thank M. Gössel and J. Vilser for stimulating discussions during the preparation of this paper.

5. References

/1/ Budnik, P., and D. J. Kuck: The organization and use of parallel memories. IEEE Trans. Comput. C-20 (1971), pp.1566-1569

/2/ Shapiro, H. D.: Theoretical limitations on the use of parallel memories. Univ. Illinois, Dept. Comp. Science, Report R-75-776, (1975)

/3/ Lawrie, D. H.: Access and alignment in an array processor. IEEE Trans. Comput. C-24 (1975), pp.1145-1155

/4/ Lawrie, D. H., and Ch. R. Vora: The prime memory system for array access. IEEE Trans. Comput. C-31 (1982), pp.435-442

/5/ Rebel, B., and M. Gössel: Ein paralleler Speicher. Report, ZKI der AdW, Berlin (1972)

/6/ Gössel, M., and B. Rebel: Parallel memory with recursive address computation. Proc. Conf. Parallel Computing '83, Berlin. (Ed.: M. Feilmeier, Elsevier Sci. Publ. 1984), pp.515-520

/7/ Wijshoff, H. A. G., and J. van Leeuwen: The structure of periodic storage schemes for parallel memories. IEEE Trans. Comput. C-34 (1985), pp.501-505

/8/ Shirakawa, H.: On a parallel memory to access trees. Unpublished manuscript. 1984

/9/ Gössel, M., and B. Rebel: Data structures and parallel memories. (to be presented at PARCELLA '86, Berlin)

/10/ Horowitz, E., and S. Sahni: Fundamentals of Data Structures. Comp. Science Press. Woodland Hills (Ca.) 1976

ON THE POWER OF CELLULAR PARALLELISM
(Extended Abstract)

A. Hemmerling [1]

0. The cellular automaton or cellular space is one of the oldest models of parallel computation /24/. A cellular automaton can be simulated by a Turing machine in linear space and with a polynomially bounded overhead in time. Therefore it has not the computational power of the modern mathematical models of "full" parallelism (e.g. alternating Turing machines /1/). These belong to the second machine class for which the so-called parallel computational thesis, Parallel PTIME=Sequential PSPACE, was established, see /22/ for details. On the other hand, it was pointed out in /2/ that the practically realizable ("realistic") parallel computing devices satisfy the relation Realistic Parallel PTIME (SPACE) = Sequential PTIME (SPACE).

The advance of VLSI technologies enables the implementation of large cellular multiprocessor systems. In recent years much work was done in order to characterise the computational power of several cellular computation models (/4/,/5/,/6/,/11/,/12/). In the first place the systolic automata of various kinds are considered, but very often there is an equivalent type of one-dimensional cellular automata or iterative automata. The computational power of one-dimensional and multidimensional cellular and iterative automata was already investigated in many earlier papers, e.g. /3/,/7/,/9/,/13/,/19/,/20/,/23/,/17/. They can be regarded as the off-line and the on-line model, respectively, of the cellular computation.

In the present sketch we survey relationships between (space, time) complexity classes of multidimensional cellular and iterative automata and of the corresponding types of Turing machines. Furthermore, linear-space and real-space simulations of multidimensional automata by one-dimensional ones and a real-space and real-time simulation of one-dimensional multitape Turing machines by cellular or iterative automata are given.

The basic ideas of these results but the last one were already sketched in /7/,/10/; the last result, at least for the on-line case, is also already known, see /19/,/17/. Nevertheless, there has not been any survey of such linear-space simulations up to now. Remark that there are subtle simulation techniques which improve some of our results with respect to the time complexity. That applies both to the fast simulation of multidimensional Turing machines by low dimensional ones (/15/,/16/ and Theorem 6i) and to the real-time simulation of multidimensional multitape

[1] Sektion Mathematik der Ernst-Moritz-Arndt-Universität
DDR-2200 Greifswald, Jahn-Strasse 15 a

or multihead Turing machines by iterative arrays (/17/ and Theorem 7ii). But all these techniques require non-linear overhead in workspace. For the importance of linear-space simulations see /18/.

We consider only the deterministic models of automata, but the results easily extend to the nondeterministic case.

1. An alphabet is a non-empty, finite set X which does not contain the blank symbol §. For any positive integer d, by a d-dimensional word (d-word) over X, we mean a finite connected d-dimensional pattern of symbols from X. More formally, the partial mappings r from $\underline{I}^d$ into X with connected finite domains, dom(r), are called d-representations over X, and a d-word is an equivalence class of such representations, w=[r], with respect to the equivalence relation defined by

$$r_1 \sim r_2 \longleftrightarrow \exists (z_0 \in \underline{I}^d)\ r_1 = \{(z+z_0,x):\ (z,x) \in r_2\}.$$

Connectedness is meant with respect to the von Neumann neighbourhood; here every cell $z \in \underline{I}^d$ has the 2d neighbours $z+\underline{e}_1,\ldots,z+\underline{e}_{2d}$ which differ from z in just one component by ± 1. Let $\underline{E}_d = \{\underline{e}_0=(0,\ldots,0),\underline{e}_1,\ldots,\underline{e}_{2d}\}$. We only consider non-empty words $w \neq [\emptyset]$. $|w| = card(dom(r))$ is the size of the d-word w=[r]. Let X_d^+ denote the set of all non-empty d-words over X.

A linear ordering $\preccurlyeq$ in $\underline{I}^d$ is defined by

$$(i_1,\ldots,i_d) \preccurlyeq (j_1,\ldots,j_d) \longleftrightarrow i_1=j_1 \wedge \ldots \wedge i_d=j_d$$
$$\vee\ \exists (k<d)\ i_1=j_1 \wedge \ldots \wedge i_k=j_k \wedge i_{k+1}<j_{k+1}.$$

A d-dimensional cellular automaton (d-CA) over X is given by a local transition function $C:\ (X \cup \{\S\})^{2d+1} \longrightarrow X \cup \{\S\}$, where $C(\S,\ldots,\S)=\S$. The corresponding global transition function $\overline{C}$ removes the representation r by $\overline{r}=\overline{C}(r)$ defined by $\overline{r}_\S(z) = C(r_\S(z), r_\S(z+\underline{e}_1),\ldots,r_\S(z+\underline{e}_{2d}))$ $(z \in \underline{I}^d)$, where $r_\S = r \cup ((\underline{I}^d - dom(r)) \times \{\S\})$ for any representation r.

A d-CA accepts its input word w=[r] by the state (that means, the inscription) of the cell $\min_\preccurlyeq(dom(r))$. For it, a set $X_0 \subseteq X$ of accepting symbols is fixed. Then we say that w is accepted [in space s(n) and time t(n) for functions $s,t:\ \underline{N}^+ \longrightarrow \underline{N}^+$,] if there is an integer k [$\leq t(|w|)$] such that $\overline{C}^k(r)(\min_\preccurlyeq(dom(r))) \in X_0$ [and $card(\bigcup_{i=0}^{k} dom(\overline{C}^i(r))) \leq s(|w|)$].

A set $W \subseteq X_d^+$ is recognized by a d-CA over some superalphabet $\overline{X} \supseteq X$ in space s(n) and time t(n) if this d-CA accepts all d-words of W in space s(n) and time t(n) but it does not accept any d-word of $X_d^+ - W$. Let $CA_d(s(n),t(n))$ denote the family of all d-word sets (d-languages) which can be recognized by a d-CA in space s(n) and time t(n). Remark that $s(n) \geq n$ if this complexity class is non-empty.

A d-dimensional Turing machine (d-TM) consists of a finite-state control unit joined with a read-write head scanning a cell $z \in \underline{I}^d$ in each step. Depending on the current inscription of this cell and on the internal state of the control unit, the machine changes this inscription and the internal state and moves the head to one of the neighbouring cells $z+\underline{e}_i$. We omit the formal details of the definition.

A d-TM starts with its initial state and with the head on the minimal cell, $\min_{\preccurlyeq}(\mathrm{dom}(r))$, of the given input word $w=[r]$. It can accept the input by entering a special accepting state. We say that the machine accept the input w in space s(n) and time t(n) if the accepting state is entered after $k \le t(|w|)$ steps and the number of cells used until this step (i.e. the number of cells from dom(r) together with the positions of the head in these steps) is bounded by $s(|w|)$.

Like the complexity classes for d-CAs, we define the family $TM_d(s(n),t(n))$ of all d-languages which can be recognized by a d-TM in space s(n) and time t(n).

We use the O-notation for complexity bounds in the usual sense.

<u>Theorem 1:</u>

i) $CA_d(s(n),t(n)) \subseteq TM_d(O(s(n)),O(s(n)\cdot t(n)))$,

ii) $TM_1(s(n),t(n)) \subseteq CA_1(\ s(n)\ ,\ s(n)+t(n)\ )$,

iii) $TM_2(s(n),t(n)) \subseteq CA_2(\ s(n)\ ,\ O(s(n)+t(n))\ )$,

iv) $TM_d(s(n),t(n)) \subseteq CA_d(\ s(n)\ ,\ O(\ n^5+s(n)+t(n)\ )\ )$ for $d \ge 3$.

Inclusion i) is well-known for d=1, see /21/,/12/. A TM simulates one step of a CA by twofold crossing over the corresponding representation and the neighbouring cells. (Without loss of generality we assume that the blank symbol never arises on a non-blank cell, hence the representation remains connected during the work of the CA.) During the first crossing the TM computes the new inscriptions but preserves the old ones, too. In the second crossing the new inscriptions are put here. For the multidimensional case, the crossings are implemented by an algorithm for searching d-dimensional labyrinths, see /7/.

The simulation of a TM by a CA is straightforward. But after reaching the accepting state of the TM, in the CA a corresponding signal is to send to the cell $\min_{\preccurlyeq}(\mathrm{dom}(r))$ to enter an accepting symbol here. Moreover, the simulation has to start with the initial position $\min_{\preccurlyeq}(\mathrm{dom}(r))$ for the head of the TM. For one-dimensional representations r, this cell can be recognized in one step of the CA. But for $d \ge 2$, this recognition is a non-trivial problem related to the so-called queen bee problem in CA theory /20/. It can be solved (by a bounded CA) in time $O(|[r]|)$ for d=2, see /25/, but in time $O(|[r]|^5)$ for $d \ge 3$, see /8/. //

2. The CAs and TMs considered in the previous section are off-line computation models, the entire input is given at the start of the computation. Now we deal with the corresponding on-line models, for which the input is presented rather sequentially.

Let the Turing machine have a d-dimensional worktape which is empty at the begin of the computation. The input is given on a special tape scanned by a read-only input head. We assume that some dimension d_0 of the input tape is fixed in the following and that the control unit of the machine also controls the moves of the input head (with some fixed restrictions, possibly). The input is accepted if the machine enters an accepting state. This machine model will be called d-dimensional input

Turing machine (d-IM).

The corresponding cellular model is the d-dimensional iterative automaton (d-IA). Here the input head works like for a d-IM, but it is controlled by the state of a certain fixed cell z_0 of the d-dimensional worktape. Our input mode is somewhat more general than for the iterative automata considered in /3/, but by fixing corresponding restrictions we can also get exactly Cole's type of automata. For all cells $z \neq z_0$, the inscription is changed according to a local transition function $C: (X \cup \{\S\})^{2d+1} \longrightarrow X \cup \{\S\}$ like for a d-CA, but the new inscription of cell z_0 and the move of the input head at each step are obtained by a special function $C_0: (X \cup \{\S\})^{2d+1} \times (Y \cup \{\S\}) \longrightarrow (X \cup \{\S\}) \times \underline{E}_{d_0}$, where Y denotes the alphabet of the input tape. At the begin of the computation the worktape is empty. The input is accepted if the cell z_0 gets an accepting symbol sometime during the computation.

Like for d-TMs and d-CAs, we define the complexity classes $IM_d(s(n),t(n))$ and $IA_d(s(n),t(n))$, respectively. These are the families of all d_0-languages which can be recognized by d-IMs and d-IAs, respectively, within time t(n) and using no more cells on the worktape than permitted by s(n).

<u>Theorem 2:</u>

i) $IA_d(s(n),t(n)) \subseteq IM_d(\ O(s(n))\ ,\ O(\ s(n)\cdot t(n)\ )\ )$,

ii) $IM_d(s(n),t(n)) \subseteq IA_d(\ s(n)\ ,\ t(n) + O(\ s(n)\ )\ )$.

This follows from the proof of Theorem 1. Because the cell z_0 is already distinguished from the other cells in a d-IA, we don't need a solution of the queen bee problem for the proof of inclusion ii). //

3. In order to simulate multidimensional automata by one-dimensional ones, we define an encoding of the d-words by 1-words. A 1-word

(0) $\quad u = (x_0, \underline{e}_{i_0})(x_1, \underline{e}_{i_1}) \ldots (x_l, \underline{e}_{i_l}) \in (X \times \underline{E}_d)_1^+$

is called a d-linearization if

(1) $\quad \sum_{j=0}^{l} \underline{e}_{i_j} = (0,\ldots,0) \quad$ and

(2) $\quad$ from $\sum_{j=k_1}^{k_2-1} \underline{e}_{i_j} = (0,\ldots,0)$ it always follows that $x_{k_1} = x_{k_2}$ $\quad (0 \leq k_1 < k_2 \leq l)$.

Then, for any $z_0 \in \underline{I}^d$, the set $r = \left\{ (\ z_0 + \sum_{j=0}^{k-1} \underline{e}_{i_j}\ ,\ x_k\ ) : k = 0,1,\ldots,l \right\}$ is a d-representation, and u is called a linearization of the d-word [r].

The intuitive background is that the second components $\underline{e}_{i_j}$ of the letters of u define a cyclic path $P_{z_0,u} = (z_0, z_1, \ldots, z_l, z_{l+1})$, where $z_k = z_0 + \sum_{j=0}^{k-1} \underline{e}_{i_j}$ $(0 \leq k \leq l+1)$. This path covers the domain of r. The first components x_j give the inscriptions of the cells.

u is called a simple linearization if, furthermore, the following two conditions hold:

(3) $\quad$ If $|u| > 1$, then $\underline{e}_{i_j} \neq (0,\ldots,0)$ for all $j = 0,1,\ldots,l$.

(4) $\quad$ If $0 \leq j < k \leq l$, then $(z_j, z_{j+1}) \neq (z_k, z_{k+1})$.

Condition (4) means that the path $P_{z_0,u}$ crosses every directed edge in the graph $(I^d , \{(z,z'): z\neq z', z-z' \in \underline{E}_d \})$ at most once.

Lemma 1: Every d-word has a simple linearization.

For example, such a linearization can be obtained by crossing the domain of a representation of the given d-word according to the labyrinth algorithm of Tarry, see /7/. //

Remark that $|u| \leq 2d \cdot |w|$ if u is a simple linearization of w.

For a d-language W, let $\mathcal{L}_{[0]}(W)$ denote the set of all [simple] linearizations of d-words from W.

Lemma 2: For every alphabet X, $\mathcal{L}(X_d^+), \mathcal{L}_0(X_d^+) \in TM_1(n , O(n^2 \log n))$.

In order to recognize $\mathcal{L}_{[0]}(X_d^+)$, a 1-TM tests in time n whether the input word u belongs to $(X \times \underline{E}_d)_1^+$ [and whether condition (3) holds].
Now let u have the form (0). Then, for every index $k_1 \in \{0,\dots,l\}$ and all $k_2 \in \{k_1+1,\dots,l\}$, the 1-TM checks condition (2), and (for $k_1=0$ and $k_2=l$) also condition (1). To do this, for every $k_2 > k_1$ the machine computes the value $\sum_{j=k_1}^{k_2-1} \underline{e}_{i_j}$. Let the coordinates of this sum be noted in binary representation on special tracks of the tape with the last digits at the cell containing letter $(x_{k_2}, \underline{e}_{i_{k_2}})$ of u. These representations are shifted by one cell to the right for the test of the next k_2. Then the tests for fixed k_1 can be performed in $O(n \cdot \log n)$ steps, hence the whole procedure takes $O(n^2 \cdot \log n)$ steps. [During this procedure condition (4) can also be checked.] //

Theorem 3: Let s be a non-decreasing function.

i) $W \in TM_d(s(n),t(n)) \longrightarrow \mathcal{L}_{[0]}(W) \in TM_1(s(n), O(n^2 \log n + t(n) \cdot s(n) \cdot \log s(n)))$,

ii) $W \in CA_d(s(n),t(n)) \longrightarrow \mathcal{L}_{[0]}(W) \in TM_1(s(n), O(n^2 \log n + t(n) \cdot s^2(n) \cdot \log s(n)))$.

To prove assertion i), let M_d be a d-TM recognizing the d-language $W \subseteq X_d^+$. We sketch the work of a 1-TM M_1 which recognizes $\mathcal{L}_{[0]}(W)$. Given an input $u=(x_0,\underline{e}_{i_0})\dots(x_l,\underline{e}_{i_l})$, M_1 tests whether $u \in \mathcal{L}_{[0]}(X_d^+)$. If yes, it enters a cell of a letter $(x_{k'}, \underline{e}_{i_{k'}})$ in u such that
$\sum_{j=0}^{k'-1} \underline{e}_{i_j} = \min_{\leq}(\{ \sum_{j=0}^{k-1} \underline{e}_{i_j} : k=0,1,\dots,l \})$. Now M_1 begins the simulation of M_d.

For the simulation of one step of M_d, M_1 has to put here the new inscription of the scanned cell everywhere in the present linearization where this cell occurs. (We assume that these new inscriptions are non-blank always.) This can be done within $m \cdot \log m$ steps if m is the size of the current linearization. Then M_1 tests whether the new position of the head of M_d is already in the domain of the d-representation corresponding to the current linearization ($m \cdot \log m$ steps). If yes, M_1 enters a corresponding cell. Otherwise, M_1 inserts such cell into the current linearization at a cell corresponding to the old position of the head. More precisely, if the (old) head position corresponds to the letter $(x'_j, \underline{e}_{i_{j'}})$ in the current linearization u', then M_1 replaces this letter by the word $(x'_j, \underline{e}_{i'})(B, -\underline{e}_{i'})(x', \underline{e}_{i_{j'}})$ if the head of M moves in direction $\underline{e}_{i'}$.

The letter $(B,-\underline{e}_{i},)$ corresponds to the new head position. This insertion takes O(m) steps for shifting a corresponding part of the linearization u'.

For every new cell used by M_d, the linearization is elongated by two cells during this simulation. If the input u is a linearization of the d-word w, we have $m \leq |u| + 2\cdot(s(|w|)-|w|) \leq s(|u|) + 2\cdot s(|w|) \leq 3\cdot s(|u|)$, because $|w| \leq |u|$. Therefore, we get the time bound $O(n^2 \cdot \log n + t(n)\cdot s(n)\cdot \log s(n))$ and the space bound $O(s(n))$ for M_1. Using the standard technique of packing of symbols, one gets a real-space simulation.

The simulation of one step of a d-CA by a 1-TM M_1 is quite similiar. In a first period, M_1 computes the new inscriptions for every cell occurring in the present linearization and also for all its neighbouring cells. These inscriptions are noted (preserving the old inscriptions) on each cell. This computation takes $O(m^2 \cdot \log m)$ steps. Then, in a second period, a linearization of the new representation of the CA is put here. (We assume that non-empty cells remain non-empty.) To do this, M_1 inserts the new cells always at the first possible place in the linearization in a way described above. This also takes $O(m^2 \cdot \log m)$ steps. Finally, in O(m) steps, the new inscriptions can be put here. //

<u>Theorem 4:</u>

i) $IM_d(s(n),t(n)) \subseteq IM_1(s(n) , O(t(n)\cdot s(n)\cdot \log s(n)))$,

ii) $IA_d(s(n),t(n)) \subseteq IM_1(s(n) , O(t(n)\cdot s^2(n)\cdot \log s(n)))$.

This follows from the proof of Theorem 3. Here the simulating 1-IM works with simple linearizations of the contents of the worktape of the simulated d-IM or d-IA. //

4. The time bounds of the simulations of the previous section can be improved if we use (one-dimensional) multitape Turing machines (1-MTM).

A 1-MTM has k one-dimensional tapes each with one read-write head, for some $k \geq 1$. It starts with the input word on the first tape and the corresponding head on the first symbol of the input. (One can assume that this is a read-only head.) All the other tapes are empty. In each step the machine reads the symbols in the cells scanned by the heads, and depending on these symbols and the internal state, it gets a new state, inserts new symbols in the cells scanned and moves the heads. It accepts an input by a special state. Let $MTM_1(s(n),t(n))$ denote the family of all 1-languages which can be recognized by a 1-MTM within space s(n) and time t(n). The exact definition is quite usual and can be omitted, remark only that the space is the maximal number of cells used by the several tapes. Obviousely, $TM_1(s(n),t(n)) \subseteq MTM_1(s(n),t(n))$.

<u>Lemma 3:</u> For every alphabet X, $\mathcal{L}(X_1^+), \mathcal{L}_0(X_1^+) \in MTM_1(n , O(n^2))$.

Indeed, a 1-MTM can perform the computation of the value $\sum_{j=k_1}^{k_2-1} \underline{e}_{i_j}$ in the proof of Lemma 2 by d special tapes working as counters. Then this computation does not require extra time. //

Similarly, modifying the proof of Theorem 3, one obtains

<u>Theorem 5:</u> Let s be a non-decreasing function.

i) $W \in TM_d(s(n),t(n)) \longrightarrow \mathcal{L}_{\angle 07}(W) \in MTM_1(\ s(n), O(n^2+s(n)\cdot t(n))\ )$,

ii) $W \in CA_d(s(n),t(n)) \longrightarrow \mathcal{L}_{\angle 07}(W) \in MTM_1(\ s(n), O(n^2+s^2(n)\cdot t(n))\ )$. //

Analogously to the 1-MTM, we define the one-dimensional multitape input Turing machine (1-MIM) which has an input head scanning the d_0-dimensional input, and some one-dimensional worktapes. The corresponding complexity classes are denoted by $MIM_1(s(n),t(n))$. Then we have

<u>Theorem 6:</u>

i) $IM_d(s(n),t(n)) \subseteq MIM_1(\ s(n)\ ,\ O(\ s(n)\cdot t(n)\ )\ )$,

ii) $IA_d(s(n),t(n)) \subseteq MIM_1(\ s(n)\ ,\ O(\ s^2(n)\cdot t(n)\ )\ )$. //

Inclusion i) follows already from the proof of Theorem 1, version I, in /16/

5. Finally we remark that multitape Turing machines can be simulated by cellular automata in real space and real time.

<u>Theorem 7:</u>

i) $MTM_1(s(n),t(n)) \subseteq CA_1(\ s(n)\ ,\ t(n)\ )$,

ii) $MIM_1(s(n),t(n)) \subseteq IA_1(\ s(n)\ ,\ t(n)\ )$.

Unfortunately, there is no space here to give a full sketch of the basic idea of the proof. For i) one can assume that every tape of the given 1-MTM works as a pushdown. The simulating 1-CA uses one track for each pushdown, in a further track it notes the current state of the 1-MTM:

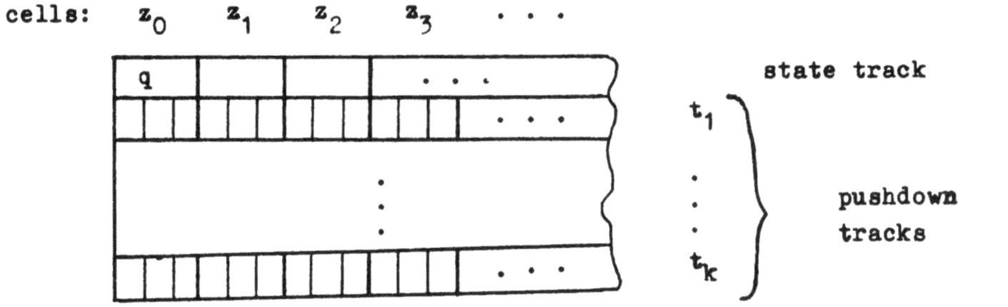

Every cell contains three registers in each pushdown track. During the simulation the CA tries to fill exactly two registers in each of the first cells of the pushdown tracks by non-blank symbols. //

<u>Remark:</u> It is known that multihead Turing machines can be simulated by multitape machines without space and time loss /14/. Therefore, also a real-space and real-time simulation of (one-dimensional) multihead Turing machines by 1-CAs or 1-IAs follows from our result.

<u>Corollary:</u> The assertions of Lemma 3 and Theorems 5 and 6 hold also for the complexity classes CA_1 and IA_1 instead of MTM_1 and MIM_1, respectively.

This follows immediately from Theorem 7. //

Theorem 7ii) seems to be proved already by Cole, see the corresponding remark in /17/, /19/. The real-time simulation given in /17/ of multidimensional multihead Turing machines by multidimensional iterative arrays requires non-linear overhead in space.

References

/1/ Chandra,A.K.,D.C.Kozen,L.J.Stockmeyer: Alternation. JACM 28 (1981), 114-133.

/2/ Chazelle,B.,L.Monier: Unbounded hardware is equivalent to deterministic Turing machines. TCS 24 (1983),123-130.

/3/ Cole,S.N.: Real-time computation by n-dimensional iterative arrays of finite-state machines. IEEE Transactions C-18 (1969),349-365.

/4/ Culik II,K.,J.Gruska,A.Salomaa: Systolic trellis automata. Intern.J. Computer Math. 15 (1984),195-212 and 16 (1984),3-22.

/5/ Culik II,K.,A.Salomaa,D.Wood: Systolic tree acceptors. RAIRO Inf. theor. 18 (1984),53-69.

/6/ Gruska,J.: Systolic automata-power,characterizations,nonhomogeneity. LNCS 176 (1984),32-49.

/7/ Hemmerling,A.: Zur Raumkompliziertheit mehrdimensionaler Zellularräume und Turing-Automaten. EIK 15 (1979),143-158.

/8/ Hemmerling,A.: Concentration of multidimensional tape-bounded systems of Turing automata and cellular spaces. Fundamentals of Computation Theory FCT'79. Berlin 1979,167-174.

/9/ Hemmerling,A.: Turing-Automaten,Systeme von Turing-Automaten und Zellularräume in mehrdimensionalen Speichermedien. Dissertation B. EMA-Universität Greifswald 1979.

/10/ Hemmerling,A.,G.Murawski: Zur Raumkompliziertheit mehrdimensionaler Turing-Automaten. Zeitschr. f. math. Logik u. Grundl. d. Math. 30 (1984),233-258.

/11/ Ibarra,O.H.,S.M.Kim: Characterizations and computational complexity of systolic trellis automata. TCS 29 (1984),123-153.

/12/ Ibarra,O.H.,S.M.Kim,S.Moran: Sequential machine characterizations of trellis and cellular automata and applications. SIAM J. Comput. 14 (1985),426-447.

/13/ Kosaraju,S.R.: On some open problems in the theory of cellular automata. IEEE Transactions C-23 (1974),561-565.

/14/ Leong,B.L.,J.I.Seiferas: New real-time simulations of multihead tape units. JACM 28 (1981),166-180.

/15/ Loui,M.C.: Simulations among multidimensional Turing machines. TCS 21 (1982),145-161.

/16/ Pippenger,N.,M.J.Fischer: Relations among complexity measures. JACM 26 (1979),361-381.

/17/ Seiferas,J.I.: Iterative arrays with direct central control. Acta Informatica 8 (1977),177-192.

/18/ Slot,C.,P.van Emde Boas: On tape versus core;an application of space efficient hash functions to the invariance of space. Report 84-06, University of Amsterdam (1984).

/19/ Smith III,A.R.: Real-time language recognition by one-dimensional cellular automata. JCSS 6 (1972),233-253.

/20/ Smith III,A.R.: Introduction to and survey of polyautomata theory. Automata,Languages,Development,ed. by A.Lindenmayer,G.Rozenberg, Amsterdam 1976,405-422.

/21/ Trachtenbrot,B.A.: Algorithmen und Rechenautomaten. Berlin 1977.

/22/ van Emde Boas,P.: The second machine class; models of parallelism. Parallel computers and computations,ed. by J.van Leeuwen,J.K.Lenstra, Amsterdam 1985,pp-

/23/ Vollmar,R.: Algorithmen in Zellularautomaten. Stuttgart 1979.

/24/ von Neumann,J.: Theory of self-reproducing automata. Univ. of Illinois Press,Urbana 1966.

/25/ Smith III,A.R.: Two-dimensional formal languages and pattern recognition by cellular automata. 12th IEEE Conf. SWAT (1971),144-152.

THE HOMOGENEOUS STRUCTURES FOR OPTIMAL CONTROL PROBLEM SOLVING

I.A.KALYAEV, A.V.KALYAEV*

INTRODUCTION

An essential drawback of known methods of optimal control problem solving is their orientation for using sequential computers [1] . This brings to some difficulties in using similar methods while controlling high-speed processes. The present paper suggests the other approach to the optimal control problem solving which is oriented to be realized on the basis of high-speed homogeneous computer structure of an parallel type.

PROBLEM PRESENTATION

The traditional problem presentation treats the optimal control problem in the following way [2] . Suppose that the control object state is described by the point $x=\{x^1, x^2, \ldots, x^n\}$ in the n -dimensional phase space X , where $x^i (i=1,2,\ldots,n)$ are some parameters specifying the object behaviour. It is assumed that the object behaviour can be controlled by the change of some parameters $u^j (j=1,2,\ldots,s)$ forming the S-dimensional control space U . The movement object law can be written in the form of differential equation system

$$\begin{cases} \frac{dx^1}{dt}=f^1(x(t), u(t)) \\ \frac{dx^2}{dt}=f^2(x(t), u(t)) \\ \cdots\cdots\cdots\cdots \\ \frac{dx^n}{dt}=f^n(x(t), u(t)) \end{cases} , \qquad (1)$$

where $x(t)=\{x^1(t), x^2(t), \ldots, x^n(t)\}$ is a vector-function of the object state;

$u(t)=\{u^1(t), u^2(t), \ldots, u^s(t)\}$ is a vector-function of controls. Two points x_0 and x_K are specified in the phase space X . The first point defines the current object state, and the second one - the target object state. It is necessary among all the controls $u(t)$, transfering the phase point from the x_0 state to the x_K state to find out such a control, for which the functional

*The Taganrog Radio Engineering Institute, USSR

$$J = \int_{t_0}^{t_K} f^0(x(t), u(t))\,dt \tag{2}$$

takes the minimal value. Here, t_0 - is the initial moment of the object movement, and t_K - the moment of x_K target state. The control , allowing to solve this given problem is referred to as the optimal control, and its corresponding phase trajectory $x(t)$ as the optimal trajectory.

PROBLEM FORMALIZATION

Let's put into the discrete model of the phase space X the regular graph $G(Q, Y)$ whose verteces $q \in Q$ correspond to the space discrete points X , and the ribs $y \in Y$ simulate the direct phase trajectory between the neighbouring discrete points (Fig.1).

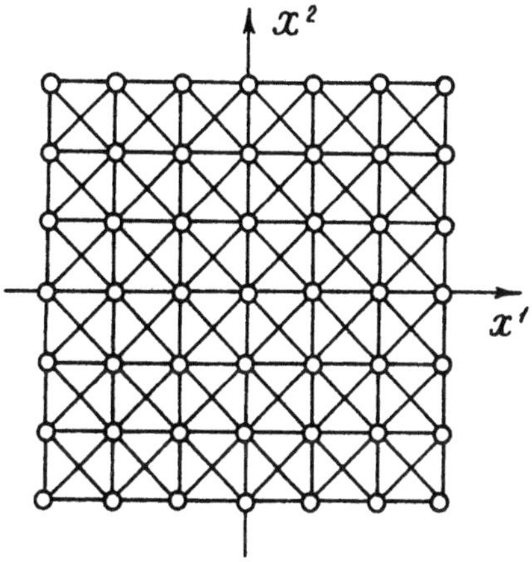

Fig.1.

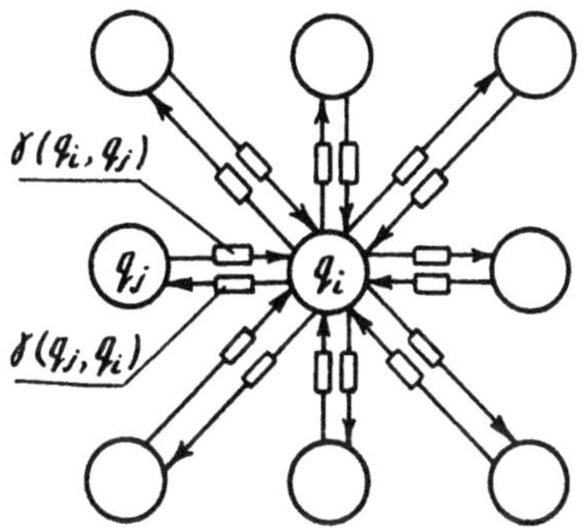

Fig.2.

Let's attach the weight $\gamma(q_i, q_j)$ to each arc $y(q_i, q_j) \in Y$ connecting the verteces q_i and q_j . The weight $\gamma(q_i, q_j)$ is equal to the functional J when the phase point transfers from the x_i state to the x_j state along the phase trajectory simulated by the arc $y(q_i, q_j)$, that is :

$$\gamma(q_i, q_j) = \min_{u_i(t) \in U} \int_{t_i}^{t_j} f^0(x_p(t), u_i(t))\,dt \tag{3}$$

where t_i - is the moment of the initial movement of the phase point state x_i ;

t_j - is the moment of the target state x_j ;

$x_p(t)$- is the phase trajectory simulated by the arc $y(q_i, q_j)$;

$u_i(t)$ - is the control transferring the phase point from x_i to x_j along the trajectory $x_p(t)$.

Besides the control $u_i(t)$ minimizing the functional (3), is attached to the arc $y(q_i, q_j)$.

In the terms of such a model the phase trajectory between the points x_0 and x_K is defined by the specified path at the graph $G(Q, Y)$, that connects the corresponding verteces q_0 and q_K. In this case the total arc weight that belongs to this path will be equal to the value of the functional J at the corresponding phase trajectory. Thus, the problem of the optimal phase trajectory brings to the problem of the search for the path between the verteces q_0 and q_K at the graph $G(Q, Y)$ having the minimal total weight of the arc which belongs to them. Such a path in the graph we call minimal. In this case the control sequence $u_0(t)$, $u_1(t), \dots, u_K(t)$ attached to the arcs of this path, will define the optimal control which transfers the phase point from the state x_0 to the state x_K.

The practical usage of such a method may bring to the difficulties because of the complication of arc weight calculating $\gamma(q_i, q_j)$ of the graph $G(Q, Y)$ according to the expression (3). The weight calculating procedure may be sufficiently simplified taking into account that the points x_i and x_j corresponding to the verteces q_i and q_j are the neighbouring ones of the phase space.

Thus the differential equation system (1) when the phase point transfers from x_i to x_j along the straight line $x_p(t)$ can be approximately substituted by the difference equation system of the form :

$$\begin{cases} \dfrac{x_j^1 - x_i^1}{\Delta t} = f^1(x_i, u_i) \\ \dfrac{x_j^2 - x_i^2}{\Delta t} = f^2(x_i, u_i) \\ \dots\dots\dots\dots \\ \dfrac{x_j^n - x_i^n}{\Delta t} = f^n(x_i, u_i) \end{cases} \tag{4}$$

and the functional (3) can be substituted by the expression :

$$\gamma(q_i, q_j) = \min_{u_i \in U} \left[f^0(x_i, u_i) \cdot \Delta t \right], \tag{5}$$

where $x_i = \{x_i^1, x_i^2, \dots, x_i^n\}$ is a parameter vector at the moment t_i ;

$x_j = \{x_j^1, x_j^2, \dots, x_j^n\}$ is a parameter vector at the moment t_j ;

$u_i = \{u_i^1, u_i^2, \dots, u_i^s\}$ is a control parameter vector at the moment t_i ;

$\Delta t = t_j - t_i$ is the time period during that the phase point transfers from x_i to x_j .

Let's find Δt . Note that since $\Delta t > 0$ the following conditions appear from the system (4).

$$sign(x_j^\kappa - x_i^\kappa) = sign(f^\kappa(x_i, u_i)) , \quad \kappa = 1, 2, \dots, n \tag{6}$$

The time Δt can be approximately defined as :

$$\Delta t = \frac{D}{V} , \tag{7}$$

where $D = \sqrt{\sum_{\ell=1}^{n} (x_j^\ell - x_i^\ell)^2}$ - is the Decart distance between points x_i and x_j in the phase space X ;

$V = \sqrt{\sum_{\ell=1}^{n} (f^\ell(x_i, u_i))^2}$ - is the module of the object phase rate vector.

Adding the expression (7) to (5) we have :

$$\gamma(q_i, q_j) = \min_{u_i \in U} \left(f^0(x_i, u_i) \cdot \sqrt{\frac{\sum_{\ell=1}^{n} (x_i^\ell - x_j^\ell)^2}{\sum_{\ell=1}^{n} (f^\ell(x_i, u_i))^2}} \right) . \tag{8}$$

Thus to define the weight value $\gamma(q_i, q_j)$ it's necessary to specify the function minimum (8), given that the conditions (6) are met. If these conditions are not met under vector $u_i \in U$, then the transfer of the phase point from the state x_i to the state x_j along the trajectory $x_p(t)$ is physically impossible. In the model of phase space - the graph $G(Q, Y)$ such a transfer must be simulated by the arc having the unlimited weight, i.e. in this case it is necessary to take $\gamma(q_i, q_j) = \infty$.

THE HOMOGENEOUS CONTROL SYSTEM

According to all the mentioned above, the optimal control problem brings to the problem of the minimal path in the graph $G(Q, Y)$ between the verteces q_0 and q_K. The latter problem can be easily solved with the homogeneous structure (HS).

For this purpose the structure cell, related with the neighbour cells matching the graph topology is to be put to each vertex q_i of the graph $G(Q, Y)$ given that the weight $\gamma(q_i, q_j)$ of the arcs $y(q_i, q_j) \in Y$ (Fig.2) must be simulated by the time delays. Also, each HS cell must contain the memory register set where the control vectors u_i attached to the arcs $y(q_i, q_j)$ issued from the verteces q_i are stored. Then, if in such a structure the signal wave is generated in the cell that corresponds to the vertex q_K then the wavefront will achieve the cell q_0 through the path having the minimal time delay. This path to the HS will correspond to the minimal path in the graph $G(Q, Y)$ between the verteces q_0 and q_K and hence, define the optimal phase trajectory . In case when we fix the link in the cell q_0 from where the first propagation wave signal has come in the cell we can specify the initial section of optimal trajectory. Then the vector u_i attached to the arc of the graph $G(Q, Y)$ corresponding to the given link will specify the object control at the initial section of the optional trajectory.

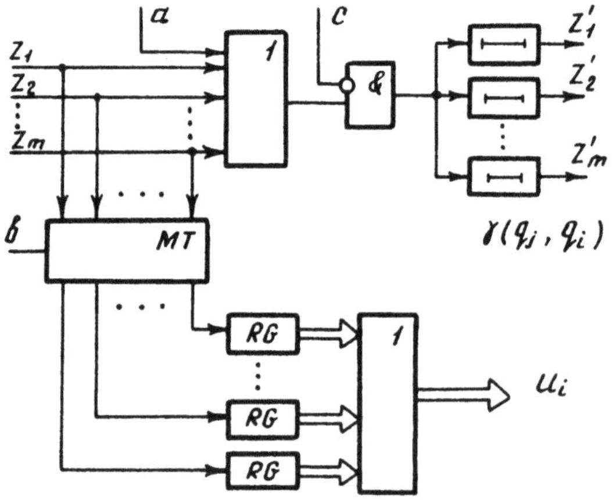

Fig.3.

The figure 3 illustrates the function scheme of that HS cell. The signal $a = 1$ going to the cell q_K comes through the AND and OR elements, in case when the signal $c = 0$ delays in the delay lines for the time proportional to the weights $\gamma(q_i, q_j)$ of the corresponding graph arcs $G(Q, Y)$ and then proceeds to the input Z of all cells, linked with the given one. In its turn each cell input Z_k $(k = 1, 2, \ldots, m)$, where m is the local degree of the graph verteces the single signal has come to, let it pass to the neighbour cell input with the corresponding time delays. Thus the propagation signal wave occurs in the system. The first single signal that has come to the input Z of the cell q_0 is fixed with the multistable trigger MT prepared for action by the signal $b = 1$. As a result of it a single signal $k-th$ trigger input through which the control parameter vector u_i is read and given to the output cell from the register RG_k . The signal $C=1$ coming parallel to all structure cells is used to reset the HS.

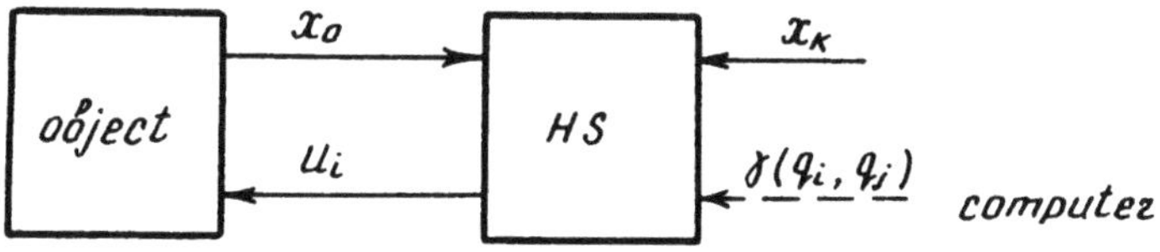

Fig.4.

Taking into account these considerations the optimal control system can be organized in the following way (Figure 4). Before the system activation you must define the weights $\gamma(q_i, q_j)$ of the graph arcs with expression (8) and the corresponding time delays are set in the HS. In that case the vectors u_i minimizing the expression (9) are stored at the memory registers of the corresponding structure cells. These procedures can be performed under computer. After that the system is ready to act.

Then, the cells q_K and q_0 are specified in the HS corresponding to the initial and target object states x_K and x_0 . The first cell generates the wave signals at the structure, and the second one fixes the link that the first of the propagation wave signals has come from. The control vector attached to the given link is read from the corresponding cell register q_0 and is transferred to the HS output to be processed by the object executive units. After that the system work cycle retries taking into account the new current object control state and so on up to the object achieves the target state x_K . In this case the value of the functional (2) resulted from the movement object, will approach the minimal one. If the target state x_K of the object is changed then the new cell is specified at the structure that corresponds to the new movement target, that becomes the signal wave generator. Finally the object will move to the new target.

As we have considered above the target object state x_K is an unambiguous. In the more general case a target state set $X_K \subseteq X$ can be specified. In this case the optimal control problem implies the search for such a control $u(t)$, that would transfer the phase point from x_0 to one of the set states X_K and minimize the functional (2) . The latter problem is easily solved with the same HS.

To do this it's necessary to generate the signal wave from all the HS cells that correspond to the set states X_K. Then the cell q_0 is achieved by the signal which has come first along the path having the minimal time delay. This path to the HS corresponds to the optimal phase trajectory from the point x_0 to one of the set point X_K at which the functional J is minimal. That is why as a result of the HS activity, the control object achieves the state that belongs to the set X_K through the optimal phase trajectory.

CONCLUSION

The method of the optimal control system construction based on the HS has some important advantages. The fastacting of HS is the first advantage. According to the researches [4] the work cycle time is in the range of $10^{-4} - 10^{-5} s$. This allows the usage of such HS for controlling the fast processes.

Secondly the periodical wave propagation to the HS allows the system to function under the conditions when the object movement target is not changed dynamically. To do this you must set the new cell at each HS work cycle as the generating one and corresponding to the new target object state. In this case the initial optimal trajectory section is fixed each time to the current target. Such a HS work cycle is very important for addition task solving.

Thirdly, one of the advantages of this method is the possibility to re-adjust the HS for controlling the different objects. For this purpose you must only change time delays at HS links and also the control vectors at the cell registers according to the graph-model $G(Q, Y)$ of the phase space of the new control object. To enable such an adjustment the reprogrammable delay lines must be used at the HS (refer to (4) about this information). This enables to use the same HS to control the different types of objects.

However we must note that all these advantages are due to the phase space descrete model usage and entering some admissions that can make the given decision to some extent "rough". One of the disadvantages of this method is the incrementation of the number of the HS cells in accordance to the incrementation of the object phase space dimension. The last point is partially compensated for the high homogeniety and the simplicity of the HS cell structure. This fact gives the enormous perspectives for the realization of the whole HS on the single SLSI. Such researches are now underway [5].

The results of the practical implementation or the given optimal control system construction method based on HS allows to make conclusion about its high effectiveness [4,5].

REFERENCES

1. Moiseyev N.N. "The theory elements of optimal systems", "Science", 1975, p.p. 526.
2. Pontryagin L.S., Boltyansky V.G., Gamkielidge R.V., Mischenko E.F. "The mathematical theory of the optimal processes", Mathemat.literature, 1961, p. 391.
3. Voevodin V.V. "Linear algebra", "Science", 1980, p. 400.
4. Kalyaev A.V., Kalyaev I.A., Noskov V.P., Chernuchin Y.V. "The homogeneous control system of the adaptive robots", "Electronic industry", 10, 1981, p.p.12-23.
5. Chernuchin Y.V., Noskov V.P., Kalyaev I.A. and others, "The microprocessors control system of the transport robot", Microprocessor facilities and systems, 6, 1984, p.p. 70-72.

THE PARALLELIZATION INDEX OF SYNCHRONOUS SYSTEMS

By Christoph Meinel[1)]

ABSTRACT

The parallelization index $\pi = \pi(\mathcal{S})$ of a synchronous system $\mathcal{S}$ is the maximal number of independent interleaved streams of computation performed by $\mathcal{S}$. Its importance lies in the fact that it gives the maximal speed-up factor, which can be obtained by using different, only slightly modified copies of the original system $\mathcal{S}$ and by letting them operate in parallel. Such parallelizations are an important design tool for circuits destined e.g. to perform real time computations. In the present paper we (i) determine this parallelization index from the inner structure of the system and compute it efficiently in time almost linear in the number of edges of $\mathcal{S}$ and (ii) give a design strategy for generating systems $\hat{\mathcal{S}}$ speeded up by factors $d, d|\pi$ compared with $\mathcal{S}$. Allowing certain, for practical reasons unessential time translations of the system, the maximal speed-up factor π can also be reached, which improves previous results obtained e.g. by Leiserson/Saxe/3/.

1. SYNCHRONOUS SYSTEMS AND TIMING GRAPHS

A synchronous system $\mathcal{S}$ is a set of points to which some computational devices are attached, such as combinatorial logic, shift registers (which are assumed to be globally clocked) which are connected by a certain interconnection structure. Let $P_1, \ldots, P_r$ be the input nodes and let P_0 be the unique output node. After an initialization of the system $\mathcal{S}$, i.e. an assignment of initial values to the registers of $\mathcal{S}$ the system $\mathcal{S}$ is ready to work. That means $\mathcal{S}$ will start its computation if it gets input data via the input nodes $P_1, \ldots, P_r$ from the external world. Let us assume that the system receives the input $x_s^{(t)}$ via the input node P_s, $1 \leq s \leq r$, in the t-th clock period. These input signals and the signals output by the registers proceed in any clock period along all possible connections through the functional elements performing their computations up to the next register. (Note that for formal mathematical reasons in our model the directions of the connecting edges will be interpreted as the demand for information. Therefore, the signals move in opposite direction through the edges.) For more

Sektion Mathematik, Humboldt-Universität, Berlin, DDR-1086 Berlin, PO Box 1297

details we refer to /6/.

By dep $f^{(t)}$ we denote the set of input data $x_s^{(j)}$, $1 \leq s \leq r$, which the output of f in the t-th clock period depends on (formally).

For preparing decisions on relocating or reducing and multiplying registers, timing graphs have proved to be the appropriate structure. Such a timing graph $G_f = (V_f, E_f)$ of a synchronous system describes only the interconnection structure of the functional elements and the output and input nodes, and records the number of interleaved registers merely as an edge label λ . The retiming operations /3/ on f introduced (explicitly) by Leiserson and Saxe can be described within G_f by assigning certain integers (the <u>lags</u>) u_P to its nodes P ($u_{P_0} = u_{P_s} = 0$ for $1 \leq s \leq r$) indicating the number of registers that are removed from all edges ending in P and that are added to all edges starting in P. Let us only mention that the R-lengths $\lambda(e)$ of cycles e of G_f and the differences of R-lengths of two paths with a common starting and a common end point remain unchanged under any retiming operation.

Further let us introduce the technique of time translation of synchronous systems, the application of which allows, in most cases, much better retiming results and better speed-up factors for parallelizing synchronous systems. Thereby, the effect of such a <u>timing translation</u> $\tau = \tau_{u_1,\ldots,u_r}$, $u_s \in \mathbb{Z}$, on a synchronous system f with r input nodes processing r input streams $x_1^{(IN)},\ldots,x_r^{(IN)}$ is that of shifting the s-th input stream $x_s^{(IN)}$ in time by u_s clock ticks, i.e., the timing graph $G_{\tau_{u_1,\ldots,u_r} \cdot f}$ of the time translated system $\tau_{u_1,\ldots,u_r} \cdot f$ equals the timing graph G_f of f with the only exception that the u_s are added to all edges ending in the input node P_s, $1 \leq s \leq r$. Physically, $\tau_{u_1,\ldots,u_r} \cdot f$ can be obtained by adding ($u_s \geq 0$) or deleting ($u_s < 0$) $|u_s|$ registers to or from all edges ending in P_s, $1 \leq s \leq r$, respectively, or by changing the input time regime in another way.

To illustrate the value of time translations in optimizing synchronous systems by retiming, look at the following rather trivial, but suggestive example:

f with G_f :

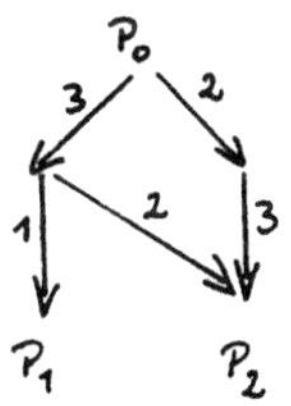

$\tau_{3,4} f$ with $G_{\tau_{3,4} f}$:

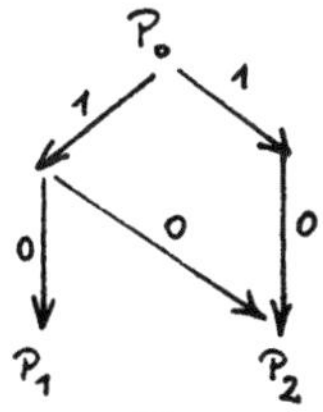

Inside f retiming does not help to reduce the needless registers but in $\tau_{3,4} f$ this is possible without difficulty.

The value of this time translation technique in speeding-up synchronous systems by their parallelization will become obvious in the following.

2. THE PARALLELIZATION INDEX AND ITS EFFECTIVE COMPUTATION

As already mentioned the parallelization index $\pi = \pi(f)$ of a synchronous system f is the maximal number of independent, interleaved streams of computation performable by f. Since the claim that $\pi | l$ if dep $f^{(t)} \cap$ dep $f^{(t+l)} \neq \emptyset$ for a $t \in \mathbb{N}$ guarantees that the π streams of computation performed during the π series $(n\pi + k)$, $n \in \mathbb{N}$, of clock periods, $0 \leq k < \pi$, depend only on their "own" data input in the corresponding series of clock periods, and, further, that the different interleaved streams of computation process different data (which follows from the quite obvious fact that $\pi | l$ for all l with dep $f^{(t)} \cap$ dep $f^{(t+l)} \neq \emptyset$ for a $t \in \mathbb{N}$ implies that the dependence sets dep $f^{(t)}$, dep $f^{(t+1)}$,..

..,dep $f^{(t+\pi-1)}$ are pairwise disjoint), the parallelization index $\pi = \pi(f)$ can be defined mathematically by

DEFINITION:

The parallelization index $\pi = \pi(f)$ of a synchronous system is the maximal number d dividing any l for which a $t \in \mathbb{N}$ exists with

$$\text{dep } f^{(t)} \cap \text{dep } f^{(t+l)} \neq \emptyset.$$

Instead of describing the parallelization index by means of the input-output behaviour of the system f let us determine this from the internal structure of f.

PROPOSITION 4:

The parallelization index $\pi = \pi(f)$ equals the greatest common divisor of the differences of R-lengths of paths of f leading from the output node P_0 to one of the input nodes P_s, $1 \leq s \leq r$,

$$\pi = \text{g c d } \{(\lambda(p') - \lambda(p)) | p, p' : P_0 \longrightarrow P_s,\ 1 \leq s \leq r, \text{ paths in } f\}$$

PROOF: The assumption follows directly from the fact that dep $f^{(t)} \cap$ dep $f^{(t+l)} \neq \emptyset$ for a $t \in \mathbb{N}$ is equivalent to the existence of two paths $p, p' : P_0 \longrightarrow P_s$ from the output node P_0 to one of the input nodes P_s, $1 \leq s \leq r$ with $\lambda(p') - \lambda(p) = l$.
If $x_s^{(j)} \in$ dep $f^{(t)} \cap$ dep $f^{(t+l)}$ for a $t \in \mathbb{N}$, then there exist two paths $p, p' : P_0 \longrightarrow P_s$ with $\lambda(p) = t-j$ and $\lambda(p') = t+l-j$ via which f gets the input $x_s^{(j)}$ in the t-th and in the (t+l)-th clock period, respectively, and which have an R-lengths difference of $\lambda(p') - \lambda(p) =$ $= t+l-j - (t-j) = l$. Reversely, if $p, p' : P_0 \longrightarrow P_s$ are two paths in f leading from the output node P_0 to one of the input nodes P_s, $1 \leq s \leq r$, with R-lengths difference $l = \lambda(p') - \lambda(p)$, then, for example, dep $f^{\lambda(p)} \cap$ dep $f^{\lambda(p')}$ = dep $f^{\lambda(p)} \cap$ dep $f^{\lambda(p)+l} \neq \emptyset$ holds because f gets $x_s^{(0)}$ in the $\lambda(p)$-th clock period via the path p and in the $\lambda(p')$-th clock period via the path p'. $\boxslash$

Now let us have a closer look at the determination of the parallelization index π. If f is a cyclic system, then π is the greatest common divisor of an infinite number of differences of R-lengths of paths $p, p' : P_0 \longrightarrow P_s$ ($1 \leq s \leq r$)! Nevertheless, because of the fact that the R-lengths of all cycles of $\mathcal{f}$ are multiples of π we can reduce this number to a finite one.

LEMMA 2:

Let $c : P \longrightarrow P$, $P \in \mathcal{f}$ (more exactly $P \in G_{\mathcal{f}}$), be a cycle, then π divides the R-length $\lambda(c)$ of c

$$\pi | \lambda(c).$$

PROOF: Let $c : P \longrightarrow P$ be a cycle of $\mathcal{f}$ and let $p_1 : P_0 \longrightarrow P$ and $p_2 : P \longrightarrow P_s$ be two paths from the output node P_0 to P and from P to one of the input nodes P_s, $1 \leq s \leq r$, which do exist because of our restriction to input-output connected systems. Then we have two paths $p, p' : P_0 \longrightarrow P_s$

$$p := p_1 p_2 \text{ and } p' := p_1 c p_2$$

with $\lambda(p) = \lambda(p_1) + \lambda(p_2)$ and $\lambda(p') = \lambda(p_1) + \lambda(c) + \lambda(p)$.
Since $\pi | (\lambda(p') - \lambda(p))$ and since $\lambda(p') - \lambda(p) =$
$= \lambda(p_1) + \lambda(c) + \lambda(p_2) - (\lambda(p_1) + \lambda(p_2)) = \lambda(c)$, we obtain $\pi | \lambda(c)$. ☒

Let us call a path $p : P_0 \longrightarrow P_s$ of $G_{\mathcal{f}}$ from the output node P_0 to an input node P_s, $1 \leq s \leq r$, reduced if

$$\text{supp}(p') \neq \text{supp}(p) \text{ for all paths } p' : P_0 \longrightarrow P_s$$

with $\lambda(p') < \lambda(p)$. Hence, if $p : P_0 \longrightarrow P_s$ is a path of $\mathcal{f}$, then the reduced path $\hat{p} : P_0 \longrightarrow P_s$ to p is the path of minimal R-length with $\text{supp}(\hat{p}) = \text{supp}(p)$. However, if $\hat{p}$ and $\hat{p}'$ denote the reduced paths to the paths $p, p' : P_0 \longrightarrow P_s$, $1 \leq s \leq r$, then the latter lemma implies

$$\lambda(p) = \lambda(\hat{p}) + n\pi \quad \text{and} \quad \lambda(p') = \lambda(\hat{p}') + n'\pi$$

with $n, n' \in \mathbb{N}$ since a path and its reduced version differ at most in some cycles covered by the original path but not by the reduced one. Consequently, since

$$\pi | (\lambda(p') - \lambda(p)) \text{ iff } \pi | (\lambda(\hat{p}') - \lambda(\hat{p}))$$

the following Proposition is proved.

PROPOSITION 5:

The parallelization index $\pi = \pi(\mathcal{f})$ of a synchronous system equals the greatest common divisor of all differences of R-lengths of reduced paths from the output node P_0 to a common input node P_s, $1 \leq s \leq r$,

$$\pi = \text{g c d} \{(\lambda(p') - \lambda(p)) | p, p' : P_0 \longrightarrow P_s, 1 \leq s \leq r, \text{ reduced paths}\}.$$

☒

In order to obtain a further drastic reduction of the number of differences of R-lengths that we have to take into account when computing, the parallelization index $\pi = \pi(\mathcal{S})$ of a synchronous system $\mathcal{S}$, we convert $\mathcal{S}$ by retiming and time translation into a certain system $\mathcal{S}'$ with $\lambda'(P,Q) = 0$ for almost all edges (P,Q) of $\mathcal{S}'$. Since the following lemma says that retimings and time translations do not influence the value of the parallelization index, we can compute π within $\mathcal{S}'$, which will be much easier than its determination within the original system $\mathcal{S}$.

LEMMA 3:

(i) Let $\mathcal{S}$, $\mathcal{S}'$ be two synchronous systems such that $\mathcal{S}'$ is a retimed version of $\mathcal{S}$. Then $\pi(\mathcal{S}') = \pi(\mathcal{S})$.

(ii) Let $\mathcal{S}$, $\mathcal{S}^{*}$ be two synchronous systems such that $\mathcal{S}^{*}$ is a time translated version of $\mathcal{S}$. Then $\pi(\mathcal{S}^{*}) = \pi(\mathcal{S})$.

PROOF:

(i) $\pi(\mathcal{S}') = \pi(\mathcal{S})$ directly follows from the fact that

$$\operatorname{dep} \mathcal{S}^{(t)} = \operatorname{dep} \mathcal{S}'^{(t)}$$

for all $t \in \mathbb{N}$, which was proved in Prop. 2. and,

(ii) $\pi(\mathcal{S}^{*}) = \pi(\mathcal{S})$ for $\mathcal{S}^{*} = \tau_{u_1,\ldots,u_r}\mathcal{S}$ can be obtained from the observation that

$$\operatorname{dep}(\tau_{u_1,\ldots,u_r}\mathcal{S})^{(t)} = \left\{ x_s^{(j-u_s)} \mid x_s^{(j)} \in \operatorname{dep} \mathcal{S}^{(t)},\ 1 \le s \le r \right\},$$

which was made in Prop. 3. $\boxtimes$

Now let us convert a given system $\mathcal{S}$ by retiming and time translating it into a system $\mathcal{S}'$, in which it is much easier to compute the parallelization index π than within $\mathcal{S}$ itself. For this, let us fix a spanning tree $T_{\mathcal{S}} = (V_{\mathcal{S}}, T)$, $T \subseteq E_{\mathcal{S}}$ of the timing graph $G_{\mathcal{S}} = (V_{\mathcal{S}}, E_{\mathcal{S}})$ of $\mathcal{S}$ rooted in the output node P_0 of $\mathcal{S}$. Obviously, firstly, such a tree $T_{\mathcal{S}}$ exists because $\mathcal{S}$ was assumed to be input-output connected, and, secondly, all input nodes P_s, $1 \le s \le r$, are leaves of $T_{\mathcal{S}}$ because these nodes are the only ones in $V_{\mathcal{S}}$ with an empty valency set. From graph theory it is well-known that every edge of $E_{\mathcal{S}} - T$ closes an elementary cycle if $G_{\mathcal{S}}$ is regarded as an undirected graph for a moment. The importance of these $|E_{\mathcal{S}} - T| = |E_{\mathcal{S}}| - |V_{\mathcal{S}}| + 1$ elementary cycles lies in the property that all cycles of $G_{\mathcal{S}}$ can be obtained by combining some of them /7/. Now we will retime and time translate $\mathcal{S}$ into a system $\mathcal{S}'$ such that all edges of T are labelled under λ' in $G_{\mathcal{S}'}$ by 0. This is possible by assigning the lag $u_P := \lambda(q_P)$ to a point P of $G_{\mathcal{S}}$ if $q_P : P_0 \longrightarrow P$ is the unique path from P_0 to P existing in the spanning tree $T_{\mathcal{S}}$. If we retime $\mathcal{S}$ by these lags and if we apply the time translation $\tau = \tau_{u_{P_1},\ldots,u_{P_r}}$, then we obtain the desired system $\mathcal{S}'$, whose parallelization index $\pi = \pi(\mathcal{S}')$ equals that of $\mathcal{S}$ because of Lemma 3

$$\pi = \pi(\mathcal{S}') = \pi(\mathcal{S}).$$

But in $\mathcal{S}'$ one obtains π easily as the greatest common divisor of the $|E_{\mathcal{S}}| - |T|$ R-lengths of the remaining edges $e \in E_{\mathcal{S}} - T$

$$\pi = g\ c\ d\ \{\lambda'(e)\ |\ e \in E_{\mathcal{S}} - T\}\ .$$

(Recall that $|E_{\mathcal{S}}| - |T| = |E_{\mathcal{S}}| - |V_{\mathcal{S}}| + 1$ since $T_{\mathcal{S}}$ is a spanning tree of $G_{\mathcal{S}}$.)

This is true since the R-lengths of all paths of $\mathcal{S}'$ are sums of 0 and the $\lambda'(e)$, $e \in E_{\mathcal{S}} - T$ and, therefore, the differences of the R-lengths are sums or differences of these $\lambda'(e)$, $e \in E_{\mathcal{S}} - T$. Since the values of the R-lengths of cycles and the differences of the R-lengths of two paths with a common starting point and a common end point remain unchanged under retiming and time translation, a further reduction of the complexity of the computation of the parallelization index π is not possible.

In order to determine the complexity of the outlined algorithm recall that the timing graph $G_{\mathcal{S}} = (V_{\mathcal{S}}, E_{\mathcal{S}})$ was obtained from the synchronous system $\mathcal{S} = (m, l)$, $m = (Z, X, d)$ by reducing all points P with $l(P) = R$. Therefore it holds that

$$n := |V_{\mathcal{S}}| = |Z - l^{-1}(R)| \leqq |Z|\ .$$

Furthermore,

$$|E_{\mathcal{S}}| \leqq |X|\ n,$$

since the correspondence of edges $(P, Q) \in E_{\mathcal{S}}$ from $G_{\mathcal{S}}$ to the first edge (P, x) of the path in $\mathcal{S}$, which defines the edge (P, Q) of $G_{\mathcal{S}}$, is one-to-one because the fan-in of points $P \in l^{-1}(R)$ was assumed to be 1. Altogether, one obtains

$$|\{\lambda'(e)\ |\ e \in E_{\mathcal{S}} - T\}| = O(n).$$

It is quite obvious that the complexity of the outlined method for computing the parallelization index of a synchronous system is determined essentially by the construction of the spanning tree $T_{\mathcal{S}}$ of $G_{\mathcal{S}}$, which is possible in time $O(n\alpha(n))$ /4/, where α denotes an almost linear function (namely, an inverse of a variant of the Ackermann function from recursion theory) and by the computation of the greatest common divisor of the $O(n)$ values $\lambda'(e)$, $e \in E_{\mathcal{S}} - T$. However, this is possible in time $O(n + \lg \lambda'_0)$ if $\lambda'_0 = \min \{\lambda'(e) | e \in E_{\mathcal{S}} - T\}$ /3/. Since λ'_0 is not greater than the total number of registers of $\mathcal{S}$ and since, in a typical circuit, this number is much less than exponential in the number of edges, we can compute the parallelization index π in almost linear time in the number $n = |V_{\mathcal{S}}|$ of vertices of $G_{\mathcal{S}}$.

THEOREM:

The parallelization index $\pi = \pi(\mathcal{S})$ of a synchronous system can be computed by fixing a spanning tree $T_{\mathcal{S}} = (V_{\mathcal{S}}, T)$ of the timing graph $G_{\mathcal{S}}$ of $\mathcal{S}$ rooted in the output node P_0 and retiming and time translating $\mathcal{S}$ such that the R-lengths $\lambda'(e)$ of all edges $e \in T_{\mathcal{f}}$ vanish in the arising system $\mathcal{f}'$. Then

$$\pi = \gcd \{\lambda'(e) \mid e \in E_{\mathcal{f}} - T\} .$$

The complexity of the procedure is almost linear in the number $|V_{\mathcal{f}}|$ of the points of $\mathcal{f}$, to which functional elements are assigned. ☐

To illustrate the outlined method for computing the parallelization index of a synchronous system look at the following example. Let $\mathcal{f}$ be a system with the timing graph $G_{\mathcal{f}}$. Fixing e.g. the spanning tree $T_{\mathcal{f}}$ we obtain the lags u_P for all $P \in G_{\mathcal{f}}$, given in the picture. After the application of the corresponding retiming and time translation we obtain a system $\mathcal{f}'$ with the timing graph $G_{\mathcal{f}'}$:

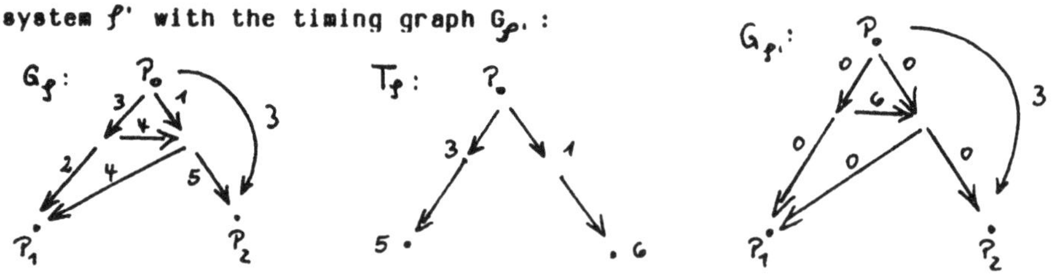

Indeed, the computation of the parallelization index $\pi = \pi(\mathcal{f}')$ of $\mathcal{f}'$, which equals the parallelization index of $\mathcal{f}$ because of Lemma 2, is very easy, one obtains $\pi = 3$.

3. SPEEDING UP SYNCHRONOUS SYSTEMS BY FACTORS d DIVIDING THE PARALLELIZATION INDEX π

After having computed the parallelization index $\pi = \pi(\mathcal{f})$ of a synchronous system $\mathcal{f}$ one knows that $\mathcal{f}$ performs π independent, interleaved streams of computation. This knowledge can be used in order to design systems $\hat{\mathcal{f}}$ to any d, $d|\pi$ which get the input data $x_1^{(kd)},\dots,x_r^{(kd)},\dots,x_1^{((k+1)d-1)},\dots,x_r^{((k+1)d-1)}$ $(k \in \mathbb{N})$ of d consecutive clock periods at once and perform d of the π independent streams of computation in parallel. One "only" has to reduce the number of the registers of $\mathcal{f}$ by the factor 1/d, to take d copies of such a register reduced version of $\mathcal{f}$ and let them operate in parallel. Then $\hat{\mathcal{f}}$ is speeded up by the factor d compared with the original system $\mathcal{f}$ because it performs the computation of d consecutive clock periods kd,...,(k+1)d-1 in the k-th clock period.

Let us have a closer look at the only critical point of this speed-up strategy, namely the reduction of registers. To see how that is possible without essential changes of the computational behaviour recall that retiming operations do not influence the global input-output behaviour of a synchronous system, and that time translations cause only changes in the input time regime. Therefore the transition from $\mathcal{f}$ to a system $\mathcal{f}'$ outlined in the last paragraph remains without essential changes on the computational behaviour. Since $\pi = \gcd \{\lambda'(e) \mid e \in E_{\mathcal{f}} - T\}$ and $\lambda'(e) = 0$ for $e \in T$, we know that the R-lengths of all edges of $\mathcal{f}'$ are multiples of any d with $d|\pi$. Hence, within f' a reduction of the number of the registers by the factor 1/d, $d|\pi$ is possible without difficulty. Following /3/ let us denote this register reduced version of f' by $1/d\,f'$. Obviously, the stream of computation performable by f' during a series $(\mathbb{N}\pi + j)$, of clock periods $j<\pi$ can be performed by $1/d\,f'$ during the clock periods $(\mathbb{N}(1/d)\pi + j \bmod d)$. Hence, we obtain a system $\hat{f}$ performing the same computation as f , but which is speeded up, compared to f , by a factor $d, d|\pi$, by taking d copies of $1/d\,f'$ and letting them operate in parallel. In most cases, instead of $1/d\,f'$ one takes a version of $1/d\,f'$ which is - in some sense - optimized by retimings and time translations in order to build $\hat{f}$. Let us illustrate this speed-up strategy by the example given in the last paragraph:

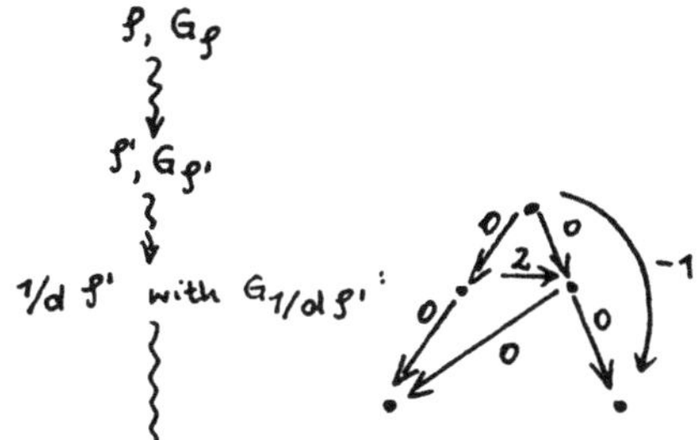

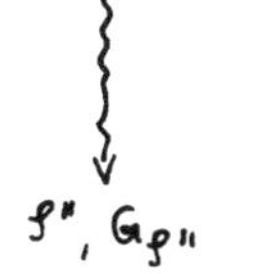

suitable retiming and time translating in order to optimize the system (e.g. to shorten the clock period or to obtain nonnegative R-lengths).

Then $\hat{f}$ is a system with the timing graph $G_{\hat{f}}$:

$G_{f''}$ $G_{f''}$ $G_{f''}$.

Before summarizing our result let us only remark that without the technique of time translations a synchronous system can only be speeded up by some small divisors d of π/3/ in general. For instance, in our example the maximal speed up factor reachable without time translations is 1!

THEOREM 2:

Every synchronous system f with the parallelization index $\pi = \pi(f)$ can be speeded up by every divisor d of π by letting d retimed, time translated and register reduced versions of f operate in parallel. ∅

REFERENCES:

/1/ Budach, L.; Ch. Meinel: Automata and environments. I and II EIK 18, 1982, Vols. 1/2, and 3

/2/ Kung, H.T.: Why systolic architectures?, CMU-CS-81-148

/3/ Leiserson, Ch.E., J.G. Saxe: Optimizing synchronous circuitry by retiming. FOCS or SIOC 83

/4/ Mehlhorn, K.: Graph Algorithms and MP-Completeness. EATCS Monographs on theroetical computer science, 1984

/5/ Meinel, Ch.: Structural investigations of parallel computing devices. Computer and Artificial Intelligence No. 4, 1984

/6/ Meinel, Ch.: Symbolic simulation of synchronous systems, Forthcoming in EIK, 1985

A NEURAL NETWORK MODEL FOR PATTERN RECOGNITION

Hisashi Mizuno[1)]

ABSTRACT

A neural network model for pattern recognition is proposed. This model has functions regulating shift in position and thickness of patterns. In learning as presented by this, an excitatory synapse, an inhibitory synapse and a threshold are simultaneously modified. The ability to regulate shift in position is realized by the existance of a cell plane. A cell plane consists of neurons which respond to the same feature patterns even with differences in position. For regulation of thickness, a presynaptic inhibitory modifiable connection is used. Processing for feature extraction and thickness regulation of a pattern are executed in parallel. Self-organization in the model is achieved through unsupervised learning. Its performance is demonstrated by computer simulation.

1. INTRODUCTION

With the aim of analyzing information processing mechanisms in the brain by means of models, neural network models with various functions have been proposed. One of the most impotant functions of the neural network model is pattern recognition. Models for pattern recognition must have functions that regulate such things as thickness, shift in position, rotation and size. A model having all these necessary functions has yet to be presented. Fukushima(3) proposed the Neocognitron model which has the ability to regulate shift in position.

In this paper, a neural network model that has functions regulating thickness and shift in position is presented. A cell plane is used for shift regulation. It consists of neurons which respond to the same feature patterns even with differnces in position such as presented by Fukushima(3). For thickness regulation, a presynaptic inhitory modifiable connection is used. Processing for feature extraction and thickness regulation of a pattern is executed in parallel. Self-organization in the model is achieved through unsupervised learning. Only if the training patterns are repeatedly put in the model,are the above men ioned functions performed. Behavior of the model is confirmed by computer simulation.

2. BASIC STRUCTURE OF THE MODEL

1) Tohoku Institute of Technology, Sendai-Shi, 982 Japan

The model is constructed from a feature extraction network, a thickness regulation network, a shift regulation network and a discrimination network. Fig.1 shows a blockdiagram of the model. An input pattern is simul-

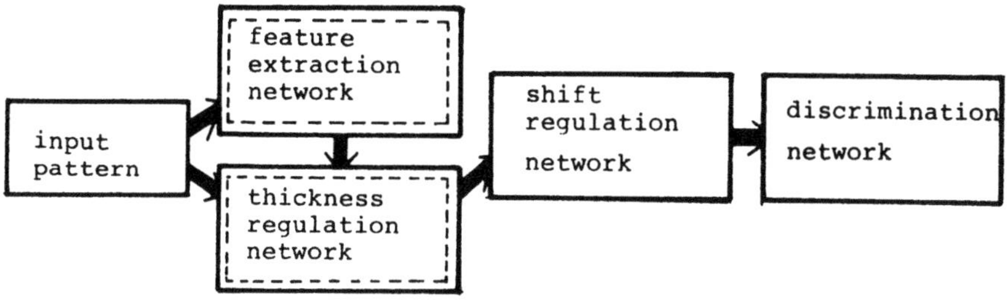

Fig.1 Blockdiagram of the model

taneously put into the feature extraction network and the thickness regulation network. The outputs of these networks are integrated and processed. A network for integration is included in the thickness regulation network. Information for feature pattern, thickness and position is integrated and processed in the shift regulation network. Recognition of the input pattern is finally performed in the discrimination network. The neurons belonging to the networks enclosed by dotted lines in Fig.1 are increased for shift regulation. Details are explained in section 2.3. As the discrimination network has the same basic structure as the feature extraction network, explanation of this is omitted.

2.1 BASIC STRUCTURE OF THE FEATURE EXTRACTION NETWORK

Fig.2 shows the basic structure of the feature extraction network. E_i

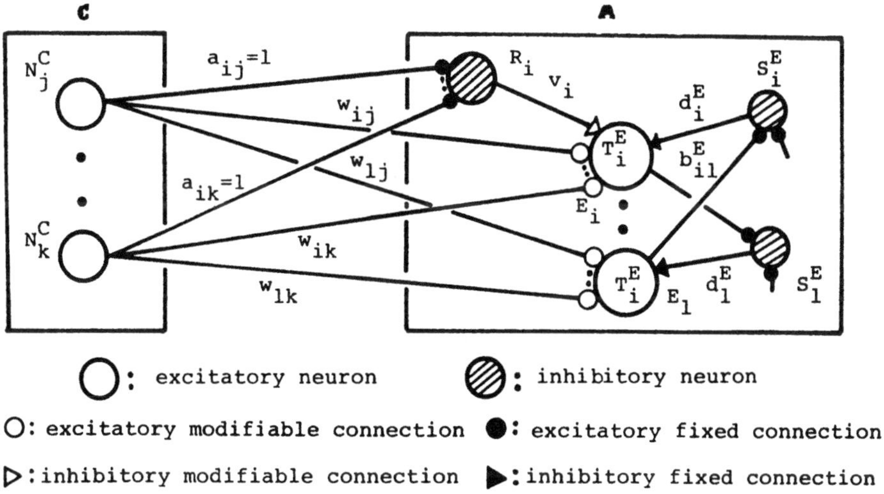

Fig.2 Basic structure of the feature extraction network

is any learning neuron. The set of neurons with which a neuron can have synaptic connections is called the connectable area of a neuron. **C** is the connectable area of E_i. **A** is the set of neurons with the same connectable area. A neuron in **C** is described by N^C. $w_{ij}, v_i, a_{ij}, d_i^E$ and b_{il}^E show the synaptic coefficients between corresponding neurons.

The output of E_i is represented by eq.(1)-(3).

$$E_i = \varphi\left(\sum_{j(j \in \mathbf{C})} w_{ij} \times N_j^C - v_i \times R_i - d_i^E \times S_i^E - T_i^E \right) \tag{1}$$

$$R_i = \sum_{j(j \in \mathbf{C})} a_{ij} \times N_j^C \quad , \quad S_i^E = \sum_{l(l \neq i, l \in \mathbf{A})} b_{il}^E \times E_l \tag{2}$$

$$\varphi(p) = \begin{cases} \alpha_2 & p > \alpha_2 \\ p & \alpha_1 \leq p \leq \alpha_2 \\ 0 & p < \alpha_1 \end{cases} \tag{3}$$

In the equations, the same symbols are used for neurons and their outputs. The learning scheme of E neurons in **A** is as follows.

(1) When a training pattern is presented in **C**, learning is achieved at that neuron which fired most strongly in **A**. In subsequent discussions, it is assumed that learning is achieved at E_i.

(2) In learning, the values of w, v and T_i^E are modified as follows.

$$\text{(a)} \quad w_{ij}(t+ t) = w_{ij}(t) + (-1)^m \times \Delta w \tag{4}$$

if $N_j^C > 0$, then m=0 and if $N_j^C \leq 0$, then m=1

$$\text{(b)} \quad v_i(t + \Delta t) = v_i(t) + \Delta v \tag{5}$$

$$\text{(c)} \quad T_i^E(t + \Delta t) = T_i^E(t) + \Delta T^E(t)$$

$$\Delta T^E(t) = \left(\sum_j N_j^C - n_s \times \alpha_2\right) \times \Delta w - \left(\sum_j N_j^C\right) \times \Delta v - \beta + (n - n_s) \times \beta \times (\Delta w - \Delta v) \times k \tag{6}$$

Here, $w_{ij}(t)$, $v_i(t)$ and $T_i^E(t)$ are the values of w_{ij}, v_i and T_i^E at t. Δw, Δv and β are constants given as parameters. N is the number of fired neurons in **C**, n_s is the number of fired neurons with saturated synaptic coefficients and k is the number of times learning has occured.

The explanation of this learning scheme is given in the literature(4) in detail. The set of E neurons, R neurons and S^E neurons is called the **E** layer which is divided into local areas with differnt connectable areas. E neurons belonging to the same local area have the same connectable area. In the model for computer simulation of chapter 3, the **E** layer in the feature extraction network is divided into 9 local areas. An E neuron has the subpattern of a input pattern as the connectable area. On the other hand, all E neurons belonging to the discrimination network have the same connectable area that consists ofoutputs of the shift regulation network.

2.2 BASIC STRUCTURE OF THE THICKNESS REGULATION NETWORK

Fig.3 shows the basic structure of the thickness regulation network. It is constructed from the **P** layer and the **L** layer. The **P** layer contains P neurons and S^Pneurons. It is divided into local areas with different connectable areas. The number of local areas in the **P** layer is the same as that in the **E** layer. Each local areas in the **P** layer has a correspond-

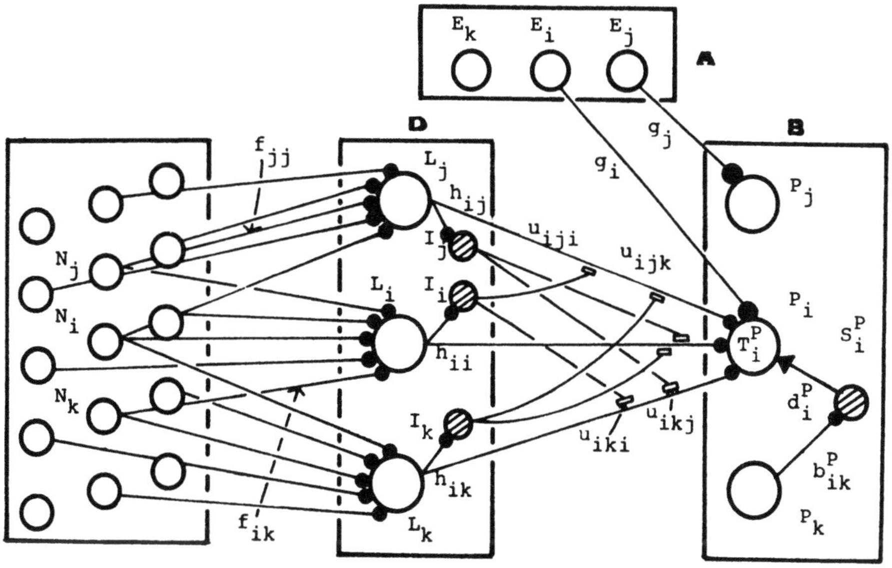

▭ : pre-synaptic inhibitory modifiable connection

Fig.3 Basic structure of the thickness regulation network

ing local areas in the **E** layer. The number and set of coordinates of neurons contained in a local area in the **P** layer are the same as those of the corresponding local area in the **E** layer. In Fig.3, **B** corresponds with **A**. Any P neuron has a set of L neurons as its connectable area. The **L** layer consists of L neurons and I neurons. The output of I_i is the same as that of L_i. A P neuron belonging to **B** has **D** as the connectable area. U_{ijk} is the presynaptic inhibitory modifiable coefficient among P_i, L_j and I_k. This means that if u_{ijk} has large value, I_k inhibits information tannsfer from L_j to P_i, and if u_{ijk} has small value, I_k cant inhibit imformation transfer. F_{ij} is the fixed excitatory synaptic coefficient between L_i and N_j. Among f_{ii},f_{ik} and f_{ij}, the following relations exist : $f_{ii} > f_{ik} (i \neq k)$, $f_{ik} = f_{ij} (i \neq j, i \neq k)$. The function of the model for thickness regulation is dependent on the area of N neurons with which L neuron can connect. In computer simulation in chapter 3, any L neuron will connect to the N neurons when the coordinate differences between the L neuron and the N neurons are less than 2. G_i, h_{ij}, d_i^P and b_{ik}^P are the synaptic coefficients between corresponding neurons. The threshold of L_i is . The outputs of L neurons and P neurons are represented by the following equations.

$$L_i = \varphi(\sum_j f_{ij} \times N_j - \theta_i^L), \quad L_i = I_i \tag{7}$$

$$P_i = (\sum_{j(j \in \mathbf{D})} h_{ij} \times L_j \times (\prod_{k(k \neq j)} [1-(I_k/L_j)^3 \times u_{ijk}]) + g_i \times E_i - d_i^P \times S_i^P - T_i^P \tag{8}$$

$$S_i^P = \sum_{j(j \neq i, j \in \mathbf{B})} b_{ij}^P \times P_i \tag{9}$$

In eq.(8), [v] means that if $v \geq 0$, [v] = v and if $v < 0$, [v]=0.

The learning scheme of P neurons in **B** is as follows.

(1) When a training pattern is given in **D**, learning is achieved at that neuron which fired most strongly in **B**. In subsequent discussions, it is assumed that learning is achieved at P_i.

(2) In learning, the values of u_{ijk} and T_i^E are modified as follows.

(a) $u_{ijk}(t + t) = u_{ijk}(t) + m \times \Delta u$

if $L_j \geq I_k > 0$ and $L_j \geq \gamma$, then m= -1, if $I_k > L_j$ and $I_k \geq \gamma$, then m =1

and any other case, then m = 0 (10)

(b) $T_i^P(t + \Delta t) = T_i^P(t) + \Delta T^P(t), \quad \Delta T^P(t) = P_i(t) - T_i^P(t) - \delta$ (11)

Here, Δu, γ and δ are constants given as parameters. As shown in (2), the values of u_{ijk} is decreased by learning.

In this network, E_i functions for P_i as supervisor. In the first stage, P_i dosn't fire due to presynaptic inhibition by I neurons. If P_i receives input from E_i, P_i fire and initiates learning. The detailed discussion can be found in the literature(5).

2.3 BASIC STRUCTURE OF THE SHIFT REGULATION NETWORK

Fig.4 shows the basic structure of the shift regulation network. It is constructed from the E_i plane, the P_i plane and the **M** layer. The E_i plane is increased in the **E** layer in the feature extraction network. The E_i plane has E_j in the **E** layer as a core neuron. The set of E planes is called the **E** cell plane. The number of E planes in the **E** cell plane is the same as that of E neurons in the **E** layer. Any neuron in E_i plane is described as ${}^SE_{ij}$ except for E_i. Similarly, the P_i plane is increased in the **P** layer in the thickness regulation network, the P_i plane has P_i neuron in the **P** layer as a core neuron, the set of P planes is called the **P** cell plane, the number of P planes in the **P** cell plane is the same as that of P neurons in the **P** layer, and any neuron in P_i plane is described as ${}^{S}P_{ij}$ except for P_i. Any neuron in the E_i plane connects to the neuron having the same coordinate in the P_i plane. It is learned that all the neurons belonging to the same plane have input synapses of the same

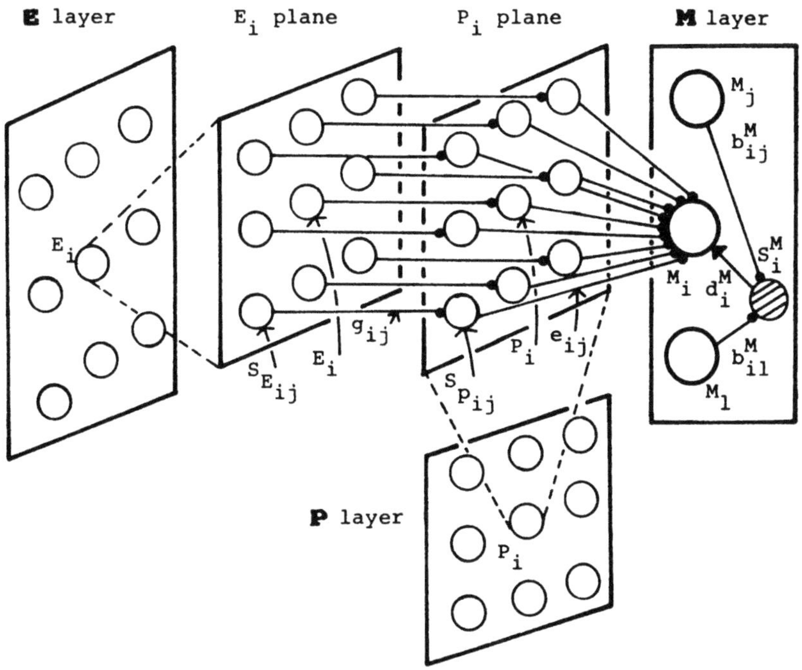

Fig.4 Basic structure of shift regulation network

spacial distribution and only the positions of presynaptic neurons are shifted in parallel. The function for shift regulation depends on the number of neurons in one plane. In computer simulation presented in chapter 3, one plane consists of 25 neurons. The **E** cell plane and the **P** cell plane are divided into local areas in the same manner as in the **E** layer and the **P** layer respectively, except that the E_i plane in the **E** cell plane corresponds to the E_i neuron in the **E** layer and the P_i plane in the **P** cell plane corresponds to the P_i neuron in the **P** layer. The **M** layer consists of M neurons and S^M neurons. M_i in the **M** layer has excitatory fixed connections with any P neurons in the P_i plane. The number of M neurons in the **M** layer is the same as that of P planes in the **P** cell plane.

The outputs of M_i in the **M** layer is represented by eq.(12) and (13).

$$M_i = \varphi\left(\sum_j e_{ij} \times {}^{S}P_{ij} - d_i^M \times S_i^M - \theta_i^M \right) \tag{12}$$

$$S_i^M = \sum_{j \neq i} B_{ij}^M \times M_j \tag{13}$$

Learning in the **E** plane and the **P** plane is performed in each local area as follows.

(1) When a training pattern is given in a connectable area, representatives are selected in each plane with the same connectable area. In the first stage of learning, Core neurons are selected as representatives. In the training processes, the neurons which fired most strongly in each plane are selected as representatives.
(2) Learning is achieved in that plane which has the representative that fired most strongly among the representatives with the same connectable area.
(3) In the learning plane, the synaptic coefficients and threshold of the representative are reinforced by the learning scheme mentioned in section 2.1 or 2.2, and simultaneously, other neurons reinforce their thresholds and synaptic coefficients between the input neurons which have their positions shifted in parallel from those of the inputs to the representative. Behaivior of this network is demonstrated by computer simulation in chapter 3.

3. COMPUTER SIMULATION

The model used for computer simulation is as follows.
The dimensions of the input pattern and L layer are 25 X 25. The dimensions of the E layer in the feature extraction network and the discrimi-

Fig.5 The patterns used for computer simulation

nation network, and those of th P layer are 27 $\times$ 27. the E layer in the feature extraction network, the P layer and the M layer are all divided into 9(3$\times$3) local areas. The dimensions of a local area are 9 $\times$ 9. The E layer in the discrimination network has one local area(27$\times$27). The values of parameters and fixed synaptic coefficients are set as $\alpha_1 = 0.01$, $\alpha_2 = 1.0$, $\Delta w = 0.3$, $\Delta v = 0.15$, $\beta = 0.4$, $\Delta u = 0.7$, $\gamma = 0.5$, $\delta = 1.5$, $g_{ij}(g_i) = 1.0$, $f_{ii} = 1.0$, $f_{ij}(i=j) = 0.1$, $h_{ij} = 1.0$, $u_{ijk} = 0.7$, $\theta_i^L = 0.2$, $\theta_i^M = 0.5$, $e_{ij}(e_i) = 1.0$, $a_{ij} = 1.0$, $b_{ij}^M = b_{ij}^P = b_{ij}^E = 1.0$, $d_i^M = d_i^E = d_i^P = 1.0$.

For computer simulation, 5 patterns were put into the model as training patterns. The number of times learning occuered was 10. Fig.5 shows the patterns used for computer simulation. On each row in Fig.5, the left most patterns were used as the training patterns and other patterns were put into the model after learning. In the discrimination network, different E neurons responded to different training patterns and the same E neurons responded to the patterns on the same rows in Fig.5.

It is confirmed from the result of computer simulation that the model has the functions regulating thickness and shift in position.

4. CONCLUSION

This paper presented a neural network model with functions regulating thickness and shift in position. Behavior of this model was confirmed by computer simulation. This model is characterized by presynaptic inhibitory modifiable connections used for realizing thickness regulation, by processing for feature extraction and thickness regulation which are executed in parallel, and by the learning scheme used in the feature extraction network and the dicrimination network.

Hereafter, we aim to improve this model such that it can be applied to the regulation of rotation and the handwriting of letters.

References

[1] Rosenblatt,F.: Principles of neurodynamics. Washington: Spartan Books i962.

[2] Fukushima,K.: Neural network and self-organization. Kyoritsu Publ.Co. 1979.

[3] Fukushima,K.: Neocognitron; A self-organizing neural network model for a mechanism of pattern recognition unaffected by shift in position. Biol.Cybernetics.,36,pp.193-202(1980).

[4] Mizuno,H.: Pattern separability of an analog threshold neuron model. Trans.(A) IECEJ,J67-A,5,pp447-454(1984).

[5] Mizuno,H.: A neural network model with a function regulating thickness for pattern dwscrimination. Tras.(A) IECEJ,J69-A,9,pp.920-927 (1985).

WORST CASE BOUNDS FOR INDEPENDENT TASK SCHEDULING

Erik H. D'Hollander[1)]

Abstract

The problem of assigning N independent tasks to p processors is addressed. Worst case scheduling bounds for general list-algorithms are derived and the special case of the Longest-Processing-Time-First algorithm is treated in more detail. It is shown that under modest assumptions concerning the tasklength distribution, all list schedulers will generate asymptotically optimal results when the number of tasks grows indefinitely. The bounds are illustrated by simulation results for fixed and variable tasklengths.

1. Introduction

Scheduling tasks on MIMD-type processors has received widespread attention for many years. Since the problem itself is NP-complete in its general form, many suboptimal algorithms have been developed, for dependent [3, 8] as well as for independent tasks [4, 7, 11]. Some of the algorithms for independent task scheduling were optimized for equal task duration times [11], interprocessor communication overhead [4] or preemptive execution [7]. Other algorithms assume a statistical distribution of tasklengths and derive various strategies in order to obtain the minimal expected time to finish all tasks [10, 2]. An important aspect of these results is how the algorithms behave in the worst case. In this paper we develop a tight worst case bound for general list-algorithms, applied to the independent task scheduling problem. A well known bound was derived earlier by Graham [8], only based on the number of processors. He proved this bound to be the best possible. In the present approach we include the task duration to derive a new bound, which relates the worst case time to the minimal execution time. This bound proves that any list algorithm will produce an asymptotic optimal schedule when the number of tasks grows indefinitely.

[1)] State University of Ghent B-9000 Ghent, Belgium, Department of Electrical Engineering, St.-Pietersnieuwstraat 41

2. Problem Formulation

The problem is stated as follows. Given:

- A set of N tasks, $J = \{ T_1, \ldots, T_N \}$;
- A weighting function Θ, mapping J on R^+, such that $\tau_i = \Theta(T_i)$ represents the execution time of task T_i;
- A number of p identical processors.
- Independent tasks, in other words there are no precedence constraints or priorities between the tasks.

Find a partition of tasks, $A_1, A_2, \ldots, A_p$ over the p processors so that the maximal execution time,

$$t_{max} = \max_{i=1}^{p} \left(\sum_{\tau_j \in A_i} \tau_j \right)$$

is minimized.

3. List Algorithms

The partitioning problem is NP-complete [9] and therefore requires a sub-optimal heuristic algorithm. Intuitively it is appealing to assign the largest tasks first, since this allows a greater freedom for handling the inequalities at the end. The Longest-Processing-Time-First algorithm (LPT) is based on this principle:

- Order the tasks according to decreasing execution times;
- Assign the tasks consecutively to the first processor available.

This is a list-algorithm, i.e. the tasks are arranged in list before they are assigned to the processors in that order. List algorithms differ only in the way the list is ordered. Unless stated otherwise, the bounds in this paper are valid for <u>all</u> list algorithms, that is for an arbitrary ordering of tasks. Altough no list ordering is the best in all cases [8], the LPT algorithm generally is expected to give better results. E.g. consider a set of 7 tasks with decreasing execution times [8, 7, 5, 3, 2, 2, 1]. Execution according to the LPT-algorithm takes 10 time units, while the reversed list requires 12 units (Fig. 1).
In contrast with the optimal enumerative algorithms, requiring an exponential calculation time, the LPT algorithm only takes $O(n.\log_2 n)$ operations for the ordering and $O(n.(p-1)/2)$ operations for the assignment.

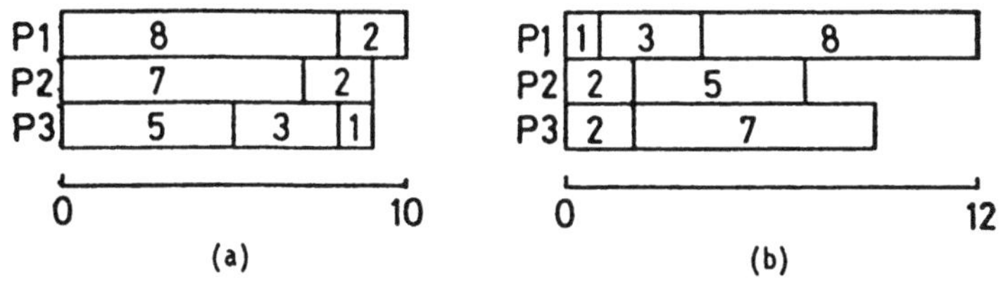

Fig. 1. Two list schedules: a) longest processing time first;
b) shortest processing time first.

4. Worst case bounds

The efficiency of an heuristic algorithm can be measured from its worst case behavior with respect to the optimal solution. Graham [8] found an upper bound for the maximal execution time of the LPT agorithm, t_{LPT}, which only depends on the number of processors p:

$$t_{LPT}/t_{opt} \le 4/3 - 1/(3p) \cdot \tag{1}$$

Here t_{opt} represents the scheduling time of the optimal schedule. This bound is best possible, if no assumptions are made on the tasklength distribution. It shows that the LPT algorithm always generates solutions within 33.3% of the optimum. However, it is possible to demonstrate that under mild conditions for the number of tasks N and the tasksize τ_i, all list-algorithms generate asymptotically optimal solutions for a large number of tasks.

Assume N tasks T_i, $i=1, \ldots, N$ with execution times τ_i and starting times t_i. A lower bound for the execution time of N tasks on p processors (N>p) is always:

$$t_{min} = \left(\sum_{i=1}^{N} \tau_i \right)/p. \tag{2}$$

This minimum is reached only when all processors are active during the interval $(0, t_{min})$. Now denote by $T_{l1}, \ldots, T_{lp}$ the last tasks which are executed on each processor. Define the longest execution time of these tasks $\tau_{l,max}$:

$$\tau_{l,max} = \max_{j=1}^{p} \tau_{lj}. \tag{3}$$

In each list-algorithm, the task $T_{1,max}$ is assigned to the first available processor, at time $t_{1,max}$. In the worst case, this task is the last task to start execution. This means that, until that time, all processors are busy executing the N-1 other tasks. Define the average tasklength

$$\tau^{*} = (\sum_{i=1}^{N} \tau_{i})/N \qquad (4)$$

then one has the following upper bound for the starting time of $T_{1,max}$:

$$t_{1,max} < (N\tau^{*} - \tau_{1,max})/p. \qquad (5)$$

Consequently, any list-algorithm has the following upper bound for its finishing time t_L :

$$t_L < t_{1,max} + \tau_{1,max} \qquad (6)$$

and substituting eq. (5) into eq. (6) one finds:

$$t_L < (N\tau^{*} + \tau_{1,max})/p \qquad (7)$$

Substitution of the minimal execution time t_{min} (eq. 2) and introducing the average tasklength (eq. 4) leads to:

$$t_L/t_{min} < 1 + ((p - 1)\ \tau_{1,max})/(N\tau^{*}) \qquad (8)$$

This is a tight bound, since it is always possible to construct an example in which all processors finish the execution of the first N-1 tasks simultaneously. In that case one has $T_N = T_{1,max}$ and this task starts at the upper bound given by eq. (5). In order to compare this bound with the Graham bound for the LPT algorithm, note that always $t_{opt} > t_{min}$, $p.t_{opt} > N\tau^{*}$ and also that eq. (8) holds for any list-algorithm, and therefore certainly for the LPT algorithm. This gives:

$$t_{LPT}/t_{opt} < t_L/t_{opt} < t_L/t_{min} < 1 + ((p - 1)\ \tau_{1,max}/(p.t_{opt})$$

Both bounds are represented in Fig. 2. The two bounds cross for

$$t_{opt} = 3\ \tau_{1,max} \qquad (10)$$

Note that eq. (8) actually relates the list schedule time to the absolute minimal execution time t_{min} given p processors, whereas eq. (1) relates the the LPT time to the optimal schedule time t_{opt}.

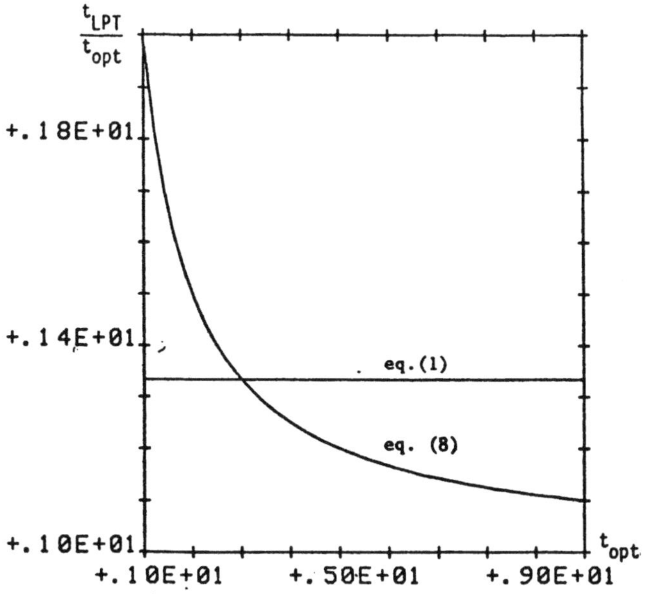

Fig. 2. Worst case bounds for the LPT-algorithm with $t_{1,max}$ = 1 and p>10.

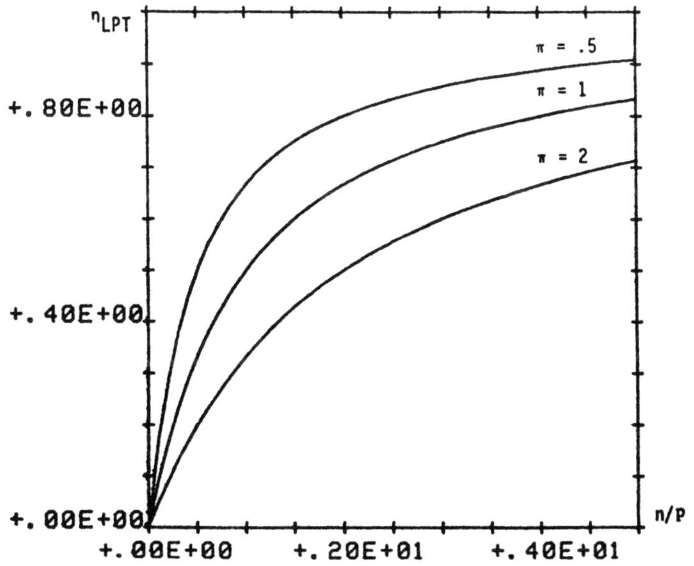

Fig. 3. Worst case LPT performance in function of N/p for various tasklength ratios π.

5. Performance characteristics

Since the LPT algorithm clearly has a lower worst case scheduling bound due to a smaller $\tau_{1,max}$, we will now further consider its performance with respect to the absolute minimal execution time on p processors, t_{min}. Define the scheduling performance η_{LPT} as:

$$\eta_{LPT} = t_{min}/t_{LPT} \tag{11}$$

From eq. (8) it follows that the worst case performance depends on N/p, the average number of tasks per processor and $\pi = \tau_{1,max}/\tau^*$, the ratio of the longest termination task on each processor to the average task duration; this gives:

$$\eta_{LPT} < 1/(1 + \pi p/N) \tag{12}$$

The effect of the two parameters N/p and π is shown in Fig. 3.

6. Simulation results

6.1. Constant task duration times

First consider the case where all task duration times are equal, i.e. π = 1. A simulation of 32 random problems, each consisting of an arbitrary number of tasks scheduled on 4 processors, is shown in Fig. 4.

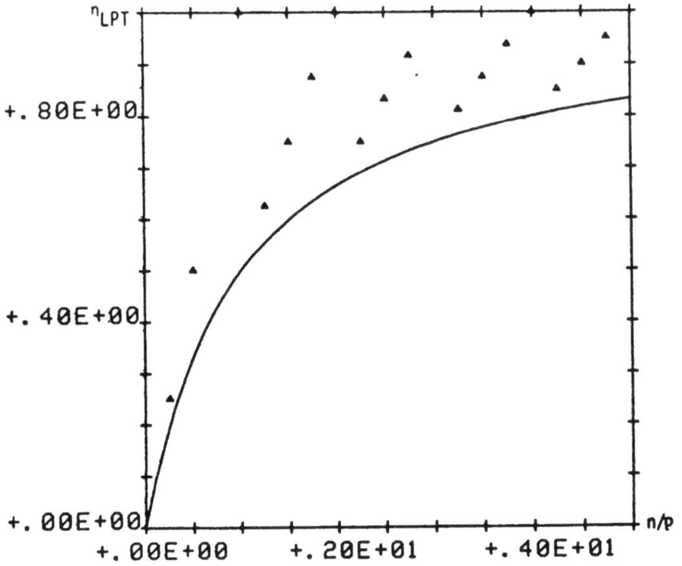

Fig. 4. Simulation of schedules on 4 processors with constant task duration times. Solid line indicates worst case bound.

In this case, the exact performance bound can be calculated easily:

$$\eta_{LPT} = (N/p)/(\text{ceiling}(N/p))$$

Note that the worst cases are close to the lower performance bound.

6.2. Variable task duration times

Here the tasklength ratio π can take any positive value. Since the LPT algorithm assigns the smaller tasks at the end, this lowers $\tau_{1,max}$ and improves the performance, as is shown in a random simulation in Fig. 5. Here 32 random problems were generated, consisting of independent tasks with uniform distributed tasklengths in the interval [2, 18]. In order to estimate the impact of the tasklength ratio on the performance, the following statistical lower bound is derived. Assume the tasks have a uniformly distributed tasklength distribution and are assigned in decreasing order of duration time. Then $T_{1,max}$ is the p-th last task assigned to a processor, and its task duration can be estimated from a linear interpolation between the minimal and maximal task duration times, τ_{min} and τ_{max}: $E[\tau_{1,max}] = \tau_{min} + (p-1)/(N-1).(\tau_{max} - \tau_{min})$. With $\tau^* = (\tau_{min} + \tau_{max})/2$, the average task duration ratio π can be estimated:

$$E[\pi] = [\tau_{min} + 2(p/N).(\tau^* - \tau_{min})]/\tau^* \tag{13}$$

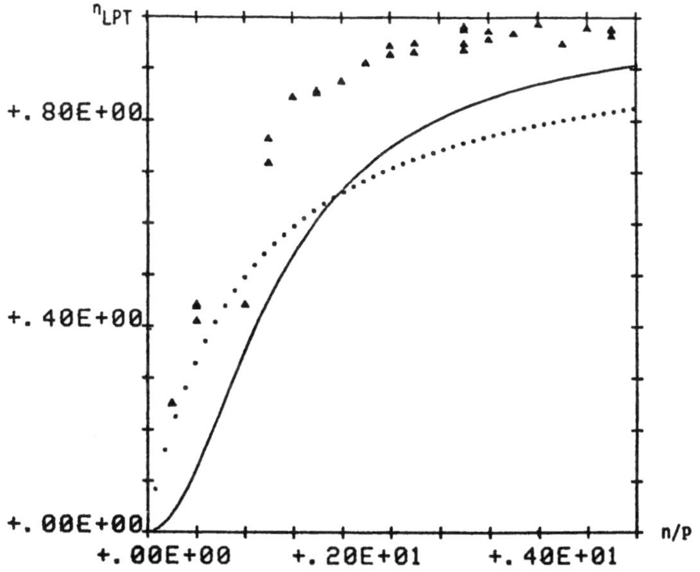

Fig. 5. Simulation with uniform distributed task duration times. Solid line indicates the estimated worst case bound, dotted line is the worst case bound for constant duration times.

Substitution of eq. (13) into eq. (12) yields an estimate on the lower scheduling bound for uniform distributed task lengths, which is depicted as the solid line in Fig. 5. For comparison, the lower bound for constant duration times is represented as the dotted line.

The simulation results as well as the lower bounds demonstrate that uniform distributed tasklengths generally allow better scheduling than fixed task duration times when the number of tasks per processors exceeds 2.

7. Conclusion

List algorithms provide a low cost heuristic for the scheduling of independent tasks. The Longest-Processing-Time-First algorithm has a better worst case behavior, because the smallest tasks are assigned at the end and this proves to be a good choice. However, when the number of tasks is a multiple of the number of processors, any list-algorithm will generate asymptotically optimal schedules. The closeness to this optimum depends on the ratio of the largest versus the average tasksize and on the number of tasks versus the number of processors.

References

[1] Adam T.L., Chandy K.M., Dickinson J.R., "A comparison of list schedules for parallel processing systems", Comm. of the ACM 17, 12, 685-690, 1974

[2] Bruno J., Downey P., Frederickson G.N., "Sequencing Tasks with Exponential Service Times to Minimize the Expected Flow Time or Makespan", Journal of the ACM 28, 1, 100-113, 1981

[3] Coffman E.G. Jr., Garey M.R., Johnson D.S., "An Application of Bin-Packing to Multiprocessor Scheduling", SIAM J. Comput., 7, 1, 1-17, 1978

[4] Cornett D.H., Franklin M.A., "Scheduling independent tasks with communications", Technical Report MF1, 1978

[5] Fernandez E.B., Lang T., "Computation of Lower Bounds for Multiprocessor Schedules", IBM Journal 19, 5, 435-444, 1975

[6] Fernandez E.B., Lang T., "Improving the Computation of Lower Bounds for Optimal Schedules", IBM Journal 21, 3, 273-280, 1977

[7] Gonzalez Teofilo, "Preemptively scheduling set of n independent jobs on m processor open shop", IEEE Trans. Comp. 28, 10, 782-786, 1979

[8] Graham R.L., "Bounds on certain multiprocessing anomalies", SIAM Journal on Applied Mathematics, 17, 2, 416-429, 1969

[9] Karp R.M., "Reducibility among combinatorial problems", in "Complexity of Computer Computation", Plenum Press, NY, 85-104, 1972

[10] Kruskal C.P., Weiss A., "Allocating Independent Subtasks on Parallel Processors", IEEE Trans. on Software Engineering, to appear, 1986

[11] Lang Tomas, Fernandez E.B., "Scheduling of Unit-length independent tasks with execution constraints", Information Processing Letters, 4, 4, 95-98, 1976

USING THE DATA FLOW APPROACH IN A MULTI-PROCESSOR SYSTEM

Eng. Antje Dziolloss and Eng. Iavor Antonov [1)]

In the first section the principles of data flow used in the presented system are explained. The next section concerns with the hardware structure of the proposed data flow architecture It is shown, how a data flow program is represented in the machine. The execution of a program is described in the third section. In the last section a data flow language based on the theoretical concept of attribute grammars is presented and it is shown, how a data flow graph can be derived from an attribute grammar.

1. Principles of the data flow approach

In the last years the VLSI technology gave the possibility to support the development of multi-processor systems with novel architectures, e.g. architectures that are able to exploit the inherent parallelism of the programs. The resulting computers can be classified as either data driven or demand driven [TREL82]. In the recent years a number of data flow machines was realized (MIT, NNT, LAU-system, University of UTAH et. al.). The research at the Technical University of Dresden began in 1984.

Pure data flow systems are based on data driven principle:

- An operation can only be executed if all operands are available (asynchronity).
- All operations are functions without side-effects (functionality).

The program for data flow computers are data flow graphs. The nodes of these graphs are operations and the arcs represent the flow of data tokens frome one operation to the next one. Data flow systems differ the way, they handle reentrant code. Reentrant code are all subgraphs that can be entered concurrently by iteration or procedure invocation. The system to be described in this paper is developed as a dynamic one. Every procedure invocation is allowed and a work copy is done.

---

1) TU Dresden Sektion Informationsverarbeitung
DDR-8027 Dresden Mommsenstr. 13

2. Hardware structure of the data flow computer

In the most of the data flow projects instruction packets are sent to processor elements for execution. One instruction packet contains a fixed number of arguments and a destination address, in which the result is to be stored. In this case the processor elements haven't a connection to the memory which contains the instructions and so composite data types can't be handled [DENN79, BRAI85]. The memory management, recursive procedure calls and the code copying cause also definite difficulties. In the DATAFLEX-1 project [AKIY84] there is an extra processor for these purposes, but when the program often demands a procedure call or code copying this processor is overloaded.
In the presented data flow architecture to prevent these faults a well known classic multi-processor system is taken in which the processor elements P and the front-end processor I/O are connected with memory segments M by a switching network, so that each processor element can access each memory segment. A data driven feedback loop is added to the system as it is shown in fig.1. This loop consists of a ready instruction sieve S, FIFO-queue Q and a ring distributor R.

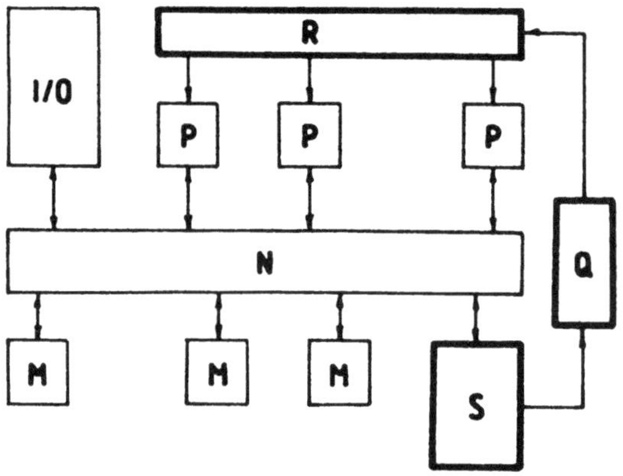

Fig.1 The data flow architecture

Each processor element can be of classic type, two-processor system with floating point co-processor, pipeline or data flow computer or any other type. A node interpreter is loaded in each processor element during the initialization process. It determines the set of the operations which are available for the data flow machine level language. The internal representation of a data flow graph consists of the program which is stored in the memory segments and the program table which stands in the internal memory of the ready instruction sieve. The program consists of a set of fields which describe all the nodes in the data flow graph and for all arcs memory cells for the values of the simple data types or a pointer to the field in which composite data types are stored. In the program table there is for every node a line. Each line consists of a column for a reference to the appropriate node description in the memory segments and a second column for a flag word. For each arc in the data flow graph there are two flags: one flag belongs to the exit of the node which the arc leaves and the other flag to the entry of the node in which the arc enters. These flags give the appropriate information about the data flow on the arcs. All flags for the leaving arcs and all flags for the entering arcs corresponding to a node are joined in a flag word. Fig.2 shows the internal representation of the data flow graph for the expression -((a+b)*(c+d)). V1-V8 denote the memory cells for the values of the data tokens, D1-D4 the node descriptions. P1-P4 are references to the lines of the nodes in the program table. Pi(j) is a reference to the jth flag of exit or entry of the predecessor respectively successor node.

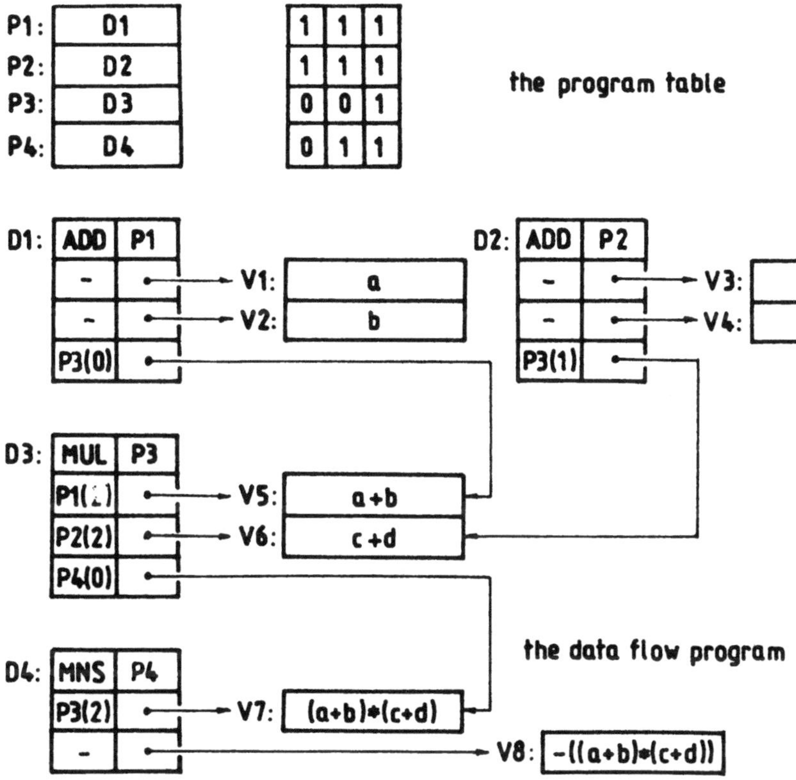

Fig.2 The internal representation of the data flow graph

The firing rule is restricted by allowing only one token to reside on each arc at any time in order to omit undesired data outrunning and to avoid expensive realization of queues before each node:

- all operands are available, i.e. all entries are occupied.
- all exits are free, i.e. there are no tokens on all arcs leaving the node.

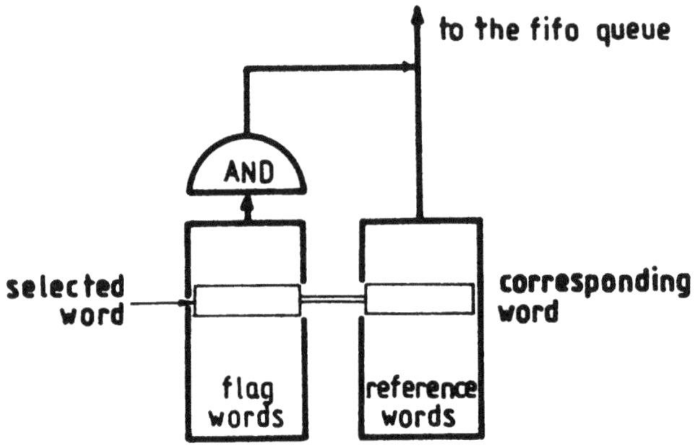

Fig.3 The ready instruction sieve

The selection of the ready nodes is done by the ready instruction sieve using the programm table and namely its second column for the flag word. By each access from each processor element the corresponding flag word is tested by an AND-gate for "all ones". If the test is true, the corresponding reference to the node description is sieved and transmitted to the FIFO-queue (fig.3). From the output of the FIFO-queue the reference is transmitted to a ring distributor which distributes it to a free processor element. The ring distributor is shown in fig.4 and consists of parallel registers connected to a ring with a multiplexer. A peripherial register to each processor is connected radial to the ring. The reference is sent as data token to the ring distributor and comes through the multiplexer in the register ring with a set valid data flag added to each of the registers. When the valid data flag from one peripherial register is cleared and when a set flag on the corresponding ring register has occured, the data is moved to the peripherial register and its valid data flag on the ring register is cleared. As clock for shifting in the ring distributor is used the system clock. The reference from the peripherial register of the ring distributor is used from the corresponding processor element to take the node description field from the memory segments. The node is interpreted by the node interpreter. It uses the argument references in the node description to take the argument values, calculates the results and stores them to the places refered by the description. It handles the corresponding flags in the program table to mark accepted data on the entering arcs and the presence of data on the arcs which leave the node. For this purpose the processor elements access the internal memory in the ready instruction sieve and thereby the next instructions are sent to execution.

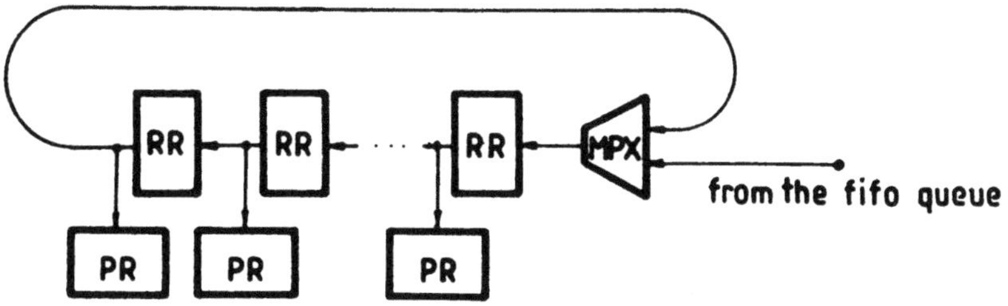

Fig.4 The ring distributor

3. Execution of the data flow programm

After the initialization the internal memory of the ready instruction sieve and the ring distributor are cleared. The processor elements are blocked. The program table is loaded into the internal memory of the ready instruction sieve. After this the processor elements are deblocked and the execution of the program begins. Every access to the flag word of one node (including the loading of the program table causes a check for all flag set. The unused flags in the flag word must be set by default to one. By firing the ready instruction sieve resets the flags of the appropriate node, i.e. all entries are free and all exits occupied. While the node operation is executed the exit flags of the predecessor nodes and the entry flags of the successor nodes are set, i.e. the exits of the predecessor nodes are free and the entries of the successor nodes are occupied. The firing and execution of the multiplication node from fig.2 is illustrated below.

The program table before firing of node 3:

		0	1	2
P1:	D1	X	X	0
P2:	D2	X	X	0
P3:	D3	1	1	1
P4:	D4	0	X	d1

and after firing:

		0	1	2
P1:	D1	X	X	0
P2:	D2	X	X	0
P3:	D3	0	0	0
P4:	D4	0	X	d1

after the execution of node 3:

		0	1	2
P1:	D1	X	X	1
P2:	D2	X	X	1
P3:	D3	0	0	0
P4:	D4	1	X	d1

meaning of the flags: entry flags 0/1 - entry free/occupied
exit flags 0/1 - exit occupied/free
x - meaning of the flag isn't significant
d1 - default one.

4. A data flow language based on attribute grammars

In many data flow projects the construction of data flow machines is connected with the developement of special data flow languages, e.g. the language VAL on the MIT. Data flow languages imly on the one side a high degree of inherent parallelism by the lack of side-effects and on the other side they offer practicable methods for leading off data flow graphs from the programs.

A language based on the principles of attribute grammars is proposed. Attribute grammars were introduced by Knuth as "a simple technique for specifying the 'meaning' of languages defined by context-free grammars" [KNU68]. There are some proposals of using attribute grammars as programming language [KAT81] and the advantages follow directly from the theoretical concept:

1. Attribute grammars support stepwise refinement.
   The underlying context-free grammar describes the decomposition of the problem in subproblems. The principles of the structured programming are realized, because context-free grammars provide all means of structured programming like sequence, alternative and recursion. The attributes represent the inputs and outputs of some decomposition. By them can be described general dependencies among decompositions. The attribute grammars are expanded by the decomposition conditions which are connected with every rule of the context-free grammar and depend from the attribute values of the rule. In terms of the decomposition conditions one can decide, whether an alternative decomposition rule is to be applied.
   Thereby an attribute grammar can be used for
   - software specification
   - compiler construction.
2. Attribute grammars involve principles of data flow languages [ACK82]:
   - functionality
   The attribute grammars are free from side-effects. The values of the attributes are specified rulewise in terms of other attribute values of the rule. For every attribute instance (attributes at the nodes of the decomposition tree - the term decomposition tree is used in analogy to the term parse tree). The value is computed only once. Other objects than attributes are not treated. The decomposition realizes a mathematical mapping of the values of the input attributes to the values of the output attributes.
   - single assignment rule
   To a variable may be assigned only once a value. This is accomplished by evaluation of the attribute instances as explained before.
   - locality of effect
   By rulewise specifying the values of the attributes the effects are

restricted to the rules of the context-free grammar.

3. Dependencies among the attributes imly a data flow along decomposition tree.

For leading off the data flow graph a modified approach of generating procedures KAT84 for absolutely noncircular attribute grammars is used. Therefore the analysis of possible in-out relations of the attributes all over the attribute grammar for building up the augmented attribute dependency relations for every rule is necessary.
The data flow graph is constructed symbolwise. We build a procedure for every out-attribute of every decomposition symbol.
The nodes of the procedure are:
- the evaluation of the in-attributes on the right sides of the alternative rules of the decomposition symbol
- the evaluation of the appropriate out-attribute of the decomposition symbol in all rules
- the invocation of the procedures for the evaluation of the out-attributes on the right sides of the alternative rules.

An arc connects two nodes that evaluate the values of two attributes if between these attributes there is a dependency.
Thereby it can be exploited
- the inherent parallelism in the expressions for evaluating the values of the attributes,
- the parallelism of evaluation of mutually independent attributes.

The language design mirrors the theoretical concept of attribute grammars. Fig.5 gives a short survey of the syntactic structure of a module.
- Alternative rules are enclosed in if-then-elif-fi constructions.
- For every decomposition symbol the in- and out-attributes and their types must be specified.
- Subdecompositions can be represented in modules and used by others.
- The language provides strong typing: There are given three elementary types - <u>int</u>, <u>bool</u>, <u>char</u>. The user can define new types by using type constructors like <u>array</u>, <u>record</u>, <u>stream</u>.
- The language is open-ended, because the set of operations isn't predefined.
- Operations and types can be defined in the library (available in all modules) or in some particular module (available only in that module).

Below is shown the program for the factorial which consists of only two alternatives:

```
module fac :  fac ( in int n  out f ):
              if  n>1  then  fac ( in n-1  out f1 ),  f:=n*f1
                       else  f:=n
              fi
eludom
```

```
module                 ::= module  decomposition_symbol:
                                   [external_modules]
                                   [typdefinitions]
                                   [operationdefinitions]
                                   {decompositions} *
                           eludom
decompositions         ::= decomposition_symbol
      ([in{type{in_attribute}*,},*] out{type{out_attribute}*,}*,):
      {alternative_rule  I  rule_body
alternative_rule       ::= if  decomposition_condition
                               then  rule_body
                           [elif  decomposition_condition
                               then  rule_body]*
                               else  rule_body
                           fi
rule_body              ::= decomposition_symbol
                           ([in{expression}*,] out{out_attribute}*,) I
                           attribute:= expression I
                           alternative_rule
```

Fig.5 Syntactic structure of a module

The data flow system presented in this paper under simulation now in order to determine its performance. The language is to be implemented to provide data flow graphs for the simulator. Thereby different algorithms can be executed including list processing.

References

[ACK82] Ackermann, W.B.: Data Flow Languages. IEEE Computer 15(1982)2

[AKIY84] Akiyama, M.; Yamashita, M.; Misu, T.: DATAFLEX-1 .. An Experimental Data Flow Computer Controlled Electronic Switching System. Proceedings of the ISS '84 Florence, May 84

[BRAI85] Brailsford, D.F.; Duckworth, R.I.: The MUSE Machine-an Architecture for Structured Data Flow Computation. New Generation Computing No.3, OHMSHA, LTD. and Springer Verlag 85

[DENN79] Dennis, J.B.; Leung, C.K.C.; Misunas, D.P.: A highly parallel processor using a data flow machine language. Techn. Rep. CSG Memo 134-1, Lab. for Computer Science, MIT 1979

[KAT81] Katayama, T.: HFP: A Hierarchical and Functional Programming Based on Attribute Grammars. 5th. Conf. on Software Eng. 1981

[KAT84] Katayama, T.: Translation of Attribute Grammars into Procedures ACM Transactions on Programming Languages and Systems 6(1984)3

[KNU68] Knuth, D.F.: Semantics of Context-Free Languages. Mathematical Systems Theory 2(1968)2

[TREL82] Treleaven, P.C.; Brownsbrigde, D.R.; Hopkins, R.P.: Data-Driven and Demand-Driven Computer Architecture Computing Surveys, Vol.14, No.1, March 1982

ORTHOGONAL COMPUTER AND ITS APPLICATION TO SOME GRAPH PROBLEMS

Bernadetta Otrubová and Ondrej Sýkora [1/]

0. Introduction

In this paper we describe a model of an orthogonal machine coinciding in the main features with a realized computer /1/. We show, that the computation times of the machine is polynomially equivalent to the computation time of the so called vector machine/2/ that means, it is from the second machine class as it is defined e.g. in /3/. Then we present algorithmic solutions to some graph problems on the machine.

1. Model of the orthogonal computer and its membership in the second machine class.

Firstly we introduce the definition of the vector machine of Pratt and Stockmayer. Vector machine is composed from a set of registers partitioned into two disjoint sets: vector registers R1,R2,... and index registers I1,I2,... Assume that the contents of a register is a Boolean vector what is a sequence of bits written from right to left. The length of a Boolean vector is the number of significant bits i.e. it is the length of the shortest initial segment of the vector, whose removal would make the remaining part of the vector constant. The contents of a vector register is considered as the vector register and the contents of an index register as the binary representation of a number. Assume that there exist an infinite tape with the input of a length n and at the beginning of a computation the whole input information is on the tape. The following instructions are defined on the registers of the vector machine: R:= constant vector, an instruction to load a constant Boolean vector into a register R; Rk:=~Ri, Ik:=~Ii and Rk:= Ri op Rj, Ik:= Ii op Ij, where op is a "bitwise parallel" Boolean operation; Rk:= Ri ↑ Ij (Rk:= Ri ↓ Ij), which shifts Ri left (right) a distance given by Ij, when shifting left the vacated positions are filled with 0's and when shifting right, the bits shifted out are discarded, the result is stored into Rk; Ik:=Ii ↑ 1, Ik:= Ii ↓ 1 for multiplication by 2 and integer division on index registers; R=0 and R≠0,(I=0 and I≠0) are predicates for testing whether R is 0 everywhere (whether I is equal to 0). Orthogonal processing corresponds to processing of vectors and/or bit

1/ Institute of Technical Cybernetics, Slovak Academy of Sciences, Dubravská cesta, 842 37 Bratislava, Czechoslovakia

slices. Our orthogonal machine is a model of an parallel computer /1/ with this feature, although it has further interesting features as cyclic shifts and flips on the blocks of the length of any power of 2 and the possibility to create a vector with only the first 1 (from the right) in a register and to determine its position.

Orthogonal machine is composed also from the vector and index registers, and the input is on a tape, but the set of instructions is different. Let BRk be the k-th bit-slice, i.e. all k-th bits of the vector registers. Besides the possibility of loading a constant Boolean vector in a vector register R or a bit-slice BR there are also the load instructions between register and bit-slices: Rk:=BRi; BRk:=Ri. Besides the predicates as before, there are also predicates for bit-slices. The shift instruction set is composed from the cyclic shifts, by 2^l positions left or right on 2^m long blocks, where $m > l$, on the vector registers or on the bit-slices according to the corresponding index register: Rk:= Ri $\uparrow\downarrow$ Ij, BRk:= BRi $\uparrow\downarrow$ Ij whereby the cyclic shift is represented in Ij by the value $2^m - 2^l$. The flip instructions set contains the flips on the blocks of length of a power of 2 of vector registers or bit-slices of the vector registers: Rk:=Ri $\otimes$ Ij, BRk:= BRi $\otimes$ Ij whereby the flips are realized on blocks of the length of the smallest power of 2 greater than the number in index register Ij. Assume in Ij there is a number: $2^{i_1} + 2^{i_2} + \ldots + 2^{i_m}$. Then the flip is a shuffle of the bits in the blocks which can be got as a matter of fact as the sequence of cyclic shifts $2^{i_1+1} - 2^{i_1}$, $2^{i_2+1} - 2^{i_2}$, ..., $2^{i_m+1} - 2^{i_m}$ in any order. Finally, there is the instruction of creating a vector with only the first 1 (from the right), in the vector register or in the bit-slice of the vector registers (from up down): Rk(Ij):= resv (Ri), BRk(Ij):= resv (BRi) whereby in Ij there will be its bit position.

To a vector or an orthogonal machine with a program there is assigned a finite directed graph with one start vertex and a set of accepting vertices and with edges each labeled with one assignment instruction or predicate. If the program mentions m registers, then a configuration consists of a node of the graph and the current contents of the m registers. A computation of the machine is a path in the graph. The time of a computation is its length i.e. we use uniform cost criterion. The space of a computation is the maximum, over all configurations during the computation, of the sum of the lengths of the vectors in the configuration.

The membership to the second machine class is defined /3/ by the polynomial equivalence in the time. We show that if the input is of the length n and $T(n) \geq \log n$, then T(n)-time bounded vector machine can be simulated on an orthogonal machine in $O(T^2(n))$ time and T(n)-time bounded orthogonal machine can be simulated on an vector machine in $O(T^3(n))$ time.

Theorem: Vector machine and orthogonal machine are from the same machine class.

Sketch of the proof.

Firstly, to simulate the instructions of the vector machine on the orthogonal machine one needs only to simulate the arbitrary noncyclic shifts. To simulate a shift, by 2^i to left, one can use the cyclic shift with code 2^j-2^i where $2^j \geq 2^i+$ length of the vector in the register and then mask out the first 2^ibits of the register. To create such a mask and all masks of a length 2^l, where $0 \leq l < i$, one is to set in a vector register 1 at the first bit position, then use cyclic shift $2^1-2^0$to the left and by oring the original mask with the shifted one, there is created the mask of the length 2. Let us assume we have created a mask of the length 2^l. By the cyclic shift $2^{l+1}-2^l$to the left and by oring the mask with the shifted one, there is created a new mask of the length 2^{l+1}. I.e. by O(i) steps one can generate all masks of the length 2^l, $0 \leq l \leq i$. Arbitrary shift by a number $k = 2^{i_1} + 2^{i_2} + 2^{i_m}$is simulated by the composition of the cyclic shifts $2^j-2^{i_1}, \ldots, 2^j-2^{i_m}$ where $2^j \geq k+$ length of the vector (one can assign to each vector register an index register where the actual length of the vector is indicated;we omit details here) and then by masking out the first k bits. Similarly can be simulated a shift to right. In this case the masks used by the cyclic shifts have to be shifted too. As the length of a vector in a computation of the vector machine can be $k^T + n$, where k is constant, any shift can be simulated in at most $O(\log(k^T+n))$ time on the orthogonal machine. Therefore if $T(n) \geq \log(n)$, T(n) - time bounded vector machine can be simulated on an orthogonal machine in $O(T^2(n))$ time.

To simulate the work of the orthogonal machine on the vector machine one need to simulate the "bit-slice"processing, cyclic shifts,flips, and the resv instruction. If the orthogonal machine uses more than one register,one can arrange all significant bits of the vectors of the registers in the vector v of a register of the vector machine.As in the time t there is no vector or bit slice longer than k^t+n, where k is a constant (given by the greatest original shift),all significant bits of the corresponding configuration are in the vector v of length $(k^t+n)(k^t+n)$. There are k^t+n blocks by k^t+n bits. Each block is assigned to one possibly used register of the orthogonal machine and all bits from the same position in the blocks represent possibly used a bit-slice. Because of working only with a block of v we need to construct a mask of the length k^t+n (this requires $O(\log(k^t+n))$time).

If there is to simulate a cyclic shift 2^j-2^i to the left,one needs to construct a mask of the type$\ldots 1^i 0^{j-i} 1^i 0^{j-i} \ldots 1^i 0^{j-i}$ of $\log(k^{t+1}+n)$ length (if the border of the cyclic shift block does not coincide with the border of the blocks of vector v) and to spread the original blocks to the new positions. The spreading can be done in $O(\log(k^{t+1}+n))$ time. By using the shift to left, and with mask, then shift to right, negation of the mask, and with the new mask and by or-ing the results one can get the shifted vector in a block of v. The construction of the mask requires $O(\log(k^{t+1}+n))$ instructions again. If there are some instructions with bit-slices, one can use a matrix transposition of /2/ to have the same access to the bit-slices as to the vectors before. The transposition requires $O(\log^2(k^t+n))$ time.

The flips can be simulated according to their definition by $\log\log(k^t+n)$ succesive cyclic shifts. That's why each flip can be simulated in at most $O(\log(k^{t+1}+n)\log\log(k^{t+1}+n))$ time.

The instruction resv can be realized as follows. We start with a mask of length 1. Then the and is realized with the corresponding block of v. We test if the resulting vector is not zero. Duplicate the mask and repeat the process until the resulting vector is not zero. Then the first 1 is in the interval between the last length of the mask and the half of the length. Then repeat the process on the interval, etc. The process requires $O(\log^2(k^t+n))$ time.

From the whole simulation one can see that if $T(n)\geq\log n$, then $T(n)$-time bounded vector machine can be simulated on an orthogonal machine in $O(T^3(n))$ time.

2. Application of the orthogonal machine to some graph problems.

In this section we shall point at application of the orthogonal computer to the following graph problems: finding connected components, transitive closure, verifying an articulation vertex and a bridge, finding a minimum spanning tree and the shortest resp. the longest paths between a vertex and the other vertices. For these problems more solutions have been suggested on various models of parallel computers e.g. /4,5,6,7/.

We use the following graph terminology. Let the graph be couple $G=(V,E)$, $E\subseteq V\times V$. $V=\{v_1,\dots,v_n\}$ is the set of graph-vertices and $E=\{e_1,\dots,e_m\}$, where $e_i=(v_j,v_k)$, is the set of edges. A minimum spanning tree (MST) of weighted graph is a spanning tree with the minimal sum of the weights of the edges. The shortest (resp. longest) path between two vertices of a weighted graph is the path with the minimal (resp. maximal) sum of the weights of its egdes. The articulation vertex (resp. the bridge) of a graph is the vertex (resp. the edge) by the releasing of which the number of connected components increases. Two representations of graphs are used:

a/ An adjacency matrix (AM). It is an n x n matrix, whereby for the representation of its row, in case of the unweighted (resp. weighted) graph, n(resp. nw) bits suffice. The number 2^{w-1} is reserved for the case that no edge exists between two vertices of weighted graph. Lower case indices serve for matrix columns indication and upper case indices for matrix rows indication.

b/ A <u>list of edges</u> (LE). For simplicity, let every vertex be incident at least with an edge. The unweighted (resp. weighted) graph can be represented by a field in the orthogonal memory, of length m and width 2 log n(resp. 2 log n + w), where w is the number of bits necessary for coding the edge-weight.

As we want to demonstrate a real application of the orthogonal machine to graph problems we assume that at the beginning of the computation we have input data in the orthogonal memory (i.e. in the vector registers of the orthogonal machine) in such a way that each row of the adjacency matrix and each edge of the list of edges are stored in one vector register.

2.1. Finding connected components, transitive closure of graph and verifying an articulation vertex and a bridge

Input: Unweighted graph G represented by AM with "ones" on diagonal. Assume, that in the i-th column AM_i "ones" exist in i_1-th,..., i_{j_i} -th rows.

Output: Matrix B of type n x n, where in each unmasked and nonzero column B_i, one component is represented with 1's in rows with indices of the corresponding vertices /at beginning of computation B is zero/.

Intermediate variable: Bit-slice R of the length n.
The algorithm creates current components from adjacency vertices and unifies current components connected by edge. We use the mask M(resp. M') of the length n for masking the columns of AM (resp.B).

```
begin
i:=1; j:=1; M:=(1,1,...,1); M':=(1,1,...,1);
while M ≠(0,0,...,0) do R:=(0,0,...,0);
   while ∃ k:(M and AM_i)(k)= 1  do R:=R or AM_k od;
   if (B^i and M') ≠ (o,o,...,o) then
       t:= bit position of 1 in resv (B^i and M')
       while ∃ k:(B^i and M')(k)= 1 do R:=R or B_k; M'(k):=0 od;
       B_t:= R; M'(t):= 1; i:= i+1; M: =~R and M
   else B_j:= R; j:= j+1  fi
od
end
```

The algorithm requires O(n) time. The best serial algorithm /8/ is of O (m+n)-time. Hence the above algorithm renders an improvement when the number of edges is of greater magnitude than O(n).

The adjacency matrix of transitive closure can be easily got from the columns of matrix B in O(n)time which gives evident improving in comparison with the best serial algorithm of $O(n^2)$-time.

There exists the serial algorithm /8/ of O(m) time for finding all articulation vertices in a connected graph. However, serial algorithm verifying whether a vertex,is an articulation vertex is of the same complexity. This problem (resp. the problem of verifying whether an edge is a bridge) can be solved on the orthogonal machine by means of the above algorithm so that the vertex is released with all incident edges (resp. the edge is the only released) and one verifies whether the number of connected components is not increased. Such solution is of O(n)time again.

2.2. Finding minimum spanning tree of weighted graph

Input: Weighted graph G represented by LE.

Output: Bit-slice C which has set bits corresponding to the edges from MST.

Intermediate variables: Bit-slices F,P.

The algorithm is based on the following: at first the edges are sorted according to their weights in the nondescending order. The first edge belongs to MST of a connected component of G. Then by means of C the edges of MST are marked and by means of F the edges, by the addition of which there arises a circuit, are forbidden. The new edge of MST is that of the minimal weight among those not forbidden, not yet chosen into MST and which has one vertex among vertices already chosen into MST(these edges are marked by means of P). C,F and P are naturally m bits long.

<u>begin</u>
Sort the edges according to the weights in nondescending order;
C:=(1,0,0,...,0); F:=(0,0,...,0); P:=(0,0,...,0);
<u>for each</u> k:($1 \leq k \leq m$) <u>pardo</u>
  <u>if</u> ($v_{k1} = v_{11} \vee v_{k1} = v_{12} \vee v_{k2} = v_{11} \vee v_{k2} = v_{12}$) <u>then</u> P(k):= 1 <u>fi</u>
<u>odpar;</u>
Label 1: PV:= <u>resv</u> (~C <u>and</u> ~F <u>and</u> P);
<u>if</u> PV=(0,0,...,0) <u>then</u> PV:= resv (~C <u>and</u>~F <u>and</u>~P) <u>fi</u>;
<u>if</u> PV=(0,0,...,0) <u>then</u> HALT <u>else</u> C:=C <u>or</u> PV;i:=bit position of 1 in PV;
  <u>for each</u> k($1 \leq k \leq m$) <u>pardo</u>
    if ($v_{i1} = v_{k1} \vee v_{i1} = v_{k2} \vee v_{i2} = v_{k1} \vee v_{i2} = v_{k2}$) <u>then</u>
     P(k):= 1 ; <u>go to</u> Label 1 <u>fi</u> <u>odpar</u> <u>fi</u>;

```
i:= bit position of 1 in PV;
for each k ((1≤ k ≤m) ∧ C(k)= 1) pardo
 if((vi1 = vk1 V vi1 = vk2)∧(vi2 = vk1= vi2=vk2))then F(i):=1; go to
Label 1
else C(i):= 1 fi odpar;
for each k(1≤ k ≤m) pardo
if (vi1=vk1 V vi1=vk2 V vi2=vk1 V vi2=vk2) then P(k):=1 fi odpar;
if (in C there is less than n-1 "ones") then go to label 1 fi
end
```

Using Batcher's or Rudolph's /9/ sorting algorithm the 1-st step can be realized in $O(w \log^2 n)$ instruotions. The rest of the algorithm requires O(nw)time. Therefore the algorithm requires $O(wn+w \log^2 n)$time, whereby the best serial algorithms require $O(m \log \log n)$and $O(n^2)$time.

2.3. Finding the shortest resp. the longest paths from a vertex to the other vertices

Input: Weighted graph G represented by AM (when finding the longest paths there are zeros in place of 2^w-1 in AM) and a vertex v_i.

Output: Vectors $W=(W(1),\dots,W(n)$ and $P=(P(1),\dots, P(n))$,where W(j) is the sum of the weights of edges of the shortest (the longest) path between vertices v_i and v_j.By means of P(j) the shortest (the longest) path between v_i and v_j is characterized: $(v_i,\dots, v_j)=(v_{p(p(\dots p(j))},\dots,v_{p(p(j))}, v_{p(j)}, v_j)$

Intermediate variables: vectors B and W', both n bits long.

At the beginning of computation, the bit-slice B has 1 only in the i-th bit and the j-th bit is set when the shortest (longest) path between vertices v_i and vj is found. The algorithm is parallelized Dijkstra's sequential algorithm.

```
begin
B:=(0,0...,0,1,0,0,...,0);
for each j(1≤ j ≤ n) pardo W(j):= 2^w-1 odpar; w(i):= 0;
{for the longest: for each j (1≤j≤n) pardo W(j):= 0  odpar;}
for each j(1≤j≤n) pardo  P (j):=0 odpar; k:=i;
label 1:if B≠(1,1,...,1) then HALT fi; M:=~B;
for each j ((1≤j≤n)∧M(j)= 1) pardo
  W'(j):= min (W(j), W(k) + AMkj)
 {for the longest: W'(j):= max( W(j), W(k) + AM kj)}
odpar;
for each j ((1≤ j ≤n)∧M(j) = 1) pardo
  if W(j) ≠ W'(j) then W(j):= W'(j)" P(j):= kfi odpar
```

wext:= min(W(j), j: 1≤ j ≤n∧M(j) = 1);
{for the longest: wext:= max(W(j),j: 1≤j≤n∧M (j) = 1);}
k:= bit position of 1 in resv (vector with 1 in places where W(j)=wext);
B(k):= 1; go to label 1
end

The complex instructions + and min (max) require O(w) time. The algorithms requires O(wn) time, whereby the sequential one requires $O(n^2)$ time.

3. Conclusions

A new model of the orthogonal parallel computation the so-called orthogonal machine was introduced and it was shown that it belongs to the second machine class. Algorithmic solutions to some graph problems were presented. Some of them (those which are of O(n) time) are optimal for the considered inputs.

Acknowledgment
We would like to thank J.Wiedermann and J. Šturc for helpful discussions.

LITERATURE

/1/ Richter,K.: A Parallel Computer System SIMD, In:Artificial Intelligence and Information-Control Systems of Robots,I.Plander/editor/, North-Holland Publ. Comp.,Bratislava-Smolenice, /1984/, 309-319.

/2/ Pratt,V.R. and L.J.Stockmeyer: A Characterization of the Power of Vector Machines, J.Comput.System Sci. 12,/1976/, 198-221.

/3/ van Leeuwen,J. and J.Wiedermann: Array Processing Machines, In: Proceedings of the FCT'85, Lecture Notes in Computer Science, Vol.199, Springer Verlag, Berlin, /1985/, 257-268.

/4/ Atallah,M.J. and S.R. Kosaraju: Graph Problems on a Mesh-Connected Processor Array, JACM,31,/1984/,3,649-667.

/5/ Hall,J.S.; A general-purpose cam-based system, In: Kung,H.T, Sproull, B. and Steele,G. /eds./,VLSI systems and computations Carnegie-Mellon University, /1981/,379-389.

/6/ Nath,D. and S.N.Maheshwari: Parallel algorithms for the connected components and minimal spanning tree problems, Inf.Proc.Letters 14,/1982/, 7-11.

/7/ Savage,C. and J.Ja'Ja':Fast, efficient parallel algorithms for some graph problems, SIAM J. on Computing 12,/1981/ 682-691.

/8/ Kučera,L.: Combinatorial algorithms / SNTL, Praha, p.283, in Czech/.

/9/ Rudolph,L.: A Robust Sorting Network, TR of Carnegie-Mellon-University, CS-84-104,/1983/,p.22

A PARALLEL NETWORK WAVE MACHINE

Peter Sapaty and Ivan Kočiš[1)]

A new approach to the organization of high-performance knowledge base machines for parallel processing of semantic networks is presented. A corresponding concept of the parallel network machine based on wave principles as well as its kernel wave language are briefly described. Some demands to the new generation computers for efficient processing of semantic networks are discussed.

1. Introduction

Nowadays semantic networks are considered as one of the most promissing models for knowledge representation and accumulation and are widely used in modern artificial intelligence systems. However the traditional computers are often extremely inefficient for processing large semantic networks because they are based on the activity of programs whereas the main part of their environment, being occupied by data, remains passive and does not contribute to the system performance. Besides, the memory of the von Neumann computers may keep only physically unbounded facts, which is in obvious contradiction with the tightly bounded, network data structures. Modelling semantic networks in such unbounded memory results in a huge program overhead, maintaining virtually bonds among the data, which considerably decreases the system's performance.

Investigations [1,2,3] showed the efficiency for highly parallel processing of graphs and networks of principally another computational model where data processing is put directly into the data and is distributed among the data. The models with active data structures become a basis for the new generation computers for semantic networks parallel processing [4,5]. The latter may be considered as extensions of the associative computers where the cells of memory may not only process their own information but also directly communicate with other cells.

Putting the data processing directly into the data enables to obtain the data processing parallelism proportional to the volume of data bases and to delete the bottleneck that is usually produced by the data traffic between processors and memory. However existing projects of parallel machines for semantic networks processing preserve another hard bottleneck - the control one - because they are globally driven by conven-

1) International Basic Artificial Intelligence Laboratory, Institute of Technical Cybernetics of the Slovak Academy of Sciences, Dubravska cesta 9, 842 37 Bratislava, Czechoslovakia

tional serial computers executing sequentional programs. Parallelism takes place only during executing of separate instructions that are generated by the host and processed simultaneously by the whole active semantic network, maintained by parallel environment.

2. The wave approach to parallel processing of semantic networks

Alleviating the control bottleneck and putting the main part of control as well as data processing directly into the distributed data was proposed within the framework of the wave ideology [6] which consists in the following. Complex data structure such as semantic network is distributed in multiprocessor space. Besides keeping part of the network (one node, in the extreme case), each component of this space is supplied with some universal possibilities of interpreting formulas of special wave languages that permit to compose parallel navigation procedures on a semantic network of arbitrary complexity. Formulas of these languages that are propagating in the network in a dataflow mode, as the waves of messages, dynamically form directly in distributed data operational structures, which may solve, in a highly parallel manner, complex information retrieval and inference tasks.

In a very generalized form the syntax of the WAVE-0 language (a kernel of the family of wave languages) may be written as:

```
wave ::= relation {. relation}
relation ::= direction {, direction}
direction ::= {key} [repetition *] generator
generator ::= multiarc[# multivertex] | [function] (wave)
function ::= control | interference | fixation
```

where [A] means that A may be omitted, {A} means that A may be repeated zero or more times and "|" is a separator of alternatives.

As may be seen, the wave formula (or merely wave) due to its recursive definition may represent an arbitrary complex navigation structure over the semantic network. At the top level it may be considered as a chain of some complex constructs, called relations. Each relation may be subdivided into a number of directions that describe the peculiarities of wave propagations in different physical directions in the network.

The definite movement in each direction is set by a generator that may be preceded by the set of keys (these detail the operations on wavefront propagations) and a pointer of the number of its repetitions. The generator may be simple of complex. The simple generator describes a one-step wavefront movement along the semantic bonds in the net from every vertex it is applied to. This movement may be set in general by naming some multiarc that includes some (or all) elementary arcs incident to the current vertex. The multiarc may cause also parallel transition to all other vertices of the net, which enables the associative searching of the whole network from every vertex. Naming some multivertex in the generator into which the multiarc may drop, enables to narrow the space of the wavefront propagation.

The complex generator may correspond to an arbitrary bracketed wave structure that enables the recursive definition of the wave. The bracketed wave may be also considered as an argument of a number of standard functions that organize the special support of wavefront propagations by the given subformulas.

The control and interference functions make first the static or dynamic splitting of the wave, forming individually coloured separate branches. The control functions organize coordinated parallel or sequential wavefront propagations on different branches using a wide variety of logical control. The interference functions enable the intersection of different branches on the sets of vertices that are passed by corresponding wavefronts, in both classical set-theoretic manner and unrigid, fuzzy modes.

The fixation functions enable to receive results (outlined by the corresponding subformulas) in different forms: logical, quantitative, in the form of sets or bounded substructures that are cut out of the network structure (using different contexts, if needed).

Syntax and semantics of the proposed language are oriented exclusively to its distributed interpretation in active data space, without traditional host devices. The latter may be briefly explained as follows. As may be seen, at the top level the wave formula is a chain of relations: R1.R2.R3. ... .RN. First, the whole chain is passed to some virtual, host vertex (being the entrance to the network) that produces by applying to the net the head of the chain, R1, some set of vertices S1. Then to the vertices of S1 the tail of the chain, R2.R3. ... .RN, is passed from the host vertex and the new head (the relation R2) is applied to their vicinity in the net producing the new set S2. Afterwards the vertices of S2, in their turn, are supplied by the new tail, R3. ... . RN, autonomously by the vertices of S1 and so on, until the tail of the formula becomes empty.

Taking into account the recursive structure of every relation RI that may represent arbitrary complex waves, the potential possibility of concurrent wavefront propagation from every vertex in active network and also the associative access of remote vertices, the parallel multiple wavefronts may propagate all over the semantic network, being organized exclusively by the internal activity of distributed data structure. The latter may be efficiently supported by parallel distributed environment based on VLSI technology.

At the present time the WAVE-0 language is put as a basis of the project of high-performance knowledge base machine for semantic networks parallel processing. This language describes mostly the navigation structures for searching semantic networks. Adding more interpretation to this skeleton language (as it takes place in the WAVE-1 language that is currently in the design stage), we may obtain powerful new generation distributed processing languages, securing the data processing parallelism, in general, proportional to the volume of data bases.

3. Architecture of the Parallel Network Wave Machine

The present concept of the architecture of specialized Parallel Network Wave Machine (PNWM), based on wave principles, is being developed at the International Basic Artificial Intelligence Laboratory in Bratislava.

The general structure of the PNWM is shown in Fig. 1. The basis of the machine is constituted by Parallel Network Environment (PNE) containing a great number of problem-oriented Processing Elements (PE) that are organized in a regular multiprocessor space having, besides local connections with neighbours, some additional levels of interprocessor communications. This enables efficient communication not only for adjacent PEs in PNE but also for remote ones as well as the organization of different forms of distributed control.

In Fig. 2 a possible two-dimensional organization of PNE is shown where every PE is connected to four neighbours (the opposite terminal PEs in PNE are tied together forming a torus-like structure). Each PE is also able to access the two orthogonal common buses, which enables direct communication of every two processors in the same string or column. This guarantees also a simple connection for arbitrary two PEs of the PNE by means of no more than one transit PE. Such two-dimensional organization of the regular space may be easily expanded to the three-dimensional where each PE has six connections with the neighbours and exits on the three common orthogonal buses. At most two transits may be needed to establish data communication for every two processors in the three-dimensional space.

Special construction of common buses enables also to make associative request from every PE of all others in the same string or column in PNE by translational transition of messages to them. A system of orthogonal buses permits also to make the associative request of all other PEs in PNE. For instance, for the two-dimensional case of PNE this may be done in two steps: initially, the requesting PE activates all other PEs in the corresponding string (or column) in PNE, and then all activated PEs (including the requesting PE) activate, in their turn, all PEs connected to the corresponding columns (or strings).

The problem-oriented PE is a VLSI device including developed means for communication with four neighbours in PNE and exits on the two common buses (in a two-dimensional case). It contains message memory and message processor and may access the external Mass Memory (MM). The heart of PE is an interpretive processor with its own local memory and hardware realized specialized functions, special associative environment for tables searching and hardware support of virtual memory.

The PNE supports in a distributed form a semantic network knowledge base, the main part of which is resident in local memories of the interpretive processors and the rest may be loaded from the MM. The bonds among the subnets, which are put into different PEs, are maintained by sending massages between PEs in the PNE, both through regular connections in space with neighbours and also by common buses (for remote PEs) if the message transitions through local connections become impossible or inefficient.

The MM is divided into zones which may be shared by different PEs, the access to different zones may be done in parallel. Each PE also keeps the same copy of a module of the wave language microprogram interpreter. During the work of the PNWM the formulas of the wave language are not resident in some PE or in a group of them (as it usually takes place for programs in computer systems), but they are propagating as the waves of messages in a dataflow manner through the active semantic network that is directly supported by PNE. The latter works as a highly distributed and parallel network interpreter of the wave language and combines the two efficient forms of data processing: associative and dataflow. The MM works here as an extension of local memories of PEs both for keeping parts of semantic network and non-resident parts of the interpreter (the latter are shared among the different PEs).

Except PNE and MM, which play the main role in distributed wave processing of semantic networks (including the entire distributes control), there are some additional functional blocks in PNWM. They are: Language Processor (LP), transforming the user requests into the internal wave form (LP uses active network grammars, put into PNE), Planning and Control Processor (PCP) making the initial activation of PNE by putting into it the wave programs as well as watching the activity of PNE and collecting the results flowing out of PNE, and also a number of Specialized Processors (SP). The latter extend the classes of tasks that are efficiently solved by PNWM (special kinds of inference, calculation, text processing, etc.).

PCP and MM connect with PNE through the system of common buses that is included into PNE. The user usually accesses the PNWM through the LP but he can also write complex programs directly in the wave formalism and put them into PNE (through the PCP).

The described architecture of PNWM is planned to be engaged mainly in:

- Information and expert systems;
- Computer-aided design and modelling;
- Control in complex intelligent systems, such as integral robots.

4. Conclusions

We have presented a new approach to the organization of high-performance knowledge base machines for semantic networks processing which enables to put directly into the distributed data not only the data processing but also the entire distributed system control. This enables to obtain a very high level of data processing parallelism which is proportional to the volume of knowledge bases and to essentionally alleviate the bottlenecks that usually take place in parallel systems designs.

In our opinion, the new generation computers for processing of complex knowledge structures such as semantic networks should satisfy the following main conditions. They must enable to combine the associative and dataflow modes of processing that should coexist at the same time in parallel distributed environment. The multiprocessor spaces maintaining semantic networks must have a developed hierarchy of communication means among processors of local (with the neighbours in the space) and different kinds of global and associative characters.

Special powerful means for massive control of parallel distributed processes in active space are needed which may be supported by both digital and analogous mechanisms. The processors in the space should be rather universal to interpret operations on structured data, maintain virtual memory and to make non-trivial decisions in contacts with their surroundings in the space.

The topology of the interprocessor bonds in their space must have a small diameter in comparison with the number of processors in the space, taking into account the demands to regularity and planarity and also the limited number of external connections of processors, for the efficient realization in VLSI.

References

1 Chang, E.J.H.: Echo algorithms: depth parallel operations in general graphs. IEEE Trans. Software Engineering, SE-8, 4 (1982), 391 - 401.

2 Sapaty, P.S.: A structural approach to solving tasks of graph and network theory. Proc. Fifth All-Union School on parallel Programming and High-Performance Systems, Vol. 4, Kiev, 1982, 46 - 47.

3 Sapaty, P.S.: Active informational field as a model of structural solving tasks on graphs and networks. Proc. USSR Academy of Sciences. Technical Cybernetics, 5 (1984), 184 - 208.

4 Hillis, W.D.: The connection machine. The MIT Press series in artificial intelligence, Thesis (Ph.D) MIT, 1985.

5 Moldovan, D.I,,Tung, Y.-W.: SNAP: A VLSI architecture for artificial intelligence processing. J. of Parallel and Distributed Computing, Vol. 2, 2 (May 1985), 109 - 131.

6 Sapaty, P.S.: A wave language for parallel processing of semantic networks. Computers and Artificial Intelligence, Bratislava, Czechoslovakia, 4 (1986).

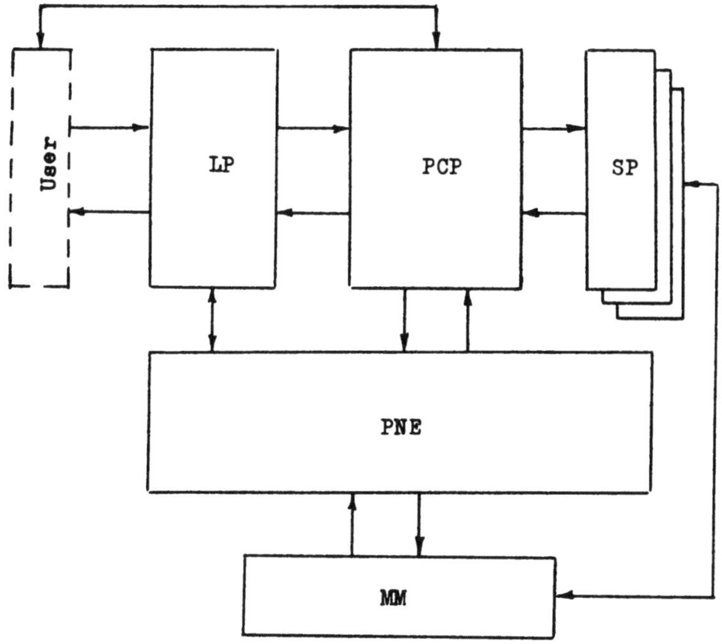

Fig.1. Parallel Network Wave Machine architecture

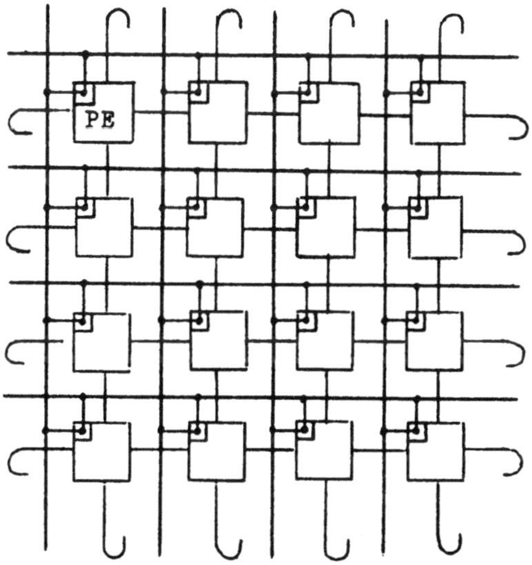

Fig.2. Parallel Network Environment

INFORMATIK · KYBERNETIK · RECHENTECHNIK

Herausgegeben von der Akademie der Wissenschaften der DDR

Zentralinstitut für Kybernetik und Informationsprozesse

Die Schriftenreihe INFORMATIK · KYBERNETIK · RECHENTECHNIK umfaßt alle Fachgebiete, die in der Hauptforschungsrichtung Kybernetik und Rechentechnik der Akademie der Wissenschaften der DDR integriert und Gegenstand der Vorlesungen und Forschungsaufträge an Universitäten und Technischen Hochschulen sind.

Folgende Themenkomplexe werden behandelt:

Automaten- und Algorithmentheorie

Informationstheorie und Automatisierung

Programmiersprachen und Rechentechnik

Datenerkennung und Datenverarbeitung

1

Dieter Bochmann/Christian Posthoff

Binäre dynamische Systeme

1981. VIII, 397 Seiten — 168 Abbildungen — 25 Tabellen — 17 × 24 cm
Lederin 68,— M (z. Zt. vergriffen)
Bestell-Nr. 7623619 (6391)

Aus dem Inhalt: Dynamische Vorgänge in binären Systemen — vorrangige Interpretation Schaltnetzwerke und Automaten — mathematische Beschreibung durch Booleschen Differentialkalkül — technische Anwendung bei rechnergestützter Analyse von Schaltnetzwerken

2

Siegfried Unger/Fritz Wysotzki

Lernfähige Klassifizierungssysteme

1981. XI, 294 Seiten — 77 Abbildungen — 8 Tabellen — 17 × 24 cm
Lederin 48,— M; Ausland 60,— M
Bestell-Nr. 7623563 (6372)

Aus dem Inhalt: Künstliche Intelligenz — psychologische Begriffslernexperimente — Klassifizierung von Objekt- bzw. Datenmengen — Wahrnehmungsprozesse — statistisch-orientierte Verfahren der Diskrimination von Verteilungen

3

Horst Völz

Information I

Studie zur Vielfalt und Einheit der Information. Theorie und Anwendung vor allem in der Technik

1982. 407 Seiten — 179 Abbildungen — 83 Tabellen — 17 × 24 cm
Lederin 78,— M; Ausland 98,— M (z. Z. vergriffen)
Bestell-Nr. 7620602 (6244/I)

Aus dem Inhalt: System und Information — formale Sprachen — Information in der Fernsprechtechnik — Speichertechnik — Optik — Sprache — Massenmedien — Psychologie — Physiologie — Informationstheorie — Versuch zur Klassifikation und Definition der Information

4

Horst Völz

Information II

Ergänzungsband zur Vielfalt und Einheit der Information. Theorie und Anwendung vor allem in der Biologie, Medizin und Semiotik

1983. XII, 370 Seiten — 184 Abbildungen — 60 Tabellen — 17 × 24 cm
Lederin 72,— M; Ausland 98,— M
Bestell-Nr. 7629690 (6244/II)

Aus dem Inhalt: Bedeutung des Informationsbegriffs in Biologie und Medizin — Genetik der Zellen — Nervensystem — Sehen — Hören — Gedächtnis — Kommunikation und Semiotik — Definition der Information

5

Programmsysteme

Anwendung — Entwicklung — Fundierung

Herausgegeben von Peter Bachmann

1983. X, 228 Seiten — 53 Abbildungen — 18 Tabellen — 17 × 24 cm
Lederin 52,— M
Bestell-Nr. 763 006 9 (6644)

Aus dem Inhalt: Programmsysteme als Hilfsmittel moderner Rechenanlagen — Architektur — Steuerung — mathematische Modellierung — Entwicklungs- und Nutzungstechnologie

6

Günter Riedewald/Jan Małuszyński/Piotr Dembiński

Formale Beschreibung von Programmiersprachen

Eine Einführung in die Semantik

1983. X, 205 Seiten — 37 Abbildungen — 16 Tabellen — 17 × 24 cm
Lederin 42,— M; Ausland 60,— M
Bestell-Nr. 763 136 0 (6720)

Aus dem Inhalt: Moderne Methoden der Programmierung — formalisierte Beschreibung von Programmiersprachen — Syntaxdefinition — Semantikdefinition — attributierte Grammatiken — algebraische Modelle von Programmiersprachen

7

Norbert Ahlbehrendt/Volker Kempe

Analyse stochastischer Systeme

Nichtlineare dynamische Systeme

1984. 335 Seiten — 37 Abbildungen — 7 Tabellen — 17 × 24 cm
Lederin 58,— M
Bestell-Nr. 763 122 1 (6714)

Aus dem Inhalt: Lineare Systeme und Markowsche Diffusionsprozesse — stochastische Differentialgleichungen — Analyse durch Funktionalreihenentwicklung — statistische Linearisierung — Volterra-Reihe aus dem Blockschaltbild — Momentenentwicklung der Verteilungsdichte — zeitliche Mittelungsmethode

8

Henning Schoch

Programmieren in PL 1

1984. 520 Seiten — 7 Abbildungen — 17 × 24 cm — Lederin 68,— M
Bestell-Nr. 763 135 2 (6719)

Aus dem Inhalt: Systematische Darstellung des vollen Sprachumfangs von PL 1 — zahlreiche Beispiele zur Veranschaulichung der Anwendungsmöglichkeiten einzelner Sprachelemente — Darlegung der wichtigsten Beziehungen zum Betriebssystem OS/ES

10

Helmut Löffler

Rechnerverbundsysteme

1984. VIII, 296 Seiten — 176 Abbildungen — 12 Tabellen — 17 × 24 cm
Lederin 54,— M; Ausland 68,— M (z. Z. vergriffen)
Bestell-Nr. 763 162 7 (6737)

Aus dem Inhalt: Architektur von Rechnerverbundsystemen — Mehrrechnersysteme — Rechnerkommunikationsnetze — Rechnernetzwerke — rechnergestützte Telekommunikationssysteme

Band 1

Inverse and Improperly Posed Problems in Differential Equations

Proceedings of the Conference on Mathematical and Numerical Methods, held in Halle Saale (GDR) from May 29 to June 2, 1979

Edited by Gottfried Anger

296 Seiten, 1979 (vergriffen)

Band 2

Fundamentals of Computation Theory FCT '79

Proceedings of the Conference on Algebraic, Arithmetic and Categorial Methods in Computation Theory, held in Berlin/Wendisch-Rietz (GDR) September 17–21, 1979

Edited by Lothar Budach

575 Seiten, 1979

Band 3

Decidability and Generalized Quantifiers

By Andreas Baudisch, Detlef Seese, Hans-Peter Tuschik, and Martin Weese

XII, 235 Seiten, 1980

Band 4

Zur Elastizitäts- und Thermoelastizitätstheorie

Potentialtheoretische Methoden in Anwendung auf verschiedene Modelle

Von Lothar Jentsch und Johannes Maul

157 Seiten, 1980

Band 5

Systems Analysis and Simulation 1980

Proceedings of the International Symposium held at Berlin (GDR) September 1–5, 1980

Edited by Achim Sydow

496 Seiten, 1980 (vergriffen)

Band 6

Nichtlineare diskrete Optimierung

von Eberhard Girlich und Michail M. Kowaljow

218 Seiten, 1981

Band 7

Completeness Problems in the Structural Theory of Automata

By Jürgen Dassow

148 Seiten, 1981

Band 8

Darstellung von Lösungen linearer elliptischer Differentialgleichungen

Von Günther Wildenhain

92 Seiten, 1981

Band 9

Introduction to the Spectral Theory of Operators in Spaces with an Indefinite Metric

By I. S. Iohvidov, M. G. Krein, and H. Langer

120 Seiten, 1982 (vergriffen)

Band 10

Nonlinear Time-discrete Systems

A General Approach by Nonlinear Superposition

By Michael Gössel

115 Seiten, 1982 (vergriffen)

Band 11

Preprimal Algebras

By Klaus Denecke

162 Seiten, 1982

Band 12

Ergodic Theory and Related Topics

Proceedings of the Conference held in Vitte/Hiddensee (GDR) October 19–23, 1981

Edited by Horst Michel

232 Seiten, 1982

Band 13

Singularly Perturbed Differential Equations

By H. Goering, A. Felgenhauer, G. Lube, H.-G. Roos, and L. Tobiska

176 Seiten, 1983

Band 14

Leben wir in einer Volterra-Welt?

Ein ökologischer Zugang zur angewandten Systemanalyse

Von Manfred Peschel und Werner Mende

233 Seiten, 1983

Band 15

Markov Decision Problems with Countable State Spaces

Optimality Criteria – Algorithms – Clustering

By Hans Michael Dietz and Volker Nollau

174 Seiten, 1983

Band 16

Stochastische Verfahren zur Suche nach dem Minimum einer Funktion

Von Ryszard Zieliński und Peter Neumann

133 Seiten, 1983

Band 17

Invertibility and Asymptotics of Toeplitz Matrices

By Albrecht Böttcher and Bernd Silbermann

200 Seiten, 1983

Band 18

Structural Induction on Partial Algebras

Introduction to Theory and Application of Partial Algebras – Part II

By Horst Reichel

205 pages, 1984

Band 19

Algebraic Methods for Toeplitz-like Matrices and Operators

By Georg Heinig and Karla Rost

212 pages, 1984

Band 20

Frege Conference 1984

Proceedings of the International Conference held at Schwerin (GDR), September 10–14, 1984

Edited by Gerd Wechsung

408 pages, 1984

Band 21

Numerical Analysis of Selected Semilinear Differential Equations

Edited by Christian Großmann, Thomas Riedrich, and Hartmut Schönheinz

203 pages, 1984

Band 22

Singular Ordinary Differential Operators and Pseudodifferential Equations

By Johannes Elschner

200 pages, 1985

Band 23

Lotka-Volterra-Approach to Cooperation and Competition in Dynamic Systems

Proceedings of the 5th Meeting of UNESCO's Working Group on Systems Theory held on the Wartburg, Eisenach (GDR) at March 5–9, 1984

Edited by Werner Ebeling and Manfred Peschel

271 pages, 1985

Band 24

Convergence Structures 1984

Proceedings of the Conference on Convergence held in Bechyně (Czechoslovakia); September 24–28, 1984

Edited by Josef Novák, Werner Gähler, Horst Herrlich, and Jan Mikusiński

254 pages, 1985

Band 25

Parcella '84

Proceedings of the II. International Workshop on Parallel Processing by Cellular Automata and Arrays held in Berlin (GDR), September 25–27, 1984

Edited by Wolfgang Händler, Tamás Legendi, and Gottfried Wolf

239 pages, 1985

Band 26

Multiobjective and Stochastic Optimization Based on Parametric Optimization

By Jürgen Guddat, Francisco Guerra Vasquez, Klaus Tammer, and Klaus Wendler

175 pages, 1985

Band 27/28

Systems Analysis and Simulation 1985
I: Theory and Foundations
II: Applications

Proceedings of the International Symposium held in Berlin (GDR), August 26–31, 1985

Edited by Achim Sydow, Manfred Thoma, and Robert Vichnevetsky

per volume 495 pages, 1985

Band 29

Parcella '86

Proceedings of the III. International Workshop on Parallel Processing by Cellular Automata and Arrays held in Berlin (GDR), September 9–11, 1986

Edited by Tamás Legendi, Dennis Parkinson, Roland Vollmar, and Gottfried Wolf

about 272 pages, 1986

Band 30

Fuzzy Sets Applications, Methodological Approaches, and Results

Proceedings of the International Workshop on Fuzzy Sets Applications cosponsored by IIASA and convened in cooperation with IAEA held on the Wartburg, Eisenach (GDR), at March 3–8, 1985

Edited by Steffen Bocklisch, Sergei Orlovski, Manfred Peschel, and Yasushi Nishiwaki

233 pages, 1986

Band 31

Mathematical Methods of Specification and Synthesis of Software Systems '85

Proceedings of the International Spring School, held in Wendisch-Rietz (GDR), April 22–26, 1985

Edited by Wolfgang Bibel and Klaus P. Jantke

245 pages, 1986

Band 32

A Model Theoretic Oriented Approach to Partial Algebras

Introduction to Theory and Application of Partial Algebras – Part I

By Peter Burmeister

319 pages, 1986

Band 33

Finite-difference Methods on Irregular Networks

A Generalized Approach to Elliptic Problems of Second Order

By Bernd Heinrich

about 200 pages, 1986

A view on international r & d activities in the field of very fast parallel processing in computers shows the increasing role of cellular and array structures. The two closely related concepts influences each other and their development has far reaching impacts on future generations of computers. A deeper understanding of these structure types enables a better algorithm-adapting of computer- and processor architectures.
The workshop Parcella '86 has gathered those scientists interested in presenting and discussing new results and ideas for parallel and distributed processing on cellular and array structures. The aim was to find common aspects of these two types of structures to deepen them and to stimulate the process of research in this field. Important information on the state-of-the-art research in the different institutions had been exchanged concerning problems and future projects.

Ein Blick auf die internationale Entwicklung der sehr schnellen Parallelverarbeitung in Rechnern zeigt die wachsende Bedeutung zellularer und feldartiger Strukturen. Beide Konzepte sind eng verwandt, beeinflussen sich gegenseitig, und ihre Entwicklung hat weitreichende Auswirkungen auf die nächsten Rechnergenerationen. Ein tieferes Verständnis dieser Strukturen ermöglicht eine bessere Anpassung von Rechner- und Prozessorarchitekturen an die Algorithmen.
Die Tagung Parcella '86 hat Wissenschaftler zusammengeführt, die an der Vorstellung und der Diskussion neuer Ergebnisse und Ideen für die parallele und verteilte Verarbeitung auf zellularen und feldartigen Strukturen interessiert sind. Es war das Ziel, gemeinsame Gesichtspunkte dieser zwei Strukturtypen zu finden, zu vertiefen und die Forschung auf dem Gebiet weiter anzuregen. Es wurden wichtige Informationen über den Stand der Forschung in den verschiedenen Institutionen über Probleme und zukünftige Projekte ausgetauscht.

ISBN 3-05-500 175-3

ISSN 0138-3019